P9-BVM-386

# Individual and Social Responsibility

A National Bureau
of Economic Research
Conference Report

# Individual and Social Responsibility

Child Care, Education, Medical Care, and Long-Term Care in America

Edited by Victor R. Fuchs

The University of Chicago Press

*Chicago and London*

VICTOR R. FUCHS is the Henry J. Kaiser, Jr., Professor Emeritus at
Stanford University and a research associate of the National Bureau of
Economic Research.

The University of Chicago Press, Chicago 60637
The University of Chicago Press, Ltd., London
© 1996 by The National Bureau of Economic Research
All rights reserved. Published 1996
Printed in the United States of America
05 04 03 02 01 00 99 98 97 96   1 2 3 4 5
ISBN: 0-226-26786-5 (cloth)


Library of Congress Cataloging-in-Publication Data

Individual and social responsibility : child care, education, medical care,
    and long-term care in America / edited by Victor R. Fuchs.
        p.      cm.—(National Bureau of Economic Research conference
    report)
    Includes bibliographical references and index.
    1. Human services—United States—Congresses. 2. Child care—
    United States—Congresses. 3. Aged—Long-term care—United
    States—Congresses. 4. Education—United States—Congresses.
    5. Medical care—United States—Congresses. 6. Responsibility—
    United States—Congresses. I. Fuchs, Victor R.
    HV91.I463   1996
    361.973—dc20                                                    95-20983
                                                                        CIP

To Isaiah

and all of his contemporaries in the twenty-first century

# Contents

# Acknowledgments

The papers and comments in this volume were presented and discussed at a National Bureau of Economic Research conference held at Stanford, California, on October 7–8, 1994. Grants from the Robert Wood Johnson and Alfred P. Sloan Foundations in support of the NBER project "The Responsible Society" are gratefully acknowledged. I also wish to thank Claire Gilchrist, Beverly Fuchs, Diane Reklis, Deborah Kiernan, Anita Samen, and Joann Hoy for their contributions to the success of the conference and preparation of this volume for publication.

Victor R. Fuchs

# I   Introduction and Overview

# Introduction

Victor R. Fuchs

The Great Health Care Debate of 1994 was like the uses of this world to Hamlet—"weary, stale, flat, and unprofitable." Not only was the debate unproductive and inconclusive; it was extremely shallow. False premises were relied on by all sides, for example, "employers bear the cost of health insurance"; "firm size is relevant when setting payroll tax rates"; and "the high cost of health care makes the United States less competitive in international trade." Economists readily understand that these assumptions are false, but virtually all the political participants framed the health care debate as if they were true. Thus, the huge expenditure of time and effort did not even serve to educate the public about the real issues of health policy (Fuchs 1994).

Is health care peculiar in this regard? Probably not. If Congress and the administration had devoted as much time to debating child care or education or long-term care, the results would probably have been equally unsatisfactory and the debate equally shallow. So why are these sectors in such deep trouble? Some analysts believe that the root problem is slow productivity growth in the economy as a whole. Greater gains in productivity, it is argued, would facilitate allocation of more resources to human services and relieve the most pressing concerns. There can be little doubt that rapid growth of real income makes it easier to fund new public programs or to expand private expenditures, but I doubt that the slowdown in productivity growth is the only, or even the primary, cause of our present difficulties. It is worth noting that many of the problems in the human services sectors intensified in the late 1960s, at a time when the economy was growing rapidly and there had been two decades of substantial gains in real income.

Victor R. Fuchs is the Henry J. Kaiser, Jr., Professor Emeritus at Stanford University and a research associate of the National Bureau of Economic Research.

The author gratefully acknowledges financial support from the Robert Wood Johnson Foundation and the Alfred P. Sloan Foundation.

Other analysts focus on perversion of the political process, which blocks the development of effective government policies. Special interests, it is said, dominate the general interest. The solution is sought in reform of campaign financing and tighter controls on lobbying. The political process does need improvement, but without wider agreement about what constitutes the general interest, it is unlikely that changes in process alone will overcome the impasse in public policy.

Despite widespread concern regarding the problems of human services in the United States, there is simply no consensus in government or among the public about how to deal with them. On the contrary, with respect to the four sectors discussed in this book there is intense disagreement over both *goals* and *means*. Are Americans spending too little or too much in each of these sectors? How could current spending be used more efficiently? Should the government's role increase or decrease? Why? What are the political, social, and economic forces that shape current policies affecting human services? Can the social sciences contribute to better policies in these sectors, and if so, how?

To address these and related questions, a National Bureau of Economic Research conference was held at Stanford, California, on October 7 and 8, 1994, with financial support provided by the Robert Wood Johnson Foundation and the Alfred P. Sloan Foundation. The invitation to the participants stated the following objectives:

1. To increase understanding of the trade-offs and complementarities among diverse goals of public policy: efficiency, justice, freedom, security

2. To increase understanding of how the pursuit of these goals involves diverse institutions: the market, government, and integrative systems such as families, religious communities, and professional organizations

3. To investigate the interactions between institutions and goals in four sectors: child care, education, medical care, and long-term care for the elderly, and to gain a deeper understanding of the relative efficacy of alternative institutions to achieve goals in specific contexts

4. To contribute to improved public policies affecting these four sectors

5. To begin to create an intellectual framework that highlights the importance of both individual and collective responsibility in the provision of human services

The twenty-three conference participants provided a wide range of expertise: applied economists with deep knowledge of each of the sectors, economic theorists, two lawyers, one physician, and three social scientists who are not economists. A Swedish economist, Assar Lindbeck, served as a general discussant, providing valuable comparative perspectives about social policies in Europe. The rapporteur for the conference was Timothy Taylor; his overview of the papers and discussion follows this introduction.

I did not contribute a paper, but as organizer of the conference I will use this introduction to present my view of the problem and an agenda for future research. In my judgment, the confused policies that plague human services, and the unproductive debates over these policies, have a systemic, generic explanation: our unwillingness and inability to discuss and resolve value issues that form the foundation of any society. What are these issues? For Raymond Aron, the French social scientist, the great unresolved problem of all modern societies is the conflict between a push for equality and the need "to produce as much as possible through the mastery of the forces of nature" (Aron 1968), a venture that requires differentiation and hierarchy. This trade-off between equality and efficiency, which is familiar to economists (see especially Okun 1975), appears with particular force in the human services sectors.

As the title of this volume suggests, the issue can also be formulated as the tension between individual responsibility and social responsibility. Both are necessary for a good society, but the current protagonists appear unwilling to acknowledge the legitimacy of their opponents' concern. The medical care debate, for instance, is about more than medical care; the child care debate is about more than child care; and so on. At the root of most of our major social problems are choices about values. What kind of people are we? What kind of life do we want to lead? What is our vision of the good society? How much weight do we want to give to individual freedom? How much to equality? How much to security? How much to material progress? If we emphasize only individual responsibility, we come close to recreating the "jungle," with all the freedom and all the insecurity and inequality that prevails in the jungle. On the other hand, if we ignore individual responsibility and rely entirely on social responsibility, the best we can hope for is the security of a well-run "zoo."

The papers and comments in this volume do not, for the most part, explicitly engage the issue of responsibility. They do, however, provide empirical and theoretical background for such engagement. A paper for each of the four sectors discusses production, financing, and distribution and considers the implications for public policy. The authors are experts in their respective fields, but the papers were written for readers who are not specialists. In recent years there have been numerous conferences about child care, about education, about medical care, and about long-term care, but rarely if ever has there been an opportunity to discuss the four sectors at the same time. Similarities and differences in the problems identified in each sector provide valuable additional insights, as do the discussions of possible solutions. While each sector is distinctive, the four also share many common characteristics; thus analysis of their problems can benefit from approaches that are not sector-specific.

With that in mind, six cross-sector papers were also invited. The authors were encouraged to be idiosyncratic, to choose themes of special interest to them, and to relate those themes to the conference agenda. Their mission was to stimulate new ways of thinking about human services through the application of economic theory, institutional analysis, and the history of social policy.

The disparate backgrounds of the participants made this a high-risk conference; the intense interactions and lively discussions, however, showed that a meeting of scholars with different interests and methodologies can produce fruitful results. Timothy Taylor's overview focuses on the positive contributions of the participants. In addition, the conference revealed gaps in current understanding of the political economy of human services in the United States, gaps that highlight the importance of future research.

## An Agenda for Research

Academic dissatisfaction with public policy debate is not a new phenomenon. In 1966 George Stigler wrote: "The controversy between conservatives and liberals in the United States is so ineffective that it is not serving the purposes of controversy. The quality of controversy is not only low, but in fact declining. And what was once a meaningful debate is becoming completely unjoined." Stigler's prescription for improvement was the collection and analysis of large amounts of information—in other words, research. He did not believe that research would eliminate all differences of opinion on public policy, but he hoped that "[a]n effective joining of the debate should put focus on our controversies and build progress into our policies" (13). It is in that spirit that I offer the following suggestions; some were derived from discussions at the conference, while others are mine alone.

### Sector Studies

The most straightforward, traditional lines of research would attempt to improve understanding of demand and supply within each of the four sectors. For example, with respect to child care, how do changes in financing (e.g., subsidies) affect decisions about child care arrangements? What are the consequences of alternative arrangements for child development? What kind of child care do parents really want (see Leibowitz, chap. 2 in this volume)? What are the implications for public policy when the preferences of parents differ from those of child care experts? Are there significant externalities associated with child care? What is the impact of current government regulations on the availability of child care and the efficiency with which it is produced?

Similar questions arise with respect to education. The nature and extent of externalities seem to require particular attention: the case for tax-financed education is predicated partly on an assumption of externalities, but James Poterba's paper reminds us that the validity of this assumption has not been the object of systematic study. The organization of production of schooling is getting and deserves considerable attention (see Hanushek, chap. 3 in this volume). Regardless of the source of finance, what are the consequences of having schooling provided through publicly owned institutions, through nonprofit organizations, or through profit-seeking firms? Indeed, future work will have to attend to more complex organizational arrangements, such as the contracting out to private firms of the operations of publicly owned schools.

The study of input and output and the relationship between the two is a standard subject in economics and in economic studies of education. These concepts, however, have often been defined narrowly, with the input assumed to be measured by the expenditures of the schools and the output measured by educational achievement. If, as seems likely, the inputs to educational achievement include much more than schooling, for example, the time and effort of students, their parents, and community resources, and if the output of the schools that is demanded by families and the community includes more than educational achievement, current claims about the declining efficiency of schools will have to be reassessed.

With respect to all these questions about education, *disaggregation* will probably prove to be very important (see Jencks's comment on chap. 3). It is not difficult to imagine that kindergarten bears more resemblance to child care than it does to the work of the university. Public policies toward higher education seem particularly ripe for reexamination by economists (see Hansmann, chap. 9 in this volume). Most higher education is publicly financed, but the classic arguments for public financing—externalities or redistribution to families with low income—are supported more by assertion than by empirical research. Most of the benefits of higher education probably accrue to the individual student, and most of the students at public colleges and universities come from middle- or upper-income families. Furthermore, even if public *financing* of higher education could be justified on efficiency or equity criteria, it does not follow that the subsidies should be used to bias the *production* of higher education toward public institutions.

Disaggregation is also called for in future work on medical care. The price elasticity and income elasticity of demand, for example, may be quite low for some medical care services but quite high for others. Problems of consumer ignorance and asymmetrical information can vary greatly, depending upon the type of medical care under discussion. Correct specification of inputs and outputs of medical care is also critical. It is now widely accepted that health outcomes depend heavily on personal behavior, the physical environment, and psychosocial factors, as well as medical care. Furthermore, much of the effort of the medical sector is devoted to providing caring, validation, and other services that are valued by patients even if health outcomes are not improved.

The traditional disaggregation of medical care research into hospital care and outpatient physician services will have to be reconsidered in the light of changes in medical finance, organization, and technology. Each year an increasing proportion of medical care is delivered by integrated health systems that provide a package of hospital care, physician services, and prescription drugs that is reimbursed on a capitation basis. Furthermore, there has been a rapid growth of ambulatory surgery and home administration of high-tech medical care that was formerly available only in hospitals. Thus, new modes of analysis, perhaps based on episode-of-illness or annual utilization of care, will have to be developed to study the health care system of tomorrow.

Probably the most under-studied sector, given its economic importance and rapid growth, is long-term care. Definitive knowledge regarding the demand for such care and efficiency in its production is scarce. Studies of policies that might reduce the impact of adverse selection and moral hazard would be particularly valuable (see Garber, chap. 5 in this volume). The most promising approach to financing long-term care appears to be a blend of private savings, private insurance, and public financing. How to achieve such a blend and how to structure incentives to achieve equity and efficiency in long-term care appear to be at least as problematic as in child care, education, or medical care.

## Interactions between Sectors

In addition to the individual sector studies discussed above, there are several promising research opportunities focusing on relationships between sectors. For example, we need to know much more about the relationship between child care and education. If, as some research suggests, the readiness of children to learn at kindergarten is a primary determinant of their educational achievement, there is clearly a need to understand what it is in the preschool experience that produces readiness to learn. The preschool years may also have significant implications for medical care. Poor child care can lead to health problems in adolescence and adulthood, such as a tendency toward obesity. It is possible that health habits and patterns of utilization of medical care are developed early in life.

The connection between education and health has been a subject of study for many decades, but much remains unclear regarding the underlying causal mechanisms. While some researchers believe that additional schooling contributes to better health through wiser use of medical care, that causal path has not been conclusively demonstrated. Similarly, it is not clear whether additional schooling causes individuals to have better health habits, or whether individuals who have better health habits are likely to get additional schooling.

There are also major opportunities for studying the interaction between medical care and long-term care. Are these services complements or substitutes? How does the answer to this question vary depending upon the type of medical care? Would it be more efficient to integrate the financing of medical care and long-term care or to keep them separate? The same question may be asked about the ownership and organization of production of these two services.

## Studies across All Sectors

In addition to research on individual sectors or interactions between two sectors, there is a need for studies that cut across all the sectors. Consider, for example, the role of nonmarket production. The possibility of substitution between nonmarket and market production within each sector has been studied, but it would also be of interest to look at the possibility of substitution of one type of nonmarket activity for another. There are significant forces that affect all nonmarket activity; thus much of the research on family and gender can and should be brought to bear on the problems of the four sectors covered in this volume. What determines the allocation of nonmarket work among the four types of services discussed in this volume and what determines its allocation among family members?

These sectors also need to be addressed from the perspective of investment in human capital. Such investment is a major factor for each of these sectors (except, perhaps, long-term care). One interesting question is how the rate of time preference of individuals and families affects their willingness to invest in each of these sectors. A related issue is the role of liquidity constraints in such investment decisions.

All of the human service sectors share the common characteristic that employment in them is predominantly female. In child care women account for over 95% of the work force; in nursing homes about 87%; in medical care there are at least three women employed for every man; and in education there are two women for every man. It would, therefore, be important to know how these sectors have been affected by the major changes in gender roles and relationships of the last thirty years. To what extent has the relative increase in women's wages and the opening up to women of occupations that were traditionally male affected the supply of labor and the costs of production in the human services sectors? To what extent has adjustment taken place in nominal wages or in the quality of the labor that is recruited? How will the inevitable retardation in the rate of growth of female labor supply affect these sectors?

Government plays a significant role in all four sectors, but the extent, locus, and form of government intervention varies greatly (see Poterba, chap. 10 in this volume). An approach to the optimal role for government that cuts across all sectors might reach different conclusions than those derived from the study of each sector in isolation. Special attention would have to be paid to the capacity of government at different levels to discharge its obligations honestly and efficiently. Such research should consider the quality of the civil service, including issues of recruitment, pay, and turnover.

It is overly simplistic to frame the question of government involvement in human services in terms of "more" or "less." At least as important are questions about the *kind* of involvement—tax credits, vouchers, direct subsidies, mandates, regulation, or direct production—and the appropriate *level* of government. To make wise policy choices, we need to know much more about economies of scale, problems of information, variability in preferences, externalities, productivity, and other economic characteristics of these sectors.

Comparative-Historical Studies

The enormous range of variation in human services across high-income, democratic nations suggests that comparative studies might provide much useful information about methods of financing and producing these services. In child care, for instance, the number of children per caregiver in France is three to four times as large as in Sweden. Does it matter? And if so, how? In some European countries child care workers have college or graduate degrees, but in the United States the average child care worker has only about thirteen years of schooling. Why the difference? And what are the consequences?

International differences in government's role in child care are particularly striking. Not only does the United States provide much less direct payment for children in the form of child allowances or mandatory paid parental leave, but it also offers much less subsidization of child care outside the home. Moreover, in contrast with other high-income countries, child-related benefits in the United States are usually means tested. These differences in child care policy stand in stark contrast to education, where the United States has been the world leader in public support, and this support is usually provided without means testing.

International differences in education take a different form. For instance, many countries have early and pervasive tracking, while American education experts question the value of such a policy. In some European countries control of education is highly centralized, but in the United States control is in the hands of local school boards and state governments. Does decentralized control actually result in much greater diversity? If not, why not? If it does, what are the advantages and disadvantages of such diversity?

Comparative studies of medical care offer a rich opportunity to learn about the effects of alternative policies because modes of finance and delivery vary greatly, even for close neighbors such as the United States and Canada. For instance, the hospital admission rate in Canada for children (ages one to fifteen) is twice the rate for the United States. At ages over sixty-five the admission rates are about equal in the two countries. What explains this age-related disparity, and what are its implications for the health of the young and the old? Other large differences between medical care in the United States and abroad that are ripe for investigation include the high proportion of specialists and the much shorter average length of hospital stay in America. Comparative studies of long-term care are very scarce, but the growing importance of this sector in all modern societies will create a need for such information.

Historical studies can be thought of at one level as another form of comparative study. For instance, a comparison of education in the United States in the 1950s with education in the 1990s, or a similar comparison for medical care, can help illuminate current problems. As with any comparative study, attempts should be made to identify the differences, to explain their origins, and to discuss their consequences. Historical studies can also be approached in another spirit, namely, that of understanding the historical development of social policy itself (see Skocpol, chap. 11 in this volume). The rising interest in "path dependency" in economics generally could be applied to the study of how current policy options are constrained by earlier decisions. For instance, starting de novo, few experts would recommend separate health insurance systems for persons under or over age sixty-five. The history of three decades of Medicare, however, makes it much more difficult to achieve a sensible, uniform policy that applies to all ages (see Aaron, chap. 4 in this volume).

Studies of Dynamic Processes

Path-dependent views of historical developments lead naturally to studies of both private behaviors and public policy making as dynamic processes. If we are to understand human services and the policies that affect them, we must consider the possibility that preferences for these services change as a result of incentive-induced changes in behavior. In this volume, for instance, Robert Frank asks us to consider how the demand for education or for medical care by the bulk of the population may "ratchet up" as consumption increases at the top. Also in this volume, Paul Romer suggests that the framing of public policies, such as Social Security, and the promises implicit in that framing, may help us understand behaviors that do not fit neatly into the narrow preference model that characterizes most economic analyses.

In the medical sector we need to understand the dynamics of a technology-insurance cycle (Weisbrod 1991) where the development of new, expensive medical technologies increases the coverage (and cost) of health insurance, and increases in insurance coverage induce further development of expensive new technologies. In education, Hirschman (1970) has called attention to a process whereby some deterioration in public education leads to the withdrawal of parents and children most concerned about school quality; their exit from public education then leads to further deterioration, further withdrawals by others, and so on.

Most sweeping of all in its implications is the idea that the habits, social norms, and ethical beliefs that constrain economic behavior in the short- and medium-term may themselves be changed in the long run by economic policies (Aaron 1994; Lindbeck 1994). Lindbeck focuses on the possible long-run effects of the welfare state on work, saving, asset choice, and entrepreneurship. The central idea, however, of the dynamic interaction among policies, incentives, behavior, and social norms could be fruitfully applied to the human service sectors.

## Concluding Thoughts

The human service sectors discussed in this volume account for roughly one-fifth of the U.S. gross domestic product. That is more than the total of agriculture, mining, construction, transportation, and public utilities; it is more than wholesale and retail trade combined; and even slightly more than all manufacturing. Thus, judged purely in dollar terms, there is a clear case for extensive attention to these sectors by economists. Moreover, careful study of how we socialize the young, train the next generation, treat the sick, and care for the old goes to the very heart of understanding American society.

The problems of research on human services, however, are formidable. Data are scarce, and, when available, uneven in quality and coverage. This can be remedied if governmental resources for data collection were reallocated to bring them into conformity with the reality of today's service economy. More troublesome is the difficulty of defining inputs and outputs in human services, concepts that are central to most economic analysis. Here a combination of theoretical and empirical work is needed to make research results more relevant for policy making. Information about the need for and quality of services is very important (see Arrow, chap. 8 in this volume), but finding the proper balance between collective provision of information and individual responsibility for acquiring it is a daunting task.

Most difficult of all is the question of values. Economic analysis usually takes values as given and discusses from both positive and normative perspectives how to maximize values given constraints of resources. In long-term analysis, however, and especially with a view to affecting public policy, it will often be necessary for economists to recognize that policies and institutions help to shape values.

Economists are understandably reluctant to prescribe values or to make normative judgments about preferences. But when economic policies affect values and preferences, and these in turn affect behavior, it is incumbent on economists to analyze the links between policies and values, and to examine the economic and social consequences of alternative value systems. In particular, this conference reinforced my belief that more explicit consideration of the tension between individual and social responsibility will contribute to a fuller understanding of private behaviors and public policies in the human service sectors.

# References

Aaron, Henry J. 1994. Public policy, values, and consciousness. *Journal of Economic Perspectives* 8 (spring): 3–21.

Aron, Raymond. 1968. *Progress and disillusion.* New York: Praeger.

Fuchs, Victor R. 1994. The Clinton plan: A researcher examines reform. *Health Affairs* 13 (spring): 102–14.

Hirschman, Albert O. 1970. *Exit, voice, and loyalty: Responses to decline in firms, organizations, and states.* Cambridge: Harvard University Press.

Lindbeck, Assar. 1994. Hazardous welfare state dynamics: Endogenous habits and norms. Mimeo.

Okun, Arthur M. 1975. *Equality and efficiency: The big tradeoff.* Washington, DC: Brookings Institution.

Stigler, George J. 1966. The unjoined debate. *Chicago Today* (University of Chicago) (winter). Reprinted in George J. Stigler, *The citizen and the state.* Chicago: University of Chicago Press, 1975.

Weisbrod, Burton A. 1991. The health care quadrilemma: An essay on technological change, insurance, quality of care, and cost containment. *Journal of Economic Literature* 29:523–52.

# 1    Overview

Timothy Taylor

The structure of this volume is straightforward. The first four papers each focus on a high-profile service industry: child care, education, health care, and long-term care for the elderly. The remaining six papers focus in various ways on how social science, and economic methodology in particular, might grapple with the sorts of issues raised by these four service industries. Each paper is followed by a discussant's comment.

This overview has three objectives. I present an overall orientation toward the volume, with brief summaries of the papers. I spend somewhat more space offering a description of the roundtable discussions that took place at the conference. This description is not exhaustive: it is one person's perspective on what it was like to attend the conference. Finally, I offer a few thoughts of my own about why the child care, education, health, and long-term care services discussed here pose special difficulties for economists and for public policy.

## 1.1   Child Care

Child care is often viewed as custodial: a service provided so that mothers can earn money in the paid labor market. This issue is important, of course; it's tied up with efforts of middle-class mothers to build economic security for their families, and it's tied up with helping poor mothers get off welfare and into work. In fact, Arleen Leibowitz makes the interesting point that welfare can be viewed as a child care program, in which the government pays many of the mothers who are most economically vulnerable to stay home and look after children.

But in her paper in this volume, Leibowitz focuses instead on the notion of

Timothy Taylor is managing editor of the *Journal of Economic Perspectives,* based at the Hubert H. Humphrey Institute of Public Affairs at the University of Minnesota.

child care as an investment in the human capital of tomorrow's adults. Her paper discusses various types of child care, issues surrounding the quality and financing of such care, and the possible role for government involvement. Leibowitz points out that the gains may be especially large for children starting off on the bottom rungs of America's socioeconomic ladder. Good-quality child care may provide a start in life that makes success in school more likely, and thus offers a start toward a middle-class economic future. Moreover, although there is less evidence on this point, child care may serve as an early intervention that helps to counteract neighborhood pathologies of crime, abuse, and children giving birth to other children. As one conference participant put it, in discussing the life of many children who grow up in poor inner-city areas, "[t]he harm is so great right now, one might choose something else just in desperation."

But if there is a general sense that improved access to child care might greatly benefit at least some children and mothers, society must develop a greater consensus on a number of issues before any substantial policy change is likely to be adopted. Some of the issues raised in the discussion at the conference went to the heart of child care policy.

For example, any public subsidy to child care is necessarily an encouragement to mothers to put their children into such programs. But how strongly should society encourage mothers to put their children into child care? Perhaps the tax credit for child care should be expanded, although this affects mainly working mothers. Perhaps a portion of Aid to Families with Dependent Children (AFDC) or child-support payments might be earmarked for child care; this would affect mainly single mothers. Perhaps, given the evidence on how child care provides relatively greater benefits to socioeconomically disadvantaged children, one might require as a condition of receiving welfare that mothers put their children into a registered child care program.

When society offers a subsidy, whether for child care or anything else, it usually comes with strings attached. At the extreme, one might envision direct federal provision of day care. However, no one at this conference spoke out in favor of such an extreme step. Some opposed anything resembling such a step with particular vehemence, arguing that a federally provided system would come loaded down with costly regulations: about types of toys; curriculum for the preschoolers; details about buildings where child care would be provided, including plumbing, electricity, entry and exit, and construction; specifications for advanced education, experience, and training for child care workers and administrators; and so on and so on.

The conference discussion among economists (many of whom are also parents) illustrated that parents have strong and differing feelings about the provision of child care. Some would prefer a well-run institution, with regular hours, professional staff, and lots of flexibility for those days when the parents are running a bit early or late. Others would prefer the proverbial middle-aged woman who loves kids and sets up a small day care establishment in her home. Still others would prefer a live-in nanny or au pair. Along with different preferences for how child care should be provided, those at the conference expressed varying preferences for how their two-year-old should best spend a day. Some would emphasize more structured and particular learning: making sure that two- and three-year-olds learn colors and shapes and counting to ten. Others prefer that their preschoolers learn to play with others and to have good associations with attending school. Social science studies have offered little guidance on the "best" sort of child care, if such care exists.

As Leibowitz points out in her paper, and the conference discussion acknowledged, families will play the key role in determining the type of care their children receive. But this raises the potential problem of segregating children at an early age, whether by income, ethnicity, type of curriculum, or some other standard. On the other side, one participant in the discussion pointed out that any segregation in day care will probably be no worse than the de facto segregation that already exists both between school districts and within schools. Given that adults are probably more integrated in their work arrangements than in their housing patterns, child care that was provided close to the workplace might end up more socioeconomically and ethnically integrated than many school districts.

## 1.2   Education

Eric Hanushek has led the way in pointing out some uncomfortable facts about the lack of any significant correlation between educational inputs and outputs. For example, U.S. education spending over the last century has increased at triple the growth rate of the gross domestic product. Real per-student expenditures quintupled from 1890 to 1940—and then quintupled again from 1940 to 1990. Yet even as the commitment of resources was rising, the performance of the U.S. educational system, as measured by a variety of standardized tests and international comparisons, has been declining.

Hanushek's paper in this volume discusses why the debate over improving the schools seems to emphasize increasing expenditures, rather than improvements in the quality of schooling. For example, many policy discussions come close to defining school quality or concerns over equity as a matter of the level or equality of spending, rather than focusing on the efficiency of that spending. Although claims are often made that education has positive externalities that justify greater spending, Hanushek points out that, when one presses for a definition and magnitude of the externalities that would result from increases in education spending above present levels, they often become vague and difficult to grasp.

Most of the discussion at the conference focused on evidence that increasing inputs to education have not bought much in the way of measurable outputs. It was noted that opponents of higher funding for education have seized on the lack of a statistical correlation, while supporters of higher funding for schools have been outraged by a conclusion that, to them, sounds like a cover-up for hard-heartedness. Such controversies often seem to surround empirical work. It's been said that a person with one watch knows what time it is, while a person with two watches can never be sure. In a similar spirit, it might be asserted that a social scientist with one regression study always knows the correct answer, but a social scientist with many regression studies can never be sure. Yet in the discussion of Hanushek's paper at the conference, the distinctions over more or less dollars seemed less black and white than they are typically presented.

If society were to contemplate a massive infusion of resources into the existing, unreformed public school system, there's no particular reason to believe that the output of schools would improve. (Of course, in these days of budgetary stringency, not many public schools are contemplating a mass infusion of resources.) However, there are certainly cases in particular school districts where more money was spent in combination with certain reforms in a way that led to improvement in test scores, dropout rates, or other measures of educational achievement. Thus, one might restate Hanushek's point to be that money alone won't save the schools. But reorganization, perhaps in combination with targeted additional money, might offer educational benefits. Even if money itself is not what improves the system, perhaps additional money can buy a willingness to change that would otherwise be absent.

Thus, rather than arguing over the level of resources, a useful discussion of educational reform might focus instead on what actual changes should take place, either with or without additional money. Among the ideas floated at the conference:

*Increase the Quantity of Education.* Hanushek points out that, in terms of years of school completed, America's level of educational attainment leveled off about two decades ago. One might increase the raw quantity of education either by providing greater encouragement for students to proceed with higher education, or increase the quantity of K–12 education with steps like longer school days, more homework, or longer school years. Of course, most of these ideas cost resources, including the time of teachers, staff, or parents.

*Improve the Quality of Teachers.* Everyone remembers the dynamic impact of a good teacher, and the frustration of trying to learn with a poor one. The present system tends to reward teachers by seniority or paper qualifications, however, rather than by the job they do in the classroom. Many proposed changes for the education system are best thought of as mechanisms for rewarding good teachers. For example, the hope behind a voucher system is that students won't be trapped with worse teachers, and can seek out better ones.

Other common proposals are to allow teachers to start their own charter schools, to encourage principals or "master teachers" to evaluate teaching directly. One powerful way to evaluate any proposal for education is to ask about the ways in which it rewards good teachers and penalizes poor ones.

*Focus the Curriculum on Modern Job Skills.* One role for education is to create a pathway into the workforce. Even without raising test scores, it may be possible to teach information and skills that will help students make this transition more smoothly. At a simple level, this could mean teaching word-processing literacy rather than typing, and spreadsheet literacy along with high school math. But at a deeper level, it may mean building ties between industry and schools—perhaps through apprenticeships—so that a high school degree once again begins to certify readiness for at least certain jobs, instead of merely proving that the student reached the age of consent without acting badly enough to be kicked out.

*Separate the Education and Social Service Budgets.* Several discussants noted that schools have taken on more and more tasks that are socially important but are not basic skills of education: security screening for safe halls and classrooms; free breakfasts and lunches; driver's education; conflict resolution; counselling; sex and drug information; after-school programs that may be best understood as day care for busy parents; and so on. Many of these programs are important and productive. As one conference participant said, education should be multidimensional, "not just aimed at buying a better car when you're forty." But there is nonetheless a danger that the tail of extra services, each one arguably useful in its own way, could end up wagging the dog of education. To clarify the trade-offs, it might be useful to budget separately for certain social functions of the schools. At worst, this would provide an additional dimension of data for social scientists to exploit; at best, it might lead to a more productive public debate over how the resources available to schools should be allocated.

*Remember the Complements to Education.* How children perform in school depends heavily on factors outside the control of the school, like parental time and involvement, decent meals, whether the child arrived in kindergarten or first grade ready to learn, whether parents are in the labor market, and whether the neighborhood is safe. Health care economists accept, almost as commonplace, the insight that reforming exercise and diet patterns would have a far greater impact on American health than any conceivable change in how the country finances medical care. Similarly, focusing on these complements to education may provide a greater boost to learning than most changes proposed for the educational system itself. In fact, Victor Fuchs has entertained the thought experiment that transferring money out of K–12 education to certain of these complements to education might increase overall learning.

## 1.3   Health Care Financing

For supporters of far-reaching reform of America's system of health care finance, 1993 and 1994 were dispiriting years. It seemed widely agreed that a system that gobbles 15% of GDP, while failing to provide health insurance for millions of Americans and threatening millions of others with lost coverage, should have some room for improvement. But after a year of intense discussion following the introduction of President Clinton's health care plan, nothing happened. Not a major reform, not a minor reform, just nothing. In fact, by the time everything was said and left undone, it wasn't even clear that health care's eighteen months in the public spotlight had enhanced America's understanding of the issues, or laid the framework for a better reform.

Henry Aaron's paper can be read as an exploration of why health care reform proved such an intractable problem. Politics played a role, of course. But Aaron argues that the key problems are central to the nature of the health care industry and the inherited patterns of how the United States provides health care. For example, new technology is driving up the cost of health care. Because of tax breaks and limited information, households have a distorted perspective on how much health insurance they need. The U.S. "system of health care" is a misnomer, Aaron argues, because of the vast number of overlapping policies and institutions, public and private, which determine how health care is provided. And yet some group has a personal stake in every one of these institutions, and thus is loath to see it changed.

Given the collapse of grand attempts at health care reform, the present agenda seems to involve thinking of smaller reforms that would be useful in themselves, and would lead toward an improved system. Aaron's paper, for example, advocates "the creation of some form of regionally based, politically legitimated, administratively capable entity (or entities) [able] to enforce order in the financing of health care." Such entities appeared in many reform proposals, both legislative and academic. In his comment, Martin Feldstein raises some other possibilities, like changing the tax exclusion for employer-provided health insurance, or medical savings plans. Other possible steps to consider included guaranteed renewal of policies, a prohibition against considering preexisting conditions, helping to build capitated health care plans (which operate with a preset annual budget), and so on.

During the discussion at the conference, however, doubts were expressed about each of these incremental steps, as well. Even if successful, it's not clear how steps like these would help the working poor who aren't presently covered and would have a hard time paying for insurance. Even if certain of the incremental reforms would work in a technical sense, it's not clear they are politically acceptable in the present poisoned atmosphere.

This conference, in October 1994, was not a cheerful time to discuss prospects for health care reform. But as Aaron points out, the problems that led to pressure for reform, like rising costs and fears of losing health insurance coverage, are not going away. In one form or another, the issues will surface again.

## 1.4  Long-Term Care

The post–World War II baby boom hit the school system in the 1950s and 1960s, and washed into the labor market in the 1970s and 1980s. Ten or twenty years into the twenty-first century, this group will start receiving Social Security. Not too many years after that, they will enter the age bracket that makes heavy use of long-term care, a broad category that covers everything from a little in-home help with meals or cleaning to institutional care in a nursing home or hospice.

Alan Garber's paper lays out the dimensions of this issue: what is actually involved in long-term care; what proportion of the population is likely to make use of such care; how Medicare and Medicaid presently cover such care; and what the options are for providing such care to the baby boom generation. Garber argues that planning for a future transfer program, from the working-age population to the elderly, is not likely to be economically or politically sustainable. Thus, the solution must be to find ways where the baby boom generation taken as a group saves the money to pay for its future long-term care needs.

Private insurance is one way in which this sort of saving might occur, but neither Garber, nor his discussant, John Shoven, nor the discussion that followed seemed very sanguine about the future of greatly expanding private insurance for long-term care. After all, why purchase insurance for catastrophic expenditures on long-term care, since Medicaid pays for such care already after an elderly person's resources are depleted? Why purchase insurance for long-term care several decades away, given the possibility that the government will create a program to finance such care? Drawing up a contract for long-term care that defines what assistance will be provided several decades in the future, under what terms, seems extraordinarily difficult. As Shoven documents, existing private contracts don't seem to offer an especially good deal to a forward-looking consumer; presumably, myopic consumers not worried about what happens a few decades in the future won't be all that interested in long-term care insurance, either.

Perhaps the most severe problem with depending on people to purchase private insurance for long-term care is that, while such care may end up as a necessity for many people, it is not a necessity that it is cheerful to contemplate. The whole notion of needing nursing home care is deeply unattractive. To many potential customers, buying insurance for long-term care sounds like a way of making sure that when you are old and withered, having difficulties dressing or feeding yourself, perhaps incontinent or senile, that you will have well-mannered, well-trained, well-dressed attendants looking after you. As one participant in the discussion put it, "I'd prefer a vial of sleeping pills and a plastic bag." I find it more pleasant to contemplate the fruits of my life insurance policy—that is, in which loved ones have a windfall income after my death—than to contemplate using a long-term care insurance policy.

But even if private insurance doesn't provide it, the need for long-term care won't go away. Without some social intervention, much of the burden seems likely to fall on the middle-aged children of the elderly who need care, and particularly on the daughters. This could have powerful implications for the labor supply of midcareer women.

The conference discussion recognized that any serious effort to deal with the coming need for long-term care must look at both benefit levels and finance. On the benefits side, a program for long-term care needs to recognize that such care forms a spectrum, ranging from providing a few meals to a person living at home to full and intensive nursing home care. Presumably, one wants to build a system where people are encouraged to be as independent as possible, to stay in the home and with their natural support system as long as possible. This framework argues for not insuring people against the milder or shorter forms of home care, like assistance in preparing meals or a one-week stay in a nursing home. (If people have insurance for receiving help around the house, the size of the program could easily overwhelm public budgets.) For those unlucky enough to have severe and ongoing long-term care needs, however, an insurance program may be useful. The challenge on the benefits side is to draw the line.

On the finance side, a program for long-term care needs to recognize that, even if one accepts the need for a system of required contributions (in the belief that private markets aren't going to meet the need), this system can still be structured in many ways. For example, it could be a general tax revenue program, a Social Security extension, a special version of medical savings plans, or some other method. These different sources of funding can easily have very different consequences for whether the program is sustainable in the long-term, or whether it has built-in momentum to overexpand, as is discussed in the papers by Paul Romer and Robert Frank in this volume.

### 1.5    Preferences, Promises, and Entitlement

Promises don't have any place in standard models of political behavior, Paul Romer points out. In such models, decisions are based on present considerations, not on words spoken in the past. Romer writes, "Promises, in the language of game theory, are just cheap talk." But clearly, in the real world, promises create in people a sense of entitlement that affects voting and the formation of policy more broadly. In turn, policy makers know that their promises do matter to some extent, and act accordingly. Romer takes on the task of explaining why rational people may have preferences that depend on the promises made by others.

Romer tackles this question by examining evidence from biology and pointing out that, in many situations, it will be useful for people to have mechanisms that help to enforce cooperative behavior. However, calling for retaliation every time someone doesn't cooperate would be an overreaction, potentially leading to a cycle of retaliation that destroys the very cooperation one is trying to build. Limiting retaliation to situations where a promise has been made can assist in building cooperation, while reducing the danger of a cycle of retaliation.

With this framework, Romer's paper uses these insights about why promises matter to reopen a set of long-standing arguments over why people vote, why negative campaigning works, why commitments and promises matter in politics, and more. In particular, he uses his argument to explain why the phrasing of promises about Social Security has been taken to be so important, both by those in favor of expanding the program and by those in favor of reining it back. His argument implies that the design of social programs and the promises surrounding their passage will influence the life expectancy of such programs, and whether they expand or contract with time.

To many economists, Romer's use of biology as evidence about rational preferences is sure to be controversial. Moreover, the idea of expanded preferences always raises a fear among economists that we are no longer testing hypotheses, but instead are making up ad hoc explanations. Of course, motivations derived from biology need to be treated with care, considered against a background of other possible motivations, and tested against a variety of empirical implications. But social scientists are not so omniscient about human motivations that they can afford to rule out any evidence that comes to hand.

## 1.6  Consumption Externalities

People judge their well-being in relation to those around them. Sometimes the effects of such relative valuations may be trivial, like envy that the neighbor's house has a nicer view. In other cases, as when one heart is available for transplant and three patients are waiting, the relative values can be life and death. In his work over the last few years, Robert Frank has illuminated these "consumption externalities"—that is, how the consumption of one person affects the utility of others. In this paper, he applies this framework to the design of programs for child care, education, health, and long-term care.

In many of these basic services, Frank argues, it is plausible that consumption externalities are significant. People want to make sure that their child's education is relatively good compared to that of other children, and that the care they receive in case of illness is as good as what most other people would receive. Consider a case where the government provides a basic level service to everyone who qualifies, like a K–12 education. What if a family, driven by the imperative for its children to be relatively a bit more educated, wants to purchase more than the basic service? Under the present system, the family can put its children into private schools, but it must then pay for 100% of their education. On the other hand, if the government provided a voucher for the value of a basic education, then a family could put its children in alternate, pricier schools and only pay the additional amount.

Frank argues that the second alternative is subject to upward drift in the quantity of service provided. People will compete to ensure that their child receives somewhat more education, and political pressure will arise for the basic amount provided to keep increasing, so that those who can spend extra do not gain a relative advantage. Moreover, courts may require a certain amount of equality in the provision of basic services like education. In this way, the design of a program and the conditions under which people are allowed either to opt out or to augment the basic package create powerful incentives for the future evolution of that program.

As was pointed out in the discussion that followed, Frank's paper can be viewed as a contribution to a set of questions that come up every time the government decides to guarantee that people receive a basic level of a particular service. If the government pays for provision of the service to everyone, without a means test, then the program looms large in public budgets, and imposes a burden on taxpayers. When the government provides the service only to a defined group—say, those up to a certain income level—then there is a "notch" problem, where a small gain in income means that one is no longer eligible for the benefit. As a result, potential recipients will try to avoid exceeding that level of income. If the government tries to circumvent the notch problem by phasing out the program gradually over a range of income levels, then the phaseout creates incentives similar to a tax. For example, if the amount of public service is reduced by 50 cents every time the recipient earns an extra dollar of income, then the recipient only gains 50 cents in income by earning a dollar, which is a fairly high marginal tax rate, especially when added to the other taxes workers pay.

Frank's argument effectively says that, even if a notch problem causes counterproductive incentives, designing a program with a notch may also act as a brake on rising public expenditures on certain services. In situations where the nation is already committing a sufficient level of resources—Hanushek and Aaron would argue that education and health care fall into this category—the notch may be a useful tool. On the other side, for industries where the resource commitment probably needs to increase—Leibowitz and Garber would argue that child care and long-term care fall into this category—then allowing people to augment a basic package may make more sense.

## 1.7   Information

Services are hard to measure. Of course, one can count the amount of time a service provider spends on certain tasks, or the amount of money spent on services, but that's not the same thing, although we sometimes pretend that it is. Two teachers or doctors may spend exactly the same time with students or patients, and yet offer an enormously different quality of service. In principle, at least, if information on the quality of service were describable and measurable, then people and suppliers could make more rational choices, and markets for services would work much better. Kenneth Arrow's paper focuses on the economics of information, and reinforces how markets will have difficulty dealing with a valuable, costly, intangible, nondepletable good like information.

On the surface, a call for better information may seem as bland as lukewarm milk-toast made with white bread. But the discussion following the paper brought out some interesting distinctions.

Society may not want to collect some forms of information, or allow that information to be used. For example, as it becomes possible to use the emerging knowledge of genetic codes to predict the likelihood of certain diseases, no one really wants to force those with an unlucky genetic profile to pay more for health insurance. Even though women live longer than men, most of the policies that sell long-term care insurance make no distinction in price between the sexes. Recently, there has been considerable press coverage of the hypothesis that racial differences are correlated with measures of intelligence; even if this were true (and the case is very far from proven), it is not clear that this information assists the functioning of society. In all of these cases, there is a conflict between treating people fairly as individuals and information about group tendencies or differences. In this context, just providing information may have results that few would welcome.

Information about the quality of services can spread in many ways: through newspaper and magazine reviews, guidebooks, professional rankings, and so on. Businesses may offer recommendations to employees, perhaps about day care options. Word of mouth from friends and neighbors can spread quickly. In some cases, individuals may be able to gather the information themselves; even if I can't put into precise and quantifiable terms whether I like my child's day care arrangement, I may still be capable of evaluating in ordinal terms whether I like it better than the alternatives. Care provided to one's children and to one's elderly parents are both somewhat visible to the naked eye. On the other hand, the quality of education being received in a school is perhaps more difficult to judge, at least in a visit of reasonable length. Moreover, it's harder for most people to change their child's school than it is to change a day care center. For most people, it is extremely difficult to judge the quality of medical care as it is provided, particularly the quality (or necessity) of costly high-tech medicine.

Although markets for information do not always develop readily, a firm's reputation can be thought of as a way of providing information about the quality of service provided. When you go to a McDonald's, you know with some accuracy the quality of the meal you'll receive. By contrast, a random burger joint involves higher variance. Even many nonprofits and public institutions, like colleges and universities, see themselves as competing for students in a way that encourages them to develop a reputation.

An alternative suggestion is that even if a consumer or society can't judge the actual quality of a service as it is provided, we can often measure some outcome of the service. For example, we might try to encourage public or private mechanisms to reward surgeons with the highest success rates, or teachers whose students make the greatest gain on standardized tests, even if we don't know exactly how these results were achieved. Of course, rewarding workers without understanding how they achieved their results is not fully satisfactory, either intellectually or practically. Whenever a particular metric is used for evaluating services, there is potential for gaming the system. For example, if teachers were rewarded according to student's test scores, they might sacrifice other forms of learning to add expertise on multiple-choice exams, or at an extreme, even encourage cheating on the exams. If long-term care providers were rewarded, say, according to a survey handed out to patients or relatives, then they might spend time lobbying patients to give them high marks, or "helping" to fill out the surveys, rather than actually providing care.

These issues are real and difficult. A single accurate measure of the quality of service provided is a will-o'-the-wisp. But even partial, incomplete, occasionally unreliable information may create incentives for service providers to try harder.

## 1.8   Organization of Production

Different institutional forms organize the incentives and flows of information in different ways. Henry Hansmann lays out how the advantages and disadvantages of public, nonprofit, and for-profit institutions determine how they are used differently in child care, education, health, and long-term care. He finds a strong expansion of for-profit provision and predicts that, just as a wave of for-profit providers has revolutionized health care in the last twenty-five years, for-profits may dramatically alter education in the next twenty-five.

The discussion that followed, led by Joseph Grundfest's comments, focused heavily on the fluidity of these organizational forms. Public organizations may function rather differently at the local, state, and federal levels. Nonprofits may either live on donations or by selling a good or service. For-profit institutions may either compete against other firms for sales to the private sector, or bid for the right to run public services like garbage collection. Of course, public-sector or nonprofit providers behave differently in the presence of competition, and differently depending on whether that competition comes from their own kind or from for-profit institutions. Moreover, as Grundfest's comment explores in detail, organizational forms can shift. Public providers can be privatized, nonprofits can take on for-profit status, or the public sector can decide to subsidize or provide directly in competition with other providers.

Amid all this turmoil, some directions seem clear. For-profit institutions are

spreading. While economists are rarely surprised by the success of the profit motive, there is reason for mild surprise in the case of the four service industries on which this volume focuses. After all, when one is searching for, say, health care, a cost-cutting for-profit institution may seem more threatening than attractive. Some would argue that making a profit from providing services like health care, education, or care for the elderly will necessarily force providers to skimp on the quality of service in the name of making a buck.

Of course, this criticism of the for-profit organizational form is not obviously true. A forward-looking for-profit firm may recognize that a reputation for skimping on services will reduce profits in the long run, and put it out of business, so it will try to build a reputation for high-quality service and innovation. By contrast, a government agency may feel that, without competition, there is little need to provide the most cost-effective and high-quality service. Apparently, at least for the present and for the sectors on which this volume focuses, the advantages of the for-profit organizational form in promoting efficiency and holding down costs are overbalancing the potential disadvantage of cut-rate service.

Even when service providers are not officially for-profit, more of them seem to be taking on a mentality of providing value for money. Even among nonprofits and public-sector providers, many discussants at the conference reported hearing talk of reinventing government, customer focus, and treating separable parts of an institution (like a university's law school) as separate cost centers. All of these are very much the sort of thinking that suffuses the for-profit sector.

## 1.9    Government in Health and Education

Economists have a neat scheme for figuring out when the government should intervene in markets. They have developed a list of market failures: cases where because of externalities, public goods, distributional concerns, information problems, or other reasons, markets either won't exist, or won't clear, or won't set prices that accurately balance social costs and benefits. This framework has proven extraordinarily useful for making judgments about the costs and benefits of policies. In his paper, James Poterba tackles the difficult question of whether market failures can also provide a framework for discussing how policies are actually chosen and implemented.

His results are frustrating, but perhaps not surprising. Principles of public finance (like taxing to offset externalities) and redistribution do not seem to be driving what services are actually provided in the areas of health care and education. Jurisdictions that appear similar have followed very different paths in providing such services, depending on what seem nothing more than quirks of history, or the interests of groups that deliver the services.

These findings are troubling to economists on several levels. If market forces are not operating, then there is little reason to believe that the choice of policies or their mix has any particular support from economic logic. It implies that when economists talk, no one is particularly listening. It implies that economic principles are largely unconnected to what has actually happened.

The conference discussion that followed raised two fronts on which these grim conclusions might be addressed. On one side, it might be possible to discover what sorts of ideas and appeals do carry weight in the public debate, and then to find ways of linking them to economic insights. Economics is a powerful tool for pointing out costs, benefits, and trade-offs; it would be surprising if this information could not be marshalled to better effect. In addition, economists should remember that market failure is not the only justification for government programs, and moderate their rhetoric accordingly. For example, market failures and measurable externalities may well be involved in policies that affect public values like patriotism, thrift, working hard, and honesty. But if economists would recognize that these values also have an independent importance of their own, they might end up doing a better job of explaining the world around them.

Either way, building a closer connection from the arguments of economists to the policies that are enacted seems a worthy goal.

## 1.10    The Politics of Social Policy

Most of the contributors to this volume are economists. Theda Skocpol is a sociologist. As she explained at the conference one evening after dinner, this doesn't mean that she thinks economists are powerless. Instead, she believes they have great power—just not in the directions that they think.

Her analysis in this paper focuses on four great waves of social reform: one involving Civil War veterans in the late nineteenth century; one involving mothers and children in the 1910s and 1920s; the New Deal of the 1930s; and the Great Society changes of the 1960s. She argues that a full understanding of these changes involves understanding how a nation comes to feel a particular sense of obligation to different groups at different times, and how existing programs grow and evolve in response to what society finds to be the especially salient arguments.

These arguments don't come in neat bunches. For example, some programs succeeded by providing a feeling that any government benefits were somehow earned by the recipients, as in veterans' benefits or Social Security. Local control of institutions, like schools and hospitals, has often helped foster their spread. The conference discussion that followed focused on a variety of public appeals that have been either successful in promoting programs—or in blocking them. For example, it is often powerful in the U.S. political system to appeal to the need for a unified society; to ask for tolerance of diversity; to rage against big bureaucracy; to draw analogies to programs that are perceived as successes (like Social Security); to point to personal health and safety (as in recent environmentalist and anticrime movements); and to appeal to "don't tread on me" individualism. As one participant noted at the conference, with only a little defensiveness, being hostile to economists, cost effectiveness, and efficiency concerns is usually a powerful way of appealing to the broad American public, too.

Skocpol's paper illuminates certain themes raised by earlier papers in the volume. For example, Romer discusses why promises might be important, while Skocpol discusses which sorts of arguments have been especially powerful in national discourse. Poterba points out that the common market failure language of economists doesn't seem descriptive of what is actually happening. Skocpol focuses on what has actually happened, and what elements of social programs appealed to the public in ways that affected the evolution of the program. What remains to be done is to discover or create links between the structured terms of art for economics and the broader terms of persuasive public discourse.

## 1.11   Thinking about Service Industries

The four industries discussed in this volume—child care, education, health care, and long-term care—are all service industries. When economists discuss such service industries, I believe that they often run into problems by focusing almost immediately on the "industry" aspects, rather than the idea of "service." Economists talk about the growth of service industries in terms of sales and employees; whether service industry jobs will all be low-paid hamburger flippers or high-paid investment bankers; how to measure productivity growth in service industries; or how the output of services affects the balance of trade and national competitiveness.

These subjects deserve considerable attention. But as economists hasten to plant their feet firmly on the hard analysis of service industries, their discussions usually overlook the softer, more humanistic idea of service. This is surprising in a way, because the ideal of service comes up often enough in academic life. Decisions about tenure for professors usually have a service component. Some colleges and universities have a service requirement for students. Every now and again, the adults in Congress propose a national service requirement for teenagers. More generally, the notion of service to others exerts a strong ethical and moral attraction in every great world religion and culture.

Of course, the tug of that moral feeling varies considerably across service industries: the ethical issues involved in giving someone a good manicure are not comparable to those of educating a child or looking after a dying cancer patient. But when the full-fledged ideal of service mixes with a capitalist economy and a democratic policy, passions are often ignited. Bloodless terms like "demand" and "supply" seem somehow too meek to convey the arguments.

Instead, the discussion begins to talk about "basic human needs" for health care or long-term care of the elderly. Providers of services like education or child care are somehow expected to do their jobs in some part because of a love for children, not in the assembly-line spirit presumed to exist in nonservice industries. Indeed, as one conference participant put it, one challenge of financing child care is to make it possible for those who really would be wonderful at looking after children to be able to make a good living doing so. The same might be said of education, or long-term care for the elderly.

The service industries on which this volume focuses touch on looking after children, and helping the sick and elderly. In all of these cases, the idea of service touches a moral chord, and leaves a resonance behind. In such a setting, where terms like "need," "love," "duty," and "justice" are hurled about, the allocation of scarce resources becomes especially contentious. Government inevitably becomes involved. But while government has considerable power to redistribute resources and to set the ground rules that organize markets, it has no magic wand to make scarcity disappear, or to make love and caring appear. Instead, it must struggle to perceive how such services are provided outside the government sector, by a combination of family, voluntary associations, and the market, and then decide upon the role that government should play. That role can range from laissez-faire, to mandating characteristics of the service without government finance, to offering government money along with mandates about service characteristics, all the way to direct government provision of certain services.

Economics often has the useful effect of taking some of the steam out of public policy debates. Arguments about environmental destruction, for example, may start out as the earth despoilers versus the tree huggers, but in the hands of economists, the argument focuses on what price accurately captures the negative externalities of certain activities. By focusing on the margin, rather than on the absolutes of unquantifiable moral judgments, economists have often been able to suggest technocratic middle-of-the-road solutions.

But for the service industries discussed in this volume, my suspicion is that economists have been too technocratic, too eager to fit the public disputes into their preset mental categories of market failure and redistribution. With service industries that touch our common humanity as closely as care for young children, teaching and education, looking after the sick and injured, and care for the elderly, this level of detachment is only a useful starting point. In the end, it will not suffice. If economists want to be relevant to the broader social debate on the evolution of these service industries, they will have to venture out on some creakier limbs. They will have to leaven their professional concern about efficiency with judgments about the justice of entitlements, the fairness of consumption externalities and who should pay, and insights about long-term political dynamics.

Of course, there is always concern that a few steps down such slippery slopes will strip the science from economics. But the papers in this volume demonstrate that such thinking can proceed with academic precision and understatement, while still capturing many of the undertones of what is touching and personal in these service industries. Moreover, an unwillingness to enter this arena will leave economists as perpetual outsiders, carping about how the world does not fit their models. In this case, the danger is that economics could lose the fundamentally social nature of its science.

# II     Human Services: Organization, Finance, and Production

# 2 Child Care: Private Cost or Public Responsibility?

Arleen Leibowitz

## 2.1 Introduction

Child care has emerged as a public policy issue because the majority of today's young mothers have taken on dual roles as labor-force participants as well as caretakers for their families. Today more than half of all mothers—even the mothers of one-year-olds—are working. The large number of mothers who are in the labor force and families' reliance on nonmaternal care for children while their mothers work have raised questions about the kinds of child care arrangements that are currently used, the quality and safety of those arrangements, the effect of child care on children, the cost of that care, and the government's role in providing or paying for child care.

Children are no longer as great a deterrent to labor supply as they have been in the past (Leibowitz and Klerman 1995). It is still true that having more children or younger children reduces the likelihood that a woman participates in the labor force (Browning 1992; Cain 1966; Carliner 1981; Gronau 1973; Leibowitz 1975; Nakamura and Nakamura 1994). However, increased labor-force participation (LFP) has been stimulated not only by lower fertility rates (Smith and Ward 1989), but also by the fact that women with children of any given age are more likely to work today than they were only two decades ago (Leibowitz and Klerman 1995). Greater market opportunities have, in turn, provided incentives for further fertility declines.

The increase in labor supply among mothers has been most dramatic for women with the youngest children. In earlier decades, LFP rose steeply at the time the youngest child entered school, because schools functioned as a source of free child care. In 1960, participation rates for married women with only school-age children (six to seventeen) were double the rates for women with

Arleen Leibowitz is a senior economist at RAND and adjunct professor at the University of California, Los Angeles.

preschool children (39% versus 19%). However, in the past three decades participation rates have grown at a fast rate even for mothers with preschoolers. In 1991, 60% of married mothers with preschoolers were in the labor force, and 75% of married women with school-age children participated (U.S. Bureau of the Census 1993). Within the preschool group, growth in labor supply has been greatest for mothers of infants and toddlers. By 1991, LFP reached high levels shortly after the birth, with more than half of the mothers (56%) working by the time their youngest child was twelve months old (U.S. Bureau of the Census 1993). Thus participation rates for mothers of one-year-olds now exceed the rates for mothers of school-age children in 1960.

This paper concentrates on the child care needs of preschool children because the increase in labor supply has been steepest for the mothers of these children and child care use has also grown rapidly for this group. Of course, the growth in after-school programs that supplement the free child care provided by schools testifies to child care needs for school-age children.[1] Nonetheless, this paper focuses on the preschool group because there is no generally available, publicly funded child care for them that functions in the way that public schools do for older children.

The purpose of this paper is, first, to understand how child care is currently provided, what it costs, how it is financed, and what defines its quality. The second purpose is to consider parental choices in an economic context, examining parents' choices of child care options (including mother care) and using data on the effect of child care on children's intellectual and emotional development to begin to describe a production function for child development. The final section of the paper addresses the question of whether there are informational, equity, or externality arguments that justify the government's taking on a greater role in public education of children who are younger than the traditional "school age."

## 2.2   Characteristics of Child Care

This section describes where children currently get care, the cost and financing of that care, and its quality.

### 2.2.1   Types of Child Care

Most preschool children whose mothers work nonetheless receive home-based child care—in their own home or in someone else's home. Data from the 1991 Survey of Income and Program Participation (SIPP; Casper, Hawkins, and O'Connell 1994) indicate that currently about a third of the preschoolers with working mothers are cared for in their own home by someone other than the mother, another third go to someone else's home, and fewer than one in ten

---

1. In 1990, 56% of children whose mothers worked and 28% of children whose mothers were not employed received some supplemental care (Willer et al. 1991).

Table 2.1          **Primary Child Care Arrangement for Preschool Children of Working Mothers, 1977–1991**

|                                 | June 1977 | Fall 1987 | Fall 1991 |
|---------------------------------|-----------|-----------|-----------|
| Number of children (1,000)      | 4,370     | 9,124     | 9,854     |
| *Type of arrangement* (%)       |           |           |           |
| Child's home                    |           |           |           |
|   Nonmaternal         | 33.9      | 29.9      | 35.7      |
|   Father              | 14.4      | 15.3      | 20.0      |
|   Other relative      | 12.6      | 8.4       | 10.4      |
|   Nonrelative         | 7.0       | 6.2       | 5.4       |
| Another home                    | 40.7      | 35.6      | 31.0      |
|   Other relative      | 18.3      | 13.3      | 13.1      |
|   Nonrelative         | 22.4      | 22.3      | 17.9      |
| Organized child care            | 13.0      | 24.4      | 23.0      |
| Mother cares for child at work  | 11.4      | 8.9       | 8.7       |

*Source:* Casper, Hawkins, and O'Connell 1994. Data for 1977 are derived from the June 1977 Current Population Survey; data for 1987 and 1991 are derived from the Survey of Income and Program Participation.

are cared for by their mother while she works (mostly in their own home). Only one-quarter of the preschoolers attend day care centers or nursery school (see table 2.1).

Although day care centers and other forms of organized child care account for only 25% of the care arrangements, such formal care has grown rapidly over a short period of time. Table 2.1 presents data from three time points, which show that, as the number of children with working mothers has increased between 1977 and 1991, the share who were cared for by organized child care grew from 13 to 23%. Considering the increased number of children in care, this implies a fourfold increase in the numbers of children in organized child care facilities over this fourteen-year period.

Offsetting the rise in organized care has been a decline in the share of children in family day care—care provided for a small group of children in a caregiver's own home. Of course, due to a more than twofold increase in the number of children in care, the total number of children in family day care situations has grown in absolute terms. In 1977 the most prevalent type of care for children whose mothers worked was care in someone else's home, which accounted for 40% of the preschool children. By 1987 the share of out-of-home care had slid to 35.6%, with most of the decline due to reductions in care by grandmothers and other relatives. Despite a slight increase between 1977 and 1987 in the percentage of children cared for by fathers, mothers generally depended less on relatives and more on the market for child care at the end of the decade. With increasing LFP for older women, grandmother care is likely to account for a shrinking share of the child care in the future.

The period between 1987 and 1991 saw reversals in the trends of the prior decade, which may be attributable to the depressed economic situation in 1991. The use of care types that are less likely to be free (organized care and nonrelative care, both inside and outside the home) declined, while relative care in the home grew. Father care shot up to account for one-fifth of all child care arrangements for preschoolers. Thus, by 1991 children were more likely to be cared for in their own home than in someone else's home.

The ideal type of child care setting depends on the child's age. Child development experts recommend that child care for very young children be in small groups with low ratios of children to providers (Kahn and Kamerman 1987; National Research Council 1990). Older children can develop well in larger groups with larger child/teacher ratios. Indeed, the majority of infants receive home-based care, which has on average smaller groups and fewer children per caretaker. About 8% of infants under one year old are cared for by their mothers at work (most often in their own home), and another 40% are cared for at home by someone else. Care in someone else's home is provided for another 40% of infants. Only 11.5% of infants are cared for in institutional settings. In contrast, a third of three- and four-year-olds are in organized care facilities (Casper, Hawkins, and O'Connell 1994).

Child care centers provide environments especially adapted to children. Nearly all child care centers are licensed, and three-quarters meet criteria set by their state regarding group size and child to staff ratios for different age groups of children (Willer et al. 1991). Most states also require childhood education for the staff (Scarr and Eisenberg 1993). In contrast, only a minority of family day care homes are licensed. As of 1988, only twenty-seven states required family day care providers to be licensed, and thirty-six states exempted from regulation family day care homes serving fewer than four unrelated children (Willer et al. 1991). It is believed that between 82 and 90% of family day care homes are unregulated (Willer et al. 1991).

Despite the lack of state regulatory oversight, unlicensed family day care homes often meet the state requirements because they care for small groups of children and use high ratios of adults to children on average (Waite, Leibowitz, and Witsberger 1991). Unlicensed family day care providers typically lack formal training in childhood education as well as advanced schooling of any kind. Licensed family day care homes tend to serve larger numbers of children than unlicensed homes, but fewer than a child care center. The National Child Care Survey and the Profile of Child Care Settings found an average group size of 7.0 children per regulated family day care home and 6.4 per unregulated home (Willer et al. 1991). Although licensed facilities must meet the state group size and safety regulations, few states impose education or training requirements on family day care providers (Scarr and Eisenberg 1993). Because most family day care is unlicensed and there is no requirement that care by relatives be licensed, much of the child care delivered is outside the purview of state regulatory authorities.

**Table 2.2          Costs of Child Care by Income Level, 1990**

|  | Working Poor | Working Class | Middle Class |
|---|---|---|---|
| % who pay for care | 27 | 32 | 43 |
| Weekly cost ($) if > 0 | 38 | 45 | 60 |
| Child care cost as % of weekly income | 33 | 13 | 6 |

*Source:* Hofferth and Chaplin 1994a.

## 2.2.2   Cost and Financing of Child Care

Many lower-wage women rely on free child care supplied by husbands or relatives. The National Child Care Survey indicates that only 27% of low-income women paid for child care and only 43% of middle-income women did so (see table 2.2). In 1991 the weekly cost of child care for a preschool child averaged $62 (Casper, Hawkins, and O'Connell 1994). Day care centers charge more ($65) than relatives ($53), but about the same as home care by nonrelatives ($62). In day care centers infant care costs more than care for preschoolers (Whitebook, Howes, and Phillips 1989).

Lower-income women are also more likely to get free care from public providers. Only 3% of Head Start programs charge fees for their services. In contrast, 39% of public-school-based programs and nearly all other programs do so (Kisker et al. 1991). Although lower-income women paid less per week for child care, their costs accounted for a larger share of their weekly income. Families earning less than $15,000 per year spent 23% of their income on child care, when they paid for care (Willer et al. 1991). Child care costs accounted for 7% of annual earnings for families with incomes between $35,000 and $49,999; it accounted for 6% of income for those earning $50,000 and more (Willer et al. 1991).

Despite the increase in the demand for child care, the hourly cost (about $1.60 per hour in 1990 for either center or family day care) remained virtually constant in real terms through the 1990s (Kisker et al. 1991). The average wages of child care workers are low and did not rise in real terms over the period 1976–86, a time of great expansion in the demand for care (Blau 1992; Phillips, Howes, and Whitebook 1991).[2] Although this constancy in prices would be consistent with a competitive market for child care services, it is not clear that the quality of child care has not declined over time. As Walker (1991) points out, it is possible that increasing demand has led lower-quality providers to enter the market.

Federal and state governments subsidize both the providers and consumers

2. Connelly (1992) suggests that the low wages of child care workers may partly result from the nonmonetary benefit of caring for one's own children at the same time.

of child care through a variety of programs. Robins (1990) calculated that the single largest government child care program is the child care tax credit, which accounted for 60% of all federal spending on child care by 1988 ($3.8 billion). This subsidy is available only to working mothers. Other federal government programs, which are expenditure-based, are available to children whether or not their mothers work.

Head Start is perhaps the most visible federally funded expenditure-based program for early childhood. When it was established in 1965, the program served primarily three- and four-year-olds with a developmentally enriching program that also met health care, nutrition, and social service needs. Although Head Start is undoubtedly one of the most popular social programs ever enacted in the United States,[3] it has never been funded at a sufficient level to reach all the children whom the legislation made eligible. In 1987 Head Start was estimated to be serving only 16% of the eligible children (Select Committee on Children, Youth, and Families 1987). Expanding the Head Start program was a priority of the Clinton administration, and the number of children served has risen in recent years from about 450,000 in 1989 to over 700,000 in 1993 (Committee on Labor and Human Resources 1994). In 1993 expenditures for Head Start grew to $2.8 billion (Executive Office of the President 1994).

While the Head Start program was designed as developmental child care for children living in poverty, other federal programs have the primary goal of facilitating women's exit from Aid to Families with Dependent Children (AFDC). These include the Job Opportunities and Basic Skills (JOBS) program, child care block grants to the states, and At Risk and Transitional Child Care, which supported an additional $2.2 billion in child care programs in 1993. Phillips (1991) notes that, although Head Start serves children from similar backgrounds, it differs fundamentally from programs like JOBS that seek to get women off AFDC. Head Start was designed as a high-quality, developmental program that attempted to meet a comprehensive range of children's needs. In contrast, JOBS and other programs like it were designed to reduce the cost of AFDC. The child care associated with these programs also tends to be low cost, and Phillips (1991) argues, of low quality.

The AFDC program itself can be considered a large government subsidy of child care by mothers. Originally established in 1935 to allow widows to stay home to care for their own children as most married women did, today it serves primarily unmarried and divorced mothers. Because AFDC income support is reduced when family income rises above a set ceiling, the program discourages market work and presumably increases mothers' child care activities at home. In recent years, however, welfare reforms have attempted to modify the discouraging effect of welfare on work by modifying child care provisions. The

---

3. In recent Senate hearings, Senator Edward Kennedy stated, "Head Start is widely regarded as one of the nation's premier social programs, on a par with Social Security and Medicare" (Committee on Labor and Human Resources 1994, 1).

Omnibus Budget Reconciliation Act (OBRA) of 1990 required states to not count as earned income for the purposes of calculating AFDC benefits up to the first $175 per month of child care expense. Further, it is likely that child care will have a prominent place in the Clinton welfare reform package.

### 2.2.3   Child Care Quality

Although the number of child care places has increased to meet the increased demands of working mothers, it is less clear what has happened to the quality of child care. The quality of child care is often measured by structural characteristics, such as child/provider ratios, group size, and educational levels of providers. Many economic studies (e.g., Hofferth and Wissoker 1992; Kisker and Maynard 1991; Leibowitz, Waite, and Witsberger 1988; Waite, Leibowitz, and Witsberger 1991) also use these measures, which were incorporated into the Federal Interagency Day Care Requirements. A 1988 study of child care centers found that structural measures of quality were related to process measures of quality based on the interactions between teachers and children. They found that small group size as well as having teachers with specialized early childhood education predicted positive and appropriate interaction between teachers and children (Whitebook, Howes, and Phillips 1989). Classrooms with lower child to teacher ratios were found to have more developmentally appropriate activity (85).

While most centers meet the licensing standards regarding group size and child/provider ratios, many provide care that fails to meet "process" standards. About one-third of all classrooms studied by the National Child Care Staffing Study fell at or below a minimally adequate rating in the ability to provide developmentally appropriate activity, while only 12% met or exceeded the "good" rating (Whitebook, Howes, and Phillips 1989). Similarly, about a quarter of the classrooms fell at or below the minimal quality rating for appropriate caregiving—a measure of teacher sensitivity, harshness, and detachment (Whitebook, Howes, and Phillips 1989).

Despite analysts' expectation that families will prefer and should pay more for "high-quality" child care, research often has not found an empirical relationship between the prices parents pay for purchased child care and its assumed quality as measured by the factors such as child/provider ratios (Waite, Leibowitz, and Witsberger 1991). Walker (1992), using data from three cities, found that parents did not pay more for child care in smaller groups or with fewer children per adult caretaker. Further, he found no price premium for providers who had more education or experience within the profession.

The lack of association between price and the regulated features of care (group size, staff ratios, and caregiver training) reflects the fact that parents report that they place greater value on other care characteristics. Parents interviewed in the National Child Care Survey in 1990 reported that they place greatest value on the interactions between caregivers and children (Hofferth and Chaplin 1994b). Indeed, an observational study of child care settings, which directly measured the quality of the interactions between children and providers, found that centers with care that was rated as "appropriate" charged higher fees. Kisker et al. (1991) also found that price is positively related to quality measured more broadly to include teacher qualifications and turnover.

The lack of a relationship between the prices parents pay and the attributes of care that are regulated by states raises the question of whether licensing provides information about characteristics that parents value. The results of the two studies that assessed the quality of the interaction between teachers and children did find a relationship to price. But Walker's analysis found that state-licensed providers did not charge higher rates.[4] This lack of association contradicts the expectation that licensing provides a signal of higher quality (Leland 1979) and suggests that the characteristics that state licensing regulates reflect only poorly the attributes that parents value in child care.

### 2.3    An Economic Perspective on Child Care

#### 2.3.1    The Demand for Child Care

Whether to care for children at home or to make other arrangements for the care of their children is a choice that families face. Therefore it is useful to consider an economic model that integrates the decision to use child care with other choices, such as whether the mother should work outside the home.

We begin with a utility framework that assumes that parents value family consumption of goods and services ($X$), their own leisure ($L$), and the healthy development of their child(ren), ($D$):

$$U = U(X, L, D).$$

Child development is produced with time inputs from parents ($t_h$), and inputs from nonparental child care arrangements ($Q_c$), as well as goods that affect child development ($X_c$):

$$D = D(t_h, X_c, Q_c).$$

Both parents' time contributes to child development. For simplicity, however, we drop the index that distinguishes parental time provided by mothers versus by fathers.

The usual constraints apply: the sum of parents' time at work, with children, and in leisure cannot exceed the total time available ($T = t_w + t_h + L$); total expenditures on consumption goods ($Xp_x$) and child care ($t_c p_c$) cannot exceed the sum of nonearned income and earnings derived from time in the market ($t_w \times w$, where $w$ represents the wage rate). $Q_c$ encompasses the time and qual-

---

4. However, Whitebook, Howes, and Phillips (1989) made cross-state comparisons of the stringency of regulations for day care centers, which are almost universally licensed. They found that parents paid higher fees in states with stiffer requirements.

ity of the child care purchased. The amount of child care purchased must be at least as great as the amount of time the parent who is the primary caretaker works. However, child care can have value because of its ability to produce child development, so even parents who do not need the custodial aspects of child care might choose to send their child to nursery school or another child care arrangement that enriched their child.

An advantage of this formulation is that it incorporates the quality of child care (as measured by its productivity in promoting child development) into the choice of whether to work. It is important to note that $Q_c$ may depend on the characteristics of the other children in the setting as well as the characteristics of the teachers, the numbers of children, and the physical surroundings. Thus the children in child care provide (positive or negative) externalities to their classmates.

This choice framework draws attention to the fact that parents weigh other attributes in addition to child care's developmental potential in choosing a particular arrangement for their child. For example, child care that is less convenient affects the amount of leisure time available to the adults in the family, and the cost of the care affects the amount of resources the family has to devote to other consumption goods (Johansen, Leibowitz, and Waite 1994).

While in theory the number of child care options available to a mother is infinite, in practice child care options fall into a small number of discrete categories. Particular child care providers supply differing proportions of characteristics that parents value—such as a developmental program, convenience, and cost. Parents, too, are heterogeneous in the value they place on these different attributes. Thus the market supplies a diversity of modes of care that "package" combinations of attributes and that are, therefore, more and less developmentally enriching, convenient, and costly (Walker 1991). For example, on average, group sizes are smaller in family day care than in child care centers, but centers are more likely to have staff with training in early childhood education.

Using this model makes it easy to understand the causes underlying the increases over time in mothers' labor supply. Not only have women's wages risen in real terms, but they have also grown relative to men's wages (Leibowitz and Klerman 1995). In addition, the price of formal child care has remained steady, which implies that women's wages also rose relative to the price of formal child care. However, it appears that free or reduced cost child care from relatives has become less available as women's wages in the market have grown generally, so it is less clear how the price of child care available from all sources (both formal and informal) has moved relative to wages.

There has been a great deal of discussion in the popular press of a lack of availability and "affordability" of child care services. The growth in market work by mothers and the related increase in number of preschool children in child care provide evidence that child care places are available. The lack of increase in the hourly cost of care suggests that new providers have entered the market to supply the additional demand. Although child care accounts for a large share of family budgets in low-income families, the economic perspective suggests that parents have found it "affordable" in the sense that they believe themselves to be better off working and using child care than not working and providing parental care.

As we would expect, there is often excess demand for subsidized child care (e.g., provided by churches or by Head Start). These sources of care may also be highly sought after because of their high quality. Thus the problem may be not accessibility, but the availability at subsidized rates of high-quality care, which the National Child Care Staffing Study found to be more costly to produce. However, that study also found that children from both low-income and high-income families attended child care centers of greater quality than did children of middle-income families, because of subsidies for poor children in high-quality centers.

### 2.3.2    Child Care as an Input to Child Development

How does child care enter into the production function of child development? Dr. Benjamin Spock, in the first edition of his classic book, *Baby and Child Care* (1946), stated the then commonly held belief that nonmaternal care had potential to harm children, and that mother care was best. More recent research shows that good care not only does no harm, but can actually provide cognitive and social benefits for children, particularly if the child comes from a disadvantaged environment.

Psychologists have identified three waves of child care research. Scarr and Eisenberg (1993) characterize the question underlying the first wave as, "How much damage is done to infants and young children by working mothers?" The second wave examines the relationship between the quality of child care and the child's outcomes. The third wave seeks to understand how other characteristics of the child or the environment (e.g., gender, center staff turnover) affect the child's experience of child care.

The first wave of studies documents the effects of day care on children's socioemotional development, particularly attachment to the mother. Belsky and Rovine (1988) find that children in day care have an insecure attachment, which they hypothesize leads to "heightened aggressiveness, noncompliance, and withdrawal in the preschool and early school years" (Belsky 1988). These findings generated a great deal of controversy, particularly because they focus on one outcome whose long-term significance was not well understood (Phillips et al. 1987).

Despite Belsky's negative findings about the detrimental effects of child care on one socioemotional outcome, there is evidence that children who attend child care centers have better outcomes in other domains, including greater verbal ability and social competence than children reared at home. Clarke-Stewart (1991) reviews the literature on development of children exposed to center care versus care in the home—by parents, sitters, or family day care providers. She concludes that children who are exposed to child care in a center are, "on the average, socially and intellectually advanced over their peers who have only been at home" (118). However, the timing of the out-of-home care may have an impact on outcomes. Blau and Grossberg (1992), for example, found that three- and four-year-old children whose mothers worked in the first year of the child's life had lower scores on a test of verbal ability. However, there was an offsetting positive effect of maternal employment (and therefore child care) during the child's second and later years.

Although many of the studies lack adequate controls for the selection of higher-quality child care for children from families of higher socioeconomic status (Zaslow 1991), similar conclusions come from analyses that randomly assign children to early childhood education programs.

The Infant Health and Development Program (IHDP) represents one of the most intensive early childhood interventions conducted as a randomized trial. In the IHDP, 377 low-birth-weight infants were randomly assigned to receive intensive home visits that helped their parents foster the child's intellectual, physical, and social development. From the time they were one year old until they reached age three, the children in this intervention group also attended a full-day, developmental child care program. The children's intellectual, behavioral, and physical progress was measured at age three and compared to that of 608 low-birth-weight infants who were randomly assigned at birth to a group that received physical monitoring only, but no child development intervention. When they were three years old, the intervention group scored significantly higher on the Stanford-Binet Intelligence Scale—a mean of 93.5 compared to 84.5 in the control group. The children receiving early intervention were only one-third as likely to score in the "mentally retarded" range on the IQ test (5.6% versus 16.9% of the randomly selected controls; Ramey et al. 1992). In addition, the mothers of the group who received home visits and day care reported fewer behavior problems with their children (IHDP 1990).

Because the IHDP combined home visits with developmental child care, it is impossible to determine how much of the gains relative to the control group relate to child care itself. Nonetheless, this study, like the Carolina Abecedarian Project that preceded it, suggests the gains in cognitive and behavioral outcomes for high-risk children that may be attainable through early childhood education. Further research is needed to determine the success of this type of early intervention with children who are at high risk of suboptimal development for reasons other than low birth weight.

Although preschool does seem to promote school readiness, some of the most important long-run effects may be in the realm of behavior. The one controlled trial with a long follow-up period, the Perry Preschool Project, found that low-IQ, low-income, black children who were randomly assigned to a developmental nursery school program and weekly home visits at age three and four showed IQ gains over the control group when they were tested at age five. The child care group did not retain beyond second grade their early cognitive gains relative to the control group. Despite the loss of gains on intelligence tests, the intervention group scored significantly higher on achievement tests and teacher ratings when they were retested at age nineteen. They also had strikingly better social and behavioral outcomes—they were significantly more likely to have graduated from high school and to be employed, and significantly less likely to have been arrested or to be receiving welfare. The girls were half as likely to have had a pregnancy (Berrueta-Clement et al. 1984). Thus it appears that the longest-lasting improvements were in the effort the children put into their studies and in the behavioral realm. Another intensive early intervention program with low SES mothers and their infants also found effects primarily in behavior rather than in improved cognitive abilities (Olds, Henderson, and Kitzman 1994).

The second wave of research emphasizes that quality of care is more important than the type of care (center versus home). Zaslow (1991) reviews a number of studies that show that higher-quality child care has significant positive effects on both short-term and long-term outcomes for children. As expected, higher-quality child care results in more positive daily experiences and better developmental outcomes for youngsters. The gain in children's school readiness and language development over the school year was found in the National Day Care Study to depend on structural quality measures such as group size and teacher qualifications (Ruopp et al. 1979). School readiness is an important outcome because it is an input to the production of learning in school, as suggested by Fuchs and Reklis (1994), who found that the single most important determinant of a state's average mathematics achievement scores was the percentage of students who were judged "ready to learn" by their kindergarten teachers.

The third wave of research addresses the fact that more advantaged children tend to be in higher-quality child care centers, by looking for interactions among child, family, and child care attributes. These analyses suggest that child care is particularly beneficial for children at risk for poor outcomes because of health risk or lack of family resources (Clarke-Stewart 1991). Child care may, however, have negative consequences for more advantaged children and for boys (Mott 1991). For example, using secondary data from the National Longitudinal Survey of Youth (NLS-Y), Caughy, DiPietro, and Strobino (1994) found that low-income children in the NLS-Y who participated in day care in their first year of life had better reading recognition scores at age five or six. Children from higher-income families and more enriched environments scored lower if they began day care in their first year. As in the wave two studies, many analyses do not account for selection bias.

Currie and Thomas (1995) deal with selection bias statistically by correcting for fixed effects of mother characteristics. After correcting for selection, they find that participation in Head Start or other preschool is significantly related to higher verbal test scores for white and Latino children, but not for African-

American children. Randomized trials also document the impact of child care for at-risk children (IHDP 1990; Ramey et al. 1992).

## 2.4    Is There a Government Role in Child Care?

Since the dawn of the twentieth century, Americans have generally accepted the norm of elementary education for all children (Folger and Nam 1967; Skocpol, chap. 11 in this volume). Can a similar case be made for a public role in providing or financing child care services for preschool children? Despite the research on the educational value of child care, most families see day care as a means of freeing the mother's time for market work. Because the mother's decision to work is a private one, it is generally assumed that the responsibility for child care services is primarily private. The largest governmental program that supports child care is the child care tax credit—which fundamentally treats child care as a work-related expense for employed mothers. Thus child care costs are seen as equivalent to union dues—a cost that one must pay in order to work.

What is the government role in this heretofore private choice? Because high-quality child care can have lasting, positive effects on the child, particularly for disadvantaged children, three rationales exist for the government role: the first relates to information, and would arise if the government had better information than parents have about the effects of child care quality on children; the second is an equity argument that all children deserve equal opportunities to receive the benefits of preschool education; and the third concerns the positive externalities for the population as a whole that could result from high-quality child care. I discuss each of these below.

### 2.4.1    Information

Walker (1991) identifies the lack of information as the "most striking difference between the child care market and the idealized perfect market" (65). He notes that most parents use providers whom they knew beforehand or get information about child care informally, from friends and relatives. These personal recommendations may be important to parents because of the weight they place on the process aspects of care, which are most easily observed by a person who has used the care. Even after using the child care service, however, it is often difficult to assess its quality. It is hard to monitor the behavior of the provider when the parents are not present, so there is always a potential for shirking on the part of providers. Parents prefer to rely on relatives for child care (Mason and Kuhlthau 1989). One reason for this may be that parents believe relatives may be less likely to shirk, because they can be more easily monitored and they may also value good outcomes for the child.

Although economists have focused on the problems caused by imperfect information about particular providers in the market, there is another sense in which information is also lacking. Parents may value child development, but lack the knowledge of the link between (more costly) high-quality child care and child development. This link is difficult to document by observation, since a child is exposed to many influences, and it is nearly impossible to attribute particular outcomes to any one source. Drawing conclusions about the effects of child care by looking at the experience of children who were exposed to child care by earlier generations of working mothers may not be valid. The growth in child care use has been so great that the children whose mothers work today are a less selective population than those of women who worked in earlier years, and child care may be of very different quality today than formerly.

This lack of information provides a rationale for the government's increasing knowledge about child care in general. In addition, the government could facilitate the operation of the market for child care services, by increasing information about the quality and availability of particular providers (Blau 1991). The government could also stimulate parental demand for high-quality child care by subsidizing programs that were known (to the government) to be high quality. This is perhaps the reason that the child care tax credit cannot be used for child care by relatives, which is of unknown quality (at least to the government). However, the rationale for the government's intervening through subsidy or direct provision of services relies primarily on equity considerations or on the presence of externalities.

### 2.4.2   Equity

Research on the early determinants of later cognitive and behavioral outcomes has begun to document the influence of early child care on children. Does the evidence that school success depends on earlier preschool experiences mean that equity demands that all children have access to an enriched preschool environment, so that they can begin school on an equal basis? We also know that parental characteristics affect school success and that child care can offset some of the deficits associated with disadvantaged backgrounds. To what extent should the government spend resources to equalize educational opportunity at the preschool level?

The economic model above suggests that parents choose the level of investments in their children, so it is expected that higher-income parents spend more resources on their children. We saw that low-income families are already spending a large fraction of their income on child care when the mother works. Whether the government should pay for early childhood education because it is a good investment is an economic question that is taken up in section 2.4.3. Whether the government should intervene to level the playing field is a political question that should be addressed by the political process.

### 2.4.3   Externalities

The empirical evidence that high-quality day care makes children more ready to learn when they go to school and that it also can have positive effects in discouraging antisocial behaviors suggests that there may be public gains over and above the private gains captured by families. If children who have been exposed to high-quality day care are easier to teach, require less remedial education, and are less likely to come into contact with the juvenile justice system or to become teenage parents, the savings to public programs in reduced schooling expense, reduced police and prison costs, and lower welfare payments might justify public support of quality day care early in life. In addition, children who are easier to teach provide positive externalities to the other children in their classroom, yielding further societal gains. Interventions early in life have the potential to be very cost-effective, because the child brings the improved human capital as an input to all future activities.

One recent evaluation of an early intervention with mothers and infants indicated that even an expensive program can be cost-effective if it is targeted at a high-risk population. Olds et al. (1993) evaluated an intensive home-visit program given to poor, unmarried, teenage mothers. Although the program was expensive ($3,246 per family), the government had net savings by the time the children were four years old because of reduced costs for AFDC, food stamps, Medicaid, and Child Protective Services and higher tax revenues from greater maternal employment, which more than offset the discounted cost of the program for poor mothers. That benefits outweigh costs, even without counting any benefits that will accrue after the child is four years old, provides a very strong argument for funding such programs. The key to the high yield of the home-visit program is targeting families who have a high probability of receiving public transfers.

Some of the greatest problems facing our society today are exactly the social and behavioral outcomes that high-quality child care seems to affect most, and the "culture of poverty" that supposedly fosters them (Wilson 1987; McLanahan and Garfinkel 1989). Indeed, if poor socialization into the norms of the overall society stimulates antisocial behaviors, high-quality child care, which has been shown to generate more positive social behaviors, might prove a cost-effective means of preventing these problems.

The costs of dealing with "acting out" behaviors such as teenage pregnancy and juvenile criminal behavior are high, yet few programs targeted at teenagers have succeeded in discouraging these behaviors. In contrast, the limited evidence available suggests that high-quality child care at early ages may help children avoid these undesirable behaviors when they are older. Thus, it is possible that child care may prove a cost-effective tool in lowering rates of teen pregnancy and criminal activities. In contrast to current punitive programs to reduce teen pregnancy and crime, for example by reducing welfare benefits or increasing jail terms, improving access to high-quality child care would actually enrich childrens' lives while reducing behaviors with negative externalities.

The Perry Preschool Project provides encouraging evidence of long-term effects, even for a high-risk group of children. However, it is important to recognize that this was a small and unique intervention. Not only was it very expensive (an average per child cost of $6,300 annually in 1986 dollars), but it also targeted children at high risk for mental retardation. Before proceeding, we would need the results of well-designed studies on larger samples of children to determine how child care affects average children and to learn how early behavioral outcomes (e.g., ability to follow the teacher's instructions) link to later actions (e.g., being law abiding).

In thinking about using high-quality child care to counteract the "culture of poverty," it is important to define child care very broadly. Child care is not just care for children of working mothers. The AFDC program can be construed as a child care program wherein the government pays low-income women to stay home to provide care for their children. As we discussed above, however, child care centers do a better job of increasing young children's intellectual skills and social development than does home care—even care by the child's mother. And this is particularly true when the mother has little education and few job skills, since children from disadvantaged families seem to gain most from high-quality day care.

When the AFDC program began, most women stayed home with their children. Equity considerations suggested that widows, the original recipients of the program, should have the same advantage. In 1946 Dr. Spock called for a program like AFDC, arguing that "[i]t would save money in the end if the government paid a comfortable allowance to all mothers (of young children) who would otherwise be compelled to work" (475). Although AFDC conformed to the prevailing beliefs about the effect of mother care and the dangers of child care, current knowledge about the benefits of child care may lead to a different conclusion. Rather than improving children's well-being by allowing even poor children to be cared for by their mothers, AFDC may now serve to promote low-quality child care by poorly skilled providers at home. One can argue on both equity and externalities grounds that child care outside the home be promoted, especially for children beyond infancy.

The proposed welfare reforms that would require that AFDC mothers seek work or training and put their children in child care may have direct positive effects on children—because day care has particularly favorable effects for disadvantaged children. However, as Phillips (1991) points out, child care that is designed primarily to facilitate an exit from welfare has tended historically to be of poorer quality than child care like Head Start, which was designed to be developmental. Although it may impose short-term costs, providing high-quality child care for children whose mothers are leaving AFDC may yield long-term gains that will offset the cost differential. Providing high-quality child care so that AFDC recipients can enter the labor force has additional benefits. The child care provides benefits directly to the children yet presents the mothers with no disincentives to work and, in fact, may stimulate work.

### 2.4.4    Who Should Pay for Child Care?

Should the government provide and finance child care, as it does for public education from kindergarten to twelfth grade, or simply subsidize its private purchase by parents, perhaps through the use of vouchers or tax credits? Or is child care a private cost that should be borne by working women or their employers? We first discuss the family's and employer's role and then discuss the government's role in paying for or providing child care.

If payment for child care were considered solely a family responsibility, child care would likely reinforce existing differentials in opportunities for preschool children. Currently, higher-income families purchase better-quality child care. The fact that low-income families have better access to more stimulating child care centers than middle-income families (Whitebook, Howes, and Phillips 1989) results from public and private subsidies that allow children from poor households to attend stimulating child care such as that provided by Head Start. Lower-income households are already spending a higher proportion of their income on child care. This suggests that, without subsidies, relying completely on private family financing of child care will tend to reinforce existing disparities in school readiness among children of different income groups.

If families alone cannot afford the type of child care that will equalize opportunities, can employers perform this function? In the United States, employers provide many social welfare benefits that governments supply in other countries. Pensions and employer-based health insurance are two prominent examples of this arrangement. As in the case of health insurance, mandating employers to pay for child care benefits may appear attractive to legislators because the costs for the service do not appear on the government ledgers (although they may erode the tax base). However, the cost of employer-mandated benefits is shifted back to the employees who receive the benefit (Gruber 1994), so that, in the long run, there is little net financial gain to the recipients. Employment-based child care would be regressive, because the mothers with the highest wages are most likely to be in the labor force (Fuchs and Reklis 1992). Yet the children who appear to benefit most from child care are those whose mothers have low levels of education and little income. Since these mothers are less likely to be employed, their children would have less access to employer-based child care.

This leaves public subsidy or provision as the two means by which government can increase the use of high-quality child care. If parental child care choices are subsidized by government—through tax credits, vouchers, or other means—we can conceptualize parents' choices using the model outlined above. According to that model, parents choose child care, as they choose their other consumption, with several goals in mind. One goal is to promote their child's development. Conflicting goals for the family include finding child care that is convenient or less costly and leaves more resources for parental leisure or consumption. A voucher lowers the cost of child care, but the entire value of the voucher may not be targeted to improving child care quality. Parents may choose to increase the convenience to themselves of the child care they choose, or they may use some of the extra resources for other purposes that increase their own utility. Because parents have these other goals, a child care subsidy becomes "fungible" and will not necessarily lead to the purchase of higher-quality child care.

Even if parents value child development as much as the government does, they may lack the information about what constitutes the most developmentally appropriate child care and may therefore be less effective agents for their child. However, the development of cognitive skills is not the only goal parents have for children. Parents also value transmission of cultural values consonant with their own; parents are probably in the best position to make these choices. Nor is it likely that governmental agencies have better information than parents about what is productive for a particular child. Parents appear to be better placed to monitor at close hand the quality of child care their preschooler receives. The lack of association between child care licensing requirements and child care prices suggests that government agencies would have great difficulty in implementing regulation that would lead to care that parents value.

Although the equity and externality arguments for child care echo the rationale for free public education at higher grades, it is probable that a combination of improved information and public finance of early childhood learning is more in keeping with the family's primacy in providing preschool experiences. The division between the public sphere and that of the family is nowhere more sensitive than with regard to young children. Certainly, in this era of "family values," we will not easily move the choice of instruction for impressionable young children far away from the family. Although families will certainly have an important role in choosing the type of care their children receive, the recent research evidence suggests that it is not necessarily optimal for families to serve as full-time caretakers for children. As I have argued above, both equity and externality considerations argue for the provision of high-quality child care to children, whether or not the mother works.

The suggestive evidence of negative effects of child care for middle-class children implies that our public subsidies of child care, which have primarily been through the child care tax credit, have primarily been designed to provide financial relief for the cost of child care. Because middle-class children benefit less than poorer children from child care, it is hard to make the case that the largest government subsidy of child care has been designed primarily to stimulate child development. Armed with emerging information on the potential benefits of child care, we should use public funds to promote quality care for disadvantaged children as well.

## 2.5 Conclusion

Many preschool children spend their days in child care. The quality of that care is an important determinant of children's later success in life. This paper has argued that for equity reasons and because child care may be a high-yield investment in children, government should have a role in improving the quality of the child care children receive and in encouraging quality preschool experiences for disadvantaged children, even those whose mothers do not work. The evidence that quality preschool is especially beneficial for disadvantaged children suggests that we need to sever the link between subsistence support for low-income children and the provision of child care for them. Children growing up in AFDC homes are doubly disadvantaged—they lack the advantages of having greater financial resources, and they often suffer from not being exposed to more enriched preschool environments available to children in out-of-home care. The expansion of the Head Start program for toddlers is a valuable step in this direction. The large payoff from programs that intervene with high-risk children in infancy suggests that it may be beneficial to begin even earlier.

# References

Belsky, Jay. 1988. The Effects of Infant Day Care Reconsidered. *Early Childhood Research Quarterly* 3:235–72.

Belsky, Jay, and Michael J. Rovine. 1988. Nonmaternal Care in the First Year of Life and the Security of Infant-Parent Attachment. *Child Development* 59:157–67.

Berrueta-Clement, J. R., L. J. Schweinhart, W. S. Barnett, A. S. Epstein, and D. P. Weikart. 1984. *Changed Lives: The Effects of the Perry Preschool Program on Youths through Age 19.* Monographs of the High/Scope Education Research Foundation, 8. Ypsilanti, MI: High/Scope Press.

Blau, David M. 1991. The Quality of Child Care: An Economic Perspective. In *The Economics of Child Care,* ed. David M. Blau, 145–74. New York: Russell Sage Foundation.

———. 1992. The Child Care Labor Market. *Journal of Human Resources* 26, no. 1:19–39.

Blau, Francine D., and Adam J. Grossberg. 1992. Maternal Labor Supply and Children's Cognitive Development. *Review of Economics and Statistics* 74:474–81.

Browning, Martin. 1992. Children and Household Economic Behavior. *Journal of Economic Literature* 30:1434–75.

Cain, Glen G. 1966. *Married Women in the Labor Force: An Economic Analysis.* Chicago: University of Chicago Press.

Carliner, Geoffrey. 1981. Female Labor Force Participation Rates for Nine Ethnic Groups. *Journal of Human Resources* 16, no. 2:286–93.

Casper, Lynne N., Mary Hawkins, and Martin O'Connell. 1994. Who's Minding the Kids? Child Care Arrangements: Fall 1991. In U.S. Bureau of the Census, *Current Population Reports P70–36.* Washington, DC: Government Printing Office.

Caughy, Margaret, Janet A. DiPietro, and Donna M. Strobino. 1994. Day Care Participation as a Protective Factor in the Cognitive Development of Low-Income Children. *Childhood Development* 65:457–71.

Clarke-Stewart, Alison K. 1991. A Home Is Not a School: The Effects of Child Care on Children's Development. *Journal of Social Issues* 47, no. 2:105–24.

Committee on Labor and Human Resources. 1994. *Partners in Creating a 21st Century Head Start.* Washington, DC: Government Printing Office.

Connelly, Rachel. 1992. Self Employment and Providing Child Care. *Demography* 29 (February): 17–29.

Currie, Janet, and Duncan Thomas. 1995. Does Head Start Make a Difference? *American Economic Review* 85:341–64.

Executive Office of the President of the United States. Office of Management and Budget. 1994. Budget of the United States Government, Fiscal Year 1995.

Folger, John K., and Charles B. Nam. 1967. *Education of the American Population.* A 1960 Census Monograph. Washington, DC: Government Printing Office.

Fuchs, Victor R., and Diane M. Reklis. 1992. America's Children: Economic Perspectives and Policy Options. *Science* 255:41–46.

———. 1994. Mathematical Achievement in Eighth Grade: Interstate and Racial Differences. NBER Working Paper no. 4784. Cambridge, MA: National Bureau of Economic Research, June.

Gronau, Reuben. 1973. The Effect of Children on the Housewife's Value of Time. *Journal of Political Economy* 81 (March–April): S168–99.

Gruber, Jonathan. 1994. The Incidence of Mandated Maternity Benefits. *American Economic Review* 84, no. 3:622–41.

Hofferth, Sandra L., and Duncan Chaplin. 1994a. *Caring for Young Children while Parents Work: Public and Private Strategies.* Washington, DC: Urban Institute.

———. 1994b. *Child Care Quality versus Availability: Do We Have to Trade One for the Other?* Washington, DC: Urban Institute.

Hofferth, Sandra L., and Douglas Wissoker. 1992. Price, Quality, and Income in Child Care Choice. *Journal of Human Resources* 27, no. 1:70–111.

Infant Health and Development Program. 1990. Enhancing the Outcomes of Low Birthweight, Premature Infants: A Multi-Site Randomized Trial. *Journal of the American Medical Association* 263:3035–42.

Johansen, Anne S., Arleen Leibowitz, and Linda J. Waite. 1994. Parents' Demand for Child Care. RAND Working Paper Series 94–13, DRU-741-NICHD.

Kahn, A. J., and S. B. Kamerman. 1987. *Child Care: Facing the Hard Choices.* Dover, MA: Auburn House.

Kisker, Ellen, Sandra L. Hofferth, Deborah A. Phillips, and Elizabeth Farquhar. 1991. *A Profile of Child Care Settings: Early Education and Care in 1990.* Washington, DC: Government Printing Office.

Kisker, Ellen, and Rebecca Maynard. 1991. Quality, Cost, and Parental Choice of Child Care. In *The Economics of Child Care,* ed. David M. Blau, 127–44. New York: Russell Sage Foundation.

Leibowitz, Arleen. 1975. Education and the Allocation of Women's Time. In *Education, Income, and Human Behavior,* ed. F. Thomas Juster. 171–97. New York: McGraw-Hill.

Leibowitz, Arleen, and Jacob Klerman. 1995. Explaining Changes in Married Mothers' Employment over Time. *Demography* 32 (August).

Leibowitz, Arleen, Linda J. Waite, and Christina Witsberger. 1988. Child Care for Preschoolers: Differences by Child's Age. *Demography* 25 (May): 205–20.

Leland, H. 1979. Quacks, Lemons, and Licensing: A Theory of Minimum Quality Standards. *Journal of Political Economy* 87:1328–46.

McLanahan, Sara, and Irwin Garfinkel. 1989. Single Mothers, the Underclass, and Social Policy. *Annals of the American Academy of Political and Social Science* 501:92–104.

Mason, Karen Oppenheim, and Karen Kuhlthau. 1989. Determinants of Child Care Ideals among Mothers of Preschool-Aged Children. *Journal of Marriage and the Family* 51:593–603.

Mott, Frank L. 1991. Developmental Effects of Infant Care: The Mediating Role of Gender and Health. *Journal of Social Issues* 47, no. 2:139–58.

Nakamura, Alice, and Masao Nakamura. 1994. Predicting Female Labor Supply: Effects of Children and Recent Work Experience. *Journal of Human Resources* 29, no. 2:304–27.

National Research Council. Commission on Behavioral and Social Sciences and Education. 1990. *Who Cares for America's Children? Child Care Policy for the 1990s,* ed. Cheryl D. Hayes, John L. Palmer, and Martha J. Zaslow. Washington, DC: National Academy Press.

Olds, David L., Charles R. Henderson, and Harriet Kitzman. 1994. Does Prenatal and Infancy Nurse Home Visitation Have Enduring Effects on Qualities of Parental Caregiving and Child Health at 25 to 50 Months of Life? *Pediatrics* 93 (January): 89–98.

Olds, David L., Charles R. Henderson, Charles Phelps, Harriet Kitzman, Carole Hanks. 1993. Effect of Prenatal and Infancy Nurse Home Visitation on Government Spending. *Medical Care* 31:155–74.

Phillips, Deborah A. 1991. With a Little Help: Children in Poverty and Child Care. In *Children in Poverty: Child Development and Public Policy,* ed. Aletha C. Huston, 158–88. Cambridge: Cambridge University Press.

Phillips, Deborah A., Carollee Howes, and Marcy Whitebook. 1991. Child Care as an Adult Work Environment. *Journal of Social Issues* 47, no. 2:49–70.

Phillips, Deborah A., K. McCartney, Sandra Scarr, and Carollee Howes. 1987. Selective Review of Infant Day Care Research: A Cause for Concern. *Zero to Three* 7:18–21.

Ramey, Craig T., Donna M. Bryant, Barbara Wasik, Joseph J. Sparling, Kaye H. Fendt, and Lisa M. LaVange. 1992. Infant Health and Development Program for Low Birth Weight, Premature Infants: Program Elements, Family Participation, and Child Intelligence. *Pediatrics* 3:454–65.

Robins, Philip K. 1990. Federal Financing of Child Care: Alternative Approaches and Economic Implications. *Population Research and Policy Review* 9 (January): 65–90.

Ruopp, R., J. Travers, F. Glantz, and C. Coelen. 1979. *Children at the Center.* Cambridge, MA: Abt Associates.

Scarr, Sandra, and Marlene Eisenberg. 1993. Child Care Research: Issues, Perspectives, and Results. *American Review of Psychology* 44:613–44.

Select Committee on Children, Youth, and Families. 1987. Programs That Work. U.S. Congress. Transcript.

Smith, James P., and Michael P. Ward. 1989. Women in the Labor Market and in the Family. *Journal of Economic Perspectives* 3, no. 1:9–23.

Spock, Benjamin. 1946. *Baby and Child Care.* New York: Pocket Books.

U.S. Bureau of the Census. 1993. *Statistical Abstract of the United States, 1993.* Washington, DC: Government Printing Office.

Waite, Linda J., Arleen Leibowitz, and Christina Witsberger. 1991. What Parents Pay For: Child Care Characteristics, Quality, and Costs. *Journal of Social Issues* 47, no. 2:33–48.

Walker, James R. 1991. Public Policy and the Supply of Child Care Services. In *Economics of Child Care,* ed. David M. Blau, 51–77. New York: Russell Sage Foundation.

———. 1992. New Evidence on the Supply of Child Care. *Journal of Human Resources* 27, no. 1:40–69.

Whitebook, Marcy, Carollee Howes, and Deborah A. Phillips. 1989. Who Cares? Child
    Care Teachers and the Quality of Care in America. Executive summary, National
    Child Care Staffing Study. Oakland, CA: Child Care Employee Project.
Willer, Barbara, Sandra L. Hofferth, Ellen E. Kisker, Patricia Divine-Hawkins, Eliza-
    beth Farquhar, and Frederick B. Glantz. 1991. *The Demand and Supply of Child Care
    in 1990.* Washington, DC: National Association for the Education of Young Children.
Wilson, William J. 1987. *The Truly Disadvantaged.* Chicago: University of Chicago
    Press.
Zaslow, Martha J. 1991. Variation in Child Care Quality and Its Implications for Chil-
    dren. *Journal of Social Issues* 47, no. 2:125–38.

## Comment     Francine D. Blau

Arleen Leibowitz does an excellent job summarizing what we know about the
provision of financing of child care and outlining the equity and efficiency
arguments for a larger government role in this area. As she points out, from a
policy perspective, the issue of child care is often examined in the context of
its impact on working parents, especially mothers. Leibowitz instead focuses
on the effect on children and in so doing clarifies an important aspect of the
potential government role in this area. As I indicate below, it is my view that
additional insights can be achieved by putting the parents back in, since child
care is intrinsically a "woman's issue" as well as a "children's issue." However,
this is not meant in any way to minimize the important contribution that Leibowitz makes with her "child-centered" approach.

Taking children as her focus, Leibowitz constructs equity and efficiency rationales for government intervention in this area that clearly and persuasively
parallel the justifications for government support of primary and secondary
education. Additionally, as Leibowitz points out, interventions early in life
have the potential to be particularly cost-effective in that children bring their
augmented human capital to all their future activities. Especially promising in
my view is the potential for early intervention to reduce antisocial behaviors
such as teen pregnancy and crime, which not only have high negative externalities, but have proved particularly intractable to other forms of intervention.
Also extremely important for similar reasons is evidence she cites suggesting
that high-quality child care can boost the learning readiness of disadvantaged
children and hence improve their educational outcomes. Based on her summary of the accumulating evidence that child care is particularly beneficial for
at-risk, low-income children, Leibowitz argues that the externalities as well as
the equity argument for government intervention to provide or subsidize child
care for this group is also strongest. In this respect her reasoning echoes that

Francine D. Blau is the Frances Perkins Professor of Industrial and Labor Relations at Cornell
University and a research associate of the National Bureau of Economic Research.

of Hanushek and Poterba in questioning whether the externality argument for government intervention in education has been applied with too broad a brush to justify government support of all levels of education. Both considerations argue for a more targeted approach, although it might be premature to adopt one without a fuller probing of potential externalities arguments applicable to higher educational levels and other income groups.

Turning to the system of child care provision in the United States, Leibowitz depicts an extremely heterogeneous system where informal arrangements, care in the child's own home or the home of a relative or nonrelative, predominate over organized care. This contrasts starkly with the much more uniform governmental provision of primary and secondary education in this country, as well as the extensive governmental provision of child care itself in some other countries, such as Sweden. Leibowitz's discussion implies that this heterogeneity is both a great strength and a great weakness of the current situation. On the one hand, as she points out, it addresses the different preferences of families and the potentially different developmental needs of young children at different ages. To this I would add that the widespread disaffection with our system of public education suggests that an excess of uniformity in provision can pose certain difficulties even for older children. On the other hand, the informal care that accounts for the majority of child care arrangements is unlicensed in the vast majority of cases and consequently, at least from this perspective, of uncertain quality.

Thus, a crucial policy issue that we face is how to maintain a desirable degree of diversity and choice in the provision of child care while assuring minimum levels of quality or, better yet, providing incentives for increasing quality of care. While Leibowitz's paper sheds considerable light on this issue, I think we still have a long way to go before it is fully resolved. A related point is the need for more research linking the inputs into the child care production process that both regulators of child care and researchers focus on as indicators of quality—for example, child/provider ratios, group size, and educational levels of providers—to measurable outcomes for children. The research that Leibowitz summarizes is certainly encouraging in this regard, but the empirical examination of this question is still in its infancy. The issue of developing appropriate, relatively easily applied indicators of child care quality will further increase in importance if government involvement in this area is expanded. More research on the relationship between child care quality and children's outcomes would also be helpful in better understanding the negative findings that have emerged for alternative care in the first year of life, which contrast with the positive results obtained for alternative care during the rest of the preschool years (e.g., Blau and Grossberg 1992). These findings may be due to the difficulty of obtaining high-quality care for infants.

Until the issues involved in providing good alternative care to infants are better understood, encouraging diversity in the types of arrangements available is especially important for this group. This includes facilitating parental care for some of this period. Indeed, in her otherwise comprehensive review of current government involvement in child care, Leibowitz has neglected the government mandates that have recently entered the picture in the form of the Family and Medical Leave Act (FMLA) of 1993, which requires up to twelve weeks of unpaid leave for new parents. (The United States in this respect has lagged behind other industrialized countries, which adopted such mandates earlier, usually with more generous leave provisions than those required under the recent U.S. legislation.)

Consideration of the FMLA raises the question of the appropriate role for employers in the provision and financing of child care, and its relationship to the broader issue of women's work status. A major factor lowering women's pay relative to men's is women's shorter and more discontinuous labor-force attachment, while employer's expectations of this pattern provide a rationale for their reluctance to hire women for jobs requiring substantial on-the-job training. Facilitating child care availability and/or lowering its cost encourages female labor-force participation, and particularly the continuity of that participation. Additionally, mandated parental leave of relatively short duration also most likely increases women's labor-force attachment. Thus, government intervention in these areas has the potential to raise female earnings relative to male earnings. This type of equity issue—the reduction of gender differences in earnings—spans the income distribution and thus might provide an equity rationale for a broader government provision or subsidy of child care rather than interventions aimed at the disadvantaged.

In failing to examine child care as a worker's issue as well as a children's issue, Leibowitz may also be too quick to dismiss a significant role for employers, though I agree with her that extensive government mandates may not make a great deal of sense. Government subsidies or tax breaks to firms for child care would encourage an expansion of the number of firms offering such benefits, either through the direct provision of child care itself or through various pecuniary benefits. This would have the indirect effect of encouraging firms to increase their investments in the firm-specific capital of their female workers, thus lowering the gender pay gap.

Along with other types of heterogeneity, the greater direct employer provision of child care that would be encouraged by subsidies might have advantages to children, as well, in the form of more effective monitoring of quality—both by the employer and by the employees who would be in closer proximity to their children than is typically the case with other child care arrangements. An additional benefit of direct employer provision is that it would encourage greater sharing of family responsibilities between parents, if, for example, child care is available at the father's place of work but not the mother's. This would mean that the father would assume responsibility for dropping off and picking up the child and that he would likely be the one on call in emergencies.

Many believe that a greater sharing of family responsibilities between parents is crucial to the advancement of gender equality in labor market outcomes. So the equity goal of reducing the gender pay gap is also furthered.

### Reference

Blau, Francine D., and Adam J. Grossberg. 1992. Maternal Labor Supply and Children's Cognitive Development. *Review of Economics and Statistics* 74:474–81.

# 3    Rationalizing School Spending: Efficiency, Externalities, and Equity, and Their Connection to Rising Costs

Eric A. Hanushek

By sheer size consideration, schools deserve the attention of policy makers. Annual direct expenditure on education has been running at about 70% of total business spending on new plant and equipment. In terms of industry comparison, educational expenditure exceeds the combined value of shipments from primary and fabricated metals and is roughly equal to shipments of transportation equipment. In terms of governmental spending, education is one-quarter of total social welfare spending—slightly less than governmental spending on all health and medical care and approaching twice the amount spent on public aid. These comparisons also illustrate common alternative ways of viewing education. It's an investment in the productive capacity of the nation; it's a raw material used in production; and it's an expenditure that from the government's viewpoint relates to general social welfare and to distributional concerns. These are all issues that will be covered later in this paper.

Nobody, however, believes that our schools are doing particularly well. Widespread dissatisfaction with the performance of schools, as opposed merely to size of the sector, has propelled education to a position high on the policy agenda. Yet the source of this dissatisfaction varies. Some people focus on student outcomes—whether the products of the schools can read and compute at an acceptable or desirable level. Others are more concerned with distributional aspects, concentrating on racial and economic differences in schooling and the rewards of schooling. Still others identify cost growth as the key problem, at least cost growth when compared to perceptions of performance of the schools. Another group focuses its attention on the role of government

Eric A. Hanushek is professor of economics and public policy and director of the Wallis Institute of Political Economy at the University of Rochester.

Victor Fuchs, Christopher Jencks, and Paul Romer provided insightful comments on a previous version that helped clarify the argument and ideas. Julie Somers provided valuable research assistance to this project.

in providing education, arguing variously that government does a poor job (in terms of costs and performance) or too good a job (in terms of introducing specific values, moral views, and the like).

As is frequently the case, a portion of the difference in viewpoints comes from differences in preferences. Some people simply value education for themselves and for others more or less than other people do, and this tends to affect the evaluation of school performance. But a substantial part of the difference comes from people looking at the same data and interpreting them differently. A good part of this seems to reflect long-standing issues about the measurement of educational outcomes, but basic analytical questions also intrude.

The analytical base for much of the current discussion is built on school attainment—simple years of school completed. This choice is convenient for both theoretical and empirical discussions and is undeniably useful in many contexts. Nevertheless, the central focus of current policy deliberation is quality of schooling, not quantity, and the arguments and analysis pertaining to quantity do not readily transfer to quality. This paper considers both quantity and quality arguments and then pursues issues of quality, particularly quality of elementary and secondary schools. Central concerns in the discussion are issues of efficiency and of equity. These issues are directly intertwined in educational debates because of the measurement and policy approaches commonly taken in distributional assumptions. Efficient spending is assumed, so that expenditure variations can be used to gauge the distribution of educational services. Obviously, if expenditure is not a good measure of educational quality, equity discussions based on expenditure can be misleading.

The central thesis of this paper is straightforward. Much of the policy discussion about education is built on a poor understanding of the underlying structure of education and schools, but the ambiguities and uncertainties lead to systematic biases toward increased spending on schools. Evidence on high rates of return to investment in quantity of schooling are translated into increased spending aimed at improving quality, yet with little assurance of actual improvement. Similarly, concerns about equity and about externalities from schooling push spending up without satisfying these objectives. A related issue, addressed at the end of the paper, is how citizens view spending in the context of their local districts. Preliminary analysis of voting on school budgets in New York State suggests no systematic relationship between performance of schools (measured in terms of student achievement) and willingness to support proposed budgets.

## 3.1    A Brief History of Schooling in America

### 3.1.1    Quantity Considerations

Economists view schooling as an investment both by individual students and by the society at large. Both incur costs and both reap rewards. For an individual student, the costs of education include the direct costs of tuition, books,

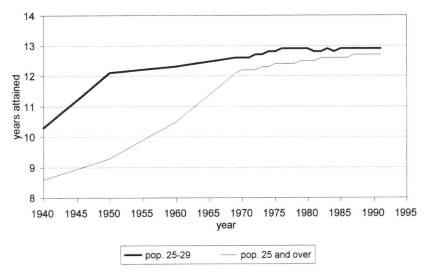

**Fig. 3.1    Median years of schooling by year: population age twenty-five to twenty-nine and age twenty-five and over**
*Source:* Current Population Survey.

and other school-related expenditures as well as the income that the student forgoes when attending school instead of taking a paying job. Similarly, society incurs direct costs in subsidizing a school system that provides free education to millions. It also forgoes the opportunity to devote to other projects the skills, people, and resources that are engaged in education. This viewpoint—regarding education as an investment—was brought into mainstream economics over three decades ago by Schultz (1961, 1963) and Becker (1993) and has been the basis of a steady stream of subsequent theoretical and empirical analyses.

A look at the history of the twentieth century suggests that schooling has generally been a good investment. Individuals have dramatically increased their own investments in education. At the turn of the twentieth century, only 6% of the adult population had finished high school. After the First World War, high school graduation rates began to increase rapidly. But changes in education work their way slowly through the overall population. By 1940, only half of Americans aged twenty-five or older had completed more than eight years of school—that is, had had any high school education at all. Not until 1967 did the median adult aged twenty-five or over complete high school.[1]

Since 1967, however, the increase in the number of years of schooling completed by Americans has slowed. The young adult population, aged twenty-five to twenty-nine, has had stable completion rates for almost two decades (see fig. 3.1). Since the overall schooling level is determined by the accumulation

1. See U.S. Bureau of the Census 1975, 1993; and Goldin 1994a, 1994b.

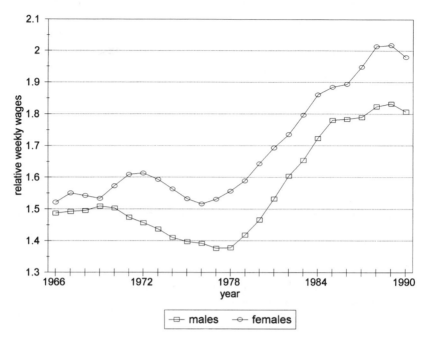

**Fig. 3.2   Ratio of wages of average college-educated to high school–educated workers: young white workers by sex**
*Source:* Author's calculations from Current Population Survey data.

of prior school attainment, this stabilized schooling has slowed dramatically the growth in schooling for the adult population as a whole. Today, the median years of school completed by Americans over twenty-five rests at slightly less than thirteen years.

The benefits of education to individuals are clear. The average incomes of workers with a high school education remain significantly above those of the less educated, and the incomes of workers with a college education now dwarf those of the high school–educated. The explosion in the earnings of college-educated workers, charted in figure 3.2, provides them with a premium of more than 70% higher earnings than a high school graduate with similar job experience.[2] Not only are wages higher for the better educated, but they also enjoy greater job opportunities and suffer less unemployment. The common interpretation is that our high-technology economy produces ever larger demands for skilled workers, workers who can adapt to new technologies and manage com-

2. More detail on the patterns of earnings can be found in Murphy and Welch 1989, 1992 and Kosters 1991. McMahon (1991) reports slightly lower private rates of return for high school completion than for college completion, although they remain substantial. These calculations all rely just on salary differentials, and greater equality in the provision of fringe benefits may act to compress the differences for total compensation. However, no analysis of schooling returns in terms of total compensation is available.

plicated production processes effectively. So for individuals, at least, the increased relative incomes of more educated people has been sufficient to offset the costs. An individual can expect significant financial benefit from extended schooling, even after appropriately considering costs.

Individuals also reap nonfinancial benefits from education. For example, there is evidence that more educated people make better choices concerning health, so they tend to live longer and to have healthier lives. There is also evidence that the children of more educated parents get more out of school. They attend longer and learn more. Such benefits of schooling simply reinforce those from the labor market.[3]

Society as a whole also benefits from education. The nation is strengthened economically by having workers with more and better skills. National income rises directly with individual earnings. Moreover, recent economic studies argue that education may provide economic benefits to society greater than the sum of its benefits to individuals—by providing a rich environment for innovation and scientific discovery, education can accelerate the growth rate of the economy.[4] The more educated are more prone to vote in local and national elections, and a better-informed and more responsible electorate improves the workings of a democratic society.[5] Increases in the level of education are associated with reductions in crime (e.g., Ehrlich 1975).

Education has also helped to achieve both greater social equality and greater equity in the distribution of economic resources. Schooling was quite rightly a centerpiece of the War on Poverty in the 1960s, and the benefits of improved schooling are demonstrated in comparisons of the earnings of different social and ethnic groups. Earnings by blacks and whites have converged noticeably since the Second World War, and much of this convergence is attributable to improved educational opportunities for African-Americans.[6] Providing an exact accounting for the benefits of education to society is difficult, because many of the benefits education provides are hard to value. But for the purposes here, it is safe to say that education has historically been a good investment both for society and for individuals.

### 3.1.2  Quality Considerations

If schooling has been such a good investment, what leads to the widespread concern about schools? For most of this century, debate over the economic consequences of schooling concentrated on the amount of school attained or,

3. Michael 1982; Haveman and Wolfe 1984; Wolfe and Zuvekas 1995; Leibowitz 1974. Many factors are unclear, however, because of questions of causality; see, for example, Farrell and Fuchs 1982.
4. See, for example, the analyses of growth in Lucas 1988, Romer 1990, Barro 1991, and Jorgenson and Fraumeni 1992.
5. The pattern of voting over time can be found in Stanley and Niemi 1994. An analysis of the partial effects of educational attainment (which are positive in the face of overall declines in voter turnout over time) is presented in Teixeira 1992.
6. See Smith and Welch 1989 and Jaynes and Williams 1989.

simply, the quantity of schooling of the population. Policy deliberations focused on school-completion rates, on the proportion of the population attending postsecondary schooling, and the like. And analyses of the benefits of schooling were most concerned with the effects of quantity of schooling—whether benefits are seen in terms of individual incomes or social benefits like improved voting behavior of citizens. For many reasons, however, today's attention is focused on the quality dimension of schooling.

As the growth in the number of years that Americans spend in school virtually stopped, many benefits that Americans might have expected from a continuously growing educational system have not materialized. Income growth has slowed,[7] and children no longer routinely surpass the earnings of their parents. Income convergence between blacks and whites also has stopped—coincident with a slowing in the convergence of the school-completion rates for the two groups.[8]

At the same time, nations around the world have increased their levels of schooling dramatically, with completion rates from secondary schools in a number of industrial competitors now rivaling those of the United States. Thus, America can no longer be easily assured of a higher quality-workforce than those of its trading partners. Both of these new realities shift the focus of the educational debate from quantity to quality. Improving the quality of schooling, or how much is learned for each year, has been seen as a possible way of counteracting the effects of U.S. slowdown in quantity of schooling.

The reason for questioning American education is straightforward. There is no evidence that increases in the quality of education are making up for the slowdown in the growth of schooling; on the contrary, declining quality may be making things worse. As described subsequently, data from a variety of sources suggest that the knowledge and skills of students are not as high as those measured in America in the past or in other nations currently. Moreover, achieving these current levels of student performance is costing much more than in the past.

The economic effects of differences in the quality of graduates of our elementary and secondary schools are much less understood than the effects of quantity, particularly with regard to the performance of the aggregate economy. The incomplete understanding of the effects of educational quality clearly reflects difficulties in measurement. Although quality of education is hard to define precisely, I mean the term *quality* to refer to the knowledge base and analytical skills that are the focal point of schools. Moreover, to add concreteness to this discussion, I will tend to rely on information provided by standardized tests of academic achievement and ability. Relying on standardized tests

---

7. See, for example, Levy and Murnane 1992 for a review of recent earnings patterns.
8. Discussion of distributional issues including earnings differences by race can be found in Smith and Welch 1989; O'Neill 1990; Kane 1990; Juhn, Murphy, and Pierce 1991; Card and Krueger 1992b; Grogger forthcoming; Levy and Murnane 1992; Bound and Freeman 1992; Boozer, Krueger, and Wolkon 1992; and Hauser 1993.

to provide measures of quality is controversial—in part because of gaps in available evidence and in part because of the conclusions that tend to follow (as discussed below).[9] Nevertheless, such measures appear to be the best available indicators of quality and do relate to outcomes that we care about.

A variety of studies of the labor market have been concerned about how individual differences in cognitive ability affect earnings (and modify the estimated returns to quantity). The early work was subsumed under the general topic of "ability bias" in the returns to schooling. In that, the simple question was whether the tendency of more able individuals to continue in school led to an upward bias in the estimated returns to school (because of a straightforward omitted-variables problem).[10] The correction most commonly employed was the inclusion of a cognitive ability or cognitive achievement measure in the earnings function estimates.[11] While focusing on the estimated returns to years of schooling, these studies generally indicated relatively modest impacts of variations in cognitive ability after holding constant the quantity of schooling.[12] In this work, there was no real discussion of what led to any observed cognitive differences, although much of the work implicitly treated it as innate, and not very related to variations in schooling.[13] Further, all of this work relied on nonrepresentative samples of the population.

The most recent direct investigations of cognitive achievement, however, have suggested generally larger labor market returns to measured individual differences in cognitive achievement. For example, Bishop (1989, 1991), O'Neill (1990), Ferguson (1993), Grogger and Eide (1995), and Murnane, Willett, and Levy (1994) all find that the earnings advantages to higher achievement on standardized tests are quite substantial. These results are derived from quite different approaches. Bishop (1989) worries about the measurement errors that are inherent in most testing situations and demonstrates that careful treatment of that problem has a dramatic effect on the estimated importance of

---

9. A substantial part of the controversy relates to the implications for effectiveness of expenditure or resource policies, as discussed below. The contrasting view emphasizes measuring "quality" by the resources (i.e., inputs) going into schooling. Most recent along this line is Card and Krueger 1992a; see also the review of the discussion in Burtless 1994.

10. See, for example, Griliches 1974.

11. The appropriate measure of earnings ability generally has received little attention, and the empirical work has tended to use any standardized test measure that is available. Therefore, differences in the results across studies may partially reflect the specific measure of ability employed.

12. This limited impact of cognitive achievement was also central to a variety of direct analyses of schooling such as Jencks et al. 1972 and Bowles and Gintis 1976. An exception to the generally modest relationship of cognitive performance and income is the work of Young and Jamison (1974). Using a national sample of data on reading competence, they find a strong influence of test scores on income for whites (but not blacks). This held in both recursive and simultaneous equations models of the joint determination of achievement and income.

13. Manski (1993) represents more recent work with this same general thrust. He recasts the issue as a selection problem and considers how ability or quality interacts with earnings expectations to determine continuation in schooling. Currently, however, no empirical work along these lines identifies the quantitative importance of selection or the interaction of school quality and earnings in such models.

test differences. O'Neill (1990), Ferguson (1993), Grogger and Eide (1995), and Bishop (1991), on the other hand, simply rely upon more recent labor market data along with more representative sampling and suggest that the earnings advantage to measured skill differences is larger than that found in earlier time periods and in earlier studies (even without correcting for test reliability). Murnane, Willett, and Levy (1994), considering a comparison over time, demonstrate that the results of increased returns to measured skills hold regardless of the methodology (i.e., whether simple analysis or error-corrected estimation).

The National Research Council study on employment tests (Hartigan and Wigdor 1989) also supports the view of a significant relationship of tests and employment outcomes, although the strength of the relationship appears somewhat less strong than that in the direct earnings investigations. It considers the relationship between the General Aptitude Test Battery (GATB), the standard employment test of the Department of Labor, and job performance. Their synthesis of a wide number of studies suggests a systematic but somewhat modest relationship with correlations to performance on the order of .2 to .4. The analysis also finds that the validity of these tests in predicting performance has gone down over time. These results, being somewhat at odds with the recent studies, may simply reflect the specialized nature of GATB.[14] Specifically, the GATB may not be a good measure of the cognitive outcomes of schools and may not correspond well to standard measures of cognitive achievement.

An additional part of the return to school quality comes through continuation in school. There is substantial evidence that students who do better in school, either through grades or scores on standardized achievement tests, tend to go farther in school (see, e.g., Dugan 1976 and Manski and Wise 1983). Rivkin (1991) finds that variations in test scores capture a considerable proportion of the systematic variation in high school completion and in college continuation. Indeed, Rivkin (1991) finds that test score differences fully explain black-white differences in schooling. Bishop (1991) and Hanushek, Rivkin, and Taylor (1995) find that individual achievement scores are highly correlated with school attendance. Behrman et al. (1994) find strong achievement effects on both continuation into college and quality of college; moreover, the effects are larger when proper account is taken of the endogeneity of achievement. Hanushek and Pace (1995), using the High School and Beyond data, find that college completion is significantly related to higher test scores at the end of high school.

I conclude from these diverse studies that variations in cognitive ability, as measured by standardized tests, are important in career success. Variation in measured cognitive ability is far from everything that is important, but it is significant in a statistical and quantitative sense.

---

14. The GATB is a very old test that may not reflect changes in the economy. It also suffers from some psychometric problems (see Hartigan and Wigdor 1989). The central purpose of the study was assessment of the Department of Labor practice of providing test information normed to racial groups.

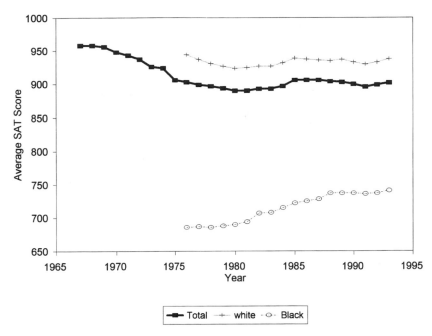

**Fig. 3.3    SAT scores: total and by race, 1967–1993**
*Source:* U.S. Department of Education 1993.

The linkage of individual cognitive skills to aggregate productivity growth is much more difficult to establish. There is no clear consensus on the underlying causes of improvements in the overall productivity of the U.S. economy, or on how the quality of workers interacts with economic growth.[15]

### 3.1.3    The Pattern of Quality Changes

First warning of problems came when national average Scholastic Aptitude Test (SAT) scores fell from the mid-1960s through the end of the 1970s.[16] As shown in figure 3.3, there has been some recovery, but it has been neither con-

15. One observation is useful, however. When looking at the history of productivity increase in the U.S. economy, several distinct time periods stand out. Productivity growth continued at some 2% per year through the 1960s, but fell off subsequently—first to 1% in the 1970s and then to virtually 0 in the 1980s. Noting that productivity changes in these time periods mirror the aggregate pattern of scholastic test scores (shown below), some have gone on to presume that the test scores are driving the productivity changes. Such could not, however, be the case—since, as Bishop (1989) makes clear, the test takers with lower scores remained a small proportion of the total labor force through the 1980s. Lower test scores in the 1980s may signal forthcoming problems, but they cannot be an explanation for past changes in the economy.

16. The SAT is subject to questioning because of the selective nature of test takers—essentially high school students who wish to go to a geographically and academically select group of schools. While some of the change in test scores can be attributed to changes in the test-taking population, it is clear that real performance changes are also included. See Congressional Budget Office 1986, 1987.

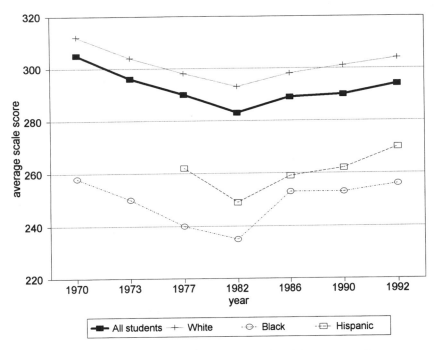

**Fig. 3.4  Science achievement as measured by National Assessment of Educational Progress: seventeen-year-olds, 1970–1992**
*Source:* U.S. Department of Education 1993.

sistent nor sufficient to return performance to its previous highs. If we compare the peak to the trough, we find that the average test taker in 1979 was performing at the 39th percentile in math and the 33d percentile in reading of the 1963 test takers. While the declines in the college admission tests (SAT and American College Test [ACT]) were among the largest, other tests also showed very significant falls.

Results from the National Assessment of Educational Progress (NAEP) are particularly significant because these are the only tests that provide data for a sampling of students that is statistically representative of the overall student population. These tests cover reading, mathematics, and science for a random selection of students of given ages. While there are some differences between different tests in the series, these data (which are summarized in figs. 3.4–3.6) suggest that the performance of the average seventeen-year-old student changed little between the early 1970s and 1992. While reading performance may be up slightly over the entire period, mathematics performance has shown no improvement, and science performance has slipped. (Note also that these tests were first employed after a substantial portion of the fall in SAT performance had already occurred, suggesting that performance stabilized at a lower level than that of the 1960s.)

Comparing the performance of whites and blacks on both SAT and NAEP

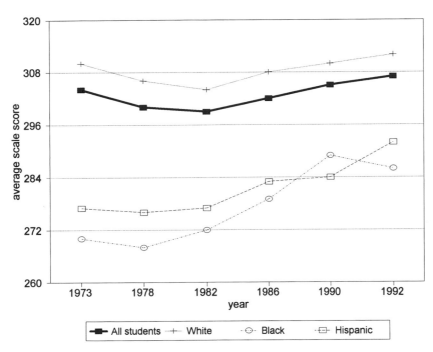

**Fig. 3.5   Mathematics achievement as measured by National Assessment of Educational Progress: seventeen-year-olds, 1973–1992**
*Source:* U.S. Department of Education 1993.

exams, two facts stand out. First, the black-white gap in performance has generally been narrowing over time. Second, the gap remains unacceptably large.

International comparisons provide a different perspective on student performance. The most telling of the several different testing projects that have been undertaken over the past three decades is the International Assessment of Educational Progress (IAEP). The IAEP results come from science and mathematics, subjects less affected by possible language and cultural differences. They also use the general tests developed for U.S. students, so any differences in curricular objectives or instructional approaches work in the Americans' favor. American students scored near the bottom, and the gap is particularly large on more complex tasks (Lapointe, Mead, and Gary 1989). As the report on the first IAEP mathematics results notes, however, the students from the United States seemed unworried by their performance: "Despite their poor overall performance, about two-thirds of the United States' thirteen-year-olds feel that they are 'good at mathematics.' Only 23 percent of their Korean counterparts, the best achievers, share the same attitude" (Lapointe, Mead, and Gary 1989, 10). A smaller and different group of countries participated in a follow-up to the IAEP in 1991 (U.S. Department of Education 1993). On this collection of tests, nine-year-old students from the United States scored in the middle of the range on the science examination and at the bottom on the mathematics

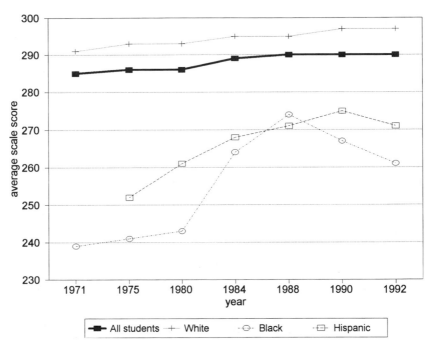

**Fig. 3.6    Reading achievement as measured by National Assessment of Educational Progress: seventeen-year-olds, 1971–1992**
*Source:* U.S. Department of Education 1993.

examination. By contrast, thirteen-year-old American students scored at the bottom in both mathematics and science. The one examination showing a somewhat different result is the 1991 Reading Literacy Study. U.S. fourteen-year-olds placed seventh out of nineteen international testing groups (U.S. Department of Education 1993). Unfortunately, no historical data exist on reading performance, so it is impossible to say anything about changes over time.

Related to concerns about the performance of the average student are questions concerning the performance of the very top students. Many suggest that the very highly skilled, for example, scientists and engineers, have a particularly important role in determining the viability of the economy and its future growth. Thus, a fall in the performance of the highest-performing students—particularly a disproportionate fall—might have especially adverse effects. While there are suggestions of a decline in top students, existing data and testing methodology make it very difficult to ascertain with confidence the extent of any such change. No evidence, however, indicates that performance of top students has improved.[17]

17. See, for example, the discussion in Educational Testing Service 1991 and Congressional Budget Office 1986.

### 3.1.4   Cost Considerations

These results have not been for lack of trying.[18] The United States has continually increased the resources devoted to public schools throughout the twentieth century. By some measures, expenditure on education has grown faster than that on health over the past two decades. Yet while health care costs are the subject of vigorous debate, the unremitting growth in educational expenditures receives only passing attention in most policy discussions. More ironically, when attention is focused on educational expenditure, it is usually to suggest that spending should rise. But educational expenditure has risen strongly and steadily in real terms throughout the century. Some of the increase is a simple consequence of the increased numbers of school-age children, but a larger part reflects active policy choices to increase expenditure on the schooling of each student—through more and higher-paid teachers, working in schools with a steadily declining pupil/teacher ratio. These increases are magnified by even larger increases in expenditure other than for instructional staff.

Between 1890 and 1990, real public expenditure on elementary and secondary education in the United States rose from $2 billion to almost $190 billion. (All monetary measures are adjusted by the GNP deflator to constant 1990 dollars; expenditure excludes capital costs.) This almost 100-fold increase was more than triple the growth rate of the GNP during the same period. Educational expenditure increased from less than 1% of the GNP in 1890 to over 3.5% of the GNP in 1990.

Spending on public schooling as a percentage of the GNP actually peaked in 1975, at almost 4%, when baby boomers reached their maximum school-going years. But demographics are only the lesser part of the story of rising educational spending. Rising per-student expenditure explains the bulk of the change in educational outlays. Figure 3.7 plots increases in per-student expenditure from 1890 to 1990. Real, per-student expenditure rose from $164 in 1890 to $772 in 1940, and on to $4,622 in 1990—roughly quintupling in each fifty-year period. The figure also separates expenditure on instructional staff—mainly teachers and principals—from other school expenditure. Today, expenditure on instructional staff accounts for roughly 45% of total school spending. In 1940, by contrast, it accounted for about two-thirds.

Three factors drive spending on instructional staff (which I frequently refer to simply as teachers). First is the absolute size of the school population, which is determined by the numbers of children of the relevant ages, by whether or not they are enrolled in school, and by their choices between public and private schools. Second are choices in the intensity of instruction—including varying average class sizes and the length of the school year. The third force driving instructional costs is wage rates and other personnel costs, most importantly

18. This section summarizes the more detailed analysis of costs found in Hanushek and Rivkin 1994.

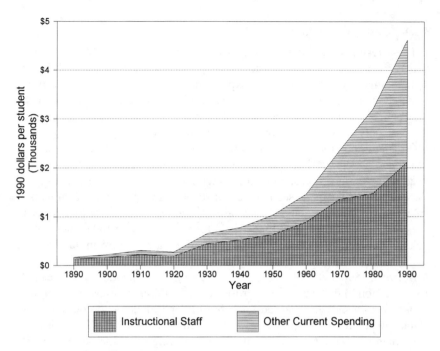

**Fig. 3.7    Real instructional staff and other current expenditure per student, 1890–1990**
*Source:* Hanushek and Rivkin 1994.

for teachers. Table 3.1 illustrates how these three separate forces have affected the growth in instructional-staff expenditure over the past century.

Over the entire century from 1890 to 1990, 29.5% of the growth in instructional-staff spending was attributed to increases in public school population, with most of that coming from pure growth in the school-age population. An almost equal share came from a rise in the intensity of instruction, most notably from declines in class sizes. Pupil/teacher ratios fell from 35 in 1890 to 25 in 1960 to 15 in 1990.[19] The remaining 42.6% of overall increases came from increases in the real wages of teachers. The aggregation across the full century, however, masks some very different periods. Specifically, 1970–90 exhibited

19. Over the century, a portion of the fall in pupil/teacher ratios can be attributed to a proportionate increase in the secondary school population. Secondary schools have maintained 20–25% lower pupil/teacher ratios, at least during the post–World War II period, so an increase in the proportion of secondary students will imply a reduction in average class sizes even if no fundamental changes occurred. At the same time pupil/teacher ratios within both elementary and secondary schools have continuously fallen over the last fifty years. Overall private school pupil/teacher ratios have been roughly equal to public school ratios, although part of this comes from aggregating over very heterogeneous situations. Private secondary schools have had lower pupil/teacher ratios, while the opposite holds at the elementary school level. Further, there is a very different mix of elementary and secondary student populations in private schools as compared to public.

**Table 3.1**    **Changes in Instructional Staff Expenditure Attributed to Input Changes by Periods, 1890–1990 (percentage)**

|  | 1890–1940 | 1940–1970 | 1970–1990 | 1980–1990 | 1890–1990 |
|---|---|---|---|---|---|
| Quantity |  |  |  |  |  |
| School-age population | 24 | 35.3 | −36.1 | −16.9 | 23.3 |
| Enrollment rate | 8 | 4 | 3.0 | 11.8 | 6.0 |
| Public school enrollment | 1.5 | −1.3 | −2.1 | −2.7 | 0.2 |
| Intensity |  |  |  |  |  |
| Pupil/teacher ratio | 10.7 | 20.3 | 85.4 | 36.1 | 20.8 |
| Days per year | 12.7 | 1.4 | 0 | 0 | 7.2 |
| Input cost |  |  |  |  |  |
| Price of teachers | 43.1 | 40.3 | 49.9 | 71.6 | 42.6 |
| Total | 100 | 100 | 100 | 100 | 100 |

*Source:* Hanushek and Rivkin 1994.

*Note:* This table uses a multiplicative decomposition of cost growth to attribute the overall increases in instructional costs to specific factors. See Hanushek and Rivken 1994.

marked declines in the school-age population (the "baby bust") with continued declines in pupil/teacher ratios and increases in teacher wages that exceeded those of the earlier periods. The net effect was the continued growth in per-pupil spending that was, in the aggregate, masked by a falling population.

The pupil/teacher ratio has declined steadily, regardless of whether the price of instructional personnel increased or decreased. While technological change has led to substitution of capital for labor elsewhere in the economy, the opposite has occurred in education. One contributing factor in the decline in the average pupil/teacher ratio might be an increase in the number of difficult-to-educate children, such as handicapped children or children from low-income families. But the general nationwide decline in the pupil/teacher ratio—which occurs across schools in communities with a wide variety of student populations—suggests that this is not the fundamental reason for change. Direct analysis of the growth in the handicapped populations also indicates that this can explain considerably less than half of spending growth (Hanushek and Rivkin 1994).

The growth in teacher salaries is also interesting. While wage increases have contributed significantly to the growth in school expenditure, teacher earnings have, at least since World War II, slipped relative to earnings opportunities elsewhere in the economy. This unfortunate situation appears to reflect simply the low growth in productivity of education relative to other sectors in the economy.[20] It is interesting, however, that schools (and, through bargaining,

---

20. The general pressures toward increasing costs in low-productivity industries is set out in Scitovsky and Scitovsky 1959, Baumol and Bowen 1965, and Baumol 1967. The interpretation in the educational industry is more complicated, however, because educated labor is both an input and an output—implying that the value of output is going up at the same time that input costs are rising.

teacher unions) have responded to cost pressures by accepting falling relative wages along with reduced pupil/teacher ratios. The pattern of wage changes is complicated and differs significantly for men and women, but increased alternative work opportunities for women is likely to put added strain on schools in the future (see Hanushek and Rivkin 1994).

Expenditure other than on instructional staff, the final component of cost growth, has had dramatic impacts on overall spending, but interpreting changes is difficult. Other expenditure grows from $0.4 billion in 1890 to $6.4 billion in 1940 and to over $100 billion in 1990. As figure 3.7 shows, other expenditure has actually risen more rapidly over the entire century than instructional-staff expenditure. On average since 1960, this noninstructional-staff expenditure per student rises at 5% per year, compared to only 3% per year for instructional expenditure. The relative growth of other expenditure is most rapid during the decade of the 1970s, when the total school-age population dropped significantly.[21] If, for example, other expenditure had grown at the same per-student rate as instructional-staff expenditure between 1960 and 1990, the 1990 per-student expenditure would have been $3,480 instead of over $4,622. This would implicitly allow for increased noninstructional-staff spending intensity because the growth of instructional-staff expenditures includes a fall in the pupil/teacher ratio of a third.

The attention that is given to other expenditure (outside of that for instructional staff) flows in part from a common interpretation that, if it does not relate to instructional staff, it must be growth of administrative bureaucracy.[22] Unfortunately, it is difficult to tell exactly what changes have occurred, let alone to judge the efficacy of any such changes. Little consistent data are available to permit any detailed analysis of what lies behind this growth. Moreover, the data that do exist are somewhat misleading, since the other category actually includes a variety of items that are conceptually part of instructional expenditure but are labeled noninstructional by accounting convention. For example, the "noninstructional" component includes employer-paid health care and retirement contributions for teachers. Other components left out of instructional-staff spending include items like books and supplies, which are legitimately part of classroom instruction. Thus, the break between instructional and noninstructional expenditure is difficult to make.

21. In terms of absolute growth rates, the decades of the 1950s and 1960s are the largest of the postwar period; this holds for both per capita expenditure and total current expenditure. During these decades, however, both instructional-staff and other expenditure were growing in parallel. During the 1970s, instructional-staff expenditure was constant in the aggregate and rose less than 1% annually on a per-student basis, while other expenditure per student grew at an annual real growth rate of 5.6%.

22. For example, former Secretary of Education William J. Bennett writes: "Too much money has been diverted from the classroom; a smaller share of the school dollar is now being spent on student classroom instruction than at any time in recent history. . . . It should be a basic goal of the education reform movement to reverse this trend toward administrative bloat and to reduce the scale of the bureaucratic 'blob' draining our school resources" (1988, 46).

### 3.1.5    Uncertainty about School Performance

The aggregate data motivate a concern about the performance of public schools. Nevertheless, they are inconclusive, because they reflect factors that go beyond just the core activities of the schools.

First, achievement is affected by a variety of influences, not just schools. Parents, friends, and others outside of the school all contribute to a student's achievement, so that the aggregate scores do not simply reflect what is happening over time in the schools. Moreover, the aggregate character of these outside factors has clearly been changing through time. It is natural to point to such things as the upsurge in immigrant populations, the increase in child poverty, and the tilt toward single-parent families as adversely affecting the preparation of students for school and the support they receive for obtaining high performance. But even the aggregate story is complicated and difficult to sort out by simple consideration of trend data. Offsetting favorable factors for education include the increased education of parents, the movement toward smaller families, and the increase in government interventions such as Head Start that are aimed at compensating for poorer family support. The net impact of these and similar factors is difficult to infer from the aggregate (see also Congressional Budget Office 1987).

Second, on the expenditure side, there also may be interpretive problems. Not all expenditure is aimed at improving performance in core areas. Thus, for example, expansion of the social agenda of schools undoubtedly takes resources but contributes little to the improvement of science ability of students (see Committee for Economic Development 1994). Similarly, as mentioned before, expenditures on handicapped children are unlikely to have much impact on average achievement scores, in part because such students are frequently excluded from routine testing. Additionally, performance at each point in time should be related to the cumulative past expenditure contributing to a cohort's schooling. The generally smooth nature of increases, however, suggests that such timing issues are not particularly important.

The import of all of these issues is to introduce caution in the interpretation of aggregate performance data. While the overall level of performance is a clear concern, the consideration of the role of schools and school policy requires further analysis. Importantly, however, more detailed consideration of the circumstances behind the aggregate data does not change the overall picture and conclusions to be drawn. The key finding of more direct evidence on school performance, described below, is that schools have a performance problem that has not been solved by increased resources for schools.

## 3.2    Conventional Policy Interpretations

This lengthy review of the data and the state of education in the United States is really meant as a preamble to the main thesis of this paper. Specifically, much of the debate and policy discussion appears based on a flawed understanding of the data that is compounded by translating observations about quantity of schooling into policy statements about quality of schooling. First, based on extensive evidence that increasing school attainment has had powerful effects on individual earnings and aggregate economic performance, many quite naturally argue for an expansion of schooling. Expanding schooling with a relatively constant level of school attainment implies devoting more resources to schools and, in effect, increasing the intensity of the resources provided to a fixed pool of students. This translation, as described in section 3.2.1, on improving quality, is unlikely, however, to yield the economic benefits presumed. Second, pursuing the objective of increased equity falls prey to similar problems. Equity is viewed in two somewhat different ways: in terms of race or income and in terms of geographic variation in school spending. Both begin with a concern about quality differences but then tend to confuse such concerns with very imperfect measurement of quality differences among schools. Third, while less central to much of the current policy debate, the notion that education is a "high externality" area provides a backdrop for many arguments aimed at changing the quality of schooling, but little evidence relates to this at all.

The unifying feature of these perspectives on school policy is the pressure generated for increased spending on schools. Each revolves around a plausible sounding and widely accepted argument for increased public support of schools. And each incorrectly applies evidence about returns to quantity of schooling to support expenditure expansion.

This paper does not, however, "test" its main thesis. Instead, it lays out the ideas as a way of organizing thinking about much of the current educational debate. As such, it tries to rationalize the existing evidence and the existing rhetoric.

### 3.2.1    Improving Quality through Expanding Resources

The most common policy proposal for dealing with the performance problems of schools described previously is to expand the resources available for schools.[23] Such proposals tend to ignore the aggregate data presented above that indicate a steady expansion of resources before and during the period of concern about lagging school performance. A common justification for increased resources is estimates of high rates of return to schooling investments, but these estimates of high rates of return rely almost exclusively on characterizations of earnings improvements from quantity of schooling. As is obvious, increasing spending on schools without a commensurate improvement in stu-

---

23. An example, typical of the large number of reform proposals appearing in the past decade, is the Committee for Economic Development (1985) statement appearing in bold on page 4, "We believe that any call for comprehensive improvement in the public schools that does not recognize the need for additional resources is destined for failure." Interestingly, Committee for Economic Development 1994 takes a very different tack, arguing that management and governance issues are much more important than additional resources if our schools are to improve.

dent performance will only decrease the rate of return on schooling (even though common methods of calculating rates of return will frequently not show such true effects).

The aggregate data on spending and performance are suggestive but far from conclusive, because, as mentioned, many other factors enter into overall changes in student outcomes over time. Much more persuasive is the evidence from a large number of detailed econometric studies of the determinants of student achievement. The econometric evidence comes from various estimates of the effects of either spending or real resources on student performance (holding constant student family background and other characteristics). These studies, initiated in response to the "Coleman Report" (Coleman *et al.* 1966), are designed to separate the various influences on student performance. The basic summary table of econometric results, reproduced from Hanushek (1989), is found in appendix table 3A.1. This table summarizes the sign of estimated coefficients for the effects of major school resources and their statistical significance. The primary determinants of variations in expenditure per students across classrooms and schools are teacher education and teacher experience—which determine teacher salaries—and pupil/teacher ratios—which determine over how many pupils the teacher's salary is spread. There is little confidence of any consistent resource effects related to these factors, based on conventional statistical standards, and many studies even suggest that increased resources are associated with decreased student performance.[24]

This evidence makes it clear that there is no systematic and consistent relationship between school resources and student performance.[25] These findings are categorized under efficiency simply because they imply that increased resources are associated with no gains in outcomes, an obvious case of economic inefficiency. The research does not imply that resources *never* could or do improve performance, just that they currently do not.[26] Most policy appeals for expanding school resources do not offer any substantial change in the organi-

24. Expenditure effects are best viewed in terms of real resource differences that vary across classrooms and schools, that is, class sizes, teacher-education levels and teacher-experience levels. A limited number of studies directly investigate measured expenditure per pupil. Since such measures are generally available only at the school district level, studies employing such measures tend to be highly aggregated and less reliable. See Hanushek 1986, 1989, 1994b. A reanalysis of the expenditure data can be found in Hedges, Laine, and Greenwald 1994, which attempts to conduct formal statistical tests combining the estimated coefficients of expenditures. As reviewed in Hanushek 1994a, 1994b, there is agreement that some schools employ resources effectively, but this does not support any broad resource-centered policies.

25. The basic articles (Hanushek 1986, 1989) provide information about the underlying studies. While a few studies were missed, this analysis attempted to include an exhaustive set of underlying estimates that met minimal criteria (published studies that included both resource and family background measures and that reported sign and significance of estimated effects). About three-quarters of the 187 studies included employ standardized test scores as the measure of student performance, while the remainder include such things as subsequent incomes, college continuation, or school dropout behavior.

26. The recent exchange on the statistical nature of the evidence (Hedges, Laine, and Greenwald 1994; Hanushek 1994a) underscores agreement that some schools appear currently to use resources effectively, while a counterbalancing set does not.

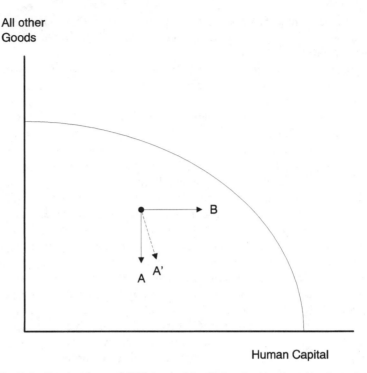

**All other
Goods**

**Human Capital**

**Fig. 3.8   Production possibilities and inefficiencies in educational production**

zation and incentives of schools, and thus the available evidence on past lack of success appears relevant for these appeals.

The general situation is best illustrated in figure 3.8. Society's resources can be devoted either to producing more human capital or to any other (public or private) good. The frontier traces the maximum consumption of all other goods, given the level of human capital chosen. But inefficient use of resources in education places us somewhere inside this possibilities curve. Pure resource or spending policies, of the type frequently proposed and pursued, appear by the evidence to lead to additional inefficiency instead of added human capital production. Thus, they tend to drive resource allocation in the direction of A. On the other hand, since elimination of existing inefficiencies can improve the amount of human capital produced without expanding additional resources, policies moving us in the direction B should be the focus of attention. The debate about interpretation of existing evidence (Hedges, Laine, and Greenwald 1994 and Hanushek 1994a) can be interpreted simply as a debate about whether spending policies might not be purely vertical but instead might move us slightly to the right as depicted by the dashed line moving in the direction A'. Even if movement toward A' could be achieved, such policies would remain very inferior to policies pushing toward B.

One way some view this evidence is that varying levels of resources may have powerful effects at low levels of investment, but, given the current amount spent on U.S. schools, there is no obvious impact. Such an interpretation is consistent with evidence that minimal levels of resources have important effects in promoting quality in the schools of developing countries (see, e.g., Harbison and Hanushek 1992). It may also help reconcile the findings of Card and Krueger (1992a) with those presented here, because their study finds significant resource impacts on earnings when variations across pre–World War II schools are considered.[27] None of this evidence suggests, however, that one should expect significant differences in student performance to follow expansion of school resources from current levels and within the current incentive structure.[28] Similar to what has been suggested for medical care, we may simply be on the flat of the performance curve, where added resources yield little marginal payoff.

Arguing simply that schooling, broadly defined, is a high-return investment does not provide adequate justification for increased direct expenditure on schools. The arguments of investments to improve quality must consider the nature of the investment in ways that arguments to expand the quantity of schooling usually do not. This confusion over returns to quantity and quality and over the kinds of investment to be undertaken has, in my opinion, quite distorted the educational policy debate.

### 3.2.2   Equity

Another thrust of the general consideration of educational policy concentrates on equity matters—the distribution of outcomes by identifiable characteristics. The historical review of schooling highlighted some of the concerns. First, the gap in measured performance by race and ethnic background is very large. Second, although not discussed, the gap in achievement by parents' education, income, and social status is likewise large. Together, these observed outcome differences (and the income and employment ramifications) have formed the basis for a large amount of the attention to schools serving disadvantaged groups.

But the educational policy debate has concentrated more on a different equity concern—that of differential spending across local school districts. Since the first decisions in the landmark school finance case of *Serrano v. Priest* in the late 1960s, attention has focused on the structure of local and state fi-

---

27. Significant controversy over the findings of Card and Krueger (1992a) and their relevance for current schools remains and is unresolved; see Burtless 1994 and other papers presented at the Brookings conference "Do School Resources Matter?" (Washington, DC, June 6, 1994). Reestimation of the basic earnings relationships by Heckman, Layne-Farrar, and Todd (1994) also suggests that the original estimates of Card and Krueger are very sensitive to sample and model specification and that the resource effects are weakened or disappear in alternative estimates.

28. An alternative set of incentives—ones emphasizing student performance—may well be able to change this situation. These arguments, nonetheless, go well beyond the scope of this paper. The evidence on performance effects is also very limited today. See Hanushek with others 1994.

nance.[29] The simple argument that now has been repeated in over half of the states is that local schools supported by local property taxes are inequitable because they make the quality of school provision dependent on the "wealth of one's neighbors." Decisions in these state cases have depended on specific state circumstances and the separate state constitutions. But there is no doubt that they have been popular in large part because supporters of the suits and judges in the cases view them as addressing the more general equity concerns—differential outcomes by race and income.[30] The attention given to Jonathan Kozol's recent book (1991) provides some evidence on that score. His book provides a vivid description of the contrast between the country's very best and very worst schools. He then suggests that bringing all schools up to the funding of the wealthiest will eliminate the racial and income disparities in student performance and lifetime success, a position that simply is not supported by the evidence. Nevertheless, this book has been featured in the popular press and is widely quoted as illustrating both the existing equity problems and the obvious solutions.

Various aspects of local inefficiencies, tax equity, interjurisdictional mobility, sorting by preferences à la Tiebout, and the like immediately spring to mind when local property taxes and different tax bases are discussed. But the educational equity aspects are less clear. In simplest terms, if the distribution of funding does not relate to the quality of schools, the equity aspects of the school financing debates and court cases that focus on spending variations are significantly less clear.

One part of the evidence and the debate needs clarifying at this point. As a general matter, it is important to recognize that schools are but one input to a student's learning and achievement. The student's own ability and motivation, the education from parents and families, and the input of community and friends each contributes.[31] The common observation that students in wealthy suburban areas who attend high-spending schools do well on standardized achievement tests frequently sends the message that duplicating those schools in poor areas will equalize achievement. In fact, the previous evidence (from econometric analysis that standardizes for parental inputs and, sometimes, individual ability differences) indicates these conclusions are wrong on two counts. First, one should not simply equate high student achievement with well-functioning schools, because the high achievement frequently just implies strong parental influences. Second, providing equal resources is unlikely to

---

29. Following a 1974 ruling in *Rodriguez v. San Antonio,* these school finance issues have been a matter of strictly state concern, and the federal government has not been involved.

30. It is generally presumed that places with low tax bases are the ones with most of the population of poor children. This presumption, however, is far from true, in large part because of the powerful influence of the distribution of commercial and industrial property on the size of the local tax base but also because of the substantial variation in incomes within most communities.

31. This discussion takes the general view that family inputs are very important but are not very manipulable from a policy viewpoint. This position probably understates some possibilities. See, for example, Fuchs and Reklis 1994 on the importance of readiness for school, which might be affected by policy interventions.

close gaps, given that schools do not consistently employ resources effectively.[32]

Most recently, these financing cases have gone one step further by introducing the concept of "adequacy." In one form, adequacy is simply an appeal for more resources. Even if a state's funding shows little variation, so the argument goes, the level of funding may be inadequate to provide high-quality schools. Such an argument was employed, for example, in a 1992 school-finance suit in Alabama where very little variation in spending was matched with a ranking of forty-seventh among the states in average expenditure in 1991.[33] Yet the evidence presented previously indicates that simple expansion of school resources is unlikely to yield much overall improvement in student performance, even though the state could clearly move up in national spending rankings.[34] A second, and somewhat more appealing, version of adequacy is that sufficient funding should be provided to ensure that all students can perform at an acceptable level. This version is more appealing because it focuses attention on student performance, but it is no more practical, regardless of one's views about appropriate social goals for equity. Its impracticality derives from an inability to specify how added resources translate into better achievement.

The primary message is that equity concerns cannot be separated from efficiency. If there is no direct way to transform resources into improved student performance, policies aimed at more equity through equalizing resources have little hope of improving equity as defined in terms of student outcomes. Policies of redistribution are not neutral, however, because seldom is there a simple change in existing funding patterns when increased equality of spending is sought. Instead of moving funds from high-spending districts to low-spending districts, changes invariably involve expansion of total spending—that is, it is easier to redistribute a larger pie. Thus, equity-inspired policies are probably best thought of in terms of their other potential purposes or effects—whether that is increasing the overall level of spending, moving toward more equal tax rates across jurisdictions, or whatever.

### 3.2.3  Externalities

A final area where policy rhetoric and evidence seem at odds involves the extent of externalities in education. In general, activities that are perceived to have significant externalities are prime candidates for increased governmental

---

32. The overall trends toward convergence of black and white test scores have led some to infer that increased compensatory spending on schools has finally begun to be seen. This conclusion is not, however, the result of explicit analysis, and it ignores other trends such as increased education of black parents, declining family sizes, and (going in the other direction) increased illegitimacy rates and stagnant incomes. Direct analyses of the effectiveness of compensatory programs does not support this as an explanation (see Mullin and Summers 1983).

33. Wyckoff (1992) provides comparative inequality measures for all states in 1987. Only four states (excluding Hawaii with its unified school system) had a lower coefficient of variation in current expenditure per pupil than Alabama. Spending by state is found in U.S. Bureau of the Census 1993.

34. See the description of projected achievement effects in Hanushek 1993.

support. As is also well-recognized, externalities are noticeably elusive, and, while optimal tax and subsidy policies in the face of externalities are well understood conceptually, few estimates of the magnitude of externalities exist anywhere. Nevertheless, if economists were polled on externalities in education, I suspect that they would substantially support the view that education involves extensive externalities.

As described previously, leading candidates for areas of external benefits involve citizen involvement in the community and government, crime reduction, family decision making and child upbringing, and economic growth. There is evidence that more schooling does have a positive impact in each of these areas. But what does that imply for the current debates?

In each area, a significant portion of the beneficial effect of education appears to come from comparing very low levels of school attainment with significantly higher levels. Thus, extensive discussions of the social benefits of schooling in developing countries would seem both warranted and correct.[35] It is difficult to have, for example, a well-informed citizenry when most of the population is illiterate. It may also be difficult to introduce advanced production technologies, at least in a timely manner, if workers cannot be expected to read the accompanying technical manuals.

On the other hand, even if accepting the importance of externalities at minimal levels, there is little reason to believe that there are constant marginal externalities.[36] Specifically, arguments about the social benefits of expanded education seem much stronger in the case of developing countries of Africa than in the case of the United States during the twenty-first century. Where half of the population has attended some postsecondary schooling, another year of average schooling seems unlikely to change dramatically the political awareness of the U.S. population. Similarly, if the average high school student scores 950 on the SAT instead of 900, I do not think many would expect noticeable changes in the identified extra social benefits of education.

My leading candidate for potential externalities of education in the United States and other developed countries would revolve around economic growth. If a highly skilled workforce permits entirely different kinds of technologies to be introduced, or to be introduced earlier in a development cycle, expanded education of an individual may indeed affect other workers in the economy.

35. Interestingly, policy discussions of education in developing countries tend to concentrate most on private rates of return and the market advantages of schooling, even though they make some reference to other social benefits such as political participation and lower fertility. See, for example, Heyneman and White 1986; Psacharopoulos, Tan, and Jimenez 1986; and Lockheed and Verspoor 1991.

36. This issue is raised by Friedman 1962 and remains for the most part in the discussions of college education in Hartman 1973 and Mundel 1973. None of these, however, provides empirical evidence on the existence or magnitude of any externalities. The early primer on externalities in education (Weisbrod 1964) concentrates chiefly on geographic spillovers and fiscal effects and downplays the issues raised here. A discussion of the magnitude of externalities that is similar to the one here is found in Poterba (chap. 10 in this volume).

Or, if improved abilities of the best students leads to more rapid invention and development of new technologies, spillovers of educational investments may result. Nevertheless, I know of little evidence that distinguishes externalities in economic growth from simply the impact of better workers and more human capital.

The consideration of externalities ties into the previous discussion by offering another argument for the expansion of resources devoted to schools that appears to me to come from inappropriate application of evidence. While externalities may support expansion of schools to provide basic literacy and numeracy, their application in the case of college education or of providing more resources to improve student quality is stretched.

### 3.3   What Supports Spending?

The motivation behind public spending on schools still remains mysterious. What determines increases in spending, and, specifically, is spending at all related to a school's performance? Here we provide a preliminary look at citizen decisions on school budgets in New York State.

New York State requires citizen approval of school budgets for a majority of school districts in the state.[37] This analysis builds on voter reactions to proposed school budgets.[38] It combines votes on school budgets with information about the district's students and parents and about student performance. The focus of this analysis is the percentage favoring the initial budget proposal of each district. The models estimated consider income and other characteristics of the population, the impact on current tax rates and the history of tax rates, and alternative measures of student test performance.

The models are meant to characterize the various influences on voter preferences for spending. Since school systems do not readily provide information on performance, even though there is mandatory student testing at various grades in New York State, alternative formulations of information employed by voters are tested. Specifically, one measure of student performance is the change in reading and math passing percentages from third grade in 1987–88 to sixth grade in 1990–91. This measure is designed to proxy value-added of schools, since these are the same cohort of students. The second measure is the simple percentage achieving passing scores on sixth-grade reading and math tests. Neither is perfect as a measure of school system performance. The

37. The "big five" districts (New York City, Buffalo, Rochester, Syracuse, and Yonkers) are dependent districts getting their budgets from the city government and are excluded from requirements for voter approval. Another group of fifty cities (a historical definition that does not uniformly include the next largest jurisdictions) are also excluded. Over five hundred districts remain with annual voting on proposed budgets.

38. This analysis considers only the first vote for a school budget. By New York law, communities can have subsequent votes (on budget proposals that are the same, higher, or lower than the initially rejected budget) after a budget is rejected. Further, districts can operate under a "contingency budget," which does not require voter approval.

first is error-prone because of intervening student mobility, while the second mixes school effects with the effects of family and peers. But the object is understanding how citizens might use available information to assess performance of their schools, and each of these measures plausibly conditions voters' views on the performance of their schools.

Table 3.2 presents two alternative models of the determinants of voter ap-

**Table 3.2**    **Explanations of Voter Approval of School Budgets for 550 New York State School Districts, 1991–1992 (*t*-statistics in parentheses)**

| Variable | Dependent Variable: Proportion Yes[a] | |
|---|---|---|
| | Value-Added Achievement | Level of Achievement |
| Proportion teachers[b] | 570.66 | 579.78 |
| | (4.0) | (4.0) |
| Public school enrollment (white)[c] | 0.074 | 0.072 |
| | (1.0) | (0.9) |
| Elderly[d] | 0.286 | 0.282 |
| | (2.7) | (2.6) |
| Median income ($1,000)[e] | $0.923 \times 10^{-3}$ | $0.889 \times 10^{-3}$ |
| | (2.1) | (2.0) |
| Tax-rate growth (1988–90)[f] | −0.038 | −.038 |
| | (−1.3) | (−1.3) |
| Requested tax-rate increase[g] | −2.860 | −2.81 |
| | (−1.9) | (−1.9) |
| Δ reading score (grades 3–6)[h] | $-0.853 \times 10^{-4}$ | |
| | (−0.1) | |
| Δ math score (grades 3–6)[i] | $-0.416 \times 10^{-3}$ | |
| | (−0.4) | |
| Reading score (grade 6)[j] | | $0.6 \times 10^{-3}$ |
| | | (0.6) |
| Math score (grade 6)[k] | | $-.107 \times 10^{-2}$ |
| | | (−1.0) |
| Constant | .411 | .461 |
| | (4.8) | (4.6) |
| $R^2$ | .063 | .064 |

[a]Proportion of voters favoring proposed school budget.
[b]Proportion of families in school district with a teacher.
[c]Proportion of white students attending public schools.
[d]Proportion of persons age sixty or more.
[e]Median household income 1989.
[f]Change in local revenues/property tax base between 1988 and 1990.
[g]Proposed change in local revenues/property tax base.
[h]Percentage of sixth graders passing reading test (1990–91) minus percentage of third graders passing reading test (1987–88).
[i]Percentage of sixth graders passing math test (1990–91) minus percentage of third graders passing math test (1987–88).
[j]Percentage of sixth graders passing reading test (1990–91).
[k]Percentage of sixth graders passing math test (1990–91).

proval, differing only by the measure of student performance. The estimated effects are very consistent across the different versions, since voters do not seem to react to either of the measures of performance. The primary result is clear: neither estimated value-added nor the level of performance is systematically related to voter approval of budgets.

The models do not explain much of the variation in voter approval with $R^2$'s of only .06. Nonetheless, a number of systematic effects do come through. Higher-income communities are more supportive of proposed budgets, as are communities with a greater proportion of elderly (population over age sixty). Communities with proportionately more teachers residing in them also tend to support proposed budgets. While less precisely estimated, voters also vote against larger tax increases in the proposed budget and are less supportive of current budgets if there has been larger past growth.

These preliminary estimates are subject to various statistical and methodological concerns.[39] Nonetheless, the lack of relationship between voter approval of expenditure and student performance raises serious questions about what does drive spending and citizen demands for school spending. Knowledge of citizen preferences is a key element in understanding the likely course of school spending.

I do believe that these results bode continued difficulty for improved political decision making in education. One interpretation of the results is that voters are quite in the dark about which schools are performing well and which are providing a good return on resource investments. An alternative is that parents in fact know well what their schools are doing and are simply less concerned about student cognitive achievement than other things. Either way one has to be concerned about prospects for "high-return" investments—those that most directly improve the skills of students and that provide most of the justification for public support of the schools.

### 3.4   Some Concluding Thoughts

The underlying story is that problems of inefficiency in the provision of education pervade most discussions. As soon as concern moves away from simple quantity of schooling, as it invariably does today in the United States, it is not possible to neglect how resources are transformed into student outcomes. Yet because of the difficulty of this and because of uncertainties about the production process, this step is frequently not taken. Instead, inappropriate use is often made of general conclusions about investments in quantity of schooling to justify spending programs aimed at quality.

Two outcomes flow from this. First, the policy debates, the court delibera-

---

39. One important issue is the low turnout for school-budget votes. This low, and certainly selective, turnout leads to concerns about measurement errors. Additionally, this analysis employs a limited range of test scores (in terms of both grade level and subject matter).

tions, and the related academic analyses all tend to founder on conflicting assumptions about how to achieve specific goals. In other words, even if everybody could agree completely about objectives, real controversy about strategy typically remains. Second, the controversy appears to be frequently resolved in favor of increased expenditure on schools. The goals and objectives—increased performance and greater equity—are legitimate and worthy of support, and there is a surface plausibility to dealing with these with greater resources. The history of spending and performance indicates disappointing results.

It is difficult for economists to think about areas that are marked by important inefficiencies of the kind described here. Economists have found notions of efficiency to be very useful, convenient, and frequently plausible. If efficiency reigns, spending levels provide a ready measure of opportunities, variations in spending speak to equity concerns, and policy can be developed directly in terms of resources devoted to the area. Each disappears with substantial inefficiency.

On the other hand, it should not really surprise economists or others to find substantial inefficiency in the delivery of schooling. Even though there are very large differences among schools and teachers, successful schools and teachers receive essentially the same rewards as unsuccessful ones. Areas of economic activity where efficient provision occurs generally involve more direct and obvious incentives for performance. With few incentives related to school outcomes, inefficiency should not be totally unexpected.

Setting out the alternative ways to address performance and equity concerns is beyond the scope of this paper. The most plausible approach, however, seems to be application of quite straightforward economic principles: align incentives with goals and evaluate alternative ways of achieving goals. These ideas, described in detail elsewhere (Hanushek with others 1994), provide ways of dealing with the cost and performance difficulties in today's schools. The important point for this discussion is that improving schools calls for radically different policies than the traditional approach of simply throwing money at schools. Ultimately arriving at the proper level of investment in schools—a level that best meets our achievement and equity goals—may cost more or less than what we are currently spending. We simply do not know the answer, given the current organization and performance of the schools.

There is every reason to believe that investment in education is a good one, yielding high returns to individuals and to society. Substantial evidence also supports using quality education as a useful tool in altering income distributions and achieving general equity goals of society. The central message here is simply that not every investment is equal. There are good and bad investments in education. Much of recent policy has pushed toward generally bad investments—those that increase costs without any substantial benefits. Little evidence suggests that the primary problem facing schools has been lack of resources, and we should not treat that as the central issue.

# Appendix

Hanushek 1989 summarizes available published econometric evidence through 1988. The selection of studies is described in that article. Subsequent reanalyses and consideration of the interpretation of these results can be found in Hedges, Laine, and Greenwald 1994 and Hanushek 1994a, 1994b.

**Table 3A.1**    **Summary of the Estimated Relationship between Student Performance and Various Components of School Expenditure (187 studies)**

| Input | Number of Studies | Statistically Significant + | Statistically Significant − | Statistically Insignificant Total | Statistically Insignificant + | Statistically Insignificant − | Unknown |
|---|---|---|---|---|---|---|---|
| Teacher/pupil | 152 | 14 | 13 | 125 | 34 | 46 | 45 |
| Teacher education | 113 | 8 | 5 | 100 | 31 | 32 | 37 |
| Teacher experience | 140 | 40 | 10 | 90 | 44 | 31 | 15 |
| Teacher salary | 69 | 11 | 4 | 54 | 16 | 14 | 24 |
| Expenditure/pupil | 65 | 13 | 3 | 49 | 25 | 13 | 11 |
| Administrative input | 61 | 7 | 1 | 53 | 14 | 15 | 24 |
| Facilities | 74 | 7 | 5 | 62 | 17 | 14 | 31 |

*Source:* Hanushek 1989.

# References

Barro, Robert J. 1991. Economic growth in a cross section of countries. *Quarterly Journal of Economics* 106 (May): 407–43.

Baumol, William J. 1967. Macroeconomics of unbalanced growth: The anatomy of urban crisis. *American Economic Review* 57 (June): 415–26.

Baumol, William J., and William G. Bowen. 1965. On the performing arts: The anatomy of their economic problems. *American Economic Review* 55 (May): 495–502.

Becker, Gary S. 1993. *Human capital: A theoretical and empirical analysis, with special reference to education.* 3d ed. Chicago: University of Chicago Press.

Behrman, Jere R., Lori G. Kletzer, Michael S. McPherson, and Morton Owen Schapiro. 1994. How family background sequentially affects college educational investments: High school achievement, college enrollment, and college quality choices. April. Mimeo.

Bennett, William J. 1988. *American education: Making it work.* Washington, DC: Government Printing Office.

Bishop, John. 1989. Is the test score decline responsible for the productivity growth decline? *American Economic Review* 79 (March): 178–97.

———. 1991. Achievement, test scores, and relative wages. In *Workers and their wages,* ed. Marvin H. Kosters, 146–86. Washington, DC: AEI Press.

Boozer, Michael A., Alan B. Krueger, and Shari Wolkon. 1992. Race and school quality since *Brown v. Board of Education. Brooking Papers: Microeconomics,* 269–338.

Bound, John, and Richard B. Freeman. 1992. What went wrong? The erosion of relative earnings and employment among young black men in the 1980s. *Quarterly Journal of Economics* 107 (February): 201–32.

Bowles, Samuel, and Herbert Gintis. 1976. *Schooling in capitalist America: Educational reform and the contradictions of economic life.* New York: Basic Books.

Burtless, Gary. 1994. Does money matter? The effects of school resources on student achievement and adult earnings. Paper presented at Brookings Institution conference, "Do School Resources Matter?" June.

Card, David, and Alan Krueger. 1992a. Does school quality matter? Returns to education and the characteristics of public schools in the United States. *Journal of Political Economy* 100 (February): 1–40.

———. 1992b. School quality and black-white relative earnings: A direct assessment. *Quarterly Journal of Economics* 107 (February): 151–200.

Coleman, James S., Ernest Q. Campbell, Carol J. Hobson, James McPartland, Alexander M. Mood, Frederic D. Weinfeld, and Robert L. York. 1966. *Equality of educational opportunity.* Washington, DC: Government Printing Office.

Committee for Economic Development. 1985. *Investing in our children: Business and the public schools.* New York: Committee for Economic Development.

———. 1994. *Putting learning first: Governing and managing the schools for high achievement.* New York: Committee for Economic Development.

Congressional Budget Office. 1986. *Trends in educational achievement.* Washington, DC: Congressional Budget Office.

———. 1987. *Educational achievement: Explanations and implications of recent trends.* Washington, DC: Congressional Budget Office.

Dugan, Dennis J. 1976. Scholastic achievement: Its determinants and effects in the education industry. In *Education as an industry,* ed. Joseph T. Froomkin, Dean T. Jamison, and Roy Radner, 53–83. Cambridge, MA: Ballinger.

Educational Testing Service. 1991. *Performance at the top: From elementary through graduate school.* Princeton, NJ: Educational Testing Service.

Ehrlich, Isaac. 1975. On the relation between education and crime. In *Education, income, and human behavior,* ed. F. Thomas Juster, 313–37. New York: McGraw-Hill.

Farrell, Philip, and Victor R. Fuchs. 1982. Schooling and health: The cigarette connection. *Journal of Health Economics* 1 (December): 217–30.

Ferguson, Ronald F. 1993. New evidence on the growing value of skill and consequences for racial disparity and returns to schooling. Malcolm Wiener Center for Social Policy, H-93-10. Harvard University. September.

Friedman, Milton. 1962. *Capitalism and freedom.* Chicago: University of Chicago Press.

Fuchs, Victor R., and Diane M. Reklis. 1994. Mathematical achievement in eighth grade: Interstate and racial differences. NBER Working Paper no. 4784. Cambridge, MA: National Bureau of Economic Research, June.

Goldin, Claudia. 1994a. Appendix to "How America graduated from high school, 1910 to 1960," construction of state-level secondary school data. NBER Historical Paper no. 57. Cambridge, MA: National Bureau of Economic Research, June.

———. 1994b. How America graduated from high school, 1910 to 1960. NBER Working Paper no. 1994. Cambridge, MA: National Bureau of Economic Research, June.

Griliches, Zvi. 1974. Errors in variables and other unobservables. *Econometrica* 42 (November): 971–98.

Grogger, Jeffrey T. Forthcoming. Does school quality explain the recent black/white wage trend? *Journal of Labor Economics.*

Grogger, Jeffrey T., and Eric Eide. 1995. Changes in college skills and the rise in the college wage premium. *Journal of Human Resources* 30 (spring): 280–310.

Hanushek, Eric A. 1986. The economics of schooling: Production and efficiency in public schools. *Journal of Economic Literature* 24 (September): 1141–77.

———. 1989. The impact of differential expenditures on school performance. *Educational Researcher* 18 (May): 45–51.

———. 1993. Can equity be separated from efficiency in school finance debates? In *Essays on the economics of education,* ed. Emily P. Hoffman, 35–73. Kalamazoo, MI: W. E. Upjohn Institute for Employment Research.

———. 1994a. Money might matter somewhere: A response to Hedges, Laine, and Greenwald. *Educational Researcher* 23 (May): 5–8.

———. 1994b. School Resources and Student Performance. Paper presented at the Brookings Institution conference, "Do School Resources Matter?" June.

Hanushek, Eric A., with Charles S. Benson, Richard B. Freeman, Dean T. Jamison, Henry M. Levin, Rebecca A. Maynard, Richard J. Murname, Steven G. Rivkin, Richard H. Sabot, Lewis C. Solmon, Anita A. Summers, Finis Welch, and Barbara L. Wolfe. 1994. *Making schools work: Improving performance and controlling costs.* Washington, DC: Brookings Institution.

Hanushek, Eric A., and Richard R. Pace. 1995. Who chooses to teach (and why)? *Economics of Education Review* 14 (June): 101–17.

Hanushek, Eric A., and Steven G. Rivkin. 1994. Understanding the 20th century explosion in U.S. school costs. Rochester Center for Economic Research (RCER), Working Paper no. 388. August.

Hanushek, Eric A., Steven G. Rivkin, and Lori L. Taylor. 1995. Aggregation and the estimated effects of school resources. RCER, Working Paper no. 397. February.

Harbison, Ralph W., and Eric A. Hanushek. 1992. *Educational performance of the poor: Lessons from rural northeast Brazil.* New York: Oxford University Press.

Hartigan, John A., and Alexandra K. Wigdor, eds. 1989. *Fairness in employment testing: Validity generalization, minority issues, and the general aptitude test battery.* Washington, DC: National Academy Press.

Hartman, Robert W. 1973. The rationale for federal support for higher education. In *Does college matter? Some evidence on the impacts of higher education,* ed. Lewis C. Solmon and Paul J. Taubman, 271–92. New York: Academic Press.

Hauser, Robert M. 1993. The decline in college entry among African Americans: Findings in search of explanations. In *Prejudice, politics, and the American dilemma,* ed. Paul M. Sniderman, Philip E. Tetlock, and Edward G. Carmines, 271–306. Stanford, CA: Stanford University Press.

Haveman, Robert H., and Barbara L. Wolfe. 1984. Schooling and economic well-being: The role of nonmarket effects. *Journal of Human Resources* 19 (summer): 377–407.

Heckman, James J., Anne S. Layne-Farrar, and Petra E. Todd. 1994. Does measured school quality really matter? University of Chicago. September. Mimeo.

Hedges, Larry V., Richard D. Laine, and Rob Greenwald. 1994. Does money matter? A meta-analysis of studies of the effects of differential school inputs on student outcomes. *Educational Researcher* 23 (April): 5–14.

Heyneman, Stephen P., and Daphne Siev White, eds. 1986. *The quality of education and economic development.* Washington, DC: World Bank.

Jaynes, Gerald David, and Robin M. Williams, Jr., eds. 1989. *A common destiny: Blacks and American society.* Washington, DC: National Academy Press.

Jencks, Christopher, Marshall Smith, Henry Acland, Mary Jo Bane, David Cohen, Herbert Gintis, Barabar Heyns, and Stephen Michelson. 1972. *Inequality: A reassessment of the effect of family and schooling in America.* New York: Basic Books.

Jorgenson, Dale W., and Barbara M. Fraumeni. 1992. Investment in education and U.S. economic growth. *Scandinavian Journal of Economics* 94, supplement: 51–70.

Juhn, Chinhui, Kevin M. Murphy, and Brooks Pierce. 1991. Accounting for the slow-down in black-white wage convergence. In *Workers and their wages,* ed. Marvin H. Kosters, 107–43. Washington, DC: AEI Press.

Kane, Thomas. 1990. College enrollments by blacks since 1970: The role of tuition, financial aid, local economic conditions, and family background. Harvard University. Mimeo.

Kosters, Marvin H. 1991. Wages and demographics. In *Workers and their wages,* ed. Marvin H. Kosters, 1–32. Washington, DC: AEI Press.

Kozol, Jonathan. 1991. *Savage inequalities: Children in America's schools.* New York: Crown Publishers.

Lapointe, Archie E., Nancy A. Mead, and W. Phillips Gary. 1989. *A world of difference: An international assessment of mathematics and science.* Princeton, NJ: Educational Testing Service.

Leibowitz, Arleen. 1974. Home investments in children. *Journal of Political Economy* 82, no. 2, pt. 2:S111–31.

Levy, Frank, and Richard J. Murnane. 1992. U.S. earnings levels and earnings inequality: A review of recent trends and proposed explanations. *Journal of Economic Literature* 30 (September): 1333–81.

Lockheed, Marlaine E., and Adriaan Verspoor. 1991. *Improving primary education in developing countries.* New York: Oxford University Press.

Lucas, Robert E. 1988. On the mechanics of economic development. *Journal of Monetary Economics* 22 (July): 3–42.

McMahon, Walter W. 1991. Relative returns to human and physical capital in the U.S. and efficient investment strategies. *Economics of Education Review* 10, no. 4:283–96.

Manski, Charles F. 1993. Adolescent econometricians: How do youth infer the returns to schooling? In *Studies of supply and demand in higher education,* ed. Charles T. Clotfelter and Michael Rothschild, 43–57. Chicago: University of Chicago Press.

Manski, Charles F., and David A. Wise. 1983. *College choice in America.* Cambridge: Harvard University Press.

Michael, Robert T. 1982. Measuring non-monetary benefits of education: A survey. In *Financing education: Overcoming inefficiency and inequity,* ed. Walter W. McMahon and Terry G. Geske, 119–49. Urbana: University of Illinois Press.

Mullin, Stephen P., and Anita A. Summers. 1983. Is more better? The effectiveness of spending on compensatory education. *Phi Beta Kappan* 64:339–47.

Mundel, David S. 1973. Whose education should society support? In *Does college matter? Some evidence on the impacts of higher education,* ed. Lewis C. Solmon and Paul J. Taubman, 293–315. New York: Academic Press.

Murnane, Richard J., John B. Willett, and Frank Levy. 1994. The growing importance of cognitive skills in wage determination. Harvard Graduate School of Education. March. Mimeo.

Murphy, Kevin M., and Finis Welch. 1989. Wage premiums for college graduates: Recent growth and possible explanations. *Educational Researcher* 18 (May): 17–26.

———. 1992. The structure of wages. *Quarterly Journal of Economics* 107 (February): 285–326.

O'Neill, June. 1990. The role of human capital in earnings differences between black and white men. *Journal of Economic Perspectives* 4 (fall): 25–46.

Psacharopoulos, George, Jee-Peng Tan, and Emmanuel Jimenez. 1986. *Financing education in developing countries: An exploration of policy options.* Washington, DC: World Bank.

Rivkin, Steven G. 1991. Schooling and employment in the 1980s: Who succeeds? Ph.D. diss., University of California, Los Angeles.

Romer, Paul. 1990. Endogenous technological change. *Journal of Political Economy* 99, no. 5, pt. 2:S71–102.

Schultz, Theodore W. 1961. Investment in human capital. *American Economic Review* 51 (March): 1–17.

———. 1963. *The economic value of education.* New York: Columbia University Press.

Scitovsky, Tibor, and Anne Scitovsky. 1959. What price economic progress? *Yale Review* 95–110.

Smith, James P., and Finis Welch. 1989. Black economic progress after Myrdal. *Journal of Economic Literature* 27 (June): 519–64.

Stanley, Harold W., and Richard G. Niemi. 1994. *Vital statistics on American politics.* 3d ed. Washington, DC: CQ Press.

Teixeira, Ruy A. 1992. *The disappearing American voter.* Washington, DC: Brookings Institution.

U.S. Bureau of the Census. 1975. *Historical statistics of the United States, colonial times to 1970: Bicentennial edition.* Vols. 1 and 2. Washington, DC: Government Printing Office.

———. 1993. *Statistical abstract of the United States, 1993.* Washington, DC: Government Printing Office.

U.S. Department of Education. 1993. *The condition of education, 1993.* Washington, DC: Government Printing Office.

Weisbrod, Burton A. 1964. *External benefits of public education: An economic analysis.* Princeton, NJ: Princeton University Press.

Wolfe, Barbara L., and Sam Zuvekas. 1995. Nonmarket outcomes of schooling. Discussion Paper, 1065–95. Institute for Research on Poverty, University of Wisconsin, May.

Wyckoff, James H. 1992. The intrastate equality of public primary and secondary education resources in the U.S., 1980–1987. *Economics of Education Review* 11 (March): 19–30.

Young, K. H., and Dean T. Jamison. 1974. The economic benefits of schooling and compensatory education. Paper presented at meetings of the Econometric Society, December.

# Comment   Christopher Jencks

Hanushek's provocative paper asks why educational spending has risen so much in recent decades. His analysis starts with two factual premises. First, individuals who invest in additional years of schooling obtain quite high returns on their investment, and these returns have risen since 1980. Second, when the government spends more on elementary or secondary education, the return is now close to zero.

Let me begin by recasting these propositions in slightly different terms. Investment mainly involves commitments of time to activities that pay off in the relatively distant future. What Hanushek calls the "quantity" of schooling is, in essence, the amount of time that students invest in their own education.[1] Per-

Christopher Jencks is the John D. MacArthur Professor of Sociology at Northwestern University.

1. Hanushek's measure of "quantity" is actually the highest grade of school or college that an individual completed. This measure weights each student's investment of time by the average number of grades that the student completed per year. But since most students complete exactly one grade per year, this measure weights most students' time equally.

pupil expenditure, in contrast, measures the amount of the time that adults invest in the average student's education, with each adult's time weighted by its monetary value. Hanushek's conclusions can therefore be restated as follows: (1) The amount of time students invest in their own education has a big effect on their subsequent earnings. (2) The amount of time adults invest in a student's education has very little effect on anything.

Hanushek's main goal is to explain why per-pupil expenditure in public elementary and secondary schools keeps rising even though the rate of return is negligible. The easy answer is that neither parents nor voters believe the returns are negligible. Many parents are willing to pay higher taxes in order to live in school districts that spend a lot on their schools. Even voters whose children are not in school often support increases in school spending, because they see such spending as an investment in the whole country's future. Hanushek believes that this faith is misplaced. I do not find the evidence he presents as persuasive as he does, but he may be right anyway.

### Test Scores and Expenditures

Until 1966, almost all Americans assumed that higher school spending led to greater mastery of the subjects taught in school. Then James Coleman and his colleagues published *Equality of Educational Opportunity,* commonly known as the Coleman Report, which found little relationship between school spending and student achievement. Most social scientists eventually accepted this counterintuitive conclusion, but few parents or educators concurred. In the past couple of years new evidence has appeared, which suggests that the public's skepticism about social science may have been well founded. To see why this might be the case, the reader should look closely at Hanushek's appendix.

Hanushek found thirty-eight published studies in which per-pupil expenditure had positive effects on student outcomes and sixteen in which it had negative effects. In two-thirds of these studies the 95% confidence interval for the coefficient of per-pupil expenditure included zero, making the coefficient insignificant by traditional standards. But the fact that a confidence interval includes zero does not prove that the true value really is zero. If the true effect of expenditures were zero, negative point estimates should be as common as positive ones. In reality, 70% of the point estimates are positive. If the true effect were zero, moreover, 95% of the confidence intervals should include zero. In reality, only two-thirds of them include zero.

Given the preponderance of positive point estimates, the most plausible inference from Hanushek's appendix is that expenditures have a modest positive effect. If the true correlation between spending and achievement is low but positive, and if most studies cover relatively small samples of schools or school districts, one would not expect most of the observed coefficients to be significant by conventional standards.

The best way to summarize a literature of this kind is not to count the number of significant coefficients but to compute the mean effect across all studies, regardless of their significance. Hedges, Laine, and Greenwald (1994) reanalyzed Hanushek's data using this approach. Averaging across all the studies that Hanushek had reviewed, they found that the coefficient of per-pupil expenditure was very large and highly significant. Indeed, the average effect was so large as to make the results seem quite implausible. Hanushek concludes from this that their analysis was flawed. I conclude that the underlying data are biased.

One likely source of bias is that Hanushek looks only at published studies. That may seem like a reasonable form of quality control, but many literature reviews have found that the effects reported in published studies tend to be larger than those reported in unpublished studies. This difference presumably reflects the fact that scholarly journals are more likely to publish studies that report significant effects. But for this bias to explain the entire surplus of significant coefficients in Hanushek's sample, we have to assume that only one study in six gets published. That seems unlikely.

A second and more fundamental problem is that the studies in Hanushek's sample are not true experiments. Instead of comparing students who had been randomly assigned to schools that spent different amounts, these studies compare students whose parents often chose their place of residence partly on the basis of what they knew about the quality of the local schools. Parents who value school achievement usually try to live in districts that spend a lot on education. Most of these parents also make a special effort to help their children learn whatever the schools teach. Hanushek's studies try to correct this source of bias by including statistical controls for parental income, education, family structure, and the like. But measures of this kind are imperfect proxies for the parental characteristics that influence residential choices and children's achievement. Because the corrections for selection bias are imperfect, these studies probably overestimate the effect of school spending on achievement. Judging by Hedges et al.'s findings, the bias is usually quite large.

One way around this difficulty is to look at what happens when school districts change their expenditures. Ideally, we should do this by tracking achievement over time in different districts, but as far as I know, nobody has done this. Instead, we have to rely on aggregate data for the nation as a whole. As Hanushek rightly emphasizes, public elementary and secondary schools have raised their real per-pupil expenditures quite steadily throughout the twentieth century. We do not have parallel data on student achievement until the 1970s, but since then it has not risen much. Nonetheless, the picture is not quite as grim as Hanushek suggests. The best evidence comes from the National Assessment of Educational Progress (NAEP), which began in 1971. Unlike other testing programs, NAEP tries to test a representative national sample of students. Its reports show that students' scores have mostly improved since 1971 but that the mean gain has been relatively small.[2]

2. The illusion that student achievement has fallen derives largely from declines in the mean score of those who take the Scholastic Aptitude Test (SAT). Unfortunately, the Educational Testing Service does not norm the SAT on representative national samples of students. Students take the

Reading and math skills probably matter more than the other things that NAEP measures, and the performance of seventeen-year-olds matters more than the performance of younger children.[3] Among seventeen-year-olds near the bottom of the distribution, reading skills improved by about a fifth of a standard deviation between 1971 and 1992. Among those in the top quarter of the distribution, there was almost no change. Overall, seventeen-year-olds' mean reading score rose by 0.10 standard deviations (National Center for Education Statistics 1994, 113).

NAEP's time series for math skills does not begin until 1978, but it tells roughly the same story as the reading series. Among seventeen-year-olds in the lower two-thirds of the distribution, math scores improved steadily from 1978 to 1992. There was no improvement among students near the top of the distribution. Overall, mean math scores rose by about 0.15 standard deviations (National Center for Education Statistics 1994, 121).

If we convert per-pupil expenditures to 1992 dollars, schools had spent a cumulative total of about $55,000 on the average seventeen-year-old by the time he or she was tested in 1992. If we make the same calculation for those tested in 1971, the total is only half as large. If nothing else had changed, therefore, we could infer that doubling real spending had raised the average seventeen-year-old's reading skills by about 0.10 standard deviations—a rather modest gain.

Taken at face value, the results for math are more encouraging. Measured in constant dollars, total outlays on seventeen-year-olds tested in 1992 were about 60% higher than total outlays on those tested in 1978. Mean math scores rose by about 0.15 standard deviations during this interval. If this relationship were really causal, we could infer that raising expenditures by 60% has about twice as much effect on math scores as on reading scores. This would not be surprising, since math skills are almost entirely dependent on what students learn in school, whereas reading skills also depend on how students spend their leisure.

But intertemporal comparisons of this kind may yield upwardly biased estimates for the same reason that comparisons between districts do. The social and economic changes that drove up school spending were linked to changes in what happened outside of school, and most of these changes would lead us to expect improvements in student achievement even if schools had not changed at all.

The Census Bureau collects data on five family characteristics that are known to influence children's test scores: the parents' education, occupation, and income; the number of adults in a child's household (two is better than one); and the number of other children in the household (fewer is better).

---

SAT only if they want to attend a college that requires it. The colleges that require the SAT have changed over time, and so have their applicant pools.

3. NAEP's time series on seventeen-year-olds is restricted to those who were enrolled in high school. But the proportion of all seventeen-year-olds enrolled in high school has not changed much since 1971, so the trend for the full cohort should parallel that for those still enrolled in school.

Parental education rose steadily during the 1970s and 1980s, as did the percentage of parents working in white-collar jobs. Real parental income was also higher from 1975 to 1992 than from 1954 to 1971, and the number of children in the average family was lower. The only indicator that changed for the worse over this period was the percentage of seventeen-year-olds living with both their biological parents. (More mothers also worked, but there is no consistent evidence that maternal employment affects teenagers' test performance.) Judging by their coefficients in cross-sectional data, the positive effects of improvements in parental education, occupation, and income and reductions in family size should have dominated the negative effect of more children's growing up in a single-parent family.

This conclusion holds for the poor as well. The proportion of all children living in families with incomes below the poverty line has risen since 1970. But those who turned seventeen in 1971 were born in 1954, and during most of their childhood the poverty rate for children was even higher than it is today. Thus if a family's purchasing power was an important determinant of its children's test scores, low-income children tested in 1992 should have done better than those tested in 1971. Today's poor children also have better educated parents and fewer siblings than their predecessors had in 1971. Only their family structure has changed in a way likely to lower test performance.

If children are learning more at home, and if real school spending has doubled, how are we to explain the fact that test scores have improved only among those in the bottom part of the distribution? The most likely explanation, I think, is that students in the top third of the distribution have not had much incentive to learn more. Although opinion leaders keep bemoaning the fact that American students score lower than their European and East Asian counterparts on math and science tests, I have not seen any evidence that elementary or secondary schools have responded to such criticism by making their curriculum more demanding. Elementary school math textbooks still proceed at the same leisurely pace as in 1960. High schools still assume that calculus is too difficult for most college-bound students. Honors classes in English and history assign no more "difficult" books today than in the past. If anything, reading lists have gotten easier.

Nor do college admissions policies reward talented students for learning more. The Advanced Placement examinations are America's closest approximation to the curriculum-based exams that European and East Asian countries use to select (and hence motivate) prospective university students. In America, elite colleges make their admissions decisions before applicants have even taken these exams. Instead of relying on tests that measure how much students learned in high school, America's top colleges rely on a combination of high school grades and the Scholastic Aptitude Test (SAT), which measures vocabulary, reading comprehension, and mastery of basic math. Ambitious high school students respond to this system by looking for teachers who gives lots of A's and by taking cram courses for the SAT, not by enrolling in courses that promise to teach them a lot.

Summarizing, I would say that (1) contrary to Hanushek, conventional "production function" studies suggest that higher spending raises test scores, but (2) these studies are probably biased, and (3) changes over time suggest that additional resources may make some difference for poor students' achievement but do not help good students.

If that summary judgment is correct, we must return to Hanushek's puzzle. If higher spending does not boost good students' scores, why do parents of talented students keep moving to districts with high school taxes? One obvious answer is that schools have many outputs. Until we have studied a lot of them, we should be cautious about assuming that parents are fools.

## Retention Rates

Next to test performance, retention rates are the most widely used indicator of how schools are doing. If most students finish high school and go on to college, parents are satisfied. Hanushek does not discuss the handful of studies that have tried to link variation in districts' per-pupil spending to variation in their students' eventual educational attainment. But his figure 3.1 suggests that increased spending has done little to improve school retention rates since 1970.

The median twenty-five-to-twenty-nine-year-old (hereafter the median "young adult") had completed twelve years of school in 1950. Forty years later the median young adult had still completed only twelve years of school. Taken at face value, this is puzzling. Schooling is heavily subsidized, and its monetary value has been rising. Thus, one would expect young people to stay in school longer even if their schools had not improved at all.

This particular puzzle is more apparent than real, however. Far more people complete exactly twelve years of school than complete any other amount. Once the median reaches twelve years, therefore, the distribution of schooling must shift a lot before the median jumps to thirteen years. In 1950, for example, only 53% of young adults had completed high school and fewer than 25% had completed a year of college. By 1990, 86% of young adults had completed high school and 45% had completed at least a year of college. This change implied a substantial increase in mean educational attainment. But the median young adult—the individual at the 50th percentile of the distribution—still had twelve years of school.

The Census Bureau has long recognized that the median is a poor measure of change in educational attainment. In an effort to deal with this problem, it does not report true medians. Instead, it reports what I will call an interpolated median. To calculate this statistic, the Bureau pretends that those who have completed any given year of school are uniformly distributed over the interval between that year and the next. Thus, if 40% of young adults have completed twelve years of school, the Bureau pretends that 4% got 12.0 years, 4% got 12.1 years, 4% got 12.2 years, and so on. This fiction allows the Bureau to report a small increase in the median whenever the proportion of young adults with twelve or more years of school rises. Hanushek's figure 3.1 shows medi-

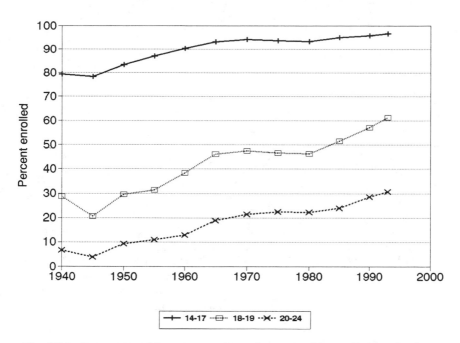

**Fig. 3C.1    Percentage of fourteen-to-twenty-four-year-olds enrolled in school, by age, 1940–1993**
*Source:* National Center for Education Statistics 1994, table 6.

ans of this kind. But while interpolated medians are better than true medians, they do not solve the basic problem. Even using interpolated medians, young adults' educational attainment does not appear to change much from 1950 to 1975, and it hardly changes at all from 1975 to 1990.[4]

If we want to know how much time young people are investing in schooling, age-specific enrollment rates are a better guide than the median number of years completed.[5] Figure 3C.1 shows such rates for individuals of various ages. Since 1945, enrollment rates have climbed for all age groups, but especially for those over seventeen. The 1970s are the main exception to this rule, and they are easy to explain.

4. In 1991, the median for young adults finally reached 13.0 years. That means half the nation's young adults had completed at least one year of college. If college enrollment climbs at the same rate during the 1990s as during the 1980s, the median young adult may well have 14.0 years of school by the end of the decade. In tables showing trends in the median, therefore, the rate of growth in educational attainment will appear to accelerate during the 1990s. Some analysts will no doubt attribute this apparent change to the fact that returns to education rose during the 1980s.

5. Enrollment rates are not ideal measures of time spent in school, because they do not take account of changes in the number of hours that enrolled students spend in class or doing homework. Among eighteen- and nineteen-year-olds, part-time students constituted 7% of total enrollment in 1970, 11% in 1980, and 19% in 1990. Among twenty-to-twenty-four-year-olds, the figure rose from 24% in 1970 to 27% in 1980 but was still 27% in 1990 (National Center for Education Statistics 1994, 178). I suspect, but cannot prove, that there was a parallel decline in time spent preparing for class, because more full-time students were working part-time for pay.

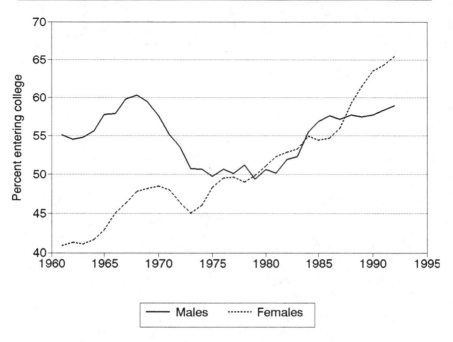

**Fig. 3C.2   Percentage of high school graduates entering college, by sex, 1961–1992**

*Source:* National Center for Education Statistics 1994, table 180.

During the 1950s and 1960s, men between the ages of eighteen and twenty-six were likely to be drafted into the army unless they were in school. As a result, more men attended college than would otherwise have done so. This was especially true in 1950–52 and 1965–71, when the country was at war and many draftees came home in boxes. Military deferments, the draft, and the Vietnam War all ended in the early 1970s. The percentage of male high school graduates entering college fell as a result (see figure 3C.2). This decline was probably accentuated by a temporary surplus of Vietnam-era BAs. When these men entered the labor market in the early 1970s, the wage differential between high school and college graduates contracted, making higher education look like a poor investment. In the 1980s, when the value of a BA began to rise again, male college attendence also began to recover.

Women were not subject to the draft, but since the mid-1960s their economic security has been increasingly threatened by the decline of marriage and the spread of divorce. Fewer women marry immediately after high school, and more of them realize that divorce may someday force them to support both themselves and their children. As a result, college attendance rates for women have risen steadily.[6]

---

6. The brief decline in college entrance rates among women in the early 1970s is a puzzle for which I have no explanation.

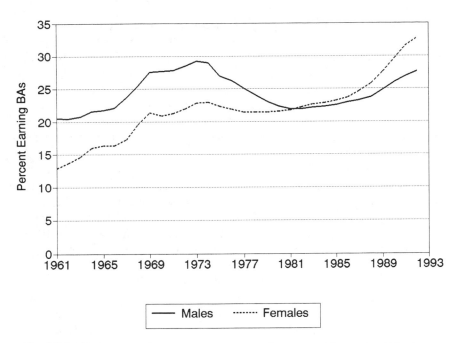

**Fig. 3C.3    Percentage of twenty-two-to-twenty-four-year-olds earning BAs, by sex, 1961–1992**
*Source:* National Center for Education Statistics 1994, tables 15 and 234.

Going straight through college is no longer the American norm. The typical BA has now been out of high school for about six years. The college entrance rates in figure 3C.2 therefore imply that graduation rates for men should have fallen from 1974 to 1979, stayed low from 1979 to 1987, and risen after 1987. Figure 3C.3 confirms this prediction.[7] By 1992, the graduation rate for men was almost back to its Vietnam-era peak. The rate for women was at an all-time high.[8]

7. The numerator for the percentages used to construct figure 3C.3 is the number of BAs awarded to individuals of a given sex in the relevant year. The denominator is a three-year moving average of the resident population between the ages of twenty-two and twenty-four in the relevant year, divided by six. Use of a three-year moving average gives the number of twenty-three-year-olds in the relevant year a weight of three, the numbers of twenty-two- and twenty-four-year-olds weights of two, and the numbers of twenty-one- and twenty-five-year-olds weights of one. This procedure comes closer to approximating the age distribution among those earning BAs than the use of any one birth cohort.

Ideally, the denominator of this ratio should include members of the armed forces living overseas, but such counts are not readily available. Omitting these individuals inflates the estimated graduation rate, especially during the Vietnam years. The calculations implicitly assume that twenty-two-to-twenty-four-year-olds were half male and half female throughout this period. The observed sex ratio rose from just under one male for every female in the 1960s to just over one male for every female in the 1990s. I assume this change mainly reflects changes in the size and composition of the overseas armed forces.

8. The fact that more young people are earning BAs is not yet obvious using the most popular trend measure, which is the percentage of young adults with such a degree. This measure shows a

Data on college entrance and graduation rates tell a quite different story from Hanushek's figure 3.1. Once we adjust for the adverse effect of ending draft deferments, college entrance rates have clearly risen for both men and women. But just as with test scores, Hanushek's basic point may still be right, because we have no solid evidence linking the rise of college entrance rates to the rise in elementary and secondary school spending. Increases in parental education, declines in family size, and the rising monetary value of a BA might well have driven up college entrance rates even if school spending had remained at its 1970 level.

A better test of the relationship between spending and retention may be the proportion of teenagers who graduate from high school. Schooling is free at this age, and the opportunity cost of staying in school is low. If higher spending had allowed schools to provide students with more services that they valued, dropout rates should have fallen. That is not what happened, at least from 1970 to 1992. At the end of the 1960s, 77% of all seventeen-year-olds were earning regular high school diplomas. By the early 1990s, the figure had fallen to 73% (National Center for Education Statistics 1994, table 99).[9]

This decline in high school graduation rates was partially offset by an increase in the proportion of high school dropouts who subsequently earned certificates of General Education Development (GEDs). These certificates are widely touted as being "equivalent" to a high school diploma. As a result, the fraction of young adults who tell the Census Bureau that they are high school graduates has risen fairly steadily, even though the percentage with real diplomas has fallen. Growing demand for GEDs among dropouts makes the decline in the true graduation rate even harder to explain. If demand for some kind of diploma is rising, and if high schools have more money to spend on programs for prospective dropouts, the dropout rate should have fallen. That fact that this did not happen strongly supports Hanushek's argument that higher spending yields few benefits that students value.

### Are We Measuring the Right Outputs?

We are left with the question of why so many parents prefer school districts that spend a lot to those that spend less. If higher spending does not raise either test scores or retention rates, what other school outputs might lead parents to choose such districts? Three possibilities deserve attention. First, schools with big budgets may teach their students all sorts of skills and information that

---

college graduation rate of 21.9% in 1975, 22.2% in 1985, 23.2% in 1990, and 23.7% in 1993 (National Center for Education Statistics 1994, table 8). Changes in this measure lag about five years behind changes in the actual graduation rate.

9. Not all high school graduates are seventeen years old, of course. But the graduation rate does not change appreciably if one compares the number of diplomas awarded to a weighted average of seventeen-, eighteen-, and nineteen-year-olds. I should also note that high school graduation rates fell after 1970 despite a modest increase in the proportion of all fourteen-to-seventeen-year-olds enrolled in school (see figure 3C.1). These two trends are not necessarily contradictory, but reconciling them might prove difficult.

standardized tests do not measure. Second, school spending may also improve students' social skills, character traits, or behavior. Third, school spending may improve the quality of students' lives while they are still enrolled in school.

*Are We Using the Right Tests?* Social scientists have traditionally measured school output using multiple-choice tests that cover basic skills like reading and math. Until recently, most of these tests were designed to minimize the impact of having attended one school rather than another. Testers would not ask students to identify Scylla or Charybdis, for example, because they knew that some schools did not teach *The Odyssey,* and they did not want to put students from such schools at a disadvantage.

Test design also reflected psychometricians' interest in measuring what they saw as unitary traits, such as "intelligence" or "mathematical skills." When test designers had to decide whether to include a given item, they did not ask whether it measured something students needed to know. Instead, they asked whether students who answered the item correctly also answered other items on the test correctly. If a given math item did not correlate well with other math items, it was discarded. This procedure had two rationales. First, it was often said that an item could not be a good measure of math skills if it did not correlate with other items that measured math skills. Second, low interitem correlations make a test less reliable.

If a math test is restricted to items that correlate highly with one another, it is likely to measure mathematical aptitude rather than mastery of specific mathematical skills. Mathematical aptitude is obviously worth measuring. But if you want to know whether schools that spend more money teach more math, aptitude tests will not always give the right answer. Suppose, for example, that affluent districts teach calculus while poor districts do not. Expenditures will then have a big effect on the number of students who pass the Advanced Placement calculus exam. But expenditures may not have much impact on basic math skills, because even students in poorly financed districts may have spent many hours in classes that teach these skills.

Since 1970, testers have begun to put more emphasis on measuring skills and information that teachers judge important. The NAEP tests try to do this, for example. But much of what we think we know about the effect of educational spending reflects the results of studies that use less appropriate tests.

*Noncognitive Outcomes.* Employers care about workers' social skills, character, and behavior on the job as well as their cognitive skills. Few employers want workers who shirk, no matter how well they spell. Nobody knows precisely which noncognitive traits matter most to employers. But we do know that test performance accounts for less than half the correlation between years of schooling and earnings. This fact suggests that individuals who stay in school must have more than their share of the noncognitive traits that employers value.

Since we do not know which noncognitive traits contribute to the correlation between schooling and earnings, we do not know whether schools with big budgets are especially good at developing these traits. If generously funded schools run more smoothly, need fewer arbitrary rules, and resolve conflicts more amicably, their alumni may become better workers. Such a pattern might help reconcile the weak relationship between changes in school spending and student achievement with Card and Krueger's (1992) finding that children born in states with high per-pupil expenditures earn more than children born in less generous states, regardless of where they live in adulthood.

*Schooling as Consumption.* When social scientists measure the effects of educational spending, they usually look for outcomes that seem likely to predict students' future success. But a large part of any school's budget is spent on making the quality of students' lives better right now. When a high school decides to build a swimming pool or a basketball court, it does not claim that this will make the school's alumni more employable. Likewise, when my suburban elementary school district decided to lengthen the school day by adding half an hour for art and music, it did not tell taxpayers or parents that this change would help children find better jobs when they grew up. It claimed that art and music would enrich the children's lives immediately. A large fraction of any school's budget should therefore be seen as consumption rather than investment.[10]

The line between investment and consumption is, of course, often quite murky. Schools may, for example, claim that they want to cut class size in order to raise achievement. The real reason for cutting class size, however, is usually that teachers and students prefer small classes. That does not mean small classes are a waste of money. It just means they should be seen partly as consumption rather than as a pure investment.[10]

Americans now spend almost a fifth of their life attending school. During these years they spend roughly a quarter of their waking hours in school. Thus, even if parents thought that school spending had no effect whatever on their children's long-term prospects, they might still choose to allocate a significant fraction of their disposable income to making their children's life at school more enjoyable. If parents reason this way, we might expect the consumption component of the education budget to rise in tandem with GDP. Trends since 1970 are consistent with such a model. Education claimed 7.6% of GDP in 1993, compared to 7.5% in 1970.

---

10. Expenditures aimed at keeping the political peace, such as bilingual education, mainstreaming slow learners, or busing students to reduce racial segregation, are also hard to classify on a consumption-investment spectrum. Schools often have future-oriented rationales for spending money on such programs, but they seldom evaluate these programs by asking whether they raise students' test scores or adult earnings. School boards establish these programs in order to resolve current social and political conflicts, and they judge the programs successful if conflict diminishes. A significant part of the increase in spending after 1970 may have been of this kind.

One might argue that education's share of GDP should have fallen after 1970, because school-age children constituted a declining fraction of the population. But Americans had fewer children partly because they wanted to spend more on each child. Thus, the fact that educational outlays rose at about the same rate as GDP might not have struck most parents as alarming even if they had known the extra money would have no long-term effect on their children after they finished school. Such consumption-oriented parents should, however, have been worried by the fact that higher spending was not lowering the dropout rate. This fact suggests that higher outlays were not even reducing the proportion of students who hated school.

**Policy Implications**

Throughout the 1980s, commentators of every political stripe complained about schools' failure to prepare their students for skilled jobs. During the 1950s and 1960s, legislators responded to actual and anticipated shortages of skilled labor by making it easier for the young to attend college. States kept tuition at public institutions low, and they built new campuses so that more students could attend college while living at home. In 1958, the federal government began offering prospective college students low-interest loans. Later, Congress authorized direct grants to low-income students.

During the 1980s, legislators followed precisely the opposite policy, asking students to pay a rising fraction of what it cost to educate them. Tuition and fees accounted for 17% of revenue at public colleges and universities in 1991, compared to 13% in 1980 (National Center for Education Statistics 1994, table 317). Legislators could have justified this change in policy by arguing that college students reap most of the benefits associated with earning a BA, so they should also pay most of the costs. But arguments of this kind were rare. Most legislators just said that the state's budget was tight, that taxpayers were unwilling to pay more, and that students would therefore have to pay the difference. This explanation sounds quite plausible. Yet as Hanushek emphasizes, fiscal austerity did not slow the growth of per-pupil spending at the elementary or secondary level. How are we to reconcile these disparate trends?

The simplest explanation is that spending patterns were driven mainly by institutional inertia rather than student demand. If we ignore changes in enrollment and look only at total outlays, spending on higher education rose slightly faster than spending on elementary and secondary education between 1970 and 1990. It is only when we take account of enrollment changes that spending patterns diverge. At the postsecondary level, enrollments rose almost as fast as total real outlays, leaving expenditure per student almost unchanged. At the elementary and secondary level, enrollment fell, making expenditure per pupil rise even faster than total spending. The results are apparent in figure 3C.4. The solid line shows that public elementary and secondary schools doubled their real spending between 1968 and 1992. The dashed line shows that col-

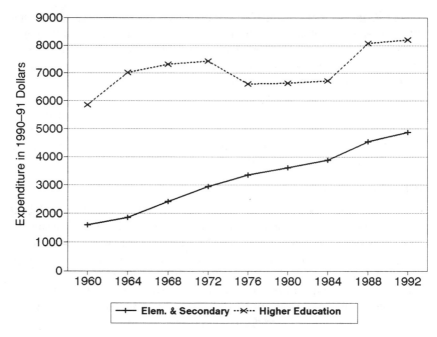

**Fig. 3C.4   Expenditure per student: elementary and secondary versus higher education, 1960–1992**
*Source:* National Center for Education Statistics 1994, table 165 and 238.

leges and universities raised their real outlays per student by only 12% during this period.[11]

I know of no empirical research comparing the social rate of return to subsidies for different levels of education. Nonetheless, I suspect that most Americans subscribe to the basic proposition with which I began this comment, which is that increasing the amount of time students invest in their own education yields higher returns than increasing the amount of time adults invest in each student's education. Thus, if the voters had been given a choice, I think most of them would have preferred to spend less money expanding the payrolls of elementary and secondary schools and more money helping high school graduates attend college. Certainly I would have favored such a policy.

Perhaps the most disturbing fact about America's present system of educational governance is that this possibility was never even discussed. Perhaps that is an inescapable cost of democracy, which puts ultimate power in the hands of people who seldom pay attention. Such a system gives politicians a strong

11. Both sets of figures are adjusted using the Consumer Price Index, which overstates inflation during the 1970s. Neither series presents a realistic picture of changes in the cost of educational inputs (e.g., teachers of constant quality). The figures for higher education cover "educational and general expenditures." Both sets of figures exclude capital investment.

incentive to postpone choices whenever possible. In education, avoiding choices led to steady growth of support for all levels of schooling, regardless of whether demand for their services was rising or falling.

## References

Card, David, and Alan Krueger. 1992. Does School Quality Matter? Returns to Education and the Characteristics of Public Schools in the United States. *Journal of Political Economy* 100:1–40.

Hedges, Larry, Richard Laine, and Rob Greenwald. 1994. Does Money Matter? A Meta-Analysis of Studies of the Effects of Differential School Inputs on Student Outcomes. *Educational Researcher* 23:5–14.

National Center for Education Statistics. 1994. *Digest of Education Statistics, 1994.* Washington, DC: Government Printing Office.

# 4     Health Care Reform: The Clash of Goals, Facts, and Ideology

Henry J. Aaron

In 1994, the United States engaged in a great, if confused, national debate on how to modify financing and delivery of health care. Despite general satisfaction with the quality of care they receive, Americans tell poll takers that their health care system is badly awry and in need of fundamental change. While in seeming agreement that something needs to be done, the public and health care experts alike seem confused and divided on just what to do.

## 4.1   Why Consensus Is Elusive

The sources of disagreement are several. First, a major goal of health care— the ability to enjoy high-quality life as long as possible—is not very well defined and is affected more by the external environment, personal behavior, and genetic inheritance than by health care. As a result, discussion of health care finance often loses focus when observers point out—correctly—that health gains from reform of health care financing will be small unless violence is controlled, housing upgraded, diet improved, drug abuse curbed, or some other change in the social environment or personal behavior achieved. It is certainly likely that such steps would improve health more than would reform of health care, and such reforms are important for other reasons as well. Furthermore, the concept of "high-quality life" is multifaceted. How large are benefits from cure of somatic disease if people live in dreadful conditions or suffer from other devastating diseases? The question takes on particular force when somatic illnesses result from personal actions—smoking, substance abuse, reckless driving, hunting, or poor diet.

Thus, debates about health care financing slide easily into a host of related questions concerning human behavior. But they are not what reform of health

Henry J. Aaron is director of the Economic Studies Program at the Brookings Institution.

care financing is about. Coherent consideration of health care financing requires that most of these issues be left for separate consideration. It also requires an awareness that health care serves important purposes other than purely medical ends, such as providing care and comfort during travail and, most notably, at life's two momentous transitions, birth and death. As Victor R. Fuchs (1979) observed, physicians and other health providers now perform important functions once the responsibility of the family or organized religion.

A second obstacle to the achievement of consensus on reform of health care financing arises from disagreements over the proper realms of individual choice and of social intervention. Once again, health status depends on many behaviors that are clearly the responsibility of individuals, not society. In addition, people disagree on whether health care is primarily a commodity, similar to VCRs and restaurant dinners, the allocation of which capitalist societies leave to individual choice, or more like voting and elementary and secondary education, the entitlement to which is a right of citizenship. Two decades ago, Arthur Okun (1975) noted that standard economic theory easily shows that welfare would be increased if people could sell votes or if military draftees could pay others to serve in their stead. Similar arguments can be adduced that people should be permitted to buy or sell organs for transplant. In each case, it is argued that a willing buyer and a willing seller will carry out a transaction only if it makes each of them better off. Yet such behavior is explicitly prohibited by law because of a widely shared belief that some things should not be bought or sold, but enforced as inalienable rights or obligations.

Thus, some observers hold that society may have an obligation to ensure that people can buy insurance at actuarially fair prices (with associated subsidies for the poor, elderly, or chronically ill, as deemed necessary), but that no further collective obligation exists. For them, the goal of reform of health care financing is to remove alleged shortcomings in the market for insurance.[1]

Others hold that public policy should ensure access to health services at prices no greater than sufficient to deter utterly frivolous use. This result can be achieved through direct public financing or private insurance—with limited copayments, deductibles, or coinsurance in either case. Private insurance can achieve universality, however, only if subsidies make it affordable for those with low incomes and if individuals or their employers (or both) are required to buy insurance, a step regarded as unnecessary or harmful by those concerned primarily with *access* to insurance.

A third obstacle to consensus is the pace of change in the technology of insurance, health care, and organization of delivery. Insurers are increasingly adept in using statistical techniques to identify individuals and groups with high expected health care costs. Biomedical research is beginning to identify

---

1. I use the mushy term "shortcomings," rather than the standard economists' term "imperfections," because some observers are concerned about asymmetric information and the possibility of instability or failure of insurance markets, while other observers are even more upset about the results of accurate experience rating, surely *not* a market imperfection.

genetic markers that predict predispositions to develop specific diseases. The power and accuracy of these procedures can only increase, perhaps very fast. These techniques have created one of the few areas of consensus in the debate about health care reform—an understanding of the perniciousness of untrammeled risk selection and unlimited underwriting by insurers. These techniques promise—or threaten, depending on one's point of view—to convert health insurance into a form of prepayment.

The advances in the technology of health care are even more dramatic than the progress in risk selection. Some of this progress rests on hardware, some on pharmaceutical products, and some on clinical technique. The net effect is to cause frequent changes in recommended courses of therapy for major diseases.

An additional dimension of change concerns the organization of the market for health care. Partly under pressure to control costs and partly from efforts to anticipate the future consequences of legislation, physicians, hospitals, and insurers are merging, reorganizing, and regrouping. How these efforts will affect the delivery and cost of care remains obscure, but they have sown uncertainty among providers and insurers regarding the future.

Confronted with this dynamism, some observers focus on health care delivery and financing as they stand, some on projections of the directions in which arrangements are evolving. The former group tends to see some problems but no crisis. Costs are high, but areas for achieving economies exist. Some people are uninsured, but the number can be reduced. Quality of care is high on the average. Sometimes physicians intervene too early and too much, and sometimes they do too little, often because uninsured patients come too late for care.

The group that attends to projections of risk selection and health technology is prone to see crisis. They see current trends leading to reduced coverage, to much increased expenditures on low-benefit care, and to deterioration in quality from poorly designed efforts to control spending. Technological dynamism creates continuing pressures on costs, which in turn generate behaviors by individuals, businesses, and governments that tend to narrow insurance coverage and access to care. Whether the reactions of public and private payers to rising costs will suffice to squeeze out low-benefit, high-cost care remains a matter of hot dispute.

## 4.2   A Few Facts

Against this background, several key facts—and disagreements about some of them—help explain why agreement on how to reform health care financing has proven so elusive.

*Fact 1.* Annual health care outlays are highly concentrated, with 1% of the population accounting for roughly 30% and 5% of the population accounting for more than half of acute-care outlays. This fact is the arithmetic expression of the simple truth that most people are healthy most of the time and healthy people consume little health care. This spending pattern holds in several countries for which data are available.

*Fact 2.* Health care technology is advancing rapidly. The degree to which scientific advances improve the quality of care varies across both technologies and patients. Typically, new medical technologies improve the diagnostic accuracy or therapeutic efficacy for many patients but are used on many other patients where the medical value is questionable. Thus, new technologies improve the quality of care for some patients and may extend the quantity of care by enabling diagnosis or treatment of patients for whom nothing similar could be done previously.[2] They also tend to be used wastefully on other patients. The long-term value of new technologies is difficult to appraise because they are used not only for current patient care but also as part of ongoing research. Part of the value of medical advance is its role in undergirding further research on new methods of patient care.

It is commonplace, even among economists, to note that advances in medical technology, unlike advances in other fields, have not reduced costs. While commonplace, this statement reflects muddled thought. First, scientific advance has not led to reduced "costs" in many fields, at least if the term "cost" is used, as in the case of medical care, to refer to total spending. Technological advance tends to reduce *price,* but not necessarily *total spending.* The price of a floating-point operation has plummeted, but total expenditures on computers have skyrocketed. The quality-adjusted price of automobiles has fallen relative to the price of most other goods, but total spending on automobiles has increased.

In the case of health care, we simply do not know whether the price of quality-adjusted medical services has risen or fallen (Aaron 1991; Newhouse 1992). No good definition of health outputs exists. In the absence of such a measure and in the face of revolutionary changes in the methods of care—that is, in the unit of output—no meaningful price index is possible. Common price indices that indicate that health prices have risen faster than other prices are

---

2. Total outlays have risen not only because medical advances make possible the treatment of previously untreatable conditions, but also because these advances often reduce contraindications for therapy and thereby increase the number of patients for whom the cost/benefit ratio of treatment or diagnosis is favorable. Furthermore, successful medical interventions raise total spending also because they often spare people low-cost deaths who then survive to absorb really expensive care for chronic illnesses—that is, for diseases that are not immediately lethal but for which the only available care is palliative or supportive but not necessarily cheap—or they make possible treatments that are curative but often very costly. Antibiotics illustrate these phenomena. They have slashed mortality and morbidity from infectious diseases among children and young adults, thereby sparing them to live until they can generate really large medical bills. They have sharply reduced the incidence among the elderly of pneumonia, once called "the widow's friend." And they have made possible aggressive and costly cancer therapies that ravage defenses against potentially lethal infections.

close to meaningless.[3] Whether health prices really have risen faster than other prices, not as fast, or have actually fallen remains quite unclear. This uncertainty is heightened by the sharp declines in length of hospital stays and the dramatic shifts of therapy from inpatient to outpatient care.

*Fact 3.* Every rich nation socializes the financing of health care in two senses. Sick patients and their families are spared most of the cost of care when ill. In addition, the actual cost of health care is only loosely related to outlays expected ex ante. Some countries socialize costs through public finance, some through private insurance. Socialization is less in the United States than elsewhere, in part because the United States covers a smaller share of costs through public budgets than do other countries, but even more importantly because private financing is largely experience rated.

*Fact 4.* Alone among rich nations, the United States imposes no effective constraint on outlays of hospitals, the locus of most acute-care health spending. The U.S. system of financing health care is perfused with moral hazard and attendant incentives for economic waste. While moral hazard is inescapable if patients bear little cost for care when ill and particularly if providers are paid on a fee-for-service basis, other countries limit moral hazard by some combination of budget and fee controls or pay providers through salary or capitation.

These four facts taken together explain why health care spending is so much higher in the United States than elsewhere and why it is rising so fast. The U.S. financing system encourages patients to seek care whenever medical benefits are deemed to be positive (some would say "nonnegative"). Rapid technological advance continuously and rapidly lengthens the menu of beneficial interventions. In both of these respects, the United States does not differ from other rich nations. The United States is unique, however, in that its reimbursement system encourages providers to render all beneficial care and perhaps more besides. This system might not lead to waste, but two conditions necessary for efficient decentralized decision making are not satisfied.

*Fact 5.* Households face incentives to purchase excessive health insurance. In addition, households would be unable to make rational decisions about either the quantity or kind of health care even if they did not buy excessive health insurance. Economists universally accept the first of these statements. The exclusion of employer-financed health insurance from personal income and payroll taxes means that, at any given level of earnings, a dollar of additional health insurance reduces income available for other consumption by less than

3. The consumer price index (CPI) for health, for example, weights hospital service and dental services similarly, although total spending on hospital services greatly exceeds that on dental services. What counts for the CPI is consumer spending. Since third-party payments cover most hospital spending but little of dental spending, direct outlays are similar.

one dollar, according to Martin Feldstein (1973).[4] Feldstein also observes that the resulting incentives encourage the purchase of insurance with inefficiently small deductibles and other cost sharing. Fuchs (1979) has suggested that people overinsure for an additional reason—to escape the need to face the kinds of marginal calculations they normally make during ordinary economic life.

The second of these statements provokes widespread opposition among general economists and some health economists as well, although I believe that except for professional economists few would regard it as other than a banal truth. The reasons can be stated in economic terms. As with many complex goods, laypersons lack expert knowledge about the indications for or the value of various health care services. Accordingly, they hire experts—that is, physicians or other health professionals—to provide advice and, in many situations, to make actual decisions for them.[5] In principle, healthy people could write contingent contracts specifying the care they want when ill.

Two facts render such contracts chimerical. First, the technical complexity of defining the physical effect of particular diagnostic or therapeutic interventions is so multifaceted that it is impossible to write a contingent contract instructing providers regarding what rational people—healthy or sick—would want when sick. Approximately ten thousand separately defined medical diagnoses exist. Many of these conditions can appear in varying degrees of severity. With respect to each of these diagnoses, patients can present with widely varying conditions, complicating conditions, history of treatment. In addition, treatment options for many conditions vary, and the medical outcomes depend on severity, patient history, and complicating conditions. Thus, a complete contract would have to deal, literally, with millions of contingencies. Further complicating the situation is the matter of cost—treatments differ widely in cost. Finally, the impressive technological dynamism of medicine means that the contract would have to be rewritten in significant ways almost continuously if patients are not to be trapped in obsolete contracts.

A second consideration indicates why contingent contracts for medical care would be of doubtful usefulness even if they could be written. The expected utility of medical services depends on actual health status and on random external events, such as whether one's spouse has died or grandchildren arrive in one's life. Thus, the utility of health services for the sick may differ from the healthy person's expectation of the utility of such services. In recognition of

4. This statement is false for the narrow range over which the earned income tax credit is rising and exceeds the payroll tax and personal income tax rates are zero. The standard work is Feldstein (1973).

5. Physicians suggest that surrendering such decision-making functions is therapeutic for the patient. When made by practicing physicians, this statement emits an aroma of self-service and self-glorification. One physician, who was accustomed to making all medical decisions himself, described the process by which, when ill, he surrendered such decision making to others and characterized this behavior as entering "the sick role."

this possibility, durable powers of attorney and advance medical directives are subject to repeal on the slightest of indications by their authors at any time and under any circumstances. As Thomas Schelling (1984) has observed, reconciling conflicting preferences of a single person at different times and under different circumstances raises problems of incommensurability similar to those raised by interpersonal comparisons of utility.

Thus, people must cede to professionals detailed decisions on medical treatment. But even decisions on how much to spend on insurance and hence on the volume of resources available to professionals is likely to be flawed. The probability of most major medical events is quite low during the usual periods over which insurance contracts are written. The evidence that individuals have flawed perceptions of low-probability events is overwhelming. Thus, a strong possibility exists that people will attach irrational weights to the low-probability events that account for most acute-care outlays. Economists should recognize that, given choices about the risks against which to insure and the degree of protection to purchase, many people will choose unwisely.

### 4.3   The Way We Are

As far as the financing of health care is concerned, "the U.S. system" is a misnomer. The congeries of financing arrangements by which payments flow to health care providers reflects ancillary consequences of policies adopted for reasons having little or nothing to do with health care and the more or less independent actions of governments, religious organizations and other charities, and private businesses and individuals. These arrangements are ill-coordinated and disorganized. Except under the most Panglossian presumption that whatever is must be best, these arrangements would never be accorded any presumption of efficiency. This state is not the well-ordered cacophony of a normal economic market, but the chaos of uncoordinated actions by people and groups that are heedless of effects on third parties.

#### 4.3.1   How We Got That Way

Irrationalities in wage controls during World War II gave employer-financed health insurance its initial push. The cost of health insurance was excluded from wartime limits on compensation, enabling employers to raise workers' pay without running afoul of wartime controls. The exclusion of employer payments for health insurance from taxable compensation under the personal income tax and the payroll tax reinforced and perpetuated the linkage of insurance to work in the post–World War II period.

The McCarren-Ferguson Act entrusted insurance regulation to the states. The Employee Retirement Income Security Act (ERISA) then blocked state regulation of self-insured health plans. It thereby encouraged self-insurance, which is simply workplace-based experience rating. More than half of those insured through work now receive coverage through self-insured plans, and the proportion is rising.

This system has the virtue of encouraging employers to pay attention to workers' health and working conditions, but it creates two serious problems. First, it encourages discrimination in hiring on the basis of age, race, sex, and disability status that civil rights statutes go to great lengths to prohibit. Second, relative to individual underwriting, it also significantly mutes workers' financial interest in their own health. Community rating deals with the first problem, and does essentially nothing to aggravate the second. Individual underwriting deals with the second problem, but drastically increases sales and administrative costs. For these and other reasons, I believe that community rating within no more than a small number of distinct categories is more efficient than extensive experience rating (Aaron 1994).

Public health care programs, particularly the federal-state Medicaid program, likewise display unmistakable signs of accident and caprice. Because Medicaid eligibility is tied in part to the design and generosity of Aid to Families with Dependent Children and of Supplemental Security Income, people who are eligible in one state would be ineligible in another. Medicaid pays for services of podiatrists, chiropractors, and Christian Science practitioners in some states but not in others. Some states limit hospitalization while others do not. Physician and hospital fees differ widely. Distinct and uncoordinated programs cover Native Americans, the military, families of the military, veterans, and federal employees.

Other historical circumstances have led to enormous variation in the way health care is delivered across the United States. While it is barely conceivable that the differences reflect differences in tastes and resource costs and availability, no one familiar with the delivery system believes that. Hospital lengths of stay differ markedly across the United States. The incidence of many medical procedures differs across states and smaller areas in ways epidemiological or demographic factors cannot explain. The penetration of health maintenance organizations (HMOs) ranges from dominance in Hawaii, through significant penetration in the western states, Minnesota, and Massachusetts, to negligible in much of the rest of the United States. Currently, the organization of physicians, connections between hospitals and physicians, and linkage among hospitals are undergoing tumultuous change. Given the long history of efforts by various groups in medicine to cultivate and defend rents, I believe one should harbor little hope that the current ferment will push the system to a social optimum.

Huge international variations in the staffing of health care systems also raise serious questions about the efficiency of organization of health care provision. In 1980, the United States employed 2.8 nurses for each physician, Canada 4.4, Germany 1.4, and Belgium 0.3 (Parkin, McGuire, and Yule 1987). While these data are stale, they differ so widely that it is virtually impossible to imagine how these systems could all be operating efficiently.

### 4.3.2  Institutional Failures

Because the financing of health care in the United States reflects countless independent decisions, many made for reasons having little or nothing to do with health, significant institutional failures should surprise no one.

*Insurance.* Insurance markets are failing for several distinct reasons. First, advances in risk analysis based on both statistics and biology are narrowing the scope of true insurance, as steadily increasing proportions of the variance in future use of medical services can be predicted on the basis of characteristics of the insured at the time the insurance contract is written. These characteristics include age, race, sex, disability status, occupation, place of residence, marital status, sexual orientation, and, most notably, past use of medical services.

Such information creates a serious problem whether or not it is equally available to the insured and the insurer. If no information asymmetries exist, then insurance becomes prepayment, transforming poor health prospects from bad fortune into a negative dowry, a lump-sum charge against personal net worth. This problem declines as the duration of insurance contracts increases, but so long as premiums reflect all available information, it remains even if a lifelong contract is mandated at conception, since health background and longevity of one's parents, siblings, aunts, and uncles are correlated with one's own subsequent health and longevity. If the insurer is less well informed than the insured, adverse selection and its attendant problems arise. As Stiglitz and Rothschild (1976) showed, a sustainable insurance market equilibrium may not exist, and complete market failure is possible. As the capacity of insurers to predict use of health care services improves, the variance in underwritten rates increases, and the likelihood that those most likely to use health care will find insurance attractive declines.

Aid for poor sick people, whether privately or publicly funded, discourages people with low actual or expected incomes from buying insurance because they can count on subsidies when ill.[6] Rich nations without exception provide such help on the principle that at least some forms of health care should be available whether the recipient can afford it or not and sometimes whether the recipient wants it or not. Thus, public and private programs discourage the poor from buying insurance privately, at the same time that tax rules encourage those who face positive personal income or payroll tax rates to buy too much insurance.

*Market or Budget Discipline.* Those who provide health care services face little economic discipline in the United States. The fact that insurance, public or

---

6. Several comments during the discussion of Alan Garber's paper (chap. 5 in this volume) remarked that the availability of Medicaid makes the purchase of private insurance for the costs of long-term care a poor investment for most people.

private, makes patients insensitive to costs is well known among economists, at least since the seminal article by Arrow (1963) and the comment by Pauly (1968), which characterized this insensitivity as "moral hazard." Physicians and other health professionals would simply be instruments for effectuating this moral hazard if they acted as perfect agents for patients. In fact, the fee-for-service reimbursement system creates strong incentives for providers to increase the problem, as the literature on physician-induced demand strongly, if inconclusively, suggests (Cromwell and Mitchell 1986; Fuchs 1986; Phelps 1986).

Theory suggests that such a payment system will produce waste—the purchase of services worth less to the user and (in the absence of significant externalities) to society than they cost society. The extent of such waste depends on the shape of benefits curves associated with the menu of available medical technologies. Concave benefits curves will be associated with considerable waste; convex curves with less. I know of no good research on how much of current medical spending represents waste in this sense. Although it is tempting to conclude that an increase in the number of available procedures and of outlays will be associated with increased waste, I know of no analysis on whether waste in this sense is increasing or decreasing. Personal experiences and studies of selected procedures suggest that waste is large. Brook and Vaiana (1989) have suggested that some procedures may be inappropriately used in as many as 30% of applications and that their use is equivocal in a similar proportion of cases.[7] One recent experiment dealt a body blow to this line of reasoning, however. One of the procedures found by Brook and Vaiana (1989) to be useless, or equivocal in half or more of all cases, was carotid endarterectomy, the surgical removal of fatty deposits from the carotid artery to minimize chances of stroke. The managers of a controlled experiment to test the efficacy of this procedure not only did not confirm this judgment, but felt obliged to terminate the experiment because the results indicated such large and positive results that failure to communicate the findings immediately to physicians would constitute an indefensible disservice to patients (Altman 1994).

The practical question is how best to reduce such waste. At first blush, it might seem that if households faced the full price of insurance (that is, if the tax distortions were repealed), the price constraints created by the requirement that insurers make nonnegative profits to remain in business would establish the requisite incentives.

This outcome requires that the regulatory powers exercised by insurers exactly offset waste from moral hazard. This result is unlikely because of multiple agency problems connecting patients to insurers, patients to providers, and insurers to providers. Physicians, in particular, are trained to act as agents for patients and to assure that they receive all *medically beneficial* care. They are

---

7. Whether "inappropriate" and "equivocal" imply "harmful," "useless," or "low-benefit" is unclear. In either case, of course, benefits should be calculated ex ante, not ex post.

not trained to weight costs against benefits, but to weigh benefits from action versus benefits from inaction. Even if the agency problems are solved, a deeper problem remains: since patients may regard as suboptimal the contracts they signed when well, accurate enforcement of these contracts by agents trying to effectuate the interests of the healthy purchasers of insurance may act in ways contrary to the revised preferences of the sick. Whose life is it anyway?

According to Aaron and Schwartz (1984), physical constraints *can* force physicians to use available resources to achieve highest medical benefits. Thus, limits on the availability of operating rooms or diagnostic or therapeutic radiological equipment *can* cause those responsible for managing these capital goods to ration efficiently. Much the same is true if hospitals work with salaried staff in critical specialities, such as cardiac surgery. In these cases, providers work at full capacity but cannot care for everyone, and medical ethics align well with social objectives of using available resources to produce highest net benefits. While such a happy result is possible, it is by no means assured unless good information on outcomes of interventions is available and widely disseminated and unless regulations or incentives make it costly to practice in violation of this information. Incentives created by limits on general medical supplies and pharmaceutical products are much less likely to produce efficient outcomes, because monitoring physician behavior in the countless small decisions comprised in normal care is probably impossible, and each physician faces a conflict between obligations to specific patients and diffuse obligations to see that total resources are efficiently used.[8]

Since capital equipment typically is purchased by provider groups, effective control over the purchase of such equipment when numerous payers are involved requires that each payer establish enforceable rules limiting access to such equipment similar to those that would arise under supply constraints. But it is not at all clear how they would go about doing so, particularly since physicians control the flow of information to the insurer.

Once again, prepaid health plans seem to provide the incentives for insurers to allocate resources efficiently. But serious obstacles stand in the way. The low quality of information makes it difficult to write clear and enforceable guidelines for when to use various medical procedures.

*Research.* Medical research, like much other research, ranges from fundamental science to highly applied product and device development. At the fundamental end of the spectrum, serious public good issues have led the United States to underwrite basic biomedical research through government grants and

---

8. At one time, the British rationed dialysis by limiting the availability of dialysis machines. The primary criterion for rationing was age, with occasional exceptions based on other considerations. According to medical testimony, this method of rationing was reasonably efficient. The ability to limit dialysis diminished when continuous ambulatory peritoneal dialysis (CAPD) replaced machine-based dialysis, because the supplies necessary for CAPD were less easily monitored and controlled.

direct research (principally through the National Institutes of Health) and through private foundations, the largest of which is the Hughes Foundation. At the applied end of the spectrum, most research is carried out by pharmaceutical companies and device manufacturers. These two forms of research are complements.

Current arrangements for financing applied research may not rise (or descend) to the level of market failure, but they *are* peculiar. A crude characterization of current arrangements would be the following: Entrepreneurs invest in a company that sells products and uses the profits from current sales to fund many diverse research projects, most of which will fail. Patents on the few that succeed enable monopoly pricing, the profits from which are then used to fund further diverse research projects, most of which will fail. But some succeed, and patents on them permit monopoly pricing, the profits from which . . . And so on, ad infinitum.

Thus, the funds to pay for applied research come from the relatively few patients who benefit from the fruits of past research. This crude characterization is inaccurate in one important detail. While the patients who consume the products of past research pay for future research through drug prices well above production cost,[9] third parties—private insurers and government programs—pay for many of these products. To the extent that third parties pay for these products, the cost of future research is effectively socialized. To the extent that patients bear the costs, however, the allocation of the cost of research raises troubling questions because vulnerable people are required to pay far more than production costs for drugs and devices that are indispensable. Inevitably, some potential users find the costs insupportable and fail to buy important or even vital products because the price exceeds production cost.

This possibility is the legitimate basis for concern about high drug prices. This concern has triggered various proposals to curb drug prices that raise serious problems of their own, because the limits threaten the profit base on which much applied research rests. According to Linda Cohen and Roger Noll (1991), since the public record in supporting applied research is poor, increased government support could not effectively replace any curtailment of private research support.

## 4.4    The Elusive Prize of Health Care Financing Reform

Public opinion polls report that Americans think something is fundamentally wrong with the U.S. health care system. A highly articulate president with unmatched capacity to explain complex issues in simple terms made reform of health care financing his major domestic initiative. The president's party

9. They also pay for high total profit margins and associated dividends and appreciation and for large outlays on sales and advertising to promote product differentiation and associated profit opportunities (U.S. Congress 1993).

controlled both houses of Congress. Yet the effort to enact major reform failed utterly. Whether one of the more limited proposals cobbled together as the 1994 legislative calendar moved to its close would have been passed if the administration had embraced it earlier will occupy doctoral students for years.

Why the 103d Congress ended without major legislation demands attention. Was the explanation bad staff work and political maladroitness? Did the administration do about as well as possible given the forces that it confronted? Or were serious mistakes committed on behalf of a cause that in any case had little chance of success? Are future efforts to reach consensus likely to fare better than those of the Clinton administration?

I shall present a number of interrelated arguments, none of which is capable of being tested definitively with the techniques economists are trained to use and to trust. These arguments cannot be so tested because each is created to correlate with observed facts. This is data mining in its most fundamental sense.

- In any democracy, times when it is possible to pass legislation restructuring a tenth or more of the economy are exceedingly rare. No such time has occurred in all U.S. history, except under the exigencies of war. We are not currently living in such a time. The willingness to contemplate far-reaching legislative change requires either extreme duress (devastation from war or economic collapse) or a high order of faith that leaders are trustworthy and capable. Neither condition is currently satisfied.
- Despite diffuse agreement on the need for major changes in the system and on the specific goals of reform, no consensus exists on the weights that should be attached to the various goals of reform or on how best to achieve those goals.
- Key underlying facts about the delivery of health care are in dispute or are unknown. Relevant facts include both actual, potentially observable behavior and estimates of how people will change behavior if incentives are modified.
- Given large vistas of ignorance and complexity, people take intellectual and political refuge in ideology, which I define for current purposes as presumptions about group and individual behavior that are weakly supported but can be overridden, at best only with powerful evidence and sometimes not even then.
- The tenth or more of the economy that is the subject of health care reform is extraordinarily messy and complicated. The result of this heterogeneity is an inescapable dilemma. A proposal for sweeping reform must be bewilderingly complex; or, if it is simple, it will produce highly disparate effects in various parts of this enormously diverse nation. Moreover, reforms that extend services to some people must produce large numbers of losers—those who must pay higher taxes if spending is increased, or those whose services or incomes are cut if spending is held constant. With the aid of generally avail-

able models, little cleverness is needed to identify the losers and use them as a cudgel to beat the proponents of change.

### 4.5 The Many Faces of Hubris

Economists, political scientists, and others who try to analyze public policy are trained to look at large trends and major problems, not to focus on uninformative specificity. To deal at the macro level requires abstraction and generalization, a suppression of detail in order to highlight the structure of the problem at hand. Students of economic regulation, for example, examine the emergence in many domains of certain behavioral regularities—for example, the tendency for regulatory capture or the inefficiencies from use of process rules rather than outcome standards. On the basis of such accumulated insight, analysts who know practically nothing about an industry can effectively criticize the decisions of people who spend their lives studying and regulating the industry. Few economists know much about how products move by barge, for example; but their ignorance does not materially impair their analyses of policies of the Interstate Commerce Commission.

Disregard for "irrelevant" detail permits policy analysts to approach public policy much like students in a military academy who analyze Lee's strategy at Gettysburg. They model the terrain, place the forces in their respective locations, move stick figures around, comment on how they might have acted, and reach conclusions about alternative strategies. It is all so intellectually challenging, so stimulating, to think that one is mentally replaying an event in which tens of thousands of soldiers died. And it is so exhilarating to imagine the reconfiguration of an industry through which close to $1 trillion of resources flow, to dream of making the world a better place by designing a superior system of paying for health care. It is so intoxicating, in fact, that one can easily forget the herculean labor necessary in a democracy to bring about large-scale changes in social policy and institutions.

This mental numbing is doubly important, as in the case of the U.S. health care system, when the object being manipulated is extremely diverse and complicated in relevant ways. Thus, reformers must beware of a kind of policy makers' narcosis, a condition in which pride (often justified) about the power of one's analytical skills deadens awareness of the distinction between, for example, talking about cutting spending by $100 billion and the practical steps necessary to make such changes happen. Between what one person has called "Lotus policy analysis" and real change lies the task of writing legislation and regulations, securing popular acceptance of proposed actions, setting up new agencies, hiring staff, and, among other things, causing half a million doctors to practice medicine differently from ways learned in medical school and repeated for years or even decades.

The history of social policy in the United States gives little comfort to those who hope to enact a single major law that will reform the U.S. health care system. With the exception of war mobilization and the desperate measures of the Great Depression, U.S. history contains no example of legislation remotely approaching the ambition and complexity of major reform of health care financing and the magnitude of change in behavior and established institutions it requires. Legislation creating land grant colleges and Social Security produced enormous ramifications, but modified or replaced few existing institutions. Economic regulation, which intrudes in much of the U.S. economy, arose piecemeal over many years.

In short, the disproportion between easy talk of fundamentally reforming health care finance, a mode of discourse abetted by the rhetorical habits of scholars, and the magnitude and complexity of the task of reforming health care financing is grotesque. The most surprising aspect of the debate about health care reform is not that consensus has been so elusive but that anyone ever expected it. The most disappointing aspect of the debate was the operation of a political Gresham's law, with epithets, oversimplification, and plain lying driving out serious debate over the complex issues that might have enlightened the electorate, even if it did not persuade their elected representatives to act.

## 4.6   Goals and Weights

The goals of health care reform, like Caesar's Gaul, are divided into three parts: cost control, extension of insurance coverage, and maintenance or improvement of quality of care. If the delivery system were thought to be efficient, the inconsistency of these goals would be transparent.

But few would place efficiency among the many virtues of the U.S. health care system. A large theoretical and empirical literature, supported—one might almost say, made unnecessary—by every observer's personal experiences testifies to widespread inefficiencies. Moral hazard induced by insurance under a fee-for-service system causes consumption of much health care with lower social benefit than social cost. Flaws in the tax system lead to excessive insurance. Both of those factors reduce incentives for providers to operate efficiently. Eliminating or reducing these inefficiencies would assuredly release resources that could be diverted to those whose access to care is now inhibited by a lack of good insurance.

### 4.6.1   Goal Trade-Offs

Not only goals but weights attached to various goals differ. Inevitably choices must be made about how aggressively to pursue cost control, how far and how fast to extend financial access, and how much quality to seek.

The relationship between efficiency and quality is particularly subtle. The term "waste" for economists encompasses two phenomena: use of resources that produce no benefits at all—services that are useless or harmful and production methods that generate costs but no added benefits—and use of resources to produce services that generate benefits worth less, in some sense, than they cost.

Elimination of the first form of waste reduces costs and, since some care is harmful, may even improve quality of care in the short run. Elimination of low-benefit, high-cost care lowers quality of care as the term is commonly used, because such economies deny to some patients care they would choose to have under current financing arrangements.

In the long run, however, eliminating both kinds of waste threatens quality of care. Expenditures on research and development of new medical procedures respond to potential sales. The elimination of waste lowers potential sales and thereby discourages profit-motivated research. Over the long run, eliminating waste is likely to reduce the flow of innovation.[10] Whether a reduction in innovation is to be celebrated (because innovation widens the scope of moral hazard and, therefore, of economic waste) or decried (because large serendipitous advances may be lost), is one of many important unknowable matters in medical financing.

Even if waste is extensive, savings may not be large enough, or may not be realizable quickly enough, to pay for the costs of extending access without short-run loss of some beneficial care, quite apart from any long-term retardation of medical advance.

### 4.6.2   Weights

Among advocates of access, cost control, and quality one can identify a wide variety of latent goals.

- Advocates for the poor, including many of the long-time supporters of government-sponsored health insurance, attach dominant weight to universal access.
- Business supporters of government involvement in health care seem motivated mostly by concern about controlling growth of costs. They seem to believe that private agents, acting alone, cannot solve problems of moral hazard—problems they see growing as the menu of diagnostic and therapeutic tools lengthens.
- Many observers, including representatives from the medical community, acknowledge that lack of financial access and rising costs are serious problems but dwell on the high quality of currently available care and warn that efforts to extend access and cut costs could impair quality, if not immediately, then over time.

10. One needs to be cautious in making such forecasts, as the essence of research is identification of unexpected production possibilities. To the extent that research activities are shaped by opportunities and incentives, the transformation of the financial environment for medical services into one that rewards parsimony might produce startling results, such as the discovery of low-cost alternatives to current methods of diagnosis or treatment.

More generally, many participants in the health care reform debate deny that curtailments in the growth of spending may necessitate trade-offs among desired ends.

## 4.7  Ignorance

When a member of Congress asked Congressional Budget Office director Robert Reischauer whether he was confident that the CBO estimates of the cost of President Clinton's health reform proposal were "in the right ballpark," Reischauer responded, "I am pretty sure they are in the same city the ballpark is in."[11] This exchange crystallized the extraordinary uncertainty surrounding the debate about health care reform—not just about the president's plan, but about any proposal for far-reaching reform.

### 4.7.1  Facts and Behavior

Reliable predictions of the consequences of major reforms of health care financing are simply impossible because information on actual use of health care services is spotty and out of date, and understanding of how people will respond to changed incentives is appallingly inadequate. Data on actual household expenditures are based on surveys that are several years old and that do not permit estimates of expenditures for substate geographical areas that played a prominent part in major reform proposals debated in 1994. Analysis of how people will respond to new organizational arrangements is unavailable because each of the major reform proposals would place people in situations never before observed. The president's plan and several others include new administrative entities—regional health alliances or health purchasing cooperatives—that exist nowhere and whose effects on the marketing of insurance or organization of care is a matter of speculation. Managed competition, a congeries of market reforms to promote cost-conscious buying, looks extremely promising on paper, but it has not run the gauntlet of legislation, regulatory drafting, and implementation. How much of the current cost advantage of HMOs, the leading managed care settings, is attributable to superior efficiency and how much to rationing, selection, or cost shifting through negotiated discounts remains unclear. In their recent review of research on HMOs, Miller and Luft concluded, "[T]he findings suggest that HMOs provide care at lower cost than do indemnity plans. Recent peer reviewed literature did not produce estimates of three other central summary indicators of managed care plan performance: the rate of growth of expenditures and the level and rate of growth of premiums" (1994, 1517). Attempts now to quantify the pace or amount of retardation in growth of spending from managed care recall Alec Cairncross's advice to economic forecasters: "Give a number or a date; never both."

While the debate is occurring, major events are taking place in the organiza-

---

11. Testimony, House Committee on Ways and Means, February 8, 1994.

tion of health care. A bewildering variety of organizations is swallowing up solo or free-standing group practices of physicians throughout much of the United States. The range of managed care settings increases daily. Managed care is being born without the aid of legislative midwives.

### 4.7.2   Cost Estimates

Uncertainty is the defining characteristic of the health care reform debate. For purely illustrative purposes, consider the question of how the medical system will respond to the extension of coverage to those who currently consume health care but do not pay for it. Providers now recover the costs of such care by charging the insured more than the full cost of care. Because Medicare and Medicaid have considerable market power, these programs also pay less than the full cost of care, according to estimates of the Prospective Payment Assessment Commission. Thus, private payers face charges for hospital services that average 31% more than the actual cost of care rendered to privately insured patients, although the excess varies widely from state to state.

The vitally important question for projecting costs concerns what will happen to charges when everyone is insured. Reimbursements will be available for previously uncompensated care. How will providers respond in setting fees? Some argue that the correct answer is that nothing will happen to the level *or* growth of fees, that total payments to providers for services currently rendered will increase because of increased insurance and that the growth of charges will be unaffected. This view implies an increase in rents, waste, or both unless some action is taken to prevent them.

This projection is open to challenge on several grounds. First, the behavior of providers should be influenced by the market conditions they face. Advocates of managed competition would argue that, in a properly structured market, insurers will sooner or later bid premiums down to offset the added revenues and then bid them down some more as pressures for efficient provision and elimination of low-benefit, high-cost services proceed. Others favor regulatory measures—premium caps, hospital budgets, or fee regulation—to avoid what they see as the doubly uncertain promise of competition as to timing and amount of savings eventually achieved.

The extension of coverage to the currently uninsured may cause charges to fall—whether through competition or regulation. Especially if they do not, the rate of growth may abate. Rents and waste may still increase, it is alleged, but not by the full amount of the windfall. On one's view about this question hinges projections of the effect of health care reform on national health care spending and on the federal budget. Given the rules of congressional budget accounting, these projections determine by how much taxes must be raised or other spending cut. Given the long history of savings claimed but never realized and the legislative responsibilities of the CBO to prevent budgetary trickery, the CBO is prepared to count as savings only what is embedded in law, not what advocates hope and claim will materialize. Thus, the political environment for the debate on health care reform depends inescapably on projections that cannot be conclusively demonstrated. These projections, in turn, influence views on the importance of regulatory measures to siphon off the windfall at the outset.

This way of looking at the issue actually understates uncertainties surrounding critical details. It ignores the important variation among and within the United States in the estimated degree to which cost shifting against private payers now occurs. Estimates indicate that the excess of payments over cost by private payers for hospital services varies widely among the states. A national view omits consideration of the wide disparity among states and localities in the distribution of the uninsured or in the proportion of patients covered by Medicaid and Medicare. Thus, the windfall to providers from the extension of coverage varies enormously from state to state. Equally important variations occur within states, a relevant fact if any legislated reform relies on substate administrative entities; the magnitude of these variations is simply unknown.

### 4.7.3   Consequences

The lack of information necessary to predict the full consequences of major reform of health care is pervasive and ineradicable. In these respects, reform of health care is not unique. The full effects of any large-scale action can never be fully foreseen. Hagiography of entrepreneurs rests on their extraordinary capacities to bear risk. National leaders and honored generals receive accolades for their capacity to guide nations and armies through dark uncertainties. The key in each case is a willingness by responsible leaders to decide on a course of action under conditions others find bewildering and on their capacity to persuade others that the larger purpose justifies the risks entailed. In the political domain, action requires consensus, which can emerge from an overpowering sense of crisis or from a concordance of views on facts and goals. When no such consensus on a larger purpose exists or when profound disagreements exist on how best to achieve those purposes, lack of information becomes paralytic. No sufficiently persuasive case for action is possible; or, to be more precise, advocates of alternative courses of action contend fratricidally on how best to proceed. Attention to principle and prudence produces inaction.

## 4.8   Ideology

All actions rest on faith. The faith is simply the inductive leap that previous regularities will continue to apply in the current case. Two centuries ago Hume showed that such inferences are not rigorously provable. When actions concern major restructuring of incentives and when information is missing at every turn, few dependable forecasts of the consequences of action are possible. Such is the case with health care reform. The result is that health care reform becomes a kind of political Rorschach test in which the images conjured up by one proposal or another reflect and reveal the observers' ideologies more than their analytical or empirical reasoning.

The ideologies in evidence in the debate about health care reform closely resemble those displayed in other political debates. The most fundamental ideological cleavage concerns who is responsible for determining whether individuals should have health insurance or not. Views are ranged along a two-dimensional spectrum. On one axis views vary on the nature of health insurance (or on access to health care—not the same thing). At one pole is the view that health insurance is an ordinary market commodity, not fundamentally different from restaurant meals or automobiles in the sense that free consumer decisions based on available household resources should govern allocation. At the other pole is the view that health insurance is a right, a perquisite of citizenship or national residence, much like suffrage, the right to attend public school, or the assurance of police protection.

For those who believe that some collective responsibilities exist regarding health care, disagreement occurs along the axis of what constitutes acceptable coverage—public hospitals for the indigent? insurance for the costs of treatment during catastrophic illness? coverage for the costs of all "routine," but not for "elective," procedures? coverage for all medical care?

This dispute, heavily shadowed by views on the role of the government in promoting egalitarian income distribution, includes the sensitive question of what rules should govern the purchase of health care outside of any government-regulated system. Should individuals be free to use their own resources to buy supplemental insurance, should such insurance be taxed or otherwise penalized, or should they be prohibited from buying such insurance? Should individuals be free to buy care outside a regulated system, should price penalties or regulatory obstacles be imposed, or should the delivery of care outside the regulatory system be flatly prohibited? This group of what I call safety-valve questions is among the most important and least studied issues that will determine the long-run viability of any government-managed system.

Ideological disputes arise also with respect to cost control. Would governmental attempts to restrain growth of spending deteriorate into ineffectual bureaucratic tangles that obstruct organizational and scientific innovation and that become the vehicles for regulatory logrolling which might even raise spending? Would such regulations, instead, slow the growth of spending, as they have done in other nations, with some possible loss of efficient innovations but with certain gains from reallocation of resources from low-benefit medical services to higher-benefit alternative uses? Should one expect cost controls to cause elimination only of low-benefit services? Not if one looks at analyses of expenditure differences among nations. But perhaps outcomes analysis will change all that.

Or take the proposed health alliances or purchasing cooperatives found in proposals both Democrats and Republicans advanced early in 1994. Experts expressed doubts that the alliances could actually be created and staffed and that data necessary for their operation could be gathered in the time allotted by draft legislation. Popular and congressional criticisms focused not on practicality but on principle. Are alliances necessary to remove current imperfections in markets for health insurance? Or, if they are mandatory and especially if they are exclusive, would they be bureaucratic golems that will stifle household choice among insurance plans and physicians? Should they be run by people knowledgeable about the health industry, thereby risking regulatory capture? Or should they be managed by people untainted by such interests, thereby courting amateurishness and ignorant blundering?

If strong alliances or cooperatives prove unacceptable, what can one expect from restrictions on the marketing practices of insurance companies? Are prohibitions on underwriting practices such as denial of coverage for preexisting conditions a reasonable extension of recognized powers to regulate insurers or an unreasonable enlargement of an authority that has already been abused, for example, by mandating coverage for particular services? Taken alone, will they expand coverage by mandatory issue and limits on premiums, or will they narrow coverage by bringing sick people into insurance pools and thereby raising average premiums? In that connection, is the ERISA exemption of self-insured plans from state regulation a desirable limit on abusive regulation or the creation of a market imperfection?

I could extend this list of "ideological" issues virtually without limit. Some may demur that these are not issues of ideology but of analysis and fact. It is surely right that these issues *could* be matters of analysis and fact. But they currently are not. Like the land of the Fisher King, whose domain stretched beyond the world known to cartographers of old, the land of ideology fills the globe of health care reform because so little of the globe is charted by fact and research.

## 4.9   Gordian Knots

One of the reasons that information about the U.S. health care system is so spotty is that the system is so intricate and varied.

Go to Great Britain, and one need only master the structure of the National Health Service system, noting that an adjunct private system has some importance in selected areas and is growing. Go to Germany, and one faces the somewhat more formidable problem of mastering the scores of employment-centered insurance plans and the organization of the delivery of care to which these plans give access.

But return to the United States, and one confronts not one but fifty-two government health plans (Medicare plus fifty-one Medicaid plans) and tens of thousands of employment-based plans. One finds intricate systems for providing free care and financing it through excess charges on private payers, and a large industry selling group insurance to employers and individual insurance to families and individuals, a delivery system that contains virtually every arrangement for providing care found anywhere else in the world and that is daily creating new ways to handle the financing and delivery of care. While financing and delivery of care may be distinct in logic, they are entangled in practice as providers become risk bearers through HMOs, preferred provider organizations, and hospital-physician networks, and as physicians and other providers come increasingly to derive their incomes form several sources.

Depending on one's ideology, this diversity is a tribute to the unique flexibility of the U.S. system and its capacity to reform itself, or it is the fibrillation of a chaotic system in extremis. Regardless of one's ideology, however, this diversity is very bad news for would-be reformers operating at the national level. Deep insight is not required to understand that the essence of national reform of the financing of health care is the establishment of *national* rules governing financing. But when practices are diverse, when these differences appear in varying degrees in different places, and when the system is changing fast in sundry ways in various places, national rules have geographically dissimilar effects.

Moreover, the diversity of practice creates vexing dilemmas for would-be planners. They can try to recognize the diverse starting points of the various communities and move the nation gradually toward some common future. Given the bewildering variety of actual practices, this approach is a recipe for impossible complexity. Or they can ignore diverse starting points and require widely varying adjustments in different areas.

The subsidy structure of the Clinton plan illustrated this dilemma. Employers were to pay for health care up to certain nationally uniform percentages of payroll, and households were to be eligible for subsidies if their costs exceeded certain nationally uniform percentages of income. In addition, the Clinton plan called for the creation of regional health alliances within which community rating would prevail. Two facts of geographical diversity make the effects of this system highly varied across the United States.

First, Medicaid patients were to be covered through the alliances. The federal government would fully reimburse the regional alliances for costs of covering the "categorically eligible" Medicaid patients—those eligible because of receipt of Aid to Families with Dependent Children or Supplemental Security Income. But the federal government would reimburse the alliances only at the community rate for the "medically indigent"—patients who become eligible for assistance because of high medical expenses. Because average costs for these patients are high, their inclusion in the group used to define community premiums would raise the community rate and require other payers to pick up the difference between the community rate and the actual cost of these patients. The proportion of Medicaid patients who are medically indigent varies widely from state to state. The additional charge imposed on private payers to cross-subsidize the medically indigent varies commensurately. The exact calculation is complicated by the maintenance of effort provisions the Clinton plan would have imposed on states.

Second, per capita health care expenditures vary widely by state, ranging from $3,031 per year in 1990 in Massachusetts to $1,689 per year in South

Carolina. These cost differences mean that the flow of subsidies under formulas based on nationally uniform proportions of payroll or income would have varied widely across alliances and states. Subsidies to companies and households in high-cost states would have been larger than those paid to similar companies and households in low-cost states.

But the effects of covering the medically indigent at the community rate are far more problematic. The premium increase from this source was expected to average roughly 20%. In alliances with large populations of medically indigent, insurance premiums for employers that now sponsor insurance would have risen more than 20%, in alliances with small populations of the medically indigent, less. The Clinton plan would have imposed regulations to inhibit such increases. The administration claimed such limits were justified because providers would have been paid for current unreimbursed care. But geographical diversity guarantees that the relationship between the added costs imposed on private payers by the community rating of the medically indigent and the added incomes to providers from covering the uninsured would not have matched up well, even if they were similar in magnitude nationally. Furthermore, it is insurers who would have been put at risk by this pairing of provisions. If providers did not cut *prices* when the uninsured were covered, insurers would have faced increased costs because the *quantity* of care for the medically indigent is higher than average.

This pair of provisions created a serious dilemma for financing of the Clinton health plan—regulate premiums stringently and risk defection by insurers from certain markets, or dispense with regulations and face the likelihood of a sharp increase in premiums that would be budgetarily and politically devastating.

I have gone into this particular provision in some detail for two reasons. First, the dilemma that flows from it is an inescapable consequence of geographical diversity. Second, while more serious than most such dilemmas, it is far from unique.

When confronted with such Gordian knots, one may try to untangle them by dealing case by case with the complexities, a sure road to legislation of unimaginable complexity. Or one may cut the knot, by imposing nationally uniform rules and damning the uneven consequences. I believe that the latter course is the only one that is manageable. But this approach runs afoul of the variant of medical ethics that Charles Schultze suggested typically guides political action: "Do not be seen to do obvious harm." This rule of political action can be suspended, but only in the presence of an overwhelming shared sense that an urgent problem demands action.

The campaign for health care reform during 1994 should be viewed in that light. It was not a debate about the Clinton plan, or the Chafee plan, or the Cooper plan, or about any other single piece of legislation. It was a debate about the status quo. Was the American public sufficiently disturbed by actual or threatened erosion of private health insurance coverage, which fell from

75% to 71% between 1988 and 1992? Were households sufficiently fearful that they would suffer the loss of some or all benefits? Could businesses be persuaded to fear capriciously and uncontrollably rising costs enough to overcome their dislike of increased government regulation? Only if these conditions were met would the public have caused elected officials to fear returning for the midterm elections empty-handed more than voting for legislation the full effect of which could not be foreseen and that would create as many losers and winners.

The job of creating these conditions fell to President Clinton and his administration, who traveled and spoke across the United States on behalf of health care reform in an effort more like a presidential campaign than usual efforts to win support for legislation. This campaign had two themes: that the status quo could not be allowed to continue, and that the Clinton plan was the way to change it. The public initially and in general terms embraced the first element of this campaign, but was divided on which of the many approaches to reform was best and eventually feared to make any change at all. The president's task was to sustain public commitment to change, to persuade the citizenry that his plan was both workable and preferable to the alternatives, including the status quo, and to block off avenues of retreat so that querulous members of Congress had to stand and fight through to compromise.

In the end, President Clinton lost this campaign. He lost it in part because of the enormous difficulty of the task, in part because of genuine flaws in his plan and blunders in its presentation, in part because critics distorted and misrepresented his plan, and in part because events ranging from international crises to charges of personal improprieties distracted popular attention. The president's plan contained structural flaws and was not implementable on the schedule proposed. Critics charged the plan with shortcomings it did not possess, for example, by alleging that the president's plan narrowed patient choice among physicians, which was the opposite of the truth.

Perhaps most fundamentally, however, the trust necessary to win approval of major reform, the full consequences of which are always unpredictable, was and is wholly lacking. Successive presidents, from Carter through Bush, and countless congressional candidates have run campaigns against official Washington, alleging perverse motivations and general incompetence throughout the federal government. For all of these reasons, the chances for far-reaching health care legislation were bleak from the outset.

With the American public unsure of the nature of the problem, distrustful of elected officials, and wildly unenthusiastic about the Clinton recipe for reform,[12] elected officials retained their preferred option—to resolve doubts in favor of tinkering rather than large-scale reform.

---

12. In recounting travels on behalf of the Clinton plan, one high administration official told me, "I have heard many things on my travels, but one phrase I have never heard: 'We have to have the Clinton plan.'"

## 4.10   Next Steps

The trends that led President Clinton to place reform of health care financing at the top of his domestic legislative agenda will not change.

Rising federal health care spending fully accounts for all of the projected increase in the federal deficit and more over the next decade. If federal spending on health care grew no faster than gross domestic product, the federal deficit would decline to less than 1% of gross domestic product by 2004. Given current projections, the deficit will reach a trough at 2.3% of gross domestic product in 1998 and then rise to 3.5% in 2004 and continue increasing.

The principal force driving up health care costs—the proliferation of medical technology—shows no signs of abating (Schwartz 1994; Schwartz and Mendelson 1994; Aaron 1991; Newhouse 1992).

Reports abound that private efforts to control costs have slowed the rise of national spending, but little evidence can be found to support such claims in the growth of health care spending as a share of gross domestic product. Health care spending deflated by the gross domestic product deflator as reported in the national income accounts rose an average 6.3% from 1980 through 1990, 5.7% from 1990 through 1992, and 5.7% in 1993. Whatever their promise for cost containment, privately initiated financing reforms have yielded little so far. For a further discussion of this subject, see Levit et al. 1994; Huskamp and Newhouse 1994; Aaron 1994.

In the face of these trends, the behavioral responses that have caused unease among the American public regarding the security of coverage are likely to intensify. Governments are likely to continue to abuse their market power as the largest purchasers to buy services at marginal cost, shifting overhead costs to private payers. Large employers and health providers with the buying clout to negotiate discounts from hospitals and physician groups will engage in a similar game. Both technological advance and intensified cost shifting will strengthen incentives for employers to cut back generous fringe benefits and to buy from suppliers with meager fringe benefits items they previously made themselves. As governments and companies yield to these temptations, the reach of private health insurance will continue to shrink.

Without some form of national action, there is little reason to think that health insurance coverage will stop narrowing or that total health care spending will stop rising at excessive rates. Restrictions on private insurance companies, such as mandatory reissue, limits on denial of insurance for preexisting conditions, or limits on premium variability will help some people to buy or retain insurance. But the net effect on coverage is unclear. These reforms bring coverage to people who have higher than average expected health care costs. The inclusion of these people in insurance pools would raise premiums for many of the currently insured. As a result, some currently insured would drop coverage. Even some who believe that privately initiated reforms will retard the growth of spending acknowledge that it will take many years for reforms to become nationally effective.

Despite these trends, the conditions under which health care reform could once again be the leading legislative priority of a Washington administration are hard to imagine. Natural political selection guarantees the extinction of candidates who revel in glorious defeats. President Clinton, having staked his administration's domestic agenda on health care financing reform, is seen to have failed in that effort. Persuading Democratic members of Congress to shoulder once again the herculean labor of working through the complexities of health care reform will likely be impossible. And Republican members of Congress are unlikely to reward a president they see as vulnerable by backing legislation he would find it congenial to sign and that members of his own party refused to embrace.

The revival of health insurance as a national issue will await the conjunction of two events. The first is intensification of the problems of rising cost and insecurity of coverage. As noted, I believe that this condition will be achieved almost automatically. The second condition is identification of incremental measures that promise comprehensible, tangible progress in solving these problems. Such reforms should be consistent with long-term, nonincremental goals, but must not, like recent proposals, promise institutional turmoil or demand broad trust of elected officials.

Progress toward the goals of universal coverage and reduction in the inflationary consequences of moral hazard will be possible only when two conditions are satisfied. The first is creation of entities capable of administering measures to achieve these goals. A key element of all of the major reform proposals is the creation of some form of regionally based, politically legitimated, administratively capable entity (or entities) that have the knowledge, data, and staff to enforce order in the financing of health care. President Clinton called such entities regional health alliances. Senator Chafee and Representative Cooper called them purchasing cooperatives. Privately proposed reforms also called for such entities, according to Alain Enthoven and Richard Kronick (1989) and Aaron (1991).

In 1994, the idea of a single administrative entity for each geographical area proved politically unacceptable. Such entities, it was feared, would limit individual freedom to choose providers, function as clumsy and unresponsive monopolies, or choke off financial innovation. Most of these fears were unjustified or could have been put to rest with simple revisions. But the idea died.

Despite its political failure, the impulse that led reformers of widely varying stance to recognize the need for such regionally based entities is solidly based. Sponsors of alliances or purchasing cooperatives had divergent visions of the powers such entities should have. But they recognized that freely operating insurance markets suffer from a variety of widely studied imperfections, most of which arise from informational asymmetries. Furthermore, the bedrock of freely operating insurance markets, the incentive to price insurance at expected cost (which takes the form of pricing based on retrospective use, so-called experience rating), produces dubious social and economic consequences (Aaron 1994).

Successful reform of health care financing requires the creation of entities capable of doing what alliances and purchasing cooperatives were expected to do—enforce rules regarding the marketing of insurance, enforce premium limits, provide subsidies to needy households, and act as conduits for the flow of funds from payers to providers. Some of these functions may, in the end, be left to other organs of government. Federal legislation or state action can create such entities. Competing alliances or cooperatives can be allowed to exist, without entirely vitiating their functions and purpose, although single entities in each geographical area have important advantages.

The second condition that must be satisfied is the realization in practice of some of the reform measures that now exist only as intellectual abstractions. The Clinton plan, for example, depended on regional alliances, which exist nowhere; subsidy payment schemes unlike those under any current program; risk-adjustment payments to insurers, of whose feasibility some scholars are highly skeptical; and the elimination of inefficiencies that, by their very existence, have defied previous efforts to economize. If, as Louis Brandeis said, the states are the laboratories of democracy, it is important to encourage states to undertake efforts to deal with these issues in a practical way. The ERISA now effectively bars states from dealing comprehensively with health care, because it bars states from regulating self-insured health plans, which now cover more than half of all workers. Multistate employers have legitimate concerns that repeal of this ERISA protection would expose them to disparate regulations in every state where they now operate. While it is important to honor these concerns, many self-insured plans are operated by employers whose operations are overwhelmingly within one state. One approach would be to allow states to regulate self-insured plans of employers that operate within one state. Alternatively, states could be limited in the stringency of rules that could be applied to multistate employers. In either case, measures to enable states to undertake programs that would test ideas bruited about as abstract intellectual principles in the debate of 1993 and 1994 would permit the next round of debate on health care reform to be based on more solid information.

## 4.11   Last Words

The health care reform debate should, but is not likely to, teach lessons to analysts and elected officials alike about the limits of far-reaching reforms in a constitutional democracy based on checks and balances. Except in periods of great upheaval, progress almost invariably is incremental, particularly when legislation requires the reconstruction of powerful existing institutions. Yet the U.S. electoral system rewards candidates who convey to electors strong visions of far-reaching change. The transition from campaigning to governing requires that newly elected officials, who have just shown by their victory that they can surmount an electoral process that is death defying, both literally and figuratively, plan with genuine humility about what they can accomplish. While recognizing that their rhetorical reach must often exceed their political grasp if they are to achieve anything, officials not yet bloodied by the real-life frustrations of governing must understand that the policies they propose cannot exceed the digestive capacity of the U.S. political system. A refusal to understand those limits is a recipe for official failure and popular disillusionment.

The U.S. health care system is now so large that measures to change it are guaranteed to generate fierce and well-financed opposition. The media, which thrive on exciting controversy, not sober debate, further obstruct the formation of consensus about how to proceed. In the case of health care, the media cannot be blamed, because no professional consensus exists on how best to reform the current system. The era in which reform of the health care system could be accomplished by one "big law" is over. The task for the future is to identify specific modest changes that do not require a grand consensus on the character of the ideal grand reform, but that will nudge the system in directions regarded as desirable. It is grubby and unexciting work, but somebody has to do it.

# References

Aaron, Henry J. 1991. *Serious and Unstable Condition.* Washington, DC: Brookings Institution.

———. 1994. Issues Every Plan to Reform Health Care Financing Must Confront. *Journal of Economic Perspectives* 8:31–43.

Aaron, Henry J., and William B. Schwartz. 1984. *The Painful Prescription: Rationing Hospital Care.* Washington, DC: Brookings Institution.

Altman, Lawrence K. 1994. Surgery Is Found to Fight Stroke. *New York Times,* October 1, 1.

Arrow, Kenneth. 1963. Uncertainty and the Welfare Economics of Medical Care. *American Economic Review* 53:941–73.

Brook, Robert H., and Mary E. Vaiana. 1989. *Appropriateness of Care: A Chart Book.* Washington, DC: George Washington University, National Health Policy Forum.

Cohen, Linda, and Roger Noll. 1991. *The Technology Pork Barrel.* Washington, DC: Brookings Institution.

Cromwell, Jerry, and Janet B. Mitchell. 1986. Physician-Induced Demand for Surgery. *Journal of Health Economics* 5:293–314.

Enthoven, Alain, and Richard Kronick. 1989. A Consumer-Choice Health Plan for the 1990s: Universal Health Insurance in a System Designed to Promote Quality and Economy. *New England Journal of Medicine,* January 5, 29–37; January 12, 94–101.

Feldstein, Martin. 1973. The Welfare Loss of Excess Health Insurance. *Journal of Political Economy* 81, no. 2, pt. 1:253–80.

Fuchs, Victor R. 1979. The Economics of Health in a Post-Industrial Society. *Public Interest,* 3–20.

———. 1986. Physician-Induced Demand: A Parable. *Journal of Health Economics* 5:367–68.

Huskamp, Haiden A., and Joseph Newhouse. 1994. Is Health Spending Slowing Down? *Health Affairs* 13 (winter): 32–38.

Levit, Katharine R., Cathy A. Cowan, Helen C. Lazenby, Patricia McDonnell, Arthur L. Sensenig, Jean M. Stiller, and Darleen K. Won. 1994. National Health Spending Trends, 1960–1993. *Health Affairs* 13 (winter): 14–31.

Miller, Robert H., and Harold S. Luft. 1994. Managed Care Plan Performance since 1980: A Literature Analysis. *Journal of the American Medical Association* 271:1512–19.

Newhouse, Joseph. 1992. Medical Care Costs: How Much Welfare Loss? *Journal of Economic Perspectives* 6:3–21.

Okun, Arthur M. 1975. *Equality and Efficiency: The Big Tradeoff.* Washington, DC: Brookings Institution.

Parkin, David, Alistair McGuire, and Brian Yule. 1987. Aggregate Health Care Expenditures and National Income: Is Health Care a Luxury Good? *Journal of Health Economics* 6 (June): 109–28.

Pauly, Mark. 1968. The Economics of Moral Hazard. *American Economic Review* 58:531–37.

Phelps, Victor R. 1986. Induced Demand: Can We Ever Know Its Extent? *Journal of Health Economics* 5:355–66.

Schelling, Thomas. 1984. *Choice and Consequence.* Cambridge: Harvard University Press.

Schwartz, William B. 1994. In the Pipeline: A Wave of Valuable Medical Technology. *Health Affairs* 13 (summer): 70–79.

Schwartz, William B., and Daniel Mendelson. 1994. Eliminating Waste and Inefficiency Can Do Little to Contain Costs. *Health Affairs* 13 (spring): 224–38.

Stiglitz, Joseph E., and Michael Rothschild. 1976. Equilibrium in Competitive Insurance Markets: An Essay on Imperfect Information. *Quarterly Journal of Economics* 90:129–49.

U.S. Congress. Office of Technology Assessment. 1993. *Pharmaceutical R&D: Costs, Risks, and Rewards.* OTA-H-522. Washington, DC: Government Printing Office.

# Comment    Martin Feldstein

Although I disagree profoundly with many of the assumptions and conclusions of Henry Aaron's paper, I think it is useful because it raises fundamental issues about health care and health care financing that economists should be considering. The decisive political and popular rejection of the Clinton health plan and of the related congressional plans in 1994 may remove proposals for the radical reform of health care financing from the political agenda during the next few years. But a half century of historic experience suggests that the issue will resurface again before long. With health care spending now exceeding 14% of GDP and soon to be the largest component of the government budget, economists should be thinking about the effects of alternative reforms in anticipation of that renewed political interest.

Martin Feldstein is the George F. Baker Professor of Economics at Harvard University and president and chief executive officer of the National Bureau of Economic Research.

It is difficult to comment on a paper like Aaron's, which is not a technical analysis but rather a carefully nuanced policy discussion. I will therefore present a more general comment that contrasts two approaches to reforming the financing and organization of health care: tax and insurance reforms aimed at strengthening the market process and individual choice versus a nonmarket approach to the provision of health care. The first of these views reflects my own attitude. Some but not all of the alternative position is relevant to the Aaron paper.

## Strengthening the Market and Individual Choice

Health care is not like other goods and services. Because a small fraction of households incur very large medical bills each year, some form of insurance is appropriate.[1] Eighty-five % of the American population now has formal insurance coverage through private or public programs, and many of those who are technically uninsured know that their medical costs will be absorbed by the providers or by government because of their low income. For those with formal insurance coverage, patients' out-of-pocket spending at the time of care is generally 20% or less of the marginal cost of providing their care. This distorts the decisions of patients and their doctors at the time of care, inducing a consumption of medical care that patients and doctors value at far less than its cost of production.

Although financial risk aversion implies that some insurance is desirable, in the second-best outcome individuals would balance the gains and losses from increased insurance such that at the margin the additional deadweight loss that results from the excess consumption of medical services would be balanced by the additional reduction of financial risk. This would lead to much larger copayments than we now observe.[2] The current excessive insurance coverage reflects the tax rules that exclude employer-financed health insurance from taxable income. The combination of a 28% marginal federal income tax rate, a 15.3% combined employer-employee Social Security payroll tax, and state income and sales taxes means that many employees choose between a dollar of employer-paid health insurance premiums and 50 cents of after-tax spendable income. The resulting revenue loss to the federal government alone is esti-

1. Aaron's comments suggest that he believes that private insurance may soon not be feasible because insurance companies will have the technological capacity to predict which individuals will incur large medical expenses. A perfectly predictable event is not insurable. Although some genetic screening now does permit identifying individuals who are more likely to develop some diseases, this relates to a very small number of examples and, while identifying higher-risk individuals, is very far from predicting those who will become ill.

2. See Feldstein and Gruber (1995) for an explicit evaluation of the welfare gain that could be achieved by shifting from existing insurance coverage to plans with substantially higher copayments. A system in which individuals select the policy that reflects their own individual tastes and risk assessments would involve self-selection problems that can be overcome in practice by the use of employer-based plans and other natural groups. Although the requirement that all members of the group choose from a limited range of insurance options reduces the welfare gain from tailoring coverage to individual preferences, the higher copayment plans can still raise welfare substantially relative to the current very comprehensive insurance.

mated to be $79 billion a year. It is not surprising therefore that individuals choose excess health insurance and therefore excess health care spending.

Some of us would like to see the government remedy this tax system distortion, hoping thereby to encourage a market in which individual preferences and individual willingness to pay would be reflected in a diversity of insurance alternatives. Without the tax distortion,[3] some individuals would want indemnity policies with high copayments, accepting the additional financial risk in order to reduce the costly distortion in the consumption of health services. Others would join prepaid groups (HMOs), accepting the risk that providers will offer less than the optimal amount of care rather than accept the high premium cost of traditional low-copayment plans or the higher financial risk of indemnity plans with large coinsurance. The key point is that this second-best outcome would reflect the diversity of individual preferences.[4]

Not all economists who have studied health care accept this as the appropriate goal for policy. Some of them would prefer a "single-payer" government monopoly at the national level, rather like the traditional English National Health Service. Others hope for a sequence of political actions that would lead eventually to some system of regionally based prepaid health care systems in which all individuals would receive the same care regardless of tastes or willingness to pay. Since individual preferences and willingness to pay are not to count under such arrangements, the government must decide the aggregate spending on health care and then leave it to physicians to use the health care budget in what they regard as the technologically best way. Since all individuals are to receive the same package of financing and benefits, the financing must be equivalent to a combination of substantial subsidies and taxes. The experience with all of the 1994 health care financing proposals indicate that such a tax would involve a sharp increase in marginal tax rates as the implied subsidy at low and moderate incomes is phased out.

### Nonmarket Solutions

Why do some health specialists propose a nonmarket solution for the financing and organization of health care? My reading of their papers suggests three reasons that alone or in combination also explain why many other health care writers favor government provision.

*A Desire for Greater Equality.* Since health care spending is a very large part of personal consumption, an increase in government finance of health spending

---

3. The tax distortion could be eliminated or reduced by ending or limiting the current exclusion of employer insurance payments from taxable income. A similar and politically more likely effect might be achieved by allowing uninsured health care to be paid for with pretax dollars.

4. Many writers on health care reform assume that the appropriate care for each individual is a technical question that physicians can answer. In reality, the combination of technological uncertainty and heterogeneous preferences means that the appropriate treatment for many conditions will depend on individual preferences and not just on medical facts. This in turn implies that the appropriate form of insurance will also differ from individual to individual. I return to this later in this comment. See also Feldstein (1995) for a discussion of this issue.

(whether directly through the budget or indirectly through a system of mandates on employers or insurance companies) could substantially equalize households' cash available for spending on other things. The experience of the 1960s showed that voters are more willing to support income redistribution disguised as specific in-kind benefits (of which the clearest example is food stamps, a cash equivalent masquerading as a feeding program) than explicit income redistribution through cash transfers.

Some health specialists regard the equality of health care as specifically desirable. They compare health care to votes, implying that complete equality is the appropriate standard. I don't see why health care is like votes. Voting directs government power over others. If your vote is effective, it is likely to affect my well-being directly. An individual's purchase of health care does not have such externalities.[5] The nature of voting is also such that an increase in the number of votes that you have reduces the value of my votes. In contrast, an increase in the amount of health care that you consume does not reduce the availability of health care to me any more than is true for other goods and services. With a time horizon of a few years or longer, health care is not specifically scarce. As the rapid growth in health care spending shows, the American economy is able to expand the resources devoted to providing health care very rapidly.

The ability to purchase better health care for oneself and one's family, like the ability to purchase better food or housing or education, is a strong economic motivator. Taking health care out of the marketplace would weaken overall economic incentives even if there were no change in the link between effort and disposable money income.

*A Distrust of Individuals' Choices of Insurance and Health Care.* It is easy to agree with the proposition that choosing health insurance and medical care involves complex decisions without jumping to the conclusion that individuals should be denied the right to choose. If the government knows what insurance is best, government experts could provide that information without requiring that we accept it. Similarly, government experts could indicate what they believe is the "right" treatment for any given condition without requiring that patients and their doctors accept that advice. Consumer ignorance provides a rationale for information, not for government control.

If it were appropriate for the government to control consumption of any type of good and service about which individuals are not fully informed, there would be few things that could not be shifted to government control. We need only think about how little individuals know about the food they eat and the cars they drive.

---

5. To the extent that health spending involves externalities, it is because of too little spending. We may all have a reason for wanting others to get at least some minimum level of care. But that is very different from wanting all care to be equal.

The government's ability to make good decisions in health insurance and health care is also very doubtful. The insurance coverage provided by Medicare and Medicaid is the most old-fashioned indemnity plan. Private industry and individual choice have been the innovators that have developed managed care, point-of-service plans, and so forth. And the Veterans Administration hospitals are models of government inefficiency in the provision of care.

*An Indifference to the Diversity of Individual Tastes.* The effects on health and longevity of diet, exercise, smoking, alcohol, and other aspects of lifestyle are widely known. Some people act in all the ways that the health experts tell us are good for us, while most of us do so to a more limited extent. People do not injure their future health and reduce their life expectancy just because of ignorance or because of an inability to afford better habits, but because they find a less virtuous lifestyle more enjoyable. The same diversity of tastes for health and for other pleasures of life suggests that, among any large group of individuals with the same income, some would want to spend more on medical care and others would want to spend less so that they could spend more on other things.

Differences in taste also extend to insurance. Just as individuals with different risk tolerances hold different investment portfolios and choose different careers, those individuals would, ceteris paribus, want different health insurance. Those individuals who want to spend more on health would also generally want more comprehensive insurance.

Many writers on health care seem to me to give no consideration at all to these differences in preferences. Like so many physicians and health planners, they appear to view the choice of medical care as a technical decision in which preferences are irrelevant. In fact, there is overwhelming uncertainty about how patients should be treated under many medical situations, uncertainty that can only be resolved with reference to patients' preferences.[6]

## The Legislative Rejection of the 1994 Health Proposals

Henry Aaron devotes a substantial portion of his paper to discussing why Congress did not enact the health care plans proposed by President Clinton, Senator Mitchell, and others. He offers several reasons, but his primary explanation is that the American public accepts a radical new government program only when the national situation is one of extreme disorder and there is a high degree of faith that the government leaders are trustworthy and capable. He concludes that neither condition prevailed in 1994 and that it was therefore

6. Consider, for example, the treatment of cancer of the breast or the prostate. Alternative treatments have different residual risks for the rest of the patients' lives and different effects on the individuals' enjoyment of life. Or consider that older people have different attitudes about the amount of care they should be given if they become very ill. Why should the government impose the same standard of care on all individuals? Why should the financing cost be the same for individuals with different tastes for health care?

impossible to enact a proposal that, as he characterizes it, was change on a greater scale than anything ever done before except the wartime mobilization of World War II.

That diagnosis suggests that a more modest series of changes could gradually gain acceptance and bring us ultimately to a system that the public was unwilling to accept in one step. I hope that the public will not be fooled into accepting radical reform in small steps.

I believe that most Americans do not favor the status quo in health care and would support a modest reform package that focuses on some of the problems of the existing private insurance system, including new rules that would prevent the exclusion of preexisting conditions for job changers and the cancellation of coverage by insurance companies. Indeed, these were the features that President Clinton emphasized in his most popular appeal: insurance that cannot be taken away. I believe that the 85% of Americans who have insurance would welcome that reform and that many of the remaining 15% would find that it permitted them to obtain and keep coverage.

But that is not what the Clinton administration or the congressional leaders, including Mitchell, Chafee, and Cooper, offered. They put forward a take-it-or-leave-it package that emphasized vast expenses and, in the Clinton plan, tight controls on government spending. Although the issues were complex, I think the American public rejected this take-it-or-leave-it offer for three reasons.[7]

First, they did not want government to limit their health spending. They might want to spend less, and they might be willing to accept such things as HMO plans and point-of-service insurance contracts that achieve lower costs, but they do not trust the government to control health care.

Second, they did not want to pay a great deal in taxes or lost wages to redistribute income to those with incomes above the poverty level who already have health insurance and who would have gotten most of the subsidies under the various plans.

Third, although they believe that no one should be denied needed health care because of an inability to pay, they did not want to pay tens of billions of dollars in taxes each year to give *formal* insurance coverage to those who now receive free care for major problems and to provide equal care for those who are now uninsured. Americans recognize that the care received by the poor, especially when they are well or have minor problems but sometimes even when they have more serious problems, is not as good as the care received by the average American family, but understand that that is true also for their housing, their food, their schools, and virtually everything else.

Looking ahead, the interesting question raised by the legislative outcome of 1994 is whether the supporters of radical take-it-or-leave-it reform in 1994 will

7. These issues are discussed in more detail in several articles that I wrote for the *Wall Street Journal* and that appear in the references to this comment.

now accept the more modest reforms of private insurance or will continue to try to hold those popular reforms hostage to their more radical agenda.

## References

Feldstein, Martin. 1993. Clinton's Hidden Health Tax. *Wall Street Journal,* November 10.

———. 1994a. A Hidden $100 Billion Tax Increase. *Wall Street Journal,* August 9.

———. 1994b. Income Based Subsidies Won't Work. *Wall Street Journal,* June 17.

———. 1994c. Mandates Would Hurt the Middle Class. *Wall Street Journal,* July 21.

———. 1995. The Economics of Health and Health Care: What Have We Learned? What Have I Learned? *American Economic Review* 85 (May): 28–31.

Feldstein, Martin, and Jonathan Gruber. 1995. A Major Risk Approach to Health Insurance Reform. In *Tax Policy and the Economy,* ed. James Poterba. NBER Working Paper no. 4852. Cambridge, MA: National Bureau of Economic Research, September.

# 5     To Comfort Always: The Prospects of Expanded Social Responsibility for Long-Term Care

Alan M. Garber

> But whoever has the greatest number of the good things I have mentioned, and keeps them to the end, and dies a peaceful death, that man, my lord Croesus, deserves in my opinion to be called happy.
>> Look to the end, no matter what it is you are considering.
>
> Solon's response to Croesus, who asked, Who is the happiest man? Herodotus, *Histories*, book 1

Longevity is a cornerstone of modern conceptions of the good life. Although the desire for a long life is not unique to modern times, the expectation that most people will live beyond sixty-five years of age is a phenomenon of twentieth-century industrialized nations. Mortality rates at the turn of the century, when life expectancy was about fifty years, implied that only about four of ten newly born American children could expect to survive to age sixty-five. By 1989 nearly eight of ten could expect to reach sixty-five (National Center for Health Statistics 1992). Yet if the happiness of a life is judged by its end, these impressive gains in longevity are a mixed blessing. Even if they have financial security, none who live to advanced ages can escape the risk that they will suffer years of discomfort, disability, and dependence before they die. Those whose final years are marked by infirmity do not keep to the end the "good things" that Solon identified as part the happy life—among them sound body, health, and "freedom from trouble." They suffer from the disabling effects of diseases and injuries that medical treatment can neither cure nor fully relieve.

Thus of the three aims of medical care in the old maxim, "To cure seldom, to relieve often, to comfort always," only comfort is achievable. Long-term care is the chief means of providing such comfort. Individual, family, and soci-

Alan M. Garber is Health Services Research and Development Senior Research Associate at the Palo Alto Department of Veterans Affairs Medical Center. He is also associate professor of medicine at the Stanford University School of Medicine and a research associate and director of the Health Care Program of the National Bureau of Economic Research.

This chapter builds on the author's research supported by the National Institute on Aging, the Henry J. Kaiser Family Foundation, the Robert Wood Johnson Foundation, and the Department of Veterans Affairs.

ety have long shared responsibility for long-term care, in a shifting and uneasy balance. Different views about both the feasibility and appropriateness of an expanded public role in providing and financing long-term care are at the center of American debates about long-term care policy, which is only one contentious aspect of broader deliberations about reforming health care. Long-term care carries special significance, though, because the people who use long-term care are often helpless, always dependent upon others, and unlikely to return to full health and function. For many of them, long-term care is a necessity, and for others, it ameliorates the effects of mental and physical decline.

Notwithstanding differences in the goals of care, in important respects long-term care is similar to other health services. Like hospital and physicians' services, it is designed to ease the burden of illness. The federal government insures a substantial fraction of the care, which is also expensive—the average cost of a year in a nursing home is about $20,000 in the United States, and is higher if Medicaid-financed stays are excluded. But long-term care fundamentally differs from other health services. The population that uses it is more sharply circumscribed, limited mainly to the severely disabled elderly. And although survival is sometimes difficult or impossible without it, long-term care is never lifesaving in the same sense that, say, emergency surgery following an automobile accident can be. Nonmarket services play an important role in long-term care, which is a close substitute for nonhealth services, such as housing and food. Much of the care is basic and humanitarian—such as shelter, food preparation, and assistance in walking and personal hygiene.

It is the mode of financing, however, that most clearly sets long-term care apart. Private long-term care insurance developed slowly and never became popular. The near absence of private insurance has been blamed as the fundamental shortcoming of long-term care financing, while the wide dissemination of insurance is regularly cast as the culprit responsible for uncontrolled growth in expenditures for physicians' and hospital services. The wider adoption of private long-term care insurance has the potential to bring to long-term care the very problems that health care reform is designed to solve, and it is unlikely to address all the real and apparent deficiencies of long-term care financing. The recognition that the failure of private insurance is not accidental must temper any hope that private insurance can be the sole means of reducing risk and improving access to long-term care. Nevertheless, I will argue that it is a promising approach to better risk protection for those persons in situations in which it is most appropriate.

The central conceptual questions confronting policies toward long-term care financing are common to all social insurance: how should any (government) policy balance insurance, savings, and redistributional features, and how should it relate to private activities? I briefly discuss below the political consequences of redistributive policies, but most of my comments address the mix between savings and insurance, and public and private financing. I will argue that the most successful policies to improve access to long-term care emphasize increased private savings. Savings alone will not be enough; because a small fraction of the elderly account for most long-term care expenditures, the savings required to self-finance such care might result in undesirably large bequests for many of the elderly. Furthermore, the poor and near-poor elderly lack the assets and income needed to save for long-term care or to purchase insurance. Finally, increased savings, or indeed any reform of financing long-term care, is not a panacea, and some of the most vexing problems of long-term care have little to do with financing. The poor quality of some nursing homes, for example, has less to do with financing than with the inability to monitor the quality of care and the weak incentives some nursing homes have to improve quality. Policies designed to encourage individual savings will not solve every problem yet, I will argue, should be central to reform efforts. Expanded insurance, for example, is unlikely to be successful as the principal mode of financing long-term care; the costs would be insupportable if insurance were not coupled with savings features, and an insurance approach that controlled costs might deter the development of promising alternatives to traditional forms of long-term care. Financing universal long-term care insurance from public dollars hardly seems feasible today, and circumstances will not be more favorable in the coming years.

## 5.1   The Basic Facts of Long-Term Care

### 5.1.1   What It Is

The constellation of services that compose long-term care range from limited home-based assistance to comprehensive care in an institution. The services are frequently targeted at the specific physical and/or mental limitations of the patient but, in contrast to most medical care, are rarely aimed at a specific disease. They aid in coping with the irreversible consequences of one or (more often) multiple diseases, rather than curing them. Although not all long-term care is of indefinite or even prolonged duration—nursing home admissions can be brief, particularly when they aid in convalescence from an acute illness or operation—even patients who use long-term care for brief periods usually need it because chronic diseases and disabilities delay or impede their recovery from an acute condition.

Long-term care is traditionally delivered either in institutional (inpatient) or community settings. Institutional services are most prominent and account for the bulk of expenditures. This category includes skilled nursing (certified by Medicare to provide an appropriate range of medical, nursing, and rehabilitative services), intermediate care (offering a narrower range of professional services), and custodial facilities (basic housing and related services for persons whose disability is severe and irreversible), along with a variety of other institutional arrangements, such as hospices (for terminal care) and board and care homes, which provide meals but no professional services. In 1985 about 1.3 million, or 4.6% of all Americans sixty-five years of age and older, could be found in a nursing home at any time (National Center for Health Statistics 1994, 193).

Community-based long-term care encompasses a diverse set of services, including home health care from a visiting nurse or physical therapist, respite care, home meal preparation or delivery, day care programs, and a host of other services. Many such formally designated home health services are covered by insurance programs. The number of elderly Americans receiving some form of paid home health services approached one million in 1992 (Strahan 1993).

Modern developments have blurred the distinctions among these categories of long-term care, and even distinctions between long-term care and acute medical services. For example, social/health maintenance organizations (SHMOs) add nursing home and related long-term care services to standard medical care benefits offered by prepaid capitated health plans. Besides applying capitation to long-term care, this approach allows the health maintenance organization (HMO) to internalize long-term care, reducing the distortion in trade-offs between covered and noncovered services. Congregate living arrangements, such as life care communities or continuing care retirement communities, combine housing and other services with features of long-term care insurance. These facilities charge high prices for entry, along with monthly fees that are typically higher than condominium fees but may also pay for board and long-term care services if the member requires them. The services, and housing, are matched to the needs of the member, so in some of the communities the person may move from a fully independent existence in an apartment, then to a facility that provides limited support services, and finally to a nursing home, all without leaving the congregate setting. Although other forms of senior housing rarely offer the full array of services of a life care community, most facilities provide some assistance, such as meal preparation, whether or not they explicitly incorporate insurance features. Such arrangements can make assisted living more attractive. Unlike typical nursing home admissions, which remove the disabled elderly from friends and often spouses, the continuum of care available in some life care communities makes it possible to remain in a nearby building despite deterioration in one's health. Furthermore, they can better integrate home health and institutional services.

Perhaps the most important form of long-term care, "informal" (nonmarket) home services, is measured poorly and does not appear in national income accounts. The National Long-Term Care Survey, which was administered to a random sample of Americans sixty-five years of age and older, revealed that 19% of Medicare recipients had functional impairments expected to last at least three months (Macken 1986), of whom 90% received some form of assistance from family members (Rivlin and Wiener 1988). Spouses and children (usually adult daughters) of the disabled elderly may spend many hours each day preparing meals, helping them to eat, bathe, and walk, and even helping them to the toilet. Family members who provide such care often reduce their own hours of paid work or leave the labor force. A study of informal home health services for terminally ill cancer patients reported that family members provided ten hours of care daily, and that one-third of the caregivers who worked at the outset of the care episode dropped out of the labor force. Even if the patient received hospice care as an outpatient, though, the terminal illness caused about 22% of the caregivers to leave their jobs. In this study, caregivers who continued working lost $605 per episode of illness, and those who left the labor force lost $2,582 (Muurinen 1986). Because few hospice patients live long, the income forgone for the care of the disabled elderly who are not in the final stages of a terminal illness is likely to be far greater. When such support is no longer available or sufficient, whether through the death of a spouse, the exhaustion of a daughter, worsening disability, or supervening illness, nursing home admission often results.

### 5.1.2   Utilization

Discussions of long-term care policy often focus on the more than one million elderly Americans in nursing homes and, to a lesser extent, the million or so who use paid home health services. But about four million elderly Americans receive informal assistance for chronic impairments. Although they may not generate expenditures for long-term care, they are at risk of doing so. Limited evidence suggests that the (age-adjusted) functional status of the elderly is improving along with life expectancy. As the baby boom grows older, however, there will be a dramatic increase in the number of people who have reached the ages at which disability is common. The cohort effect is so large that it is likely to overwhelm any improvement in age-adjusted disability rates, stimulating an increase in the use of both formal and informal long-term care.

Most research on long-term care utilization has focused on its most expensive component, nursing homes. Three questions relevant to long-term care insurance predominate in the literature: who is likely to enter a nursing home, what is the distribution of utilization, and to what extent do other (lower-cost) forms of long-term care substitute for nursing homes? A smaller literature addresses the issue that may be most critical to long-term care insurance: how price sensitive is demand?

*Predictors of Utilization*

Important predictors of institutionalization are advanced age, limitations in the ability to carry out one or more basic "activities of daily living" (ADLs), cognitive impairment, and the absence of a spouse or children who provide care (Wingard, Jones, and Kaplan 1987). As it happens, similar characteristics also predict mortality. Although the frail elderly may live with functional impairments for many years before they die, disability is associated with increased mortality. And as death nears, utilization of long-term care increases. As is well known, utilization of hospital and physicians' services increases in the last year of life. The same appears to be true of nursing home utilization, as Anne Scitovsky (1988) reported in a study of Palo Alto residents. In analyses of the National Long-Term Care Survey and the National Nursing Home Survey, Thomas MaCurdy and I (1992) found a similar pattern: in the final year of life, the very old use nursing homes much more heavily than do survivors of the same age and sex. Entry to a nursing home, then, is commonly an event that occurs in the last stages of life. These observations account for one of the difficulties in identifying people likely to enter nursing homes: those who appear to be at very high risk of institutionalization often die before they are admitted or soon thereafter. One of the most important randomized trials of interventions designed to prevent institutionalization focused on a group of elderly individuals whose disabilities were thought to place them at extremely high risk of entering a nursing home; instead, very high death rates caused nursing home utilization in the control group to fall short of expectations (Kemper 1988).

### Distribution of Utilization

The skew in the distribution of nursing home utilization, combined with its substantial cost, would seem to make long-term care insurance highly attractive. A sizable minority of Americans who reach age sixty-five can expect to enter a nursing home sometime before they die (Kemper and Murtaugh 1991; Dick, Garber, and MaCurdy 1994). Most admissions are brief, but a small fraction of the people who enter account for most nursing home care. Keeler, Kane, and Solomon (1981) were among the first to explore the mix of long- and short-stayers in nursing homes; they found that long-stayers were far more likely to have diagnoses of mental disorders and senility, while short-stayers tended to have diagnoses of fractures and cancers. According to our analyses of more recent national cohorts of the elderly, although fewer than 1% of Americans are in nursing homes at age sixty-five, 35% can expect to enter a nursing home (Dick, Garber, and MaCurdy 1994). Our results, presented in table 5.1, show that most admissions are brief. A smaller minority, however, will have very long stays. The 90th percentile of nursing home utilization is seventeen months for men and twenty-nine months for women.

### Substitution and Price Sensitivity

Of fundamental importance to long-term care policy are two questions about utilization: how well do noninstitutional services prevent or substitute for institutionalization, and how price sensitive is the demand for nursing home care? If home services are close substitutes for nursing home care, they might enable people to remain in the community and delay, if not prevent, institutionalization. Institutionalization is viewed as both an expensive and unattractive living arrangement.[1] The right set of services, delivered at the right time, might fore-

---

1. Most estimates of the cost of nursing home care include expenditures for nursing home care but not savings that result from entry, which primarily accrue from reduced housing expenses. This approach may be valid for short stays but not for prolonged institutionalization. The typical nursing home patient was living alone before admission; if she is permanently institutionalized, by definition she no longer uses housing outside the nursing home. Savings on housing expenses partially offset nursing home costs. Furthermore, many patients require around-the-clock observation or care, which likely costs far less when delivered in an institution than in the community.

**Table 5.1**              **Simulations of Nursing Home Utilization Rates**

|  | Mean | 5% | 10% | 25% | Median | 75% | 90% | 95% |
|---|---|---|---|---|---|---|---|---|
| Number of nursing home admissions | 1 | 0 | 0 | 0 | 0 | 1 | 2 | 2 |
| Male | 1 | 0 | 0 | 0 | 0 | 1 | 1 | 2 |
| Female | 1 | 0 | 0 | 0 | 0 | 1 | 2 | 2 |
| Total nursing home utlization (months) | 7 | 0 | 0 | 0 | 0 | 2 | 23 | 50 |
| Male | 6 | 0 | 0 | 0 | 0 | 2 | 17 | 37 |
| Female | 9 | 0 | 0 | 0 | 0 | 3 | 29 | 61 |
| Nursing home utilization for those with at least 1 admission (months) | 21 | 1 | 1 | 2 | 6 | 27 | 66 | 88 |
| Male | 16 | 1 | 1 | 1 | 4 | 20 | 50 | 71 |
| Female | 25 | 1 | 1 | 2 | 9 | 34 | 75 | 101 |
| Spell length of 1st nursing home admissions (months) | 14 | 1 | 1 | 1 | 3 | 14 | 48 | 69 |
| Male | 11 | 1 | 1 | 1 | 2 | 9 | 34 | 54 |
| Female | 17 | 1 | 1 | 1 | 3 | 18 | 57 | 83 |
| Age at death (months after 65th birthday) | 208 | 43 | 67 | 129 | 204 | 284 | 350 | 380 |
| Male | 186 | 38 | 61 | 115 | 183 | 252 | 317 | 352 |
| Female | 224 | 48 | 75 | 142 | 225 | 309 | 366 | 398 |

*Source:* Dick, Garber, and MaCurdy forthcoming.

stall nursing home admission. If effective, lower-cost substitutes for nursing home care were available, one might think that the elderly and their families would take advantage of them, especially because many of them would initially bear the full cost of nursing home admission. Of course, the cognitive impairment that is common among the disabled elderly might make it particularly difficult to locate appropriate home health services. But a review of the best-designed trials of home health care suggests an alternative explanation: home care does not serve as a close substitute for nursing home care. The review concluded that home care services have no impact on mortality, functional status, or nursing home utilization (Hedrick and Inui 1986). People who are admitted to nursing homes may simply need so much assistance that it is prohibitively expensive or infeasible to provide the services at home. The Channeling Demonstration was perhaps the most prominent trial of the impact of intensified community-based care on rates of institutionalization. It did not test home care directly, but rather the assignment of a case manager to the patients in the intervention group. The case manager was given the responsibility for ensuring that patients would receive the full range of home services that might benefit them, with a view toward improving function and avoiding institutionalization. Case management increased the utilization of home health services, patient satisfaction, and overall costs, but did not prevent institutionalization, death, or the deterioration of other aspects of health (Kemper 1988; Thornton, Dunstan, and Kemper 1988; Wooldridge and Schore 1988).

Studies like these, which indicate that home health services are poor substitutes for nursing homes, suggest that the price elasticity of demand for nursing home care is small. Some policy positions assume that this is the case. Nursing home stays are feared and widely seen as unpleasant, a last resort for an individual whose condition is so hopeless and needs for care so great that neither family nor formal home care services can provide them. The major goal of insurance coverage for long-term care, according to this view, is redistribution of the costs of care, not increased utilization.

On the other hand, because it shares so many of their characteristics, nursing home care would seem to substitute for housing and personal health services. Furthermore, the price of nursing home care, especially relative to the opportunity costs of informal care, would seem at the very least to affect the timing of admission and sometimes its overall duration. The limited literature on the demand for nursing home care suggests that demand is moderately price-elastic. Chiswick (1976), in an analysis of regional data, estimated the surprisingly large price elasticity of $-2.3$. Thomas MaCurdy and I found that nursing home discharge rates were highly sensitive to changes in the daily subsidy implicit in Medicare rules (as Medicare payments phased out over the course of an admission), supporting the contention that demand is likely to be highly price sensitive (Garber and MaCurdy 1992). Price sensitivity may not characterize all segments of the elderly population; for example, in our work we dealt only with Medicare-covered nursing home admissions, which are deemed at the outset to be short-term rehabilitative stays. Individuals who are admitted to nursing homes for substantially longer, with irreversible limitations in their ability to carry out routine tasks, may not be able to alter their demand substantially in response to changes in price.

### 5.1.3   Financing

Comparison of the sources of financing for long-term care and for all other personal health expenditures, as displayed in table 5.2, reveals the unique pattern of long-term care: even though government payers account for a substantially greater proportion of expenditures for long-term care, the lack of private long-term care insurance means that the fraction of nursing home expenditures borne directly by the elderly as out-of-pocket expenditures is 43%. In contrast, out-of-pocket payments account for only about 20% of other health expenditures.

Some long-term care is mixed in other categories of health expenses. Foremost among these categories are home health services, which totaled about $9.8 billion in 1991. About 87% of home health care was reimbursed by third-party payers, primarily the federal government.

To understand how there could simultaneously be concerns that public insurance for long-term care is inadequate and that government expenditures for the same purpose are excessive, it is necessary to understand the basic rules under which the two major federal health insurance programs, Medicare and Medicaid, reimburse long-term care.

**Table 5.2    Sources of Payment for Nursing Home and All Other Personal Health Care (percentage of total expenditures, 1991)**

| | Total, Billions 1991 $ | Out-of-Pocket | Private Health Insurance | Other Private | Total Government | Medicare | Medicaid |
|---|---|---|---|---|---|---|---|
| Nursing home care | 59.9 | 43.1 | 1.1 | 1.9 | 53.9 | 4.4 | 47.4 |
| Personal health expenditures, excluding nursing homes | 600.3 | 19.7 | 34.8 | 3.7 | 41.8 | 19.6 | 11.3 |

*Source:* Adapted from Letsch et al. 1992.

*Medicare Coverage of Long-Term Care*

Nearly all elderly Americans are enrolled in Medicare, which covers hospital and physician expenditures. Although it is primarily an acute-care insurance program, it pays for home health services and, under specific circumstances, nursing home care. Medicare coverage is designed to encourage nursing home use only as a substitute for hospital care, which Medicare would need to reimburse. It is not designed to ensure against prolonged institutionalization. According to a leading Medicare benefits guidebook, "inpatient services in a skilled nursing facility are an extension of inpatient hospital care, at a lower level of care than provided in a hospital but still requiring 'skilled' nursing or rehabilitation services" (CCH Business Law Editors 1994). To qualify for Medicare reimbursement, an admission must satisfy several restrictions. Medicare pays only if the nursing home is a certified skilled-nursing facility, the admission meets a prior hospitalization requirement, the nursing home stay is for the treatment of the condition that was treated in the hospital, the admission is certified by a physician, and a utilization review committee does not disapprove the stay.

If all of these conditions are met, Medicare will pay the full cost for the first twenty days of nursing home care during a benefit period. From day twenty-one through day one hundred, Medicare imposes a copayment. Often private supplemental "medigap" policies pay for some or all of the copayment, but seldom do they extend coverage beyond one hundred days, when Medicare coverage ends. These limits mean that Medicare pays at least part of the charges for a substantial fraction of short-term nursing home admissions, but accounts for a small fraction—4.4% in 1991—of nursing home expenditures.

*Medicaid*

Medicaid's role in long-term care reflects two defining characteristics: it is jointly administered by states and the federal government, and eligibility is based on need. Because the states have considerable discretion in administering the program, eligibility and coverage rules vary by state (Ruther et al. 1991). Most of the elderly who receive Medicaid benefits qualify on the basis of extraordinary health expenses, under the "spend-down" provision of many state Medicaid programs. For states that have such a provision, Medicaid eligibility is determined by an asset test and an income test; the latter requires income minus health expenditures to fall below 133% of the income level for welfare eligibility. One or a series of nursing home admissions usually account for the health expenditures for the middle-class elderly who spend down to Medicaid eligibility. That is why Medicaid pays for nearly half of all nursing home expenditures and, conversely, why nursing homes account for such a large fraction of Medicaid expenditures. National estimates of the fraction of nursing home admissions that lead to spend-down range from 14 to 18%, with about 17% of patients admitted to nursing homes spending down within six months (Rice 1989; Adams, Meiners, and Burwell 1993). Although the popular image is one of catastrophic expenses suddenly leading the middle-class elderly to lose much of what they own before qualifying for Medicaid, the usual situation may be different. According to Sloan and Shayne (1993), most of the disabled elderly who spend down are already near poverty at the time they enter a nursing home. Furthermore, assets can be transferred as well as depleted.

By transferring assets to children and other relatives, the elderly can preserve wealth when they expect to face substantial out-of-pocket copayments for either medical or long-term care. Medicaid eligibility rules not only contain strong incentives for such behavior, but have several other consequences. For example, in several states, the asset limits place the spouses of the disabled elderly at risk of impoverishment. Joint assets are subject to the spend-down, so the spouses can lose liquid assets and their homes. Newspapers reported the spectacle of long-married elderly couples divorcing in order to protect the assets of the (relatively) healthy spouse. Thus the elderly who live in states with a medically needy category of Medicaid eligibility have free insurance against the costs of prolonged institutionalization, but qualifying for Medicaid is usually unattractive. Medicaid is also criticized as a long-term care insurance program because its expenditures for the elderly became unavailable for the care of the poor, particularly poor children, who are the program's intended beneficiaries.

*Private Long-Term Care Financing*

Most private financing comes in the form of out-of-pocket payments, medigap insurance, and private long-term care insurance. Out-of-pocket payments are considerable; the other sources of private financing are not. Medigap insurance usually covers Medicare copayments and deductibles, and may pay for some of the medical expenses that Medicare does not reimburse (such as physician fees that exceed the Medicare allowed charges, or expenditures that exceed maximum Medicare reimbursement) but infrequently covers prolonged nursing home admissions. Private long-term care insurance is designed for this purpose. It is a topic of perennial interest to insurers and policymakers, but for reasons I discuss below, the interest has not been reflected in sales of the policies (Van Gelder and Johnson 1991; Rivlin and Wiener 1988).

## 5.2    What Happened to Private Long-Term Care Financing?

The existing combination of private and public financing of long-term care has few champions. Current modes of financing provide the wrong kind of protection from risk, and, at least according to advocates of expanded long-term care services, the balance of federal coverage for health care of the elderly is too heavily weighted toward hospital and physicians' services. The most striking feature of long-term care financing, however, is not a small federal role, but the near absence of private insurance coverage. Many proposals for reform call for federal initiatives to promote private insurance, or to create federal insurance that would complement private long-term care insurance. Whatever the mix of federal and private financing, though, the key issue is why private insurance markets have been slow to develop when public long-term care financing is so roundly condemned as inadequate.

Common explanations for why consumers have failed to purchase long-term care insurance include the availability of Medicaid as an alternative, high price, and restrictive benefits (Pauly 1990). Medicaid is likely to be an important substitute for private insurance; although eligibility requires asset transfer or depletion for the middle-class and wealthier elderly, Medicaid is essentially a compulsory insurance program that assures payment for extended nursing home stays. Indeed, private insurance is unlikely to be attractive to those who are not very well off, because they give up little to become eligible for Medicaid benefits. The wealthy, on the other hand, are likely to self-insure. Only people whose assets are neither too small nor too large would be candidates for private insurance. They might choose not to purchase because the policies provide too few benefits for the costs. Explanations for the limited penetration of private insurance and the unattractiveness of the policies that are available emphasize disincentives to insurers, such as adverse selection, moral hazard, and demographic uncertainty.

Affordability, never a precise concept, is especially imprecise in this context, depending as it does on the timing of purchase and liquidity of assets. Certainly the cost of an actuarially fair policy can be well beyond the means of an elderly widow who lives alone and suffers from multiple disabilities. And like a patient who tries to buy health insurance after falling seriously ill, she is unlikely to find an insurer willing to sell a low-cost policy. Another aspect of affordability is the ability to pay: older people tend to have substantial asset wealth and relatively little income. Many of their assets—particularly housing wealth—are illiquid, so it may be difficult to draw upon assets for direct payments for long-term care or for insurance. Reverse annuity mortgages and related programs have been developed to draw upon housing wealth to pay for living needs, but have not been very popular. Such mortgages may hold little appeal for the large fraction of the elderly who seem not to wish to reduce their housing equity (Venti and Wise 1990).

Insurers also face severe disincentives to marketing long-term care insurance. According to the conventional wisdom, which developed from limited survey evidence, the elderly do not purchase private insurance because they are unaware that Medicare does not cover long-term care. This explanation is puzzling, since insurers who thought the market would be profitable should have found it worthwhile to disseminate the information themselves. Furthermore, publications describing coverage rules are widely distributed. It seems more likely that the insurers had doubts about the profitability of the market. For the potential long-term care insurer, the informational asymmetries and inefficiencies that have characterized health care insurance are magnified. Bro-chures for long-term care insurance show the consequences for buyers: many policies offer thin coverage and rigorous exclusions. Potential purchasers often eschew such policies because they question their value, not affordability.

Absent universal coverage, insurers and providers that bear risk, such as prepaid health plans, will find it difficult to overcome adverse selection unless they impose restrictions on coverage or limit sales to people too young to need long-term care. Poverty, lack of social supports, and functional disability are important risk factors for institutionalization. Although insurance companies may partially observe these characteristics, the beneficiary or family member who purchases the policy knows more about the health status and level of func-tion. Any party that indemnifies, reimburses services, or directly provides care faces these same problems.

To minimize adverse selection, most insurers adjust premiums for observ-able risks. They also impose waiting periods, exclude coverage for preexisting conditions, or exclude from coverage common conditions that may be difficult to detect in early stages. Presumably a woman at age forty or fifty has little information about her future risk of nursing home admission, relative to others at the same age. At age seventy, she is much more likely than the insurer to know whether she is particularly likely (or unlikely) to enter a nursing home.

Mandatory universal insurance avoids adverse selection, but it does not inev-itably reduce the magnitude of moral hazard. In health care, moral hazard is usually defined as a price effect, that is, by paying a substantial fraction of the cost of medical care, insurance coverage increases the quantity demanded. Housing, food, personal services, and other components of long-term care are of value to nearly all the elderly, not only those who are particularly disabled or who suffer from a specific disease. The broad value of such services makes it more likely that a price subsidy will increase demand for long-term care than for physicians and hospital services, which are targeted toward treating disease.

Even if the demand for care were inelastic in the short run, the adoption and diffusion of more costly new medical technology or the wider application of existing technology could increase long-run expenditures for the treatment of specific conditions. Thus, as the price to the consumer (the copayment) falls, the quantity demanded rises, and the long-run effects are likely to be magnified by technological change.

Traditional fee-for-service health insurance relies heavily on deductibles and copayments to reduce utilization. But this approach has fallen into disfavor, largely because most Medicare recipients reinsure for the copayments and de-ductibles, and because very extensive cost sharing appears to be necessary. If anything, even a small insurance-based subsidy for housing, for example, might be sufficient to increase demand. Payers do not rely on cost sharing alone. They also assess individuals on a case-by-case basis to determine their need for care, particularly for expensive procedures. In hospital settings this process of determining "medical necessity" for a particular patient can be costly. Insurers adopt an analogous approach to long-term care, screening the enrollee for limitations in ability to carry out routine physical tasks and other factors to ascertain that a genuine "need" for long-term care exists. Such procedures are widely used and apparently have some value, but assessment of the need for long-term care services is at a primitive stage. It relies heavily on subjective reports by the family and the enrollee, who have incentives to obscure disabilities when seeking to buy insurance, and to emphasize impairments when they seek reimbursement. For many acute medical services, laboratory tests and other measures that are less subject to direct manipulation by the enrollee are available to help determine medical necessity. Comparable measures are seldom available for long-term care. Thus, despite the many instruments payers can employ to limit its effects, moral hazard is likely to remain a significant challenge to any mechanism for insuring or providing long-term care.

Some analysts argue that uncertainty about potential liability has deterred many potential insurers from offering long-term care policies. Insurers have had limited experience marketing and administering such policies, the argument runs, and there is substantial uncertainty about the length of life and trends in the disability of the elderly. Demographic projections are, of course, subject to uncertainty, and even the sign of the trend in age-specific disability is controversial. Many long-term care insurance plans allow individuals to pay premiums that vary with the age at initial enrollment, like renewable term life insurance. If the elderly live longer but age-specific levels of disability do not diminish, insurers will face unexpected liabilities. Furthermore, if spouses and children provide less care for disabled elderly in the future, the demand for paid long-term care services will grow. On the other hand, it should be possible to reinsure or otherwise mitigate the risk of larger-than-expected claims for long-term care. Furthermore, many insurers limit potential claims by setting a daily maximum payment and an upper limit on months of coverage.

If consumers expect government bodies to offer long-term care insurance in the near future, they may conclude that the public program will obviate the need for any private policy they buy. If this is an important reason for the reluctance of elderly Americans to purchase long-term care insurance, it is one that some insurers have already addressed. Some plans have arrangements to refund premiums if government policy creates insurance with similar coverage for all elderly Americans.

Private long-term care insurance may become an important source of financing despite the limited role it has played so far. Private insurance became more attractive in the late 1980s, when many plans eliminated prior hospitalization requirements for nursing home admission and promised benefits for a longer period. Exclusions for such conditions as Alzheimer's disease and for preexisting conditions became less common. Finally, a greater proportion of policies guaranteed renewability (Van Gelder and Johnson 1991). These features undoubtedly contributed to their rising popularity. The Health Insurance Association of America reported that in 1988 the number of companies selling long-term care insurance was six times the number in 1984. By December 1988 an estimated 1.1 million policies had been sold. It may be several years before growing enrollment is reflected in the share of payments covered by insurance, especially if the purchasers are in relatively good health. Thus it seems likely that private long-term care insurance, which was unattractive to purchasers because it paid benefits only under a restrictive set of circumstances, will become an increasingly important means of financing nursing home care in the next decade.

Despite the prospect of continued growth, private insurance is unlikely to provide the majority of financing for long-term care in the near future. The costs due to adverse selection can be minimized if insurance is purchased during working years, so private insurance could have had an expanded role by the time baby boomers have aged. According to simulation estimates from the Brookings-ICF long-term care financing model, at most 58% of all the elderly early in the next century could be covered by private long-term care insurance purchased during working years. Insurance purchased after retirement would cover fewer people (Rivlin and Wiener 1988). Private insurance, unless subsidized, is also unlikely to finance care for low-income, high-risk men and women, like many Medicaid enrollees.

## 5.3    Limits to Expanded Public Financing of Long-Term Care

An expanded government role is the cornerstone of many proposals for reform of long-term care financing. Some of the proposals extend well beyond financing—they would broaden regulatory powers to monitor and improve the quality of nursing home care, for example. Poor quality of care is one of many problems that long-term care reform might address; it is difficult to detect because many patients are incapable of complaining or making their complaints felt, and concerned family members have few opportunities to assess quality. As important as such issues may be, financing is the centerpiece of most proposals that would expand federal involvement in long-term care. Federal financing would yield the most direct route to achieving universal coverage. The middle-class elderly, who stand to lose substantial assets if they need nursing home care, might find universal, federally sponsored insurance appealing, while the poor and near poor, who have less to lose in qualifying for Medicaid, would be little affected.

If the federal government takes an expanded role, it would most likely be as part of a "private-public partnership." A typical arrangement would have private insurance pay for the first year of nursing home care, and government programs pay for any nursing home care exceeding one year. All such proposals, even if they assume that much of the funding will remain private, need a mechanism for funding the federal share. Universal coverage would require substantial redistribution, and just as funding issues frustrated the most ambitious recent health care reform plans, they may prove insuperable obstacles to large increases in the federal share of long-term care expenditures.

Who will pay for expanded coverage? In discussing this question, I first consider shifting some of the costs from the elderly to the working-age population, or to future generations, and then consider "budget-neutral" funding, meaning the generation that receives the coverage pays for its full costs through a combination of premiums and taxes.

### 5.3.1    Intergenerational Redistribution

The funding mechanisms for long-term care might either involve deficit spending (shifting the costs to future generations) or increased taxes on the current working-age population. I will not comment on the desirability or consequences of deficit funding to finance long-term care, except to say that neither today's political climate nor tomorrow's economic environment favor deficit financing for a new entitlement for the elderly.

Funding long-term care for current Medicare beneficiaries out of taxes imposed on the currently employed population would increase an already large subsidy that is unlikely to be maintained when current workers grow old. Despite high rates of poverty, the economic well-being of the elderly has improved absolutely and in relation to other demographic groups. For example, between 1970 and 1984 median incomes for families headed by persons between twenty-five and sixty-four years old barely changed, rising from $29,113 to $29,292 (in 1984 dollars). During the same period, median incomes for families headed by persons sixty-five years of age or older rose from $13,522 to $18,236 (U.S. Senate Special Committee on Aging 1985–86, 57). By 1992 the median income of married couples sixty-five years of age and older had reached $23,817 (Grad 1994, 36). According to Hurd (1990), in 1987 the mean household income of the elderly was about 63% of the income of households of all ages, and the average wealth in 1979 was $147,000 (including federal benefits; wealth was about $80,000 excluding Social Security, Medicare, and Medicaid). Census statistics placed 1988 median net worth at $73,000 for households whose head was age sixty-five and older, about twice the median net worth for all households (U.S. Senate Special Committee on Aging 1991). As the recipients of indexed Social Security benefits and rising Medicare payments who also live longer than previous cohorts, the elderly receive far more in benefits than they contributed to Medicare and Social Security. According to one set of estimates, a new retiree in 1990 could expect to receive $4 in Medicare payments for every $1 paid in taxes and premiums (Center for Health Economics Research 1994, 21).

Though they are far more likely to be ill and require health care than other segments of the population, the elderly have already attained near-universal coverage for hospital and physician services. In 1989 about three-fourths of them had both Medicare and private supplemental insurance. About 6% had both Medicare and Medicaid. Fewer than 1% lacked health insurance, as compared with about 16% of the rest of the population (National Center for Health Statistics 1992). Their health insurance does not completely protect them from risk, for Medicare is not fully comprehensive; it does not cover prescription drugs, and although its hospital and physician benefits are extensive, they are subject to a ceiling. In a study of the disabled elderly, Liu and colleagues estimated that catastrophic health care expenses were about as likely to be due to acute care as to nursing home care. They calculated that about 9% of disabled elderly persons with an income between $500 and $1,000 per month would have acute-care expenses exceeding 15% of income, and that about 8% and 3% of them would have comparable out-of-pocket expenses for nursing home care and drugs, respectively (Liu, Perozek, and Manton 1993). Thus universal health insurance does not guarantee comprehensive protection from financial risks that result from poor health. Nevertheless, other broad segments of the population completely lack coverage, and it seems unlikely that incremental federal dollars would first go to expand benefits for the elderly.

Working in favor of funding long-term care from tax receipts today is the size of the current cohort of working-age Americans relative to retirees. The size of the cohort, however, also makes it unlikely that any such policy will be sustainable.

The support ratio captures the salient demographics in simple terms. The elderly support ratio (one hundred times the ratio of persons age sixty-five and over to working ages) is projected to rise from about twenty-one (currently) to forty (in 2030), as the total support ratio (elderly and children under age twenty as percentage of the size of the working-age population) increases from 70 to 90. As the support ratio rises, only large and sustained productivity gains will make it feasible to rely on current taxation to finance programs for the elderly. The demographic shift coincides with the financial crises that both Medicare and Social Security face early in the next century.[2]

If current trends continue, even if there is no expansion of long-term care benefits, the shift in the age composition of the population will dramatically increase health expenditures. Between 1950 and 1990 the number of Americans sixty-five years of age and older rose from 12.2 million to 31.0 million; by 2030, according to census projections, their number will more than double again, to 69.8 million. In 1990 the elderly were about 12.5% of all Americans; by 2030 they will be just over 20% of the population. In 1987 per capita health expenditures were $5,360 for Americans sixty-five years of age and older and

2. The trust fund crisis will first affect Medicare Part A; the Hospital Insurance Trust Fund, which funds Part A, will only be able to pay benefits for about seven more years. The Old-Age and Survivors' Insurance Trust Fund is projected to be able to pay benefits for about another thirty-six years with the reallocation to the Disability Insurance Trust Fund that Social Security Trustees recommend (Social Security Bulletin 1994). Medicare Part B, which is funded from the Supplementary Medical Insurance Trust, is financed on a year-to-year basis, so is not directly subject to the depletion of trust funds. It is funded by a combination of premiums that enrollees pay and general tax revenues. Premiums cover less than one-third of program costs.

$1,286 at younger ages. Thus there will be dramatic growth in the age group that uses about four times as much health care as the general population.

In fact, the age shift may have greater effects than these figures suggest. Population growth will be concentrated at advanced ages, when health expenditures are greatest. About half a million Americans in 1950 were the "oldest old," people eighty-five years of age and older. By 1990, 1.2 million were eighty-five years and older, and by 2040 there are projected to be 13.2 million Americans in this age group (U.S. Bureau of the Census 1993). Above sixty-five years of age, expenditures continue to rise with advancing age; per capita expenditures were $3,728 at ages sixty-five to sixty-nine and $9,178 at eighty-five years and older. Simple actuarial projections of health expenditures, based on recent rates of growth in per capita expenditures by age, imply that health expenditures for the elderly will grow to untenable levels early in the next century, and will exceed $1 trillion by 2030 (Garber and MaCurdy 1992). Every serious health care reform plan proposes to avert the deepening crisis in health expenditures by slowing the growth of spending for hospital and physicians' services. Unless and until expenditure growth is held to "acceptable" levels, there will be substantial political resistance to adoption of any *new* benefits, including long-term care.

Even without broader coverage, long-term care expenditures will grow dramatically. Nursing home utilization and expenditures rise at an even steeper rate with age than overall health expenditures. Per capita nursing home expenditures increase more than twenty-fold between ages sixty-five and eighty-five, averaging $165 at ages sixty-five to sixty-nine and $3,738 at eighty-five years and older; they are about $46 for Americans between ages twenty and sixty-four (Waldo et al. 1989). Over the past decade or so, age-specific nursing home utilization appears to have declined slightly. However, the effects of the shift in the age distribution of the American population will expand the number of nursing home residents, even if the trend toward lower risk of institutionalization continues.

Why might the risk of institutionalization continue to decline? New evidence suggests that age-specific disability rates are declining. In a controversial 1980 article and subsequent writings, James Fries proposed that there is a natural limit on the attainable life span, and that more and more people will live to the maximum life span. Thus survival curves will approach the rectangular, rather than developing a longer and thicker tail of very old survivors. Along with the rectangularization of survival, Fries claimed, will come a compression of morbidity: people will spend less time sick and disabled before they die. His claims were hotly debated. It seemed obvious that, just as medical care might diminish morbidity and improve function, it would also keep alive people who either had disabilities or were likely to acquire them. For example, improved treatment of congestive heart failure might enable people with the condition to live longer, albeit with severe activity limitations. Many authors questioned whether there was evidence of compression of morbidity (see, for example, Verbrugge [1984] and Poterba and Summers [1987]). Poor data made it difficult to test Fries's hypothesis in any convincing way; most of the evidence was indirect, and there was little longitudinal data with appropriate measures of functional status or morbidity. A recent publication by Manton, Corder, and Stallard (1993), based on analysis of three waves of the National Long-Term Care Survey, offered some of the most convincing evidence that age-adjusted functional status has indeed improved over time. Although their data covered only a seven-year period during the 1980s, Manton and colleagues showed that fewer nondisabled elderly became disabled (on an annualized basis) between 1984 and 1989 than between 1982 and 1984. Furthermore, people with disabilities were less likely to acquire new disabilities in the second time period. These intriguing results have yet to be confirmed using other data, but even if they are correct, the decline in morbidity seems unlikely to be sufficiently large to offset the increases in the demand for both medical care and long-term care that will result from the aging of the baby boomers.

Thus, even if general funds could pay for long-term care of the elderly today, any such approach offers only a temporary solution, since the burden of subsidizing the care of elderly baby boomers will be heavier and will fall on a smaller population of working adults.

### 5.3.2   Can Current Beneficiaries Pay?

If redistribution across generations is infeasible, what are the prospects of financing from the population that currently receives benefits? One approach that might appeal to the elderly is to finance expanded long-term care benefits by reducing Medicare outlays for hospital and physician services; it is unlikely that they would choose to have nearly all Medicare dollars go toward conventional medical services, as they do now. However, many of the elderly believe, perhaps with good reason, that any savings resulting from a cutback in medical expenditures would be used to reduce Medicare outlays, not to fund new benefits. In any case, the results of efforts to reduce Medicare expenditures, including the Prospective Payment System (designed to limit hospital costs) and the Resource-Based Relative Value Scale (designed to reduce expenditures for professional fees), have been disappointing.

An alternative mode of intragenerational financing imposes a combination of taxes and subsidies on current Medicare beneficiaries. Such approaches preserve budget neutrality and exploit the large variance in the economic status of the elderly. A similar strategy resulted in the passage of a modest expansion of Medicare benefits in the late 1980s. That experience undoubtedly contributed to the caution with which Congress has approached health care reform under the Clinton administration.

The Medicare Catastrophic Coverage Act of 1988 was the culmination of an ambitious effort to extend Medicare benefits to long-term care and prescription drugs. During months of negotiations, the benefits were whittled away, until the package included in the act was greatly diminished in scope and expense.

It liberalized the dollar limits on payments for inpatient and physicians' services, and added a prescription-drug benefit, whose deductible was set so high that only a small minority of Medicare recipients would actually receive payments. It also included a slight expansion in long-term care coverage, raising the limit from 100 to 150 days of nursing home care per benefit period, and eliminating the requirement that hospitalization had to precede covered nursing home admissions. To preserve budget neutrality and to ensure that all the elderly would be covered, the act included a subsidy for the low-income elderly and a surtax for those with high incomes. According to a Congressional Budget Office report, in 1989, when premiums averaged $145, the program's benefits were worth $62 per enrollee. The maximum surtax, which made the total cost about fourteen times the expected value of the benefits, applied to anyone whose income exceeded $35,000. Although the act was criticized from some quarters because it did not go far enough in covering long-term care, the most devastating attack came from politically active elderly individuals who faced a large surtax to pay for benefits that most already received as part of private supplemental health insurance. Their protests, which embarrassed a number of congressmen and the leadership of the American Association of Retired Persons (AARP), led to the repeal of the act before its full implementation.

### 5.4   Making Long-Term Care More Broadly Available

Private solutions to financing long-term care remain largely unproven, and government approaches, at least for the foreseeable future, will have limited scope. Do these observations imply that there are no sustainable approaches to improving access to long-term care and to reducing the risk of catastrophic long-term care expenditures? I believe that the answer is no, but that the following considerations are essential to designing improved modes of financing long-term care.

*Financing out of general tax revenues, or any means of transfer from working-age adults to the current elderly, will offer at best transient solutions.* The large size and inadequate funding of existing entitlement programs and the rising support ratio are sufficient reasons. Resistance to any such approach will be particularly severe in the face of the improved economic status of the elderly and the worsening economic plight of the very young. Plans to use deficit financing, or to increase taxes on the working-age population, will face the general resistance to increases in taxes. They would also increase redistribution to an age group that already receives substantial benefits from government programs.

*Initiatives to promote private long-term care insurance should emphasize purchase many years before disability becomes common.* Many private long-term care insurance policies are structured like either whole-life or level-premium term life insurance. They are relatively inexpensive for people who begin purchasing coverage at a time when the probability of a claim is very low and adverse selection is unlikely to be a significant problem. Adverse selection is a far more serious problem at advanced ages, when functional impairment is frequent, because methods to screen for risk factors for institutionalization are imperfect. There would be difficulties even if adverse selection could be overcome, since actuarially fair insurance would be prohibitively expensive for many of the at-risk elderly.

*Financing long-term care by redistribution among the elderly is unlikely to be politically feasible.* As the history of the Medicare Catastrophic Coverage Act illustrates, even an immensely popular and modest expansion of benefits will meet with severe political resistance if voters perceive that its costs are too high. A comprehensive long-term care benefit, particularly if it began covering nursing home care early in an admission, would be more expensive than the provisions in the Medicare Catastrophic Coverage Act. The surtaxes needed to finance the program would not go unnoticed. Attempts to fold long-term care into a more general health care reform effort, as we recently witnessed, may make the change more acceptable politically, if only because they obscure the relationship between program costs and benefits. But unless long-term care benefits are financed by reductions in other benefits, or real efficiencies result from the general reform effort, resistance will be substantial.

Is reform likely to bring new efficiencies that reduce the size of the surtax needed to finance expansion of covered benefits? Some have argued that health care reform can reduce administrative waste, eliminate inappropriate care, and promote more efficient practice patterns. Even if these claims are valid in the context of hospital and physician services, they are unlikely to apply to long-term care. Fee-for-service insurance, coupled with tax subsidies, is widely blamed for inefficiencies and overutilization in the existing market for health care. Yet insurance-induced distortions, apart from any implicit in the Medicaid program, cannot have had comparable effects on long-term care. In fact, many reform proposals seek to duplicate traditional fee-for-service private health insurance in the long-term care market, making cost reductions and efficiency gains particularly unlikely.

*Moral hazard may be a far more significant problem in developing insurance for long-term care than for physicians' and hospital services.* Projections at the time Medicare was passed grossly underestimated future expenditures. In 1967, its first full year of operation, total Medicare expenditures were $4.2 billion. By 1991 Medicare expenditures reached $120 billion (Helbing 1992). If only changes in the size and composition of the beneficiary population, along with general price inflation, had affected Medicare outlays, expenditures would have grown far more slowly. Typical projections assume that there is no behavioral response to the price subsidy implicit in health insurance, so insurance does little to increase demand for hospital or physicians' services. If only patients who develop respiratory failure benefit from assisted ventilation in an intensive care unit, for example, a reduction in the price the patient pays for such services is unlikely to increase demand substantially.

The long-run elasticity of demand, however, can be much greater than such an example suggests. Subsidized care, with the associated increase in ability to pay for high-technology services, inexorably led to the development of new and expensive modes of health care. In the absence of widespread health insurance, many of these technologies would never have left the laboratory, or they would have been sold at lower prices. Unlike many forms of conventional medical care, long-term care often substitutes for goods and services that any elderly person might consume, such as housing, personal services, and food preparation. Innovations in housing arrangements for the elderly have increasingly blurred the distinction between housing and nursing home care; many continuing care retirement communities, for example, are designed to provide a comprehensive set of services beginning with pure housing and sometimes food services, sometimes with medical insurance, and directly providing graded levels of long-term care. Because the criteria used to determine the "need" for long-term services are less precise and more easily manipulated than, say, the diagnosis of a heart attack, the close substitutability of housing and other services means that long-term care insurance is likely to increase utilization substantially, and that the distortions will be larger than for conventional medical insurance.

*A long-term care insurance program that covers noncatastrophic expenditures will be costly.* The usual arguments about the drawbacks of first-dollar insurance coverage apply with force here. Many elderly Americans can expect to use formal long-term care, and a majority will receive informal long-term care at some time. Most will make limited use of such services. Publicly and privately financed insurance to cover such expenses will be subject to the costs that result from moral hazard, and adverse selection will raise the costs of privately provided insurance that is sold to the elderly. Such insurance offers little risk reduction at high cost.

*Any public insurance program for long-term care is likely to be most successful if it mandates universal participation and restricts coverage to catastrophic long-term care benefits.* Even for those who use it heavily, long-term care is usually less expensive than hospital and physicians' services. A small fraction of people admitted to nursing homes have stays lasting a year or longer. Although nursing home charges vary greatly within and between regions, the mean cost of an admission, even if it lasts a year, is small in relation to the wealth of many of the elderly. A program that financed only greatly prolonged nursing home stays would cost substantially less than a marked expansion of benefits for conventional medical services, or for first-dollar coverage of nursing home stays, and many of the elderly could afford to pay for the period before coverage began with a combination of savings and private insurance.

Like all other forms of long-term care insurance, the catastrophic coverage would be subject to both adverse selection and moral hazard. In every respect, however, catastrophic coverage would be much less vulnerable to such problems than would, say, first-dollar or first-day coverage. The linkage of the insurance coverage to the duration of prior use (i.e., the lack of coverage until a year or so of institutionalization) would mean that only persons who could expect to have very extensive and lengthy nursing home utilization would benefit; presumably many of these people could be identified ex ante.

Not all of the elderly would be able to pay for catastrophic insurance out of current income. Below some income and/or asset threshold, individuals could continue to be covered in the current Medicaid program, whose expenditures would fall as a large fraction of the elderly who "spent down" to qualify for Medicaid become eligible to receive catastrophic coverage under the new program. All of the usual issues about phasing in a benefit that is means tested arise here: the disincentives to save, the desired degree of progressivity, and methods to ensure the quality of care delivered under the safety net (Medicaid).

The popularity of private insurance to supplement Medicare suggests that it will be difficult to preserve the cost-sharing features of catastrophic long-term care insurance. Most Medicare recipients obtain medigap policies, which pay all or part of the deductibles and copayments, thereby eliminating the features that were designed to prevent overutilization of covered services. Tax deductibility of premiums for private policies exacerbate their overpurchase. If private supplementary insurance promoted overutilization of long-term care, long-term care coverage with provider incentives (such as capitation) would be an alternative means of controlling expenditures.

*Increased savings will be necessary to ensure adequate funding for long-term care.* A savings-based approach to financing long-term care has several advantages that insurance market reform lacks. One is the development of new alternatives to traditional forms of long-term care. Innovations such as continuing care retirement or life care communities offer a combination of housing, personal, and health services, and are designed primarily for the healthy elderly who would like to be able to stay outside institutions if they become disabled. Narrowly drawn insurance coverage would encourage traditional forms of long-term care at the expense of innovations, while broad coverage could lead to excessive moral hazard. Thus private savings mechanisms will often lead to more efficient outcomes than expanded insurance, which will lead to price distortions.

There are three major concerns with savings-based approaches: public policies designed to increase private savings for long-term care might be unsuccessful; if successful, they might lead to undesirably large bequests; and many low-income workers and the persistently unemployed would be unable to save enough money. The major form of tax-advantaged savings for long-term care that was proposed during the 1980s, called the individual medical account (IMA), was patterned after IRAs. It never attracted widespread support, in part because so few people participated in IRAs, which were clearly superior from the saver's point of view (funds from IMAs could be spent only on long-term care, whereas the proceeds from IRAs could be spent on anything). Increased savings could result in undesirably large bequests, and the wealth might not be readily annuitized if long-term care insurance markets are highly imperfect. Increased savings among those who are near poverty or already receive income support seems infeasible, and for this segment of the population Medicaid is likely to remain the principal means of financing long-term care.

Specific mechanisms for promoting savings are beyond the scope of this discussion. Increased savings will likely require an increase in the average age of retirement and may require substantial behavioral change. It seems clear, however, that insurance for long-term care will remain flawed. Increased savings, when feasible, and particularly when coupled with catastrophic insurance, may offer the greatest flexibility and limit both risk and moral hazard.

## 5.5  Conclusions

Veneration of the elderly—a central tenet of both Eastern and Western religious and cultural traditions—obliges family and society to maintain and enhance the well-being of those who are old, particularly if they need assistance. Modern industrialized societies rely heavily on social welfare programs for this purpose. The United States lacks universal health insurance for the rest of the population, but it subsidizes insurance for physician services and provides all of the elderly with hospital insurance under Medicare. Federal and private programs to insure long-term care for the elderly are considerably less well developed than Medicare, though. There is little private insurance, and Medicaid is only available to the poor, the near poor, and those who spend down. How can our humanitarian impulses to ensure access to long-term care be reconciled with the financial, demographic, and political barriers to expanding or transforming the government role?

All of the mechanisms for expanding access to long-term care by changes in financing are problematic. There are three major forms of financing: direct private payments, private insurance, and government payments. Direct private payments lack risk protection, and preparing for such payments will require sizable precautionary savings. Private and public insurance can generate substantial inefficiencies, stemming from moral hazard, poor information, and the high cost of monitoring. Adverse selection is also likely to affect any insurance program that falls short of universal participation. Any broad mandate or government program could overcome adverse selection, but would have large and politically unpopular redistributional components.

Long-term care is currently financed by a mix of all three approaches, although private insurance has had a limited role. Its role is likely to grow, especially if long-term care insurance plans are marketed to younger populations, who are less likely to be subject to adverse selection. The federal role in financing long-term care is unlikely to expand substantially, unless funds are taken from other programs for the elderly, like Medicare and Medicaid. The rapidly approaching depletion of the Hospital Insurance Trust Fund, the already large general revenue contribution to Supplementary Medical Insurance, and changing demographic largely preclude the addition of a comprehensive long-term care benefit to Medicare, unless offsetting savings can be found. The costs would be high, the inefficiencies great, and the likelihood of funding budgetary shortfalls out of taxes or premium payments small.

These realities suggest that federal policy should emphasize increased savings, rather than direct federal payments for long-term care. Policy is most likely to succeed if it emphasizes ensuring that the disabled elderly can obtain humane care, whether it comes from family members, visiting nurses, or institutions. Some will be able to rely on spouses and children for assistance, but many will eventually need formal services. Efforts to prepare should begin long before this contingency is likely to arise. Government programs should promote such efforts, because if today's workers become disabled when they are older, the federal government is unlikely to be able to shoulder a greater burden than it does now. Increased private saving and greater participation in private insurance, not a broader package of federal benefits, offer the surest protection against the financial consequences of old-age disability.

# References

Adams, E. Kathleen, Mark R. Meiners, and Brian O. Burwell. 1993. Asset spend-down in nursing homes: Methods and insights. *Medical Care* 31:1–23.

Commerce Clearing House Business Law Editors. 1994. *1994 Medicare explained.* Chicago: Commerce Clearing House.

Center for Health Economics Research. 1994. *The nation's health care bill: Who bears the burden?* Waltham, MA: Center for Health Economics Research.

Chiswick, Barry R. 1976. The demand for nursing home care: An analysis of the substitution between institutional and noninstitutional care. *Journal of Human Resources* 11:296–316.

Dick, Andrew, Alan M. Garber, and Thomas E. MaCurdy. 1994. Forecasting nursing home utilization of elderly Americans. In *Studies in the economics of aging,* ed. David A. Wise. Chicago: University of Chicago Press.

Fries, James F. 1980. Aging, natural death, and the compression of morbidity. *New England Journal of Medicine* 303:130–35.

Garber, Alan M., and Thomas E. MaCurdy. 1992. Payment source and episodes of institutionalization. In *Topics in the economics of aging,* ed. David A. Wise, 249–71. Chicago: University of Chicago Press.

Grad, Susan. 1994. *Income of the population 55 or older, 1992.* SSA Publications no. 13-11871. Baltimore: U.S. Department of Health and Human Services, Social Security Administration.

Hedrick, Susan C., and Thomas S. Inui. 1986. The effectiveness and cost of home care: An information synthesis. *Health Services Research* 20, no. 6, pt. 2:851–80.

Helbing, Charles. 1992. Medicare program expenditures. *Health Care Financing Review,* annual supplement, 1993:23–54.

Hurd, Michael D. 1990. Research on the elderly: Economic status, retirement, and consumption and saving. *Journal of Economic Literature* 28:565–637.

Keeler, Emmett B., Robert L. Kane, and David H. Solomon. 1981. Short- and long-term residents of nursing homes. *Medical Care* 19:363–69.

Kemper, Peter. 1988. The evaluation of the National Long Term Care Demonstration: Part 10: Overview of the findings. *Health Services Research* 23:161–74.

Kemper, Peter, and Christopher M. Murtaugh. 1991. Lifetime use of nursing home care. *New England Journal of Medicine* 324:595–600.

Letsch, Suzanne W., Helen C. Lazenby, Katharine R. Levit, and Cathy A. Cowan. 1992. National health expenditures, 1991. *Health Care Financing Review* 14:1–30.

Liu, Korbin, Maria Perozek, and Kenneth G. Manton. 1993. Catastrophic acute and long-term care costs: Risks faced by disabled elderly persons. *Gerontologist* 33:299–307.

Macken, Candace L. 1986. A profile of functionally impaired elderly persons living in the community. *Health Care Financing Review* 7:33–49.

Manton, Kenneth G., Larry S. Corder, and Eric Stallard. 1993. Estimates of change in chronic disability and institutional incidence and prevalence rates in the U.S. elderly population from the 1982, 1984, and 1989 National Long Term Care Survey. *Journal of Gerontology: Social Sciences* 48:S153–66.

Muurinen, Jaana-Marja. 1986. The economics of informal care: Labor market effects in the National Hospice Study. *Medical Care* 24:1007–17.

National Center for Health Statistics. 1992. *Life tables for 1989.* Hyattsville, MD: Public Health Service.

———. 1994. *Health United States, 1993.* Hyattsville, MD: Public Health Service.

Pauly, Mark V. 1990. The rational non-purchase of long-term care insurance. *Journal of Political Economy* 98:153–68.

Poterba, James M., and Lawrence H. Summers. 1987. Public policy implications of declining old-age mortality. In *Work, health, and income among the elderly,* ed. Gary Burtless. Washington, DC: Brookings Institution.

Rice, Thomas. 1989. The use, cost, and economic burden of nursing home care in 1985. *Medical Care* 27:1133–47.

Rivlin, Alice M., and Joshua M. Wiener. 1988. *Caring for the disabled elderly: Who will pay?* Washington, DC: Brookings Institution.

Ruther, Martin, Thomas W. Reilly, Herbert A. Silverman, and Deidra B. Abbott. 1991. *Medicare and Medicaid data book, 1990.* Baltimore, MD: Department of Health and Human Services, Health Care Financing Administration.

Scitovsky, Anne A. 1988. Medical care in the last twelve months of life: The relation between age, functional status, and medical care expenditures. *Milbank Quarterly* 66:640–60.

Sloan, Frank A., and May W. Shayne. 1993. Long-term care, Medicaid, and impoverishment of the elderly. *Milbank Quarterly* 71:575–99.

Social Security Bulletin. 1994. Actuarial status of the Social Security and Medicare programs. *Social Security Bulletin* 57:53–59.

Strahan, Genevieve W. 1993. Overview of home health and hospice care patients: Preliminary data from the 1992 National Home and Hospice Care Survey. *Advance Data from Vital and Health Statistics,* no. 235. Hyattsville, MD: National Center for Health Statistics.

Thornton, Craig, Shari Miller Dunstan, and Peter Kemper. 1988. The evaluation of the National Long Term Care Demonstration: Part 8: The effect of channeling on health and long-term care costs. *Health Services Research* 23:129–42.

U.S. Bureau of the Census. 1993. Sixty-five plus in America. In *Current population reports, special studies.* P23–178RV. Washington, DC: Government Printing Office.

U.S. Senate Special Committee on Aging. 1985–86. *Aging America: Trends and projections.* Washington, DC: Government Printing Office.

———. 1991. *Aging America: Trends and projections.* Washington, DC: U.S. Dept. of Health and Human Services.

Van Gelder, Susan, and D. Johnson. 1991. *Long-term care insurance: A market update.* Washington, DC: Health Insurance Association of America.

Venti, Steven F., and David A. Wise. 1990. But they don't want to reduce housing equity. In *Issues in the economics of aging,* ed. David A. Wise, 13–29. Chicago: University of Chicago Press.

Verbrugge, Lois M. 1984. Longer life but worsening health? Trends in health and mortality of middle-aged and older persons. *Milbank Memorial Fund Quarterly* 62:475–519.

Waldo, Daniel R., Sally T. Sonnefeld, David R. McKusick, and Ross H. Arnett. 1989. Health expenditures by age group, 1977 and 1987. *Health Care Financing Review* 10:111–20.

Wingard, Deborah L., Denise W. Jones, and Robert M. Kaplan. 1987. Institutional care utilization by the elderly: A critical review. *Gerontologist* 27:156–63.

Wooldridge, Judith, and Jennifer Schore. 1988. The evaluation of the National Long Term Care Demonstration: Part 7: The effect of channeling on the use of nursing homes, hospitals, and other medical services. *Health Services Research* 23:119–27.

# Comment     John B. Shoven

Alan Garber's paper provides an excellent introduction to the economics of long-term or nursing home care. There are currently some serious shortcomings in our system of financing and delivering quality long-term care in the United States. Due to the aging of the baby boom generation, however, these problems are going to be magnified many times over within the next fifty years or so. Per capita nursing home expenditures grow extremely rapidly with age. In 1989, those between ages sixty-five and sixty-nine spent an average of $165 on long-term care, while those over eighty-five spent more than twenty times as much, at $3,738 per capita. Combine this with the fact that the over eighty-five population is projected to increase by a factor of five over the next fifty years, and the topic of this paper takes on immense importance.

Garber points out in the paper that private insurance is currently only a tiny factor in the financing of nursing home stays. At first glance, this is puzzling since the need for long-term care appears to be something that should be insurable. The majority of people will not need long-term care in their lifetimes, and even for those who do spend some time in a nursing home, the average total time spent is not long and the cost is not too great. However, there is a

John B. Shoven is the Charles R. Schwab Professor of Economics and the dean of the School of Humanities and Sciences at Stanford University.

sizable minority who will need care for several years, and for them the expenses can be overwhelming. As Garber points out, however, on further thought this market suffers severely from two of the classic insurance problems: adverse selection and moral hazard. Undoubtedly, these problems at least partially account for the reason that private insurance is not a big factor in this market.

There are other reasons why private long-term care insurance has failed to develop. First, to get around the adverse selection problem, insurance companies need to enroll people long before they might need care. However, with all of the talk of the government providing long-term care in the future, why should individuals give up current consumption for future benefits that may be unnecessary? Without checking the overall market for long-term care insurance, I simply examined the policy offered by Stanford University (provided by CNA Insurance, one of the largest participants in this market). In the policy offered at Stanford, there is absolutely no provision for what happens if the government is covering long-term care by the time the policy holder needs it.

Second, there often are no inflation adjustments in the policies or guarantees that the insurance company will be solvent in the distant future. The Stanford plan comes in three sizes, offering maximum daily benefits of $90, $120, or $150 (and also maximum nominal lifetime benefits). These all sound reasonable for today's prices, but if the potential enrollees think that they might need nursing home care sometime in the 2030s, these payouts might be totally inadequate. The Stanford plan mentions making adjustments (to both cost and payouts) with future inflation, but there are no specifics whatsoever. Third, the policies cannot be actuarially fair. The Stanford policy charges men and women the same amount; one visit to a nursing home where the population is between 75 and 80% women would hint that a single pricing policy cannot be in the interest of male participants. Fourth, a significant fraction of people are myopic, particularly about unpleasant events in the very distant future. And, fifth, the policies are very expensive. I calculated how much money one could accumulate if one put aside the long-term care premiums beginning at age thirty-five and earned a nominal return of 7.5% on the money. By age eighty (not far from the median age of entry into nursing homes), the account would have grown sufficiently to finance a twenty-six month stay at the policy's maximum daily benefit. But Garber's table 5.1 tells us that the average lifetime utilization of nursing homes is only seven months. Even for the 35% of the population who will spend some time in a long-term care facility, the average utilization is twenty-one months. Clearly, many people would rather take their chances than purchase a policy with the actuarial dice so poorly arranged.

Many of the problems of private insurance provision are fundamental and cannot be solved with either increased government regulation or increased private competition. It is probably safe to say that privately purchased insurance will never be a major factor in this market. Some of the problems, particularly the moral hazard problem, also apply to government-provided insurance. I personally find persuasive Garber's suggestion that the demand elasticity for nursing home care is substantial because the services provided substitute for meals and housing expenses. A high demand elasticity translates directly into a very large moral hazard problem in this market.

It is not at all clear that the solution for long-term care financing is to try to expand the role of either private or public insurance. If we had even more widespread insurance than we do now (and Medicaid is already a very large factor in this market, paying roughly half of the total bill in the economy), the moral hazard problem could become as severe as it is in the rest of the health care industry. That is, the age-specific demand for nursing home care could increase substantially if more people are put into a situation where they or their family don't pay the incremental costs of their usage. Given the demographic outlook for nursing home demand, we cannot afford to have even higher age- and sex-specific usage.

Garber ends the paper with an analysis of alternative policies for long-term care financing. None of them will easily deal with the rapidly increasing population over eight-five, of course. Expanding either public or private insurance seems both implausible and undesirable, given the moral hazard problem. The option that bears further exploration in my opinion is the combination of government provision of catastrophic long-term care insurance (for stays longer than one or two years) with individual saving responsible for shorter stays. The incentive to save will be viable only if the government refrains from financing noncatastrophic nursing home stays. Individual or family responsibility for these costs is a viable option only if the government refuses to help those who do not provide for themselves.

# III Human Services: Theoretical and Institutional Perspectives

# 6      Consumption Externalities and the Financing of Social Services

Robert H. Frank

A 60° day in March seems warm to a resident of Minneapolis, but to a resident of Miami, such a day seems chilly. Someone earning $30,000 feels rich when she lands a job that pays $50,000, but someone who earns $70,000 feels poor when her income declines to $50,000. And whereas an American living in a one-room house with no electricity or running water feels ashamed of his circumstances, a villager in Nepal views his similar dwelling with pride.

It is well known to most social and behavioral scientists that satisfaction depends not just on absolute levels of consumption, but also on the context in which they occur. Yet economists have, for the most part, continued to model behavior as if utility depended only on absolute consumption. As I and many others have argued elsewhere, the policy implications of conventional economic models often differ sharply from those in which utility depends also on context.[1] In this essay, I explore the implications of the broader model for how we should finance social services like health care, education, child care, and long-term care. But before turning to the specifics of these issues, I will briefly review some of the evidence that utility depends on relative consumption.

## 6.1   Concerns about Relative Position

If we adopt the biologist's view that human motivation was shaped by the forces of natural selection, it is no surprise that people might care so strongly

Robert H. Frank is the Goldwin Smith Professor of Economics, Ethics, and Public Policy at Cornell University.

The author thanks Victor Fuchs and Amartya Sen for helpful discussions.

1. Of the role of context in evaluation generally, see Helson 1964; Scitovsky 1976; and Brickman, Coates, and Janoff-Bulman 1978. Authors who have investigated the policy implications of concerns about relative income include, among others, Veblen 1899; Duesenberry 1949; Hirsch 1976; Boskin and Sheshinski 1978; Layard 1980; Sen 1983; Frank 1985a, 1985b; Ng 1987; Seidman 1987; and Kosicki 1987.

about relative resource holdings. Even in a famine, for example, there is always *some* food available, and the question of who gets it is settled largely by relative wealth holdings. Relative wealth holdings have also been a decisive factor in the allocation of mates, especially in early human societies. Polygyny was practiced in nearly 1,000 of the 1,154 current and past societies for which data are available, and in these societies it was almost invariably the wealthiest males who took multiple wives.[2]

Concern about relative position is also adaptive insofar as it prods people to monitor how they are doing relative to their rivals and to boost their effort levels if they start falling behind. The alternative of operating at maximum effort levels at all times is less efficient because people tend to do better by conserving their energy when environmental conditions are not stressful, for use when the threats to survival are more immediate.

Concern about relative wealth is helpful even in interpersonal bargaining contexts. Consider, for example, an elegant experiment known as the "ultimatum bargaining game" (see Guth, Schmittberger, and Schwarze 1982). The game is played by two players, Proposer and Responder. It begins with Proposer being given a sum of money (say, $100) that he must then propose how to divide between himself and Responder. Responder then has two options: (1) he can accept, in which case each party gets the amount proposed; or (2) he can refuse, in which case each party gets zero and the $100 goes back to the experimenter.

If Proposer believes that Responder cares only about absolute wealth, his own wealth-maximizing strategy is clear: he should propose $99 for himself and $1 for Responder (only integer dollar amounts are allowed). If Proposer's assumption about Responder is correct, Responder will accept this one-sided offer because he will reason that getting $1 is better than getting nothing.

But suppose Proposer believed that Responder cares not only about absolute but also relative wealth levels. Because he finds the relative terms of the one-sided offer so distasteful, Responder might then refuse it, even though he stands to gain from it in absolute terms. The irony is that the effect of Proposer's believing that Responder cares about relative wealth is to boost substantially the amount that Proposer offers Responder. By virtue of his concern about relative wealth, Responder becomes a much more effective bargainer.

People also have good reasons to be concerned about their relative position in the income hierarchy even when they do not care how their own consumption compares to others'. As Amartya Sen has emphasized, for example, community wealth levels are an important determinant of the capabilities—and hence the amount of wealth—an individual needs to be an effectively functioning member of society (Sen 1983, 1987). Because virtually everyone in Los

---

2. See Wright 1994. Although food shortages and polygyny were common in the environment of evolutionary adaptation, they have of course become rare in modern industrial societies. Yet features of human motivation that were forged in early hunter-gatherer societies are largely still with us.

Angeles has a car, a resident of that city cannot meet even the most minimal social and employment obligations without one. Yet no one expects an Ethiopian villager to be able to transport himself across comparable distances at a moment's notice.

By the same token, there are many goods that are highly desirable in their own right, yet whose supplies are such that only the wealthiest people can have them, no matter how much national income grows. The late Fred Hirsch (1976) called these "positional goods." If everyone has the same preference for a home with a commanding view, and only 10% of the homes in the area have that feature, those homes will go to families in the upper decile of the wealth distribution, no matter how much everyone earns.

Of even more pressing concern is the desire of most parents to prepare their children to have successful lives and careers once they leave home. Positional issues arise here because a "good job," like a fast runner, is an inescapably relative concept. It is a job that offers more responsibility, better working conditions, more opportunities for growth, and higher pay than other jobs. Increasingly, entry-level jobs on the most desirable career paths go the applicants with the best educational credentials (see Frank and Cook 1995, chap. 8). This gives parents a compelling reason to make sure that their children meet or exceed community educational standards, which, in turn, requires high relative income.

Michael McGuire and his collaborators have shown that relative position may even affect fundamental biochemical processes in the nervous system (McGuire, Raleigh, and Brammer 1982; Raleigh et al. 1984). In a study involving nineteen groups of adult vervet monkeys, Raleigh et al. (1984) found that the dominant member in each group had roughly 50% higher concentrations of the neurotransmitter serotonin, which affects mood and behavior in a variety of ways. They also showed that this difference was the effect, rather than the cause, of high status.[3]

Within limits, having elevated serotonin concentrations is associated with enhanced feelings of well-being.[4] Serotonin deficiencies are associated with sleep disorders, irritability, and antisocial behavior. McGuire and his colleagues also found elevated serotonin levels in the leaders of college fraternities and athletic teams.

---

3. To do this, they removed the initially dominant animal from each group and placed him in an isolation cage. Shortly thereafter, a new individual established dominance within each group, and after roughly seventy-two hours passed, serotonin concentrations in the newly dominant animal rose to the levels seen in the formerly dominant animal. At the same time, the serotonin concentrations in the formerly dominant animal fell to the level associated with subordinate status. When the initially dominant animal was returned to the group, he reasserted dominance, and serotonin concentrations in both the originally dominant and interim dominant animals responded accordingly.

4. The drug Prozac, which increases serotonin uptake in the brain, may thus help defeat the seemingly impregnable constraint that only a fraction of the population can hope to experience the psychological satisfaction associated with high relative standing.

Additional evidence on the importance of relative position comes in the form of happiness surveys conducted over time in a variety of countries. These surveys, which ask people to report whether they are "very happy," "fairly happy," or "not happy," find that happiness levels within a country at a given moment are strongly positively correlated with position in the country's income distribution. The same studies find no long-term trends in average reported happiness levels, even for countries whose incomes have been growing steadily over time. Looking at different countries at a given point of time, the happiness surveys also find little relationship between the average income level in a country and the average happiness level reported by its citizens.[5]

These survey findings are thus consistent with the view that relative position is a much more important determinant of self-rated happiness levels than is absolute position on the income scale. Even though happiness surveys call for purely subjective responses, there is evidence that they measure a real phenomenon. For example, numerous other studies have found strong positive relationships between reported happiness levels and observable physiological and behavioral measures of well-being. People who report that they are not happy, for example, are more likely to experience headaches, rapid heartbeat, digestive disorders, and related ailments (Bradburn and Noll 1969). Self-reported happiness is strongly negatively related to clinical symptoms of depression, irritability, and anxiety (Bachman et al. 1967; Wall, Clegg, and Jackson 1978). Those who rate themselves as very happy are more likely than others to initiate social contacts with friends (Bradburn and Caplovitz 1965). People who call themselves unhappy have higher labor turnover than others (McEvoy and Cascio 1985). Self-reported happiness is also linked to longevity (Palmore 1969) and coronary heart disease (Sales and House 1971).

One final piece of evidence of the strength of concerns about relative position comes from observations of the wage structure within firms. Traditional theory says that individual wage differentials will mirror the corresponding differences in marginal productivity. Yet in virtually every case for which the relevant data are available, the wage distribution within the firm is substantially compressed relative to the corresponding marginal productivity distribution. The patterns of wage compression, moreover, are consistent with the claim that individual wage payments within the firm incorporate substantial compensating differentials based on local rank (see Frank 1985a, chap. 4).

To sum up, evidence from several disciplines strongly suggests that relative economic position is an important determinant of human satisfaction. Let us now consider the implications of positional concerns for the methods of financing social services.

---

5. Richard Easterlin (1995) reports that a positive relationship between happiness and income has recently begun to show up in cross-national data, perhaps an inevitable consequence of the communications revolution.

## 6.2 Health Care

Real health care expenditures per capita in the United States have grown more rapidly than real GNP per capita for as long as the relevant data have allowed us to measure (see Newhouse 1992, 4). As a share of GNP, health care costs have risen from only 4% in 1940 to nearly 14% today.

As Baumol and Bowen explained almost thirty years ago (1966), at least some of this increase was simply to have been expected. In the performing arts, education, health care, and other service industries, productivity grows much more slowly than in agriculture and manufacturing. This implies that the prices of services, measured in units of manufactured goods, must steadily rise.

This does not mean, however, that we literally cannot afford to buy the same services we had in the past. In a recent paper, Baumol (1993) stresses that, with rising productivity in manufacturing and with constant productivity in services, we can afford even more services than before.

Yet spiraling medical costs go beyond lagging productivity in the health care industry. Also implicated have been the expansion of access to medical services through Medicare and Medicaid; increasing reliance on insurance and other third-party payment schemes in the private sector; the growing tendency for physicians to specialize; the rise in malpractice litigation; and especially the rapid introduction of costly diagnostic and therapeutic technologies (Feldstein 1971, 1977; Fuchs 1990; Weisbrod 1991).

Whatever the causes of escalating medical costs, one of their effects has been to place medical insurance increasingly beyond the reach of low- and middle-income Americans, whose real incomes have stagnated for the past two decades. Nearly 40 million Americans, most of them from low- and middle-income groups, are currently uninsured. Although most people favor the provision of universal medical coverage in some form, the budgetary dilemma is that better access means significantly increased usage of medical services and, in turn, even greater escalation in expenditures.

Why is this really a dilemma? Perhaps the value we receive from increased expenditures on medical care is at least as great as we could expect from greater spending on other things. On examination, however, this does not appear to be the case. As Victor Fuchs has repeatedly emphasized, for example, there is no persuasive evidence that mortality and morbidity vary significantly with expenditures on medical care.[6]

To explain why, he begins by noting that most health care systems deliver those medical interventions that are known to save lives and are relatively inexpensive—antibiotics for serious infections, surgical removal of inflamed appendixes, and so on. Variations in expenditures tend to be accounted for by differences in expenditures that do not greatly affect major health outcomes.

---

6. A brief summary of his argument is contained in Fuchs 1994.

For example, systems vary substantially in the extent to which they administer treatment for essentially self-limiting conditions like colds, headaches, sprains, cuts, bruises, and gastrointestinal upsets.

Further variations come in areas for which there is no consensus on which treatment is best. Thus, for example, Canadian heart-attack victims are generally treated with the enzyme streptokinase, whereas American patients will generally be given the much more expensive TPA, even though there is little evidence that TPA works any better.

Fuchs concedes that there are some instances in which expensive treatments are known to make a significant difference in major health outcomes, but he notes that these cases make up only a minuscule proportion of total expenditures on health care. Further evidence for Fuchs's general claim comes from a recent study by Manning et al. (1987), who found that insurance policies with a large deductible provision produced between 40 and 50% reductions in health care expenditures with no measurable differences in health outcomes.

Fuchs has also stressed, however, that health care systems deliver more than just medically effective interventions. They deliver care to the sick, even when they do not cure them; and they also serve to validate the claims of seriously ill or disabled persons for support from others. We must also inquire whether these important functions might be seriously compromised by efforts to hold expenditures in check.

One of the most common means for curtailing expenditure growth has been the move from private fee-for-service physicians to prepaid group practice plans. In one early study, Richard Tessler and David Mechanic (1975) attempted to compare satisfaction levels for consumers under these alternative arrangements. They found that, although most consumers in the two groups reported being "very satisfied" with their medical services, satisfaction levels were marginally lower in the prepaid group plans.

Because of positional concerns, however, even this small difference probably overstates the cost of a societywide move to less expensive methods of delivering health care. Whether a consumer is dissatisfied when he is told he must wait three weeks for an MRI of his tennis elbow will depend, after all, on how long he expected to have to wait. Canada has fewer high-tech diagnostic devices than the United States, which results in higher utilization rates, lower costs, and longer waiting times for nonemergency patients in Canada. But since the longer waiting times apply equally to all, they do not appear to be a matter of particular concern to Canadian consumers.

In what follows, I will assume that important health outcomes are at most only weakly related to total expenditures on health care and that consumer satisfaction with health care services depends not just on the absolute quality of those services, but also on their relative quality. My point is not that people envy those who receive better care or take pleasure from the fact that they receive better care than others. Rather, it is that subjective evaluations of the adequacy of care are context-dependent. By "context," I have in mind the comparison between one person's services and another's, and the comparison between current services and those enjoyed in the past. Under these assumptions, I will now compare the following two alternative health care finance plans with respect to their prospects for holding expenditure growth in check:

> *Plan 1.* Universal membership in a basic, no-frills health insurance plan is financed out of general tax revenues. Consumers are free to join more elaborate plans that include amenities like private hospital rooms, access to new and experimental technologies, or older technologies with low benefit-cost ratios; but they must pay the full cost of the alternative plan completely out of pocket.

> *Plan 2.* A tax-financed voucher is issued to every consumer in the amount required to purchase membership in plan 1. People may then either join plan 1 or supplement their voucher with their own funds to purchase membership in more elaborate plans.

Plan 1 is analogous to the existing method of financing education in most jurisdictions in the United States. Parents can send their students to public schools financed out of tax revenues, or they can send them to private schools by paying the full private tuition out of pocket. Plan 2 resembles recent proposals to fund schooling through a voucher system. These proposals allow parents to send their children to private schools by paying only the difference between the voucher and the current private school tuition.

The essential difference between the two plans is captured by a comparison of the budget constraints they present to a representative family faced with the choice of how much health care to buy. Figure 6.1 shows a family with a pretax income of $Y$, and assumes that health care services can be produced at a constant cost of $P_m$ per unit. Under plan 1, each family pays $T$ in health care taxes and is then entitled to $Q_1 = T/P_m$ units of medical services without further payment. If it wants to enroll in a private plan that offers more than $Q_1$ units of medical services, it must quit the public plan and enroll in the private plan at a cost of $P_m$ per unit. The budget constraint facing a family under plan 1 is thus the locus ABCD in figure 6.1. The kink at B represents the fact that, to improve upon the basic plan, the family must essentially forfeit its entitlement to services under the basic plan and start purchasing medical services from scratch in the private sector. Thus, to purchase just one more unit of medical services beyond the basic plan, it must pay not $P_m$, but $T + P_m$. This is a sharp disincentive to expand beyond the basic plan, and, for the indifference map shown, the family's optimal choice is to stick with the basic plan (represented by point B in fig. 6.1).

Under the voucher system of plan 2, the family's budget constraint is the locus ABF in figure 6.1. By essentially rebating the family's tax payment $T$ in the form of a voucher, this plan enables the family to expand its coverage beyond the basic plan by spending only $P_m$ for each additional unit of cover-

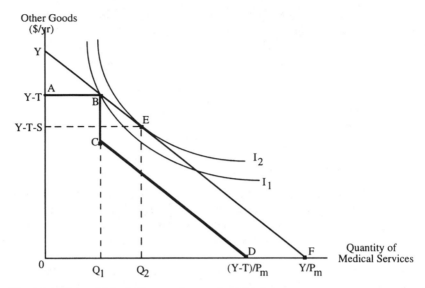

**Fig. 6.1    Financial incentives under two health plans**

age. Again for the indifference map shown, the family's best option under these terms is to expand its coverage by purchasing bundle $E$, which contains $Q_2 > Q_1$ units of medical services. What is clear, then, is that many families— possibly the vast majority of families—would purchase significantly higher quantities of medical services under plan 2 than under plan 1.

Under conventional economic models, in which satisfaction depends only on absolute consumption, this would be a difference of no concern, since families who elect more elaborate coverage would be paying the full social cost of the added coverage.[7] But things look different if satisfaction also depends on relative consumption. The fact that the voucher plan induces many families to purchase more elaborate coverage now becomes a matter of social concern, since a direct effect of their action is to reduce the satisfaction of consumers who stick with the basic plan.

Once enough consumers enroll in more elaborate health plans, features that were once considered special amenities in those plans will come, over time, to be viewed as essential. People are troubled by inequality in virtually any form, but few forms elicit such strong reactions as the perception of unequal access to "essential" medical services. In a democratic system like ours, the resulting dissatisfaction would translate into irresistible political pressures to upgrade the basic plan.

---

7. Peltzman (1973) has argued that our current method of financing public education causes many people to spend too little on education. On this view, the spending increase prompted by the move to a voucher system would be a welfare improvement.

Families would then be confronted with the option of upgrading the new, more generous, basic plan by supplementing their vouchers at the margin as before. Many would undoubtedly do so, and political pressure to upgrade the basic plan would begin anew. The voucher plan thus promises to set in motion a dynamic process that would cause even more rapid escalation in health expenditures than we have witnessed in recent decades.

In view of the evidence that spending more on health care does little to change important health outcomes, and little to enhance consumer satisfaction in the long run, the voucher plan seems a very poor bargain indeed. Under the nonvoucher plan, by contrast, there is a much clearer prospect of being able to hold the growth of medical expenditures in check.

Of course, these are not the only two plans on the table. Victor Fuchs, for example, favors a third option, in which everyone would be enrolled in a basic plan and then allowed to purchase supplementary coverage out of pocket. The desirability of this option depends critically on the price at which supplementary coverage is made available. For example, if families are permitted to supplement their basic coverage at marginal private cost, this option becomes essentially the same as what I have characterized as the voucher plan. And if the basic plan were truly a no-frills plan, most families would indeed be likely to upgrade on these terms. So just like the voucher plan, the basic-care-with-optional-upgrades plan would engage the social escalation process just described.

At the same time, Fuchs's proposal has undeniable appeal. Having grown accustomed to deluxe medical coverage under our current system, many, if not most, middle-income families might be unwilling to move to a no-frills plan. (If required to move, however, their initial dissatisfaction would diminish over time as the new context became the norm.) But political decisions are grounded largely in the here and now, and without some way of adding supplementary coverage short of starting from scratch, plan 1 might be a political nonstarter. Fortunately, a continuum of plans between plans 1 and 2 are available. What is important is that people not be allowed to upgrade the basic plan by paying only the marginal private cost of the additional features they add.

A compromise plan, for example, might be like the original plan 1 except with more elaborate coverage. This would make it more expensive at first, but would retain the critical feature of plan 1—namely, its ability to contain pressure to escalate the basic plan's coverage over time. Alternatively, a plan might be crafted along the lines Fuchs proposes: people could be permitted to purchase additional features without starting from scratch, but only by paying premiums significantly larger than the marginal private cost of those features.[8]

---

8. In cases where the marginal costs of additional services are lower than their average costs, the sellers' need to cover total costs might independently necessitate a requirement to charge more than marginal cost for upgrade features. Whether an additional premium is warranted would then depend on the strength of the consumption externalities to which the purchase of these features gives rise.

Thus, for example, if the marginal private cost of adding a rider that provided access to experimental therapies were $1,000/year, that rider could be made available at a charge of, say, $2,000. The central design goal should be to come up with a plan that can attract and maintain the allegiance of a sufficiently large majority that its features become the norm. For once large numbers of consumers elect coverage significantly beyond what is included in the basic plan, that plan ceases to be seen as "adequate" and hence becomes politically unsustainable.

## 6.3  Education

The question of how best to finance education raises many issues similar to the ones just discussed for health care. Like health care, for example, education is a service industry in which expenditures in real terms have sharply outpaced secular growth in real output. There is also some evidence that important educational outcomes do not improve significantly with increases in expenditure per pupil (see, e.g., Hanushek 1986). And perhaps even more so than in the case of health care, the adequacy of a system of education is perceived in essentially relative terms.

As noted, the current method for financing education in most jurisdictions is like the health plan 1 just discussed. Public schools are financed out of tax revenues, and parents who want to send their children to private schools must pay full market tuition out of pocket. The principal alternative to the current system is a voucher system essentially like the health plan 2 just discussed. Under this alternative, parents are given a school voucher that may be used either to enroll their children in a public school, or, with appropriate out-of-pocket supplements, to enroll them in a private school.

By making it possible to purchase small upgrades in educational quality without having to buy private schooling from scratch, the voucher plan would undoubtedly lead many families to spend more on education than is currently spent in the public schools. And since education, like medical care, is an arena in which positional concerns operate with special force, a static voucher would be difficult to sustain once substantial numbers of families had upgraded. The potential for expenditure escalation is thus precisely the same under the voucher method of financing education as it is under the voucher method for financing health care.

Before rejecting the voucher proposals in education, however, there are some important differences between the two arenas that deserve close scrutiny. Most important, despite all the legitimate criticism about limited access to the American health care system, few deny that the quality of care it delivers is among the best in the world. By contrast, the American system of public schooling ranks near the bottom of industrialized nations on virtually every important measure (see Chubb and Moe 1990). In education, there is thus a strong argument for making at least *some* changes in the status quo.

Moreover, there are persuasive arguments that the competition introduced by a voucher system might help solve many of the problems that currently plague public schools (Chubb and Moe 1990). Parents' inability to choose between schools, for example, means that public school bureaucrats have little incentive to develop innovative educational programs or to take special steps to attract and retain better teachers. Forcing schools to compete for tuition dollars could significantly alter this picture.

The question thus becomes, How can we inject additional competition into the educational arena without unleashing forces that might give rise to runaway escalation in expenditures? One solution might be to limit the applicability of the voucher to schools that held expenditures per pupil below some specified level. In functional terms, this would be similar to existing proposals that vouchers be redeemable only in public schools. A less extreme measure, similar to the intermediate health plan options discussed in the last section, would be to reduce the value of the voucher by some amount for each dollar of tuition the chosen school charged above a given threshold.

Since there is no evidence that expenditures per pupil are too small under the current system, the policy challenge is to design a voucher scheme that will introduce greater competition among schools yet not induce most parents to supplement their vouchers. As with the health care voucher plan, any plan that induces substantial numbers of families to supplement their vouchers is almost certain to launch runaway cycles of expenditure growth.

## 6.4 Child Care

Child care, once the exclusive province of the private sector, moved into the governmental arena with the introduction of the Head Start program. Although this program continues to be targeted at the children of poor households, there is growing interest in expanded public funding for preschool care programs more generally. This interest springs at least in part from the steadily growing labor-force participation rates of women with preschool children. The labor-force participation rate for mothers whose youngest child was three months old, for example, grew from less than 25% in 1975 to more than 50% in 1988 (Klerman and Leibowitz 1994, fig. 1).

To the extent that many parents are either unwilling or unable to purchase satisfactory child care on their own, there is a twofold case for greater government involvement. First, there is the issue of social justice for the children involved. Early childhood experience is known to influence important outcomes throughout life, and it seems grossly unfair for society to allow the futures of large numbers of children to be seriously compromised through no fault of their own. And second, even if justice were not a concern, we have a strong selfish interest in limiting the number of damaged people in society. Such people, after all, are more likely than others to become criminals or to require social assistance in various forms.

Suppose we grant, for the sake of discussion, a collective interest in making child care more available to those least able to afford it. What form should the government's financial assistance take? As we did in the health care and education cases, let us again suppose there are only two choices: (1) provision of basic services financed out of tax revenues; and (2) issuance of a voucher that can be used, with out-of-pocket supplements if desired, to purchase child care in the marketplace.

The first alternative invites the same set of problems that currently plague our public schools. By facilitating greater competition between child care providers, the voucher scheme would help avoid these problems. But to the extent that community standards provide the frame of reference that people use to evaluate the quality of the child care they purchase, the voucher scheme also invites the prospect of sharply escalating expenditures on child care. As in health care and education, if a substantial majority of parents supplemented their vouchers to provide more elaborate facilities for their children, these facilities would gradually become the norm, leading to political pressure to raise the existing voucher.

Whether this prospect is viewed as threatening depends on the social utility of additional expenditures on child care. In both health and education, we can be reasonably confident that we would not get much of value simply by spending more. In the child care arena our experience is much more limited. If the current problem is that most people spend far too little on child care, additional pressure to spend more might be just what we need. Even if so, however, the voucher scheme has no built-in mechanism to prevent further escalation once expenditures reached the efficient level.

As in the other arenas, many of the benefits of the voucher approach could be achieved by a modified plan that constrained parents' ability to supplement the basic voucher. Vouchers could be made redeemable, for example, only in programs that charged no more than the voucher amount. Or, more flexibly but with slightly more risk of expenditure escalation, parents could be permitted to supplement their vouchers at steep penalty rates. Thus, for example, if the basic voucher were for $500/month and parents enrolled their child in a $600/month program, they might be required to supplement their voucher not by $100, but by $200 or even $300. As before, the idea is to choose a sufficiently steep penalty that most people elect not to upgrade.

## 6.5   Long-Term Care

In the health, education, and child care arenas, people have considerable direct knowledge of community consumption standards. For this reason, voucher plans that allow upgrading at private marginal cost create the risk of runaway expenditure escalation. By contrast, community standards are much less clearly defined in the case of long-term care. Indeed, most people have no idea whether their friends and neighbors even have long-term care insurance, much less know the standard of care it might provide. Long-term care is thus an "unobservable good," a term I have used elsewhere to describe goods for which direct social comparisons are of relatively little importance (see Frank 1985a).

Although the purchase of long-term care insurance is unobservable, it and other unobservable goods are nonetheless influenced indirectly by positional concerns. Suppose, for the sake of discussion, that goods are either observable or unobservable, and that interpersonal consumption comparisons occur only with respect to observable goods. Positional concerns will then lead people to devote too much of their budgets to observable goods, and too little to unobservable goods. By this I mean that each person would obtain higher utility if all were to shift resources at the margin toward the purchase of unobservable goods.[9]

This theoretical prediction appears consistent with what we know about private purchase decisions regarding long-term care. People routinely insure their cars against theft and damage, even when they could cover such losses out of pocket without great difficulty, yet these same people generally do not insure against the loss of their earning power, a setback that few could handle satisfactorily on their own.

Unlike the health, education, and child care arenas, where voucher plans threaten to push expenditures out of control, the objective here is to induce consumers to devote more of their resources to long-term care. A voucher scheme would serve this goal nicely. The problem with leaving long-term care strictly to the marketplace is that, when consumers decide individually to increase their spending on long-term care insurance, their spending on observable goods falls relative to other consumers. But when we decide collectively to spend more on such insurance, consumption of observables falls in tandem for all consumers, which means that no one suffers a decline in relative consumption of observables.

Of course, even collective decisions to devote more resources to long-term care insurance necessarily entail absolute reductions in other categories of consumption. And to the extent that each individual's own current consumption standards help define his personal frame of reference, such reductions will not be painless. The psychological costs of adjustment, and hence the political costs of implementing the necessary reforms, are likely to be smaller if the shift of resources toward long-term care insurance occurs gradually rather than all at once.

9. Since health insurance is no more observable than long-term care insurance, the analysis suggests a parallel tendency to spend too little on health insurance. This may help explain why some 15% of all Americans, not all of them poor, currently have no health insurance. It may also explain the tendency for most governments to provide some form of social insurance for medical care.

## 6.6   Concluding Remarks

Every scheme for financing the provision of social services contains incentives that affect individual behavior. To predict how people will respond to given methods of financing health care, education, child care, or long-term care, we need reliable models of behavior. For this purpose, economists have generally employed models in which utility depends only on absolute consumption. Yet there is abundant evidence that utility depends on relative consumption as well.

I have argued that policies for financing social services have strikingly different consequences under the two models. Positional concerns operate with special force in health care, education, and child care, and policy makers who fail to take these concerns into account will fail to anticipate the potential for runaway expenditures inherent in voucher schemes in these areas. By contrast, positional concerns give rise to expenditure deficits in the long-term care arena, and policy makers who ignore these concerns are unlikely to perceive the attraction of collective efforts to steer additional resources into this arena.

If the evidence for the existence of positional concerns is so compelling, why do analysts so seldom take these concerns into account? Some have responded that, although people *do* care about relative position, they *shouldn't* care about it, and policy makers should give these concerns no more weight than, say, the concerns of sadists.[10] This is a curious position in view of the long utilitarian tradition in economics, which holds that a taste for poetry is no better than a taste for pushpins. But even if we reject envy itself as a proper basis for policy decisions, positional concerns often arise with great force even when envy plays no role. In any event, positional concerns are not going to go away. When we fail to take them into account, we often fail to achieve outcomes that everyone would prefer.

# References

Bachman, J., R. Kahn, T. Davidson, and L. Johnston. 1967. *Youth in Transition.* Vol. 1. Ann Arbor, MI: Institute for Social Research.

Baumol, W. J. 1993. Social Wants and the Dismal Science: The Curious Case of the Climbing Costs of Health and Teaching. C. V. Starr Center for Applied Economics Research Report no. 93-20. New York University. May.

Baumol, W. J., and W. G. Bowen. 1966. *Performing Arts: The Economic Dilemma.* New York: Twentieth Century Fund.

Boskin, M., and E. Sheshinski. 1978. Optimal Redistributive Taxation When Individual Welfare Depends on Relative Income. *Quarterly Journal of Economics* 92:589–600.

Bradburn, N., and D. Caplovitz. 1965. *Reports on Happiness.* Chicago: Aldine.

10. This is essentially John Rawls's position (1971).

Bradburn, N., and C. E. Noll. 1969. *The Structure of Psychological Well-Being.* Chicago: Aldine.

Brickman, P., D. Coates, and R. Janoff-Bulman. 1978. Lottery Winners and Accident Victims: Is Happiness Relative? *Journal of Personality and Social Psychology* 36 (August): 917–27.

Chubb, J. E., and T. Moe. 1990. *Politics, Markets, and America's Schools.* Washington, DC: Brookings Institution.

Duesenberry, J. 1949. *Income, Saving, and the Theory of Consumer Behavior.* Cambridge: Harvard University Press.

Easterlin, R. 1995. Will Raising the Incomes of All Increase the Happiness of All? *Journal of Economic Behavior and Organization* 27, no. 1.

Feldstein, M. S. 1971. Hospital Cost Inflation: A Study of Nonprofit Price Dynamics. *American Economic Review* 61 (December): 853–72.

———. 1977. Quality Change and the Demand for Hospital Care. *Econometrica* 45 (October): 1681–1702.

Frank, R. H. 1985a. *Choosing the Right Pond.* New York: Oxford University Press.

———. 1985b. The Demand for Unobservable and Other Nonpositional Goods. *American Economic Review* 75 (March): 101–16.

Frank, Robert H., and Philip J. Cook. 1995. *The Winner-Take-All Society.* New York: Free Press.

Fuchs, V. R. 1990. The Health Sector's Share of the Gross National Product. *Science* 247:534–38.

———. 1994. The Clinton Plan: A Researcher Examines Reform. *Health Affairs* 13 (spring): 102–14.

Guth, W., R. Schmittberger, and B. Schwarze. 1982. An Experimental Analysis of Ultimatum Bargaining. *Journal of Economic Behavior and Organization* 3:367–88.

Hanushek, E. A. 1986. The Economics of Schooling: Production and Efficiency in Public Schools. *Journal of Economic Literature* 24, no. 3:1141–77.

Helson, H. 1964. *Adaptation-Level Theory.* New York: Harper and Row.

Hirsch, F. 1976. *Social Limits to Growth.* Cambridge: Harvard University Press.

Klerman, J. A., and A. Leibowitz. 1994. The Work-Employment Distinction among New Mothers. RAND Corporation. Mimeo.

Kosicki, G. 1987. Savings as a Nonpositional Good. *Southern Economic Journal* 54 (October): 422–34.

Layard, R. 1980. Human Satisfactions and Public Policy. *Economic Journal* 90:737–50.

McEvoy, G. M., and W. F. Cascio. 1985. Strategies for Reducing Employee Turnover: A Meta-Analysis. *Journal of Applied Psychology* 70:342–53.

McGuire, M., M. Raleigh, and G. Brammer. 1982. Sociopharmacology. *Annual Review of Pharmacological Toxicology* 22:643–61.

Manning, W. G., J. P. Newhouse, E. B. Keeler, A. Leibowitz, and M. S. Marquis. 1987. Health Insurance and the Demand for Medical Care. *American Economic Review* 77 (June): 251–77.

Newhouse, J. P. 1992. Medical Care Costs: How Much Welfare Loss? *Journal of Economic Perspectives* 6 (summer): 3–21.

Ng, Y. K. 1987. Diamonds Are a Government's Best Friend. *American Economic Review* 77 (March): 186–91.

Palmore, E. 1969. Predicting Longevity: A Followup Controlling for Age. *Journal of Gerontology* 39:109–16.

Peltzman, S. 1973. The Effect of Government Subsidies-in-Kind on Private Expenditures: The Case of Higher Education. *Journal of Political Economy* 81:1–27.

Raleigh, M., M. McGuire, G. Brammer, and A. Yuweiler. 1984. Social and Environmental Influences of Blood Serotonin Concentrations in Monkeys. *Archives of General Psychiatry* 4:405–10.

Rawls, J. 1971. *A Theory of Justice.* Cambridge: Harvard University Press.

Sales, S. M., and J. House. 1971. Job Dissatisfaction as a Possible Risk Factor in Coronary Heart Disease. *Journal of Chronic Diseases* 23:861–73.

Seidman, L. 1987. Taxes in a Relativistic Economy. *Southern Economic Journal* 54 (October): 463–74.

Sen, A. K. 1983. Poor, Relatively Speaking. *Oxford Economic Papers* 35:153–67.

———. 1987. *The Standard of Living.* Cambridge: Cambridge University Press.

Scitovsky, T. 1976. *The Joyless Economy.* New York: Oxford University Press.

Tessler, R., and D. Mechanic. 1975. Consumer Satisfaction with Prepaid Group Practice: A Comparative Study. *Journal of Health and Social Behavior* 16 (March): 95–113.

Veblen, T. 1899. *The Theory of the Leisure Class.* New York: Macmillan.

Wall, T. D., C. W. Clegg, and P. R. Jackson. 1978. An Evaluation of the Job Characteristics Model. *Journal of Occupational Psychology* 51:183–96.

Weisbrod, B. A. 1991. The Health Care Quadrilemma: An Essay on Technological Change, Insurance, Quality of Care, and Cost Containment. *Journal of Economic Literature* 29 (June): 523–52.

Wright, R. 1994. *The Moral Animal.* New York: Pantheon.

# Comment     Amartya Sen

Robert Frank's paper is both interesting and insightful, and also of potential practical importance. The paper starts off in familiar territory—indeed a territory that Frank has done much to make familiar. Our sense of well-being depends greatly on our *relative* positions.[1] This important connection Frank explores in assessing different ways of financing health care, education, child care, and long-term care. With this basic relativist consideration, Frank combines a few others: the *observability* of the relative positions occupied; the *usefulness* of channeling more resources into the respective fields; and the role of *competition* in fostering efficiency in each area. I begin with presenting Frank's main arguments in terms of these general considerations applied to the respective specific spheres.

## Basic Approaches and General Considerations

There are two basic approaches in public funding of care. Plan 1 gives everyone an entitlement to some basic care, but if someone chooses to have more care than that, then he or she must pay the full cost of the alternative chosen (nothing is carried on from the basic care package). Under plan 2, however, each person is entitled to support to a fixed extent (given, for example, by the value of a "voucher"), and one could use it to purchase either the basic service

Amartya Sen is the Lamont University Professor and professor of economics and philosophy at Harvard University.

1. Frank (1985) is a far-reaching exploration of the relevance and reach of the relativist perspective. See also Hirsch (1976).

or something more expensive (paying the difference). There are many intermediate possibilities, but the main strategic contrast is between these two approaches.

The effect of plan 2 is typically to raise the overall expenditure level, particularly encouraged by the desire of each to do as well and better than others; marginal additions can be made under plan 2 without losing the basic support, as would happen under plan 1. Supplementation by some would also make the others feel—and be—worse off. And it can generate pressure for upgrading the basic entitlement itself, so that the others do not feel left far behind the supplementers. Would this be a good thing? Frank argues that the answer must vary among the distinct fields.

### Health, Education, Child Care, and Long-Term Care

When applied to health care, the expansion of medical expenditure resulting from plan 2 would not be all that productive, Frank argues, citing evidence of the ineffectiveness of additional medical expenditure in improving health or longevity (Fuchs's works bear on this claim). This suggests that plan 2 is "a very poor bargain indeed"; plan 1 has a clear advantage in the field of health care. Some compromises are considered, including a hybrid plan proposed by Fuchs (1994), whereby the upgrading of services is made more costly, without going all the way to plan 1. But intermediate plans also have intermediate problems.

In education, the same consideration applies, but Frank sees less waste in upgrading basic educational provisions in the United States (compared with that in health, where the general quality of care is already very high). This makes the argument against plan 2 in education a little less powerful. A compromise is sought, but with less of a full-blooded rejection of plan 2.

When it comes to child care, the inflationary features of plan 2 remain, but the scope for more fruitful expenditure in this field appears to be very clear. And so is the effectiveness of more competition in raising efficiency, and this would be encouraged by plan 2. The balance of advantages now shifts somewhat away from plan 1, moving in the direction of plan 2.

Finally, when it comes to long-term care, there is not only a strong need for more money being spent on it, which makes plan 2 useful, but also the well-being effects of plan 2 are less austere. The relative increase of long-term care on the part of some families need not generate the sense of being "left behind" on the part of those not able to supplement the basic provision. This is because, argues Frank, this kind of care is largely "unobservable," and the standards of care are not quite common knowledge.

### Variations and the Facts of the Case

So it turns out, in this series of arguments, that Frank arrives at quite *different* conclusions about the right way of financing distinct types of cares (health, education, child care, and long-term). But the different recommendations are all based on the same basic principles. Dissimilar conclusions result from variations in the conditions that obtain. And this indeed is a great merit of Frank's analysis, which is at once quite general (in terms of principles) and very specific (in terms of applications). Since the question is sometimes asked—explicitly or by implication—why the same rules should not apply in different spheres of social insurance and public support, Frank's line of analysis has much attraction: the rules have to be different to be faithful to the same basic principles.

While I see the force of Frank's arguments, I shall not refrain from airing some mild grumbles. First, as far as health care is concerned, it is possible that Frank is somewhat overpessimistic about the effects of more resources going to health care. While the main defects of contemporary health care arrangements in the United States clearly lie elsewhere (particularly in the absence of universal coverage and affordable health care for all), the statistics of longevity and health benefits can, to some extent, hide the positive impact of more health expenditure, particularly in reducing pain and suffering and in improving the quality of life. Also, even health care practices—not just education and schooling—can improve with more competition and more learning from each other, and there is considerable evidence that even in the United States the level of care in different hospitals (for example, in radical surgery) varies a great deal. Frank's overall conclusion may well be right, but there is some need to answer the counterarguments that can certainly be presented.

### Well-Being and Psychology

Second, when Frank analyzes the effects of relative position on one's well-being, he relies largely on the psychological sense of well-being (such as happiness, satisfaction, etc.) as the true indicator. In this sense, Frank's approach has features of classical utilitarianism. While he cites John Rawls (1971) as dissenting from this view, Rawls's counterarguments are not, in fact, terribly well presented here. Frank identifies Rawls's position with the view that "policy makers should give these [relative position–based] concerns no more weight than, say, the concerns of sadists." Rawls's arguments (and those of many other modern political philosophers) are less arbitrary than that. Rawls's reasoning turns on rejecting the exclusive status of subjective perceptions in judging well-being.

There are issues of real importance here. For example, consider a general diminution of living conditions that reduces the quality of life and effective freedoms of all, but which leaves everyone's sense of well-being (based strongly on relativist perceptions) rather unchanged, since *all* have come down together. In terms of the purely subjectivist view of well-being (to which Frank seems largely to adhere), not much would seem to have been lost in this case. But this can be seriously questioned, since everyone is *absolutely* more deprived (for example, more hungry, more insecure, and so on), even though not so in *relative* terms. There is an issue here that needs addressing.

## Types of Relativities

Finally, there is perhaps need for distinguishing among the different ways in which "relative" concerns figure in influencing our perceptions, effective freedoms, and welfare. There is, first of all, *relativity in commanding commodities:* the competition for the same facilities in which more absolute purchasing power of some would mean less relative entitlement of others. For example, in the fight for entitlement over food in situations leading to a famine, the increase in the money income of one group has often reduced the absolute command over food that others may have.

The second kind is the *relativity in generating capabilities* from a specific bundle of commodities, or from a specific level of real income. As Adam Smith has pointed out, in a country where everyone has linen clothes and leather shoes to wear, someone without them would feel poor in a way a person might not in another society in which others too don't have these things. The ability to "appear in public without shame" depends not only on one's own commodity bundle (or real income) but also on what others have.

The third kind is the *relativity in evaluating capabilities.* What we regard as minimally acceptable freedoms would tend to depend on what others standardly have. When the standard achievements go up, acceptability may also be revised upward.

Each of these three perspectives brings in relative concerns (and they actually do figure in Frank's arguments), but not for the same reason, nor in the same way. Their distinct bearings may be fruitfully separated out in extending Frank's analysis further. For example, if as a result of plan 2 there is a substantial increase in the money spent by some on health, then, given the existing *total* facilities, this may reduce the absolute facilities obtained by the others who may be competed out (relativity in commanding commodities). This can be a significant consideration, particularly in the short run.

Now consider a case in which this does not happen, perhaps because of the expansion of total supply of these facilities. But still the sense of being medically "secure" (or of having "state of the art" care) can be unfavorably affected by the escalation of care for some, even when the concrete medical facilities remain the same for others (relativity in generating capabilities). The capability of feeling medically secure does not depend only on the exact medical facilities the person enjoys, but also on relative positions.

But even when such a deprivation of capabilities does not occur, it is possible that a general expansion of medical care may lead to a change of standards in deciding on the minimally acceptable sense of medical security (relativity in evaluating capabilities). Each of these types of relations has relevance to the subject matter of Frank's paper. But they have to be distinguished, since they operate differently, and because our welfare-economic evaluation of these different types of effects may well be quite divergent.

Frank's already rich line of analysis can perhaps be somewhat further enriched in these ways. However, we must not grumble that Frank has not done more, since he has done so much.

## References

Frank, Robert H. 1985. *Choosing the Right Pond.* New York: Oxford University Press.
Fuchs, Victor. 1994. The Clinton Plan: A Researcher Examines Reform. *Health Affairs* 13 (spring): 102–14.
Hirsch, Fred. 1976. *Social Limits to Growth.* Cambridge: Harvard University Press.
Rawls, John. 1971. *A Theory of Justice.* Cambridge: Harvard University Press.

# 7     Preferences, Promises, and the Politics of Entitlement

Paul M. Romer

## 7.1   Prologue

In 1953, the U.S. Chamber of Commerce proposed a major expansion in the coverage of the Old Age and Survivors Insurance Program—the program that we now think of as Social Security. There was much room for expansion because only 55% of the workforce was covered when the Social Security Act was passed in 1935. Legislation enacted in 1950 had already expanded the coverage of the program. It brought many additional workers into the Social Security system and substantially reduced the number of quarters of covered employment that were necessary to qualify for retirement benefits. However, these changes came too late for many people. Many workers had retired before 1950. Others died without working long enough to qualify, leaving widows who were not eligible for survivors insurance. Under the Social Security Act, these unfortunate people were eligible only for Old Age Assistance, the less-generous, means-tested welfare program administered by the states.

Under the chamber's proposal, everyone over the age of sixty-five would immediately become eligible for retirement benefits. The Old Age Assistance program would be terminated. Retirement benefits would continue to be financed on a pay-as-you-go basis, using a payroll tax. All remaining workers who had not yet been brought into the Social Security system would be subjected to the payroll tax, but the tax rate would still have to be increased to pay for the expanded system of benefits.

From the perspective of the 1990s, it seems odd that a proposal for expanded social spending should come from a major business lobby. The political response this proposal provoked is equally surprising. Conservative Republicans

Paul M. Romer is professor of economics at the University of California at Berkeley, a research associate of the National Bureau of Economic Research, and a fellow of the Canadian Institute for Advanced Research.

in Congress took the initiative in promoting the chamber's plan. Daniel Reed, the conservative chairman of the Republican-controlled Ways and Means Committee, called for fundamental reexamination of the system. Carl Curtis, a Republican from Nebraska who had been critical of the evolving Social Security system, chaired the subcommittee hearings on the chamber's proposal and took the lead in promoting it in Congress. After lengthy consideration, the liberal Republicans in control of the Department of Health, Education, and Welfare in the new Eisenhower administration decided not to support it. Nelson Rockefeller, the undersecretary responsible for legislative proposals, was generally supportive of the existing Social Security system and did not want to propose any major changes to its structure. Senior citizens, even those who would become eligible for retirement benefits under the chamber's plan, did not offer any organized support for the plan.

Program executives in the Social Security Administration reacted with alarm and outrage to the hearings conducted by Curtis. As government employees, and especially as holdovers from the previous Democratic administration, they were constrained from openly attacking the merits of the proposal and the integrity of the members of Congress who supported it. However, they did feed analyses and denunciations to sympathetic policy analysts on the staff of the American Federation of Labor (AFL), who passed them on to the Washington press corps. Because the Eisenhower administration did not support the chamber's plan and because opponents were able to characterize it as a dangerous assault by enemies of the Social Security system, it never received serious consideration in Congress.

Five years later, in 1958, internal estimates prepared by the Research Department of the Social Security Administration showed that 35% of the people over age sixty-five still were not eligible for Social Security retirement benefits (Cates 1983, 72). Large numbers of them had no private source of income and refused to accept public assistance—to "go on the dole." They lived out their lives in circumstances of extreme poverty. Ultimately, the Social Security system did succeed in reducing poverty among the elderly, but demographics were an important part of the story. The poverty rate fell as the uncovered elderly died.[1]

## 7.2   Introduction and Summary of the Argument

The arguments in this paper address three types of questions. The most specific question, and the one that is easiest to answer, is why the different actors in the Social Security debate of the 1950s chose such surprising political strategies. The answer to this narrow question raises a second question that is broader and more troubling for economists, one that goes to the heart of any

1. See Derthick (1979, chap. 6) for details of the chamber's proposal and the debate it spawned. See Cates (1983, chaps. 3 and 5) for a critical evaluation of the treatment of the uncovered elderly.

analysis of political economy: What determines why and how people vote? This second question is important in its own right, but it is raised here with a view toward an even deeper and more controversial third question: How can economists and like-minded social scientists begin to address the effects that values have on policy choices and that policies have on values?

The logic behind the liberal and conservative strategies during the 1950s is clear from the historical record. Both sides in the fight over the Social Security system adopted positions that seemed to run counter to their natural interests, because they were actually fighting over something far more important than expanding benefits for the uncovered elderly. They made important tactical concessions to win the war over the public's sense of entitlement. This explanation covers the behavior of the proponents and critics of the chamber's plan, but it leaves open the question of why the elderly, especially the uncovered elderly, were absent from the debate. Observing that they were not organized then is not an explanation. It is a description of the fact that needs to be explained. We will return to this issue in the conclusion.

Conservative critics of the Social Security system were willing to accept higher current payments in hopes of limiting future growth in payments. Specifically, they were willing to accept an expansion of the Social Security program in exchange for structural changes that would keep voters from treating Social Security retirement benefits as an entitlement. The chamber's plan would dispense with the carefully crafted imagery of individual contributions and personal retirement accounts that the architects of the Social Security system had been developing for fifteen years. It would remove all pretense that there was any link between taxes paid and benefits received. It would lay bare the economic essence of the program, showing that it was a system of transfers from the young to the old. No voter believes that paying income taxes entitles the payer to cash welfare benefits. If it had been adopted, the chamber's plan would have given payroll taxes and government payments to the elderly the same political status as income taxes and welfare payments.

On the other side, the proponents of the Social Security system sacrificed the well-being of the uncovered elderly to create a system of government transfers that recipients would regard as an entitlement. Program administrators in the Social Security Administration reacted with anger and indignation to the hearing chaired by Curtis because his goal was to demolish the imagery that was at the heart of the program. He wanted to show that the previous administration had intentionally misled the public about the nature of the program. The sacrifice of the uncovered elderly was just one of several tactical concessions advocates of the system made as part of a long-run strategy for convincing people that they were entitled to payments from the government. A similar concession came in the decision to finance Social Security payments with a regressive payroll tax. President Roosevelt personally vetoed early proposals that retirement benefits be financed partially from general tax revenues. In a private remark, he later gave one of the most candid statements of the logic behind his strategy. When a visitor to the White House complained about the regressivity of the payroll tax, he explained: "I guess you are right about the economics, but those taxes were never a problem of economics. They are politics all the way through. We put those payroll contributions there so as to give the contributors a legal, moral, and political right to collect their pensions. . . . With those taxes in there, no damn politician can ever scrap my social security program" (quoted in Derthick 1979, 230).

The evidence presented in section 7.6 documents the claim that the fundamental issue in the fight over Social Security in the 1950s—in fact, the fundamental issue in the construction of the entire Social Security program—was the notion of entitlement. Both sides recognized the importance of the implicit promises that were bundled with the taxes and transfers, although conservative critics of the program were arguably slower to catch on to the importance of this issue. In light of subsequent political developments, Roosevelt and his allies in the Social Security Administration decisively won the war and imbued the Social Security program with a strong sense of entitlement. At a time when even the most radical budget cutters in Congress are afraid to even mention Social Security, it is hard to dispute the accuracy of Roosevelt's implicit model of how the political process works.

This explanation leads inexorably to the second question about the motivations that determine whether and how people vote. If the notion of entitlement is such an important political force, something important is missing from formal economic models of voting. Most conventional models of political economy summarize individual behavior with the assumption that people prefer more wealth to less. They also assume that a person will vote for a policy that would increase the voter's wealth.[2] The first assumption generally passes without comment. The second assumption is highly problematic, as many economists and political scientists have noted. But setting aside the well-known difficulty of explaining why anyone bothers to vote when the chances that one vote will matter are so small, economists are still faced with the awkward fact that their style of analysis permits no distinction between government payments that take the form of welfare checks and payments that take the form of Social Security benefits; that is, the standard model cannot distinguish between transfers and entitlements.

The models suggest that, everything else equal, voters will prefer larger payments from the government to smaller payments. From the individual's point of view, it makes no difference whether these payments are labeled "earned benefits" or "welfare payments." It makes no difference whether the voter has paid payroll taxes or not, or whether government officials made any promises about benefit payments when they collected those payroll taxes. As a result,

2. For a presentation of models of this type as applied to the analysis of voting on Social Security, see the model in Boadway and Wildasin (1989) and the models from other papers that are discussed there.

conventional models cannot accommodate the concept of entitlement, the issue that was the paramount concern of both the proponents and critics of the evolving Social Security system.

In a model of repeated interaction between two people, concepts such as reputation and punishment strategies can be invoked to give meaning to everyday concepts such as a promise or an entitlement. But in situations in which millions of voters interact with a small number of elected officials, it makes no sense to assert that any individual voter sets out to establish a reputation for toughness or to punish bad behavior by the government.

In an effort to go beyond the limitations of existing models of political economy, section 7.3 starts by briefly summarizing some of the early discussion in political science about formal models of voting. It recapitulates the conclusion that emerges from this literature—that economists and political scientists must modify the assumption that maximizing wealth is a good summary description of the motivation of an individual voter. Stated more explicitly, we have to go beyond the assumption that conventional consumption goods are the only arguments in a person's utility function and allow the act of voting to be a consumption activity that provides utility. As many political scientists have emphasized (see, for example, Aldrich 1993 and Jackman 1993), this does not signal a retreat from rational-choice models. It is merely a refinement of the objective function that a rational voter seeks to maximize.

Section 7.4 shows how an extended model of individual preferences can be used to formalize Roosevelt's implicit model of political dynamics. It shows that there are good reasons to expect that people will care about promises made to them by others and that they will be willing to incur a cost to punish someone who has made and broken a promise. The act of making, then breaking, a promise induces a taste for punishing the offender.

A desire to express anger by voting against a politician can motivate some people to go to the polls and can influence how they vote, but there are many other factors that motivate voting. Someone may feel a sense of duty or may enjoy the satisfaction that comes from demonstrating to others that one is a good citizen. Nevertheless, if anger is a potential motivation, it may be a particularly important one to study because it can be manipulated by politicians who behave strategically.

If people are angrier when a promise has been broken, it is possible to give content to the notion of an entitlement. An entitlement is a set of transfer payments that are bundled together with an explicit, credible promise from the government about the duration and level of future payments. If a politician such as Roosevelt can create an entitlement for a large number of people, this decisively changes the subsequent political dynamics. If a successor reduces the payments under the entitlement program, this will induce anger and a taste for retribution in large numbers of voters. These voters will act on this taste by voting against the successor.

The quotation from Roosevelt cited above, together with the actions of his administration documented in section 7.6, provides direct support for the claim that creating a sense of entitlement was a paramount concern for the people who developed the Social Security system. Under the assumption that they knew what they were doing, their actions offer indirect evidence that the hypothesized form of preferences with a built-in taste for punishment is correct. But there is also direct evidence that bears on the nature of preferences. Section 7.5 points to evidence ranging from the behavior of animals, to experimental economics, to recent political developments, all of which support the notion that something like anger is an important source of motivation. The laboratory experiments are particularly relevant because they decisively refute the claim that statements about preferences cannot have scientific content.

The questions addressed here in the context of the Social Security program are directly relevant for other social policy issues. A positive analysis of the policies that governments have adopted, or might adopt, in areas such as child care, education, health care, and long-term care must take account of the fact that government policies are outcomes from a political process. If we cannot understand the forces that have driven the politics of the relatively well established and relatively well studied Social Security program, there is little hope that we will be able to understand the politics of new areas of social policy.

## 7.3   Voting and Preferences

The probability that one vote will be decisive is very low in elections with realistic numbers of voters. Suppose that the number of people who will vote is equal to $2n + 1$. Fix a particular voter, and assume that all other voters will vote in favor of a particular candidate with probability $q$. For simplicity, assume that this voter's vote is decisive only in the case of a tie. The probability that the other $2n$ voters will split evenly between the two alternatives is

$$\Pi = \frac{2n!}{n!^2} q^n (1 - q)^n.$$

For large values of $n$ and values of $q$ that differ from one-half, this probability is very small.

The largest values for $\Pi$ arise in the case where $q$ is equal to one-half, so that all other voters are equally likely to vote for or against this voter's preferred candidate. Consider an election for a seat in the U.S. Senate in which the total number of other voters, $2n$, is 2 million people. The probability of a tie is about .0004. In a presidential election in which 50 million people vote, the probability is reduced to .0001. If $q$ differs from one-half, the values for $\Pi$ are even smaller. Suppose that a voter has a prior probability distribution on the value of $q$ that is uniform over the interval (.4, .6). Ex ante, the outcome in the election is still a toss-up, but now there is a reasonable chance that the actual vote will not be close. In this case, the values for $\Pi$ fall by a factor of more than one hundred. (See Brennan and Buchanan 1984 for additional calculations along these lines.)

Political theorists have long understood the problem that this poses for simple theories of voter participation. Let $U(y)$ denote an indirect utility function defined over the disposable income $y$ that is available to the consumer after all taxes or transfers from the government. If people maximize $U(y)$ when they make their decision about whether to vote, even a small cost from voting— something like $1—will be orders of magnitude larger than the expected increase in $y$ that comes from voting for the candidate who offers this voter the best package of taxes and transfers.

Starting at least with Downs (1957), formal theorists have argued that there must be other components to the utility function that influence the decision to vote. In the terminology used here, they rely on an extended preference model, a model that lets preferences depend on arguments other than the standard consumption goods that are implicit in the function $U(y)$. Implicitly or explicitly, they proceed along the following lines: Let $x$ denote the decision about whether to go to the polling station and $W(x)$ denote the utility from voting. If voters maximize $U(y) + W(x)$, then the small cost of voting can be offset by the utility associated with this act.

Riker and Ordeshook (1968, 1973) formalized this additional term in the utility function and gave it empirical content. They suggested, for example, that a voter may care about the size of the margin by which a candidate wins. They use this observation to explain why, for example, many people bothered to vote for Lyndon Johnson in his landslide victory over Barry Goldwater. They also acknowledge that other aspects of preferences like a sense of duty or a strong sense of affiliation with a particular political party may contribute to the direct satisfaction that a person gets from the act of voting. They provide evidence that their augmented model is consistent with the evidence, but as Barry (1970) notes, almost all of the explanatory power comes from the $W(x)$ term in the utility function.

Fiorina (1976) takes this kind of analysis one step further. In his analysis, the utility for a representative voter may be written as $U(y) + W(a, v)$. The variable $a$ captures the party affiliation of the voter. Suppose that the absolute value of $a$ represents the intensity of the identification and the sign represents the party, positive for Democrat and negative for Republican. Let $v$ denote the candidate for whom the voter voters, with $v = 1$ representing a vote for the Democratic candidate and $v = -1$ a vote for the Republican.

The act of going to the polling station, $x$, and the candidate for whom the voter votes, $v$, both have an effect (albeit a very small one) on the expected wealth of the consumer. Fiorina refers to these as the instrumental aspects of voting. He calls the effects that $a$ and $v$ have as arguments of $W$ the expressive aspects of voting. He treats the party affiliation variable $a$ as a state variable that is determined by the voter's history, one that is given at the time of an election. The crucial assumption in Fiorina's analysis of participation is that there is an interaction between $a$, and $v$ in the function $W$, a positive cross-partial derivative. If $v$ and $a$ line up and if $a$ is large in absolute value, then the utility from choosing to vote will be larger. In everyday language, having a strong affiliation with a political party and voting for that party together make the act of going to the polls more satisfying. In the language of consumption theory, $a$ and $v$ are complements.

As Aldrich (1993) concludes in his survey of the literature on voter participation, there is no escape from the conclusion that, to understand voting, it takes a broader theory of preferences. There is room for dispute about what the arguments of $W$ should be and about how strong the interaction effects between these arguments and other choice variables might be. But there is no reasonable alternative to a term like $W$ that depends on arguments other than wealth and conventional consumption.

As a result, the remaining debate is not about the presence of a term like $W$, but rather about the nature of the arguments of this function. On a priori grounds, some theorists follow Riker and Ordeshook, and maintain that the utility function $W$ depends only on the act of voting $x$, not on how the vote is cast. This approach uses an extended model of preferences to explain why people vote, but it preserves the traditional instrumental theories about which alternative they vote for. Duty gets people to the polls, but once they are there, wealth maximization determines how they vote.

The alternative is to follow Fiorina and allow for the possibility that the extended preference approach is important for understanding not just why people vote but also how they vote. Other arguments besides the act of voting, $x$, enter in the function $W$, arguments such as the vote choice $v$ and party affiliation $a$. If one starts from a general formulation that allows for the possibility that arguments other than wealth can influence how people vote, one then can use both theory and evidence to test assertions about $W$.

It is in this spirit that this paper considers additional arguments that could appear in the utility function. The variables considered in what follows capture the effects that promises and anger can have on how people vote. These variables can coexist with more traditional variables like a sense of duty or party affiliation, but for simplicity these other variables are suppressed because they are not central to the analysis that follows.

As Fiorina's analysis shows, extended preference models can be tested like any other model. He finds evidence that affiliation does indeed influence voter turnout. These models are consistent with the general methodological approach of rational choice. As Aldrich emphasizes, they do not make political theory less interesting or reduce the degree to which strategic calculation plays a role in political outcomes. On the contrary, they explain important forms of strategic behavior by politicians that cannot be captured in the narrow preference models. Economists who are interested in positive theories of politics should therefore be willing at least to consider the evidence that is relevant for evaluating arguments in the utility function besides wealth when they engage in discussions of political economy.[3]

There is nothing unusual about this line of investigation. Despite occasional claims to the contrary, economists do consider both theory and evidence about the nature of human preferences. Two examples illustrate the issues involved. The first centers on intergenerational altruism. For many years, economists treated altruistic acts between close kin in the same way that they treated altruistic acts between people who are not related. Gifts from parents to children were lumped together with gifts from individuals who support public broadcasting. It was behavior that obviously took place, but it was placed outside the bounds of mainstream economists.

It is hard to say exactly when the change took place, but over the course of the 1970s, economists changed views on gifts to close kin.[4] Before, the utility function of a parent could have as arguments only those goods that the parent directly consumed. By the end of the 1970s, the assumption that the consumption of children or their utility levels could also enter as arguments in the utility function of the parents passed largely without comment. There are empirical and theoretical debates about how strong this effect is and about what its implications are in areas like public finance, but there is no longer any disagreement about the notion that a taste for altruism toward children is an inherent aspect of human preferences that economists can and should study.

With a bit of a lag, this change followed the development of the notion of kin selection in evolutionary biology.[5] Because the biological basis for the economic theory of intergenerational altruism was rarely discussed in economics papers, it is difficult to trace the direct effects that developments in biology had on thinking in economics. Nevertheless, it seems to have played an important role. In a very short time, economists recognized that people had to have preferences that induced them to give valuable resources to their offspring. Otherwise, we would not have survived as a species.

In this period, what seems to have changed was the theory, not the evidence. Once economists had a theory about why preferences toward children should be the way they are, they proceeded to study the theoretical and empirical questions that this new assumption about preferences raised.

Another revealing example in economics arises in the context of preferences toward risk, and in this case it has been the evidence that has driven recent developments. Traditionally, economists relied on a mixture of introspection

---

3. Some economists clearly are willing. See, for example, Brennan and Lomasky (1985). In a separate paper, Lomasky (1985) develops a different model of the political dynamics of Social Security. His claim is that voters get a small psychic benefit from voting for a program that they perceived to be a good program.

4. Robert Barro's article on government debt (1974) seems to have marked a crucial turning point in the professional attitude toward this issue.

5. William Hamilton published the pioneering paper on kin selection in 1964.

about the plausibility of various axioms and logical deduction to support various assumptions about the nature of preferences over risky consumption bundles. For many years, the expected utility hypothesis was the only formal model of such preferences, but in the last ten years, a variety of alternative theories about preferences have been proposed. In this case, the observation that the preferences we observe must be the result of a process of biological evolution does little to guide our choice between the alternatives. Increasingly, what does help us choose is how well they account for the growing body of evidence that is emerging from laboratory experiments. (See Harless and Camerer 1994 and Hey and Orme 1994 for recent summaries of progress in testing the different assumptions about preferences.)

If we ignore what economists say about the study of preferences and look at what they do, it is clear that they make progress in understanding preferences in the same way that they make progress in any other area—by making use of theory and evidence. Theory plays an important role in delimiting the areas of investigation and setting the agenda for types of evidence to collect and study, but it is the accumulation of evidence that ultimately determines which assumptions survive and achieve broad professional support.

### 7.4   A Preference-Based Theory of Promises and Revenge

As noted above, the aspects of preferences that seem to be necessary to understand Roosevelt's model of politics relate to promises and punishments. People can threaten punishment for two distinct reasons. A person who has no underlying taste for imposing a punishment may consciously adopt a strategy that involves threats of punishment because the threats have strategic value. She may make good on the threats because they have instrumental value, in a repeated game, for example. Alternatively, a person can have a taste or desire for punishing others that is triggered by a particular sequence of events. In this case, a person carries out the threats because it is satisfying to do so.

It is this second possibility that is relevant for the discussion that follows. Much of the behavior we observe, both in the field and in the laboratory, makes sense only if we admit that people sometimes have a taste for punishing others in particular circumstances. Most of the arguments that follow are directed at specifying just what these circumstances might be. But before turning to this issue, we must address the question of why a taste for punishing others might have evolved in humans.

There are two reasons why people might have a hardwired taste for punishing others instead of a general-purpose cognitive capacity that lets them adopt threat strategies when they are useful. The first reason is that specialized, hardwired mechanisms are relatively efficient at solving evolutionary design problems. One of the reliable lessons from the study of artificial intelligence is that general problem solvers are very slow and inefficient compared to specialized mechanisms.

To illustrate the practical implications of this general lesson, consider the evolutionary problem of getting people to eat the right kinds of objects from their environment. Like other animals, we have hardwired tastes that guide this process. We could have been endowed with a preference for surviving and with general problem-solving capabilities for evaluating which objects to eat, but this would apparently have been less efficient. (If this cognitive approach to deciding what to eat had efficiency advantages over the preference-based approach, all animals would have been under strong selection pressure to develop the kinds of brains that humans have.) Hardwired tastes let information about valuable foods accumulate across many generations. Long ago, evolution stored the information that sweets and fats are good sources of calories somewhere in the parts of our DNA that supply the code for our food preferences. If we were endowed only with a general problem-solving mechanism, we would have to start from scratch in each generation relearning this fact, or rely on extensive and time-consuming training from other members of the species to get this simple message across.

Now consider the evolutionary problem of implementing a strategy such as tit for tat in a repeated game. Humans could have been given the kind of general-purpose cognitive capacities that are assumed in most of economic analysis and left to infer that this strategy (or some more complicated strategy) would be a good one to follow in a particular repeated game. Alternatively, they could have been given hardwired tastes that give them a desire to implement the punishment phase of a strategy after an opponent behaves opportunistically. Repeated strategic interaction with other humans was surely an important part of our evolutionary past. A taste for punishing defection or opportunism, analogous to our taste for sweets and fat, might have emerged from the selection pressures that resulted from hundreds of thousands of years of social interaction in small hunter-gatherer bands. In a game against nature, parts of our strategy for eating are coded in preferences. In a game against other people, parts of our strategy for cooperating and punishing might also be coded in preferences.

There is a second reason why a hardwired taste for punishing others might be more valuable than a general cognitive capacity for making strategic calculations. In some settings, a threat to punish someone who defects from cooperation will not be credible. After defection takes place, it may not be in the interest of the person who issued the threat to carry through with the punishment. If someone has a strong taste for punishment that is triggered by defection from cooperation, he will incur a cost to punish the defector in cases in which someone making cognitive calculations might not.[6] This kind of taste can support cooperation in circumstances such as one-shot games where cooperation might otherwise be impossible. As a result, this taste can enhance sur-

---

6. This explanation of emotion as a solution to commitment problems has been advanced by Frank (1988), Hirshleifer (1987), and Posner (1981), and no doubt by many others.

vival for the person who possesses it and for all members of a small band if they all possess it.

It does not follow, however, that this kind of taste will necessarily evolve or that it will survive for long if it does evolve by chance. The problem here has been long recognized in discussions about the evolution of altruism. A population with preferences that are beneficial to the group may be susceptible to entry by new individuals who have different kinds of preferences. Someone who seems to have a taste for punishment, but does not have this taste, gets the deterrent value without ever having to pay the cost of punishing someone else.[7]

For the purposes of the arguments that follow, it does not matter which of these two reasons explains why the taste for punishing opportunism is hardwired. All that matters is that the taste for punishing was built into our preferences just as the taste for sweets and fats was. This matters because preferences presumably have changed very little in the last few thousand years, even as our economic environment has changed almost beyond recognition. Think again of food preferences. Our hardwired tastes for fats and sweets still express themselves, even though many of us face serious health risks from consuming too many calories. In the same way, a taste for punishing others that evolved in circumstances where all social interactions took place in repeated encounters among small numbers of people may now express itself in circumstances where it too has no value.

The role for promises then enters because a taste for punishing others may have been adaptive in some circumstances in our evolutionary past, but it may have been quite harmful in other circumstances. Ideally, people would be able to turn the taste for punishing opportunism on and off as appropriate for the situation. If tastes were invariant over time, this would pose a problem for a taste-based mechanism for solving problems of deterring opportunistic behavior. But tastes are not invariant. They can change over time. More specifically, they exhibit obvious state- or history-dependence. Think again of food tastes. On top of our general tastes for sweets and fats, we have powerful mechanisms that induce history-dependence in our food tastes. For example, we form long-lasting aversions to strong tastes that we are exposed to before a bout of nausea.

The extensive form game in figure 7.1 illustrates why it would be useful for the intensity of the taste for punishment to depend on the act by someone else of making a promise. In this game, there are gains from cooperation. Depending on the magnitude of the parameter $x$, there may also be incentives for defection. This game can be interpreted as a food-sharing game that was played repeatedly in our evolutionary past. It can be divided into upper and lower branches that are identical except for the terminal payoffs. For the moment, ignore the initial decision by player 1 about whether to make a promise. Start at the point on each branch where player 2 can decide to share food or to pursue autarky. The only difference between these two branches is that the preferences

7. See Frank (1988) for a discussion of this point and of possible ways to address it.

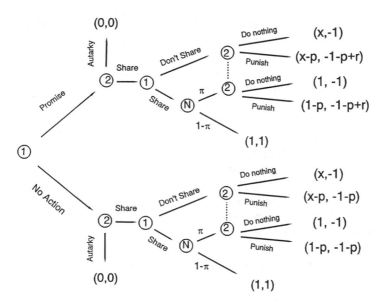

**Fig. 7.1    Opportunism and punishment in a food-sharing game**

of player 2 are different. For now, treat them as separate games played by 1
against different player 2s.

Assume that player 2 has a large quantity of nonstorable food from a hunt.
He can eat it all, or he can share half of it with player 1, who has no food in
the initial period. In the next period, player 1 will catch a similar large quantity
of food, and player 2 will have none. If they both eat their own catches, they
each receive a baseline utility of 0. Suppose that player 2 decides to share his
food. After collecting his prey, player 1 can then defect and eat it all or set
some of it aside for player 2, who will arrive later. If player 1 sets aside some
food for player 2, nature intervenes. With probability $\pi$, a large animal comes
and takes the food being stored for player 2. Assume that $\pi$ is small.

If player 2 comes back and there is food for him, both players are better off
than they would be if they had not shared the food. They get the payoffs
(1, 1) instead of the baseline payoffs (0, 0) because they can smooth their food
consumption and eat after both hunts. If, on the other hand, player 2 comes
back and there is no food for him, he faces a decision about whether to punish
player 1. The dashed line connecting the two nodes indicates that player 2 cannot tell whether player 1 did not share or player 1 did share and the random
draw from nature was bad. If he does inflict a punishment, for example by
starting a fight, this imposes a direct cost $p$ on both players.

The player 2 on the top branch has a taste for punishment that is indicated
by the additional term $r$ (for revenge) in his payoffs. Player 2 gets this psychic
payoff when he inflicts punishment on player 1 in circumstances in which
player 2 feels wronged. In principle, player 2 could also consider taking re-

venge after they have successfully cooperated, but in this case there would be no psychic payoff $r$, and player 2 would not choose to punish. Along the lower branch, player 2 never feels satisfaction from punishing player 1, even in cases in which things have turned out badly for him because of a bad draw by nature.

Throughout, we will maintain the assumption that $r$ is greater than $p$ and that $p$ is larger than $x - 1$. This means that the taste for punishment is strong enough to give the player 2 on the top branch of the game an incentive to punish player 1, even though doing so inflicts a cost $p$ on himself. It also means that punishment deters opportunism.

In this game, the critical parameter is $x$, the payoff for player 1 when he defects. Consider first a case in which $x$ is smaller than the payoff of 1 that player 1 gets from cooperation. (Imagine, for example, that the amount of food from each hunt is twice what one person can eat and that refraining from sharing imposes direct costs on player 1.) In this case, player 1 will always want to cooperate. If the probability $\pi$ of a bad draw from nature is small, both players will prefer the cooperative outcome in which each player shares. Player 2 will suffer occasional losses because of bad draws from nature, but the gains from cooperation outweigh these costs. In this case, the players clearly want to play along the lower branch. This avoids punishments when draws from nature are bad.

Now consider the case in which the payoff $x$ is larger than 1. The best state of affairs for both players would be to play along the upper branch. It is better for both players if player 2 has a taste for revenge. In the absence of a taste for revenge, it is no longer possible to sustain cooperation when $x$ is large. This is bad for both players, for they both are stuck with the autarky payoffs (0, 0). If they could sustain cooperation, the sharing payoffs (1, 1) will occur with probability $1 - \pi$, and the unfortunate outcome with punishment, which generates payoffs of $(1 - p, -1 - p + r)$ will arise with probability $\pi$. If $\pi$ is not too large, both players would prefer the cooperative outcome to the autarky outcome.

With the exception of $r$, all of the payoffs in this game have a direct positive effect on survival. They can be thought of as being measured in units of calories of food energy. The psychic payoff $r$ that player 2 sometimes enjoys from punishing player 1 has no direct positive effect on survival. The point of the arguments given above is that this taste for punishment can have an indirect effect that is positive because it deters player 1 from abandoning the strategy of cooperation. This is the case when $x$ is greater than 1. Any costs associated with carrying out the punishments might therefore be outweighed by the gains. The point illustrated by the game in the figure is that the comparison might also go the other way. When $x$ is less than 1, both players will be better off if player 2 has no taste for punishment. In this kind of world, the ideal arrangement would be for player 2 to have a taste for punishment that is activated only in those circumstances where $x$ is large. The challenge is to arrange for this kind of contingent behavior under the assumption that a taste for punishment is hardwired into preferences.

Faced with these different possible values for $x$, it is in the interest of both players to find a way to selectively "turn on" the taste for punishment in player 2. One way to do so is suggested by the first stage of play by player 1. Moving back to this stage, the game suggests that communication between the players in the initial stage can influence the preferences that player 2 ultimately expresses. Specifically, if player 1 says to player 2 that he promises that some food will be available after the second hunt, this statement by itself could activate the taste for revenge in player 2. Suppose that the full game starts with player 1 making a promise to player 2, so now we are on the upper branch. If player 2 arrives to find no food after player 1 has promised that food will be there, player 2 may have a strong sense of having been wronged and a strong desire for revenge. This sense and this desire might be absent if player 2 arrived at the same node on the lower branch; that is, player 2 might not feel any taste for revenge if he finds no food after unilaterally deciding to share, in circumstances in which player 1 has made no promise about whether he will reciprocate.

Because of the assumption that $p$ is large enough to deter defection by player 1 and that $r$ is even larger so that the threat of punishment is credible along the upper branch, cooperation can be sustained after player 1 has made his promise. Because $\pi$ is small but positive, there will occasionally be misunderstandings, cases when player 2 imposes punishments even though player 1 has cooperated. Nevertheless, it may be a cost worth paying if the gains from cooperation are high.

Of course, if $\pi$ were too high or if $x$ were low, player 1 could simply refrain from making a promise that he might not be able to keep. That is the value of a mechanism that makes the taste for punishment contingent not just on a bad outcome for the person who expresses this taste, but also on an act like a promise by his partner. It lets the players avoid invoking the revenge mechanism in states where it would not be helpful, but lets them turn it on in cases where it would be helpful. If the gains from cooperation are high, and if situations where deterring opportunism is frequently an important issue, it would be advantageous to be a person like player 2.

The discussion here has been given in the context of a one-shot game. The implied advantage of the hardwired taste for preferences is the second of the two advantages noted above. These preferences make some kinds of threats credible. As has already been noted, it is an open question whether these kinds of preferences could have emerged from the process of human evolution. Alternatively, this one-shot game could be embedded in a repeated game. In this case, the taste for punishing others might simply be a mechanism for implementing a particular Nash equilibrium strategy in the repeated game. Regardless of its origins, the relevant question for the behavior of modern voters is how people with these kinds of preferences might behave when they are put into the evolutionarily novel context of an industrial democracy.

This story seems to violate the useful methodological assumption that consumer preferences are stable. However, it is possible to specify a utility function that is stable. The strategy is the same as the one followed by the early political scientists, to include additional arguments in the utility function. Let *promise* denote the action of player 1 in the first round. It takes on the value of "make a promise" or "do nothing." Let *food* indicate what player 2 observes when he comes to collect his food after the second hunt. Let *punish* denote the act by player 2 in the last stage. It can take on the values "inflict punishment" or "do nothing." Finally, let $c$ represent survival-related payoffs, measured as before in calorie equivalents. Under the assumptions used so far, the amount of food that player 2 gets to eat, the timing of when he gets to eat it, and the punishment he inflicts will all affect $c$. In a way that is symmetrical with the preferences that reflect voter affiliation that were used above, the stationary utility function for player 2 can be written in the form $U(c) + W(food, punish, promise)$.

This utility function is an example of what Gary Becker has called metapreferences. As Becker has argued in his development of the extended-preference approach to human behavior, the crucial assumptions about metapreferences are concerned with cross derivatives.[8] In traditional economic language, these are assumptions about complementarity. They are analogous to the assumption noted above, about complementarity between party affiliation and voter turnout. The crucial assumption in the analysis here is that $W$ does not increase when *punish* increases unless *promise* takes the value "made a promise" and *food* takes on the value "no food available."

The approach followed here is closely related to the work on fairness by Rabin (1993) and the underlying theory of psychological games outlined by Geanakoplos, Pearce, and Stacchetti (1989). In a more formal and more general setting, these papers pursue the goal of introducing new, empirically relevant arguments into the utility function of economic agents. Rabin, in particular, tries to develop an explanation for punishment and its mirror image, reciprocal altruism, in a one-shot game. In Rabin's model, the payoffs that an agent receives and the strategies that the player adopts are functions not only of the underlying material payoffs (the payoffs that are measured in calories here) but also of beliefs that a player has about the motivations of other players. Technically, the description of the game outlined in this paper avoids the introduction of beliefs or intentions and makes the payoffs a function of actions (making a promise) and observables (finding no food). These actions have the unusual property that they have no effect on material (i.e., calorie) payoffs.

---

8. For examples in this line of work, see Stigler and Becker (1977) on the general approach; Becker and Murphy (1988) and Becker, Grossman, and Murphy (1994) on addiction; Becker and Murphy (1993) on advertising; Becker and Mulligan (1993) on the endogenous discount rates; and Mulligan (1993) on determinants of the intensity of intergenerational altruism.

The alternative approach pursued in Rabin's work lets preferences depend on the intentions of the other agent and allows actions and observables to matter only to the extent that they signal intentions. This deeper strategy introduces fundamental conceptual issues that have not yet been fully resolved. It would make it possible to deal with deeper questions about how our own cognitive inferences about the intentions behind the acts of others interact with our preferences. Once this richer style of analysis is fully developed, the arguments in this paper based on actions alone can presumably be extended to take advantage of it.

## 7.5   Evidence on Extended Preferences

The prediction from the model outlined above is that people have a taste for revenge that can be activated or primed by an act like a promise. The taste can then be triggered by an opportunistic act or by an outcome that is interpreted as an indicator of an opportunistic act. The theoretical arguments try to suggest that this kind of assumption does not blatantly contradict basic facts about selection. They suggest that the hypothesized form of preferences could have had survival value relative to standard preferences that do not exhibit a state-dependent taste for retribution. But this kind of abstract argument can only get one so far. The theory should be understood primarily as a justification for looking at the evidence to see whether humans do have a taste for revenge, and whether it is contingent on acts such as a promise made by others followed by subsequent opportunism.

There is abundant direct evidence suggesting that people do have a taste for revenge. For example, after surveying the available evidence from ethnographies, Daly and Wilson (1988) conclude that "lethal retribution is an ancient and cross-culturally universal recourse" for people who have been seriously harmed by others. In modern societies, the individual desire for revenge is suppressed by the state, but vestiges of it still show through. People pay money to play video games that simulate the experience of being attacked and taking violent revenge. They also pay to watch movies in which someone the audience cares about gets hurt by some bad person. The emotional payoff comes from watching the bad person suffer a violent punishment in the end. There is also evidence suggesting that a taste for revenge is present in nonhuman primates such as chimpanzees (see, for example, de Waal 1989, 205–7). People who study animal behavior call this behavior "moralistic aggression" and distinguish it from other kinds of aggression. A key stimulus for this type of behavior is the failure by one animal to reciprocate after the other has been helpful.

Recent political developments offer indirect evidence that bears on the model outlined here. Following the 1994 midterm elections, exit polls and most postelection analysis both suggest that anger was a potent motivating factor in this election. In contrast to the recent downward trend, turnout nationwide was up compared to the last midterm elections, increasing from 36.5%

to 38.7%. In the notably nasty race between Oliver North and Charles Robb, turnout was up a remarkable 16%.

As the experience with expected utility theory suggests, the best cross-check on a theory about preferences is evidence from controlled experiments. At least one experiment designed to test for expressive aspects of voting behavior has been attempted (Carter and Guerette 1992). As the authors note, the results from this particular experiment are unclear because of problems in the experimental design, but presumably better experiments can be constructed. One of the advantages of a theory that can be stated explicitly in terms of actions and payoffs in a game form is that it is possible to play the game in a controlled laboratory setting and observe the outcomes. So far, the precise game outlined above has yet to be tested in an experiment, but in principle it could be. Meanwhile, we can take advantage of related experiments that were developed for different reasons but that bear directly on the extended-preference approach outlined here.

The most relevant evidence comes from the Ultimatum game and its close relative, the Dictator game.[9] The Dictator game is very simple. Player 1 is given the opportunity to divide a fixed sum of money $s$ between herself and an unknown player 2. After the money is divided, the players take their shares, and the game is over. The prediction from most economic models is that player 1 will take all of the money. This is in fact what happens, if the game is set up to assure player 1 that her choice will not be known to anyone else. The evidence suggests that people prefer more money to less but that they also care about what others think of their behavior.

The Ultimatum game adds a second stage in which player 2 has a chance to respond. In this game, player 1 gets to propose a split of the amount $s$. In the second stage, player 2 can accept or reject the proposed split. If player 2 accepts, the players are given the amounts proposed by player 1. If player 2 rejects the split, both players receive nothing. In a representative version of the experiment, the total amount to be split is $10 and the splits must be made in units of $1. The traditional narrow-preference model makes an unambiguous prediction about the outcome of the Ultimatum game. Player 1 will propose a split that gives $1, the smallest allowable positive unit of money to player 2. Player 2 will then accept the proposed split because some money is preferred to no money. The game is of interest to economists because the prediction is so clear-cut and repeated experiments have shown that the observed behavior is significantly different from the prediction. Many of the offers proposed by player 1 are close to 50–50 splits. For the purposes of the discussion here, the interesting observation is that player 2 will often reject a split that differs too much from a 50–50 split, even if it means giving up several dollars of income.

The rejections by player 2 fit naturally in the framework outlined above. Player 2 has a taste for revenge that is triggered by opportunistic behavior by

9. For a summary of results from experiments with the Dictator game and the Ultimatum game, see Davis and Holt (1993) or Camerer and Thaler (1995).

player 1. It is worth sacrificing a few dollars to be able to punish a player 1 who behaves opportunistically and demands too much. It is interesting to note that people assigned the role of player 1 also seem to have the right model of the behavior of player 2. When they are given an anonymous opportunity to take all the money in the Dictator game, they do so significantly more often. But when they play the Ultimatum game, they restrain themselves because they know that player 2 will punish them if they push too hard.

Some economists who would like to preserve the narrow-preference model have criticized these kinds of experiments by saying that the stakes in the typical experiment are small and by claiming that other kinds of behavior should emerge when the stakes are larger. This is an easy proposition to test. At least for the Ultimatum game, the available evidence suggests that the stakes do not matter. The behavior is about the same when people divide $100 as when they divide $10. The irony in this charge is that it is sometimes made by economists who support instrumental explanations of voting, where the stakes are many orders of magnitudes smaller.

If the model of the taste for revenge that is outlined above is correct, people should be sensitive to the actions that do not have any direct effect on material payoffs. Other experiments suggest that this is the case. For example, if it is revenge rather than a general sense of fairness that motivates the rejections in the second round, player 2 should be less likely to reject an uneven split if it is the result of a random device rather than a choice made by player 1. Results in Blount (1994) confirm this prediction. Other aspects of the general context may also be relevant. For example, if one of the two players earns the right to be the divider (for example by winning a trivia contest in an earlier round of play), the dividers ask for a large share of the total, and the second-round players acquiesce. Davis and Holt summarize these kinds of results by saying that "economically irrelevant procedural details can have a significant effect on the bargaining behavior, especially when such details alter the perceived symmetry of the situation" (1993, 267). According to the model from the last section, what these "economically irrelevant procedural details" are doing is turning up or down the intensity of the taste for revenge. That is, they are providing clues about the nature of the strategic interaction that will take place. Our emotional commitment mechanisms are sensitive to these clues. In these terms, we can give a new interpretation to the game in figure 7.1. It predicts that the outcome will depend very strongly on the economically irrelevant procedural detail of whether player 1 makes a promise at the start of play. Of course, this kind of detail is economically irrelevant only if one takes a very narrow view of preferences and assumes that a promise does not influence anyone's behavior.

## 7.6   The History of the Social Security Program

The most striking aspect of the history of the Social Security system is the remarkable amount of attention that all sides devoted to issues that most economists would dismiss as "economically irrelevant procedural details." In retrospect, it is clear that the small core of people who led the Social Security system through its first four decades had a more acute awareness of the political salience of these details and were more successful at manipulating them to their advantage. But from a very early stage, at least some of the critics of the system also recognized that the implicit and explicit promises hidden in these details would determine the political future of the Social Security system.

Because of a historical accident, we have detailed evidence about how calculated the attempt was to build up the insurance imagery that was at the heart of the strategy for making Social Security benefits into an entitlement. The architects of the system feared a Supreme Court challenge to an explicit attempt by the federal government to set up a retirement system. Because the federal government clearly has the power to raise taxes and make spending decisions, the Social Security Act of 1935 described a new system of payroll taxation and a set of old-age benefits that would be paid to some citizens. The act never makes any explicit link between these two parts. Words like *insurance* and *contribution* do not appear.

At the time of the 1938 Supreme Court decision that upheld the constitutionality of the 1935 act, Wilbur Cohen was working as an aid to Robert Altmeyer, the chairman of the Social Security Board. Cohen was perhaps the most important person in the development of the system. He was a central participant in all the major developments of the system from the time of its creation up through his participation on the Greenspan commission in the 1980s. He later recalled his reaction to the Supreme Court decision upholding the constitutionality of the 1935 act. "I recall walking down the steps of the Supreme Court building in a glow of ecstasy. . . . When I got back to the office I obtained Mr. Altmeyer's approval to send out a memo to the staff stating that because of the decision, we could now call the old age benefits program 'old age insurance.' . . . The American public was and still is insurance-minded and opposed to welfare, 'the dole,' and 'handouts'" (quoted in Derthick 1979, 199).

Cates (1983, 32–33) uses excerpts from public information pamphlets to illustrate how the system's rhetoric changed immediately after the Supreme Court decision was handed down:

[From a 1937 pamphlet produced before the Supreme Court decision]
The United States Government will send checks every month to retired workers . . . under the old-age benefit plan. . . . The same law that provides these benefits for you and other workers sets up certain new taxes to be paid to the United States Government.

[From a 1938 pamphlet written after the decision]
Your [Social Security card] shows that you have an insurance account with the U.S. Government—Federal old age and survivors insurance. This is a national insurance plan for all workers in commerce and industry. . . . taxes are like the premium on any other kind of insurance.

Achenbaum (1986, 35) observes that Roosevelt himself participated in this effort, claiming that people eligible for benefits "could be likened to the policy holders of a private insurance company." The Social Security Amendments passed by the Congress in 1939 made the changes in terminology that had already been implemented within the Social Security bureaucracy official. At the insistence of the program officials within the agency, the insurance language was incorporated into the law. The Old-Age Reserve Account established in the 1935 act was renamed the Old Age and Survivors Insurance Trust Fund. The original taxes were repealed and the new insurance "contributions" were imposed under the Federal Insurance Contributions Act (FICA). As Achenbaum observes, "[A]ny dispassionate analysis of the 1939 debate over social security must recognize that there was a gap between what policymakers were doing and what they said."

It was this gap that Curtis threatened to expose to broad public view with his hearings on the Chamber of Commerce's plan. Altmeyer, who had just stepped down as the commissioner of social security, wrote to Representative Curtis refusing to appear before his committee. He accused Curtis of being hostile to the entire concept of social security, noting that "you contend that [the] old-age and survivors insurance system is not insurance, although it is so designated in the law itself." Altmeyer eventually was subpoenaed. In his responses to questions from the committee, he eventually admitted that some of the language about a "contract" between beneficiaries and the government was misleading. After the hearings, the literature distributed by the Social Security system did tone down some of its insurance rhetoric (Cates 1983, 84). Nevertheless, it is remarkable how consistent and persistent the early leaders of the program continued to be in their defense of the insurance imagery. Derthick (1979, 199) reports the following testimony by Cohen before the U.S. Senate in 1961:

> *Senator Wallace F. Bennett.* My idea of a contribution is something that I myself take out of my pocket and hand to somebody. It is not, it does not apply to what somebody else takes out of my pocket, and I think this is a tax . . .
>
> *Mr. Cohen.* You have to change the law then because it says it is the Federal Insurance Contributions Act.

Unfortunately for Cohen, there was someone at those hearings who had heard this justification before and knew the history of how the insurance language got into the law.

> *Senator Carl T. Curtis.* Who told us to do that, Wilbur? I remember the day it happened.
>
> *Mr. Cohen.* I think it was a good idea, Mr. Curtis.

In the end, the repeated conservative attacks on the logic of the position that the Social Security proponents adopted seem to have had little effect. There is certainly no evidence that they changed the political debate surrounding the program. The conservatives seemed to have missed the deeper significance of what was going on, or not to have known how to respond. In this deeply political battle, it did not work to fight rhetoric with logic. It was not the logic of the arguments made by leaders of the Social Security system that influenced the behavior of voters. It was the promise itself that changed the behavior of the listeners. Logic had nothing to do with it.

In a vague and indirect fashion, Cohen himself tried to make this point in a 1971 debate with Milton Friedman: "Mr. Friedman calls a lot of the things he doesn't like about the social security system rhetoric. And that gets me to a point that I want to stress. My point is that economists do not determine all of the choices and options and attitudes prevailing in this nation. People do live by rhetoric. . . . True, if you are an economist, you may exclude all matters of politics from your thinking. But to do so is not reality" (Cohen and Friedman 1972, 54–55).

From the beginning in 1935 until the mid-1970s, the Social Security system underwent a process of steady and significant expansion. To the original retirement benefits, benefits for surviving spouses and children were added in 1939. The coverage of the system and the level of benefits were substantially increased in 1950. Disability benefits were the most important direction for expansion during the rest of the 1950s. After disability coverage was introduced in 1956, planning for coverage of medical expenses began within the Social Security Administration. The Eisenhower administration then in power did not support the extension of the system to cover medical care, but work on the various plans proceeded and eventually culminated in the Medicare legislation of the mid-1960s. The push for increased cash benefits—the next priority—culminated in the substantial benefit increase of 1972.

Along the way, the possibility of retiring with reduced benefits at age sixty-two was added, and the coverage of the system was steadily expanded. Originally, planners anticipated that the combined tax on workers and firms of less than 6% would be sufficient to finance the system when it was fully mature. We have now reached a level of more than 15% on a much higher real wage base, and it has probably not reached its maximum. There is genuine uncertainty about how high the tax rate might have to go to cover the large benefit payments that will be required when the baby boom generation begins to retire in the third decade of the next century.

This remarkable pattern of consistent expansion was made possible in large part because program advocates and sympathetic politicians were able to make long-term, self-fulfilling promises about future tax and benefit payments. At each stage in the expansion, the advocates were able to commit the government to an upward-sloping time profile of new benefit payments and an even steeper upward-sloping profile of tax obligations. Because the initial increase in benefits was larger than the initial increase in taxes, the initial stages of expansion were generally popular and posed little political risk.

A crucial element in this program of expansion was the ability of decision makers to tie the hands of future politicians. When the full cost of previously enacted benefits eventually became apparent—when previously scheduled tax increases went into effect or expenditures exceeded revenues and some kind of adjustment had to be made—there was always a risk that policy makers would respond by cutting back on benefits instead of implementing the required tax increases. This is why the ability to create a sense of entitlement was so important. At every stage, the proponents of expansion were able to promise that a given level of benefits would be paid. And merely by making that promise, they were able to make it come true. When they told people that they had earned their benefits as a matter of right, people believed them. If those rights were threatened, they reacted with anger. When the Reagan administration finally proposed in 1981 that Social Security benefits be cut, primarily through a 25% reduction in the benefits available for early retirement, everyone learned how politically potent these promises were.[10]

## 7.7 Conclusion

Some economists and political scientists use the tools of economics to formulate positive models of political action. This is a difficult area, so it is no slander on people who have worked there to claim that there is room for improvement. Many other economists have taken the seemingly easier path of normative analysis. By examining various kinds of market failures, these economists claim to identify policies that would permit efficiency gains if they were adopted. Without making any claims about which policies *are* adopted, these economists identify policies that *should* be adopted. That is, they claim that if the identified policies were adopted, it would be possible to make everyone better off. Even this kind of analysis must ultimately confront deeper questions about preferences.

Imagine that economists really were philosopher kings. Imagine that they could bypass the political system, draw up policies, and implement them. Small, seemingly irrelevant details like the difference between transfer payments and entitlements might ultimately have a very big impact on the preferences, and therefore on the behavior, of the citizens in a nation. One of the puzzles noted in the beginning was that the typical elderly widow who was not eligible for survivors benefits did not participate in the debate about Social Security in the 1950s. But this was perfectly rational behavior. She had no ability to influence the outcome. At that time, she also lacked any sense that she had been wronged—that promises had been made and not kept—so she had no taste for writing angry letters, protesting, or making a special effort to vote against the people who opposed a plan that would have given her a windfall. As the prologue reminds us, sixty years ago policy makers were constrained because many poor people refused to accept assistance payments from the government. Today, we face a different constraint. Large numbers of affluent old people are primed for action, ready to explode in a spasm of anger at

10. See Light (1985) for a description of the furious response that this suggestion provoked.

any suggestion that the transfer payments they receive from the government be reduced.

The arguments presented here suggest that this change in the preferences or values of large numbers of people was an inevitable, intentional side effect of the way that the Social Security program was designed and implemented by the Roosevelt administration. This change in values represents a possible cost of the policies adopted then. Many people count the redistribution of income that the Social Security program achieved among the most important accomplishments of social policy in the United States. For them, this benefit may very well outweigh any costs associated with increased public perceptions about entitlement. For others, the costs of the program may seem too high. The point here is that it is not possible to weigh all the costs and benefits of this program or any other policy program without taking account of all of its effects, including its effects on values and politics.

Important, long-lasting changes in values and behavior might follow from proposed government programs in the areas such as health care and long-term care. Economists who focus only on incidence may see little difference between an employer mandate and a worker mandate concerning health care coverage. The long-run effects of these two arrangements might nevertheless be very different. They could induce very different beliefs about individual responsibility and entitlement, and these could substantially affect voting, future policy debates, and the other aspects of social life in important ways.

Presumably, even an economist who ignores how policies get adopted, who is engaged only in a purely normative analysis of the costs and benefits of various policies, would want to take account of the effects that these policies can have on values. Changes in values are one of the outcomes that the citizens of a nation care about, both for their own sake and because of the secondary effects they can induce. Economists who are interested in the positive analysis of politics and political economy will be particularly interested in how these changes in values influence subsequent political dynamics.

The goal of shaping values was arguably the driving motivation behind the widespread adoption of the most important social policy in the early history of the United States—mandatory attendance at public schools. Hunches and dim intuitions about the effects that policies have on values are driving the current debate about welfare reform. Questions about values are beginning to be addressed in discussions of reform of social welfare programs in Europe (Lindbeck 1994). Other economists have noted how much richer our policy advice would be if we could address questions about values (Aaron 1994; Aaron, Mann, and Taylor 1994). What is missing is not the will or the interest but the tools with which to begin an analysis of values.

There are many subtleties and ambiguities that need to be explored if we are to study values, but several things are clear: State-dependent preferences that allow for arguments capturing a broad range of actions or beliefs about the intentions of others offer a feasible framework for beginning to address questions about values. As Becker's analysis suggests, this framework can make use of conventional tools such as a stable underlying utility function and complementarity between different arguments in this function. In principle, the study of values need not be any more difficult conceptually than the study of party affiliation in the analysis of turnout. What we need to do is identify state variables analogous to party affiliation that capture what we mean by values, and begin to study how these variables affect other choices. There is also reason to hope that continued experimentation in the laboratory will slowly accumulate a rich body of evidence that can be used to test all theories about preferences, including ones about the deeper preferences we label values. Given the importance of the topic and the potential for headway, it would be a shame if economists held back from pursuing these questions because of a misconception about what constitutes good science when we study people.

# References

Aaron, Henry J. 1994. Public Policy, Values, and Consciousness. *Journal of Economic Perspectives* 8:3–21.

Aaron, Henry J., Thomas E. Mann, and Timothy Taylor, eds. 1994. *Values and Public Policy.* Washington, DC: Brookings Institution.

Achenbaum, W. Andrew. 1986. *Social Security: Visions and Revisions.* Cambridge: Cambridge University Press.

Aldrich, John H. 1993. Rational Choice and Turnout. *American Journal of Political Science* 37:246–78.

Barro, Robert J. 1974. Are Government Bonds Net Wealth? *Journal of Political Economy* 82:1095–1117.

Barry, Brian M. 1970. *Sociologists, Economists, and Democracy.* Themes and Issues in Modern Sociology series, ed. Jean Floud and John Goldthorpe. London: Collier-Macmillan.

Becker, Gary S., Michael Grossman, and Kevin M. Murphy. 1994. An Empirical Analysis of Cigarette Addiction. *American Economic Review* 84:396–418.

Becker, Gary S., and Casey B. Mulligan. 1993. On the Endogenous Determination of Time Preference. University of Chicago. Manuscript.

Becker, Gary S., and Kevin M. Murphy. 1988. A Theory of Rational Addiction. *Journal of Political Economy* 96:675–700.

———. 1993. A Simple Theory of Advertising as a Good or a Bad. *Quarterly Journal of Economics* 108:941–64.

Blount, Sally. 1994. The Role of Causal Attributions and Elicitation Mechanisms in the Tradeoff between Absolute and Comparative Payoffs in Social Decision Making. University of Chicago. Mimeo.

Boadway, Robin, and David Wildasin. 1989. Voting Models of Social Security Determination. In *The Political Economy of Social Security,* ed. B. A. Gustafsson and N. Anders Klevmarken. Amsterdam: North Holland.

Brennan, Geoffrey, and James Buchanan. 1984. Voter Choice. *American Behavioral Scientist* 28:185–201.

Brennan, Geoffrey, and Loren Lomasky. 1985. The Impartial Spectator Goes to Washington. *Economics and Philosophy* 1:189–211.

Camerer, Colin, and Richard Thaler. 1995. More on Ultimatum and Dictator Games. *Journal of Economic Perspectives.*

Carter, John R., and Stephen D. Guerette. 1992. An Experimental Study of Expressive Voting. *Public Choice* 73:251–60.

Cates, Jerry R. 1983. *Insuring Inequality.* Ann Arbor: University of Michigan Press.

Cohen, Wilbur J., and Milton Friedman. 1972. *Social Security: Universal or Selective?* Washington, DC: American Enterprise Institute.

Daly, Martin, and Margo Wilson. 1988. *Homicide.* New York: Aldine de Gruyter.

Davis, Douglas P., and Charles A. Holt. 1993. *Experimental Economics.* Princeton, NJ: Princeton University Press.

Derthick, Martha. 1979. *Policymaking for Social Security.* Washington, DC: Brookings Institution.

de Waal, Frans. 1989. *Chimpanzee Politics.* Baltimore: Johns Hopkins University Press.

Downs, Anthony. 1957. *An Economic Theory of Democracy.* New York: Harper and Row.

Fiorina, Morris P. 1976. The Voting Decision: Instrumental and Expressive Aspects. *Journal of Politics* 38:390–415.

Frank, Robert. 1988. *Passions within Reason: The Strategic Role of the Emotions.* New York: Norton.

Geanakoplos, John, David Pearce, and Ennio Stacchetti. 1989. Psychological Games and Sequential Rationality. *Games and Economic Behavior* 1:60–79.

Hamilton, William D. 1964. The Genetical Evolution of Social Behavior: Parts 1 and 2. *Journal of Theoretical Biology* 7:1–52.

Harless, David W., and Colin F. Camerer. 1994. The Predictive Utility of Generalized Expected Utility Theory. *Econometrica* 62:1251–90.

Hey, John D., and Chris Orme. 1994. Investigating Generalizations of Expected Utility Theory Using Experimental Data. *Econometrica* 62:1291–1326.

Hirshleifer, Jack. 1987. On the Emotions as Guarantors of Threats and Promises. In *The Latest on the Best: Essays on Evolution and Optimality,* ed. John Dupré. Cambridge: MIT Press.

Jackman, Robert W. 1993. Rationality and Political Participation. *American Journal of Political Science* 37:279–90.

Light, Paul. 1985. *Artful Work: The Politics of Social Security Reform.* New York: Random House.

Lindbeck, Assar. 1994. Hazardous Welfare State Dynamics. Institute for International Economic Studies, University of Stockholm. Mimeo.

Lomasky, Loren. 1985. Is Social Security Politically Untouchable? *Cato Journal* 5:157–75.

Mulligan, Casey. 1993. On Intergenerational Altruism, Fertility, and the Persistence of Status. Ph.D. thesis, University of Chicago.

Posner, Richard A. 1981. *The Economics of Justice.* Cambridge: Harvard University Press.

Rabin, Matthew. 1993. Incorporating Fairness into Game Theory and Economics. *American Economic Review* 83:1281–1302.

Riker, William H., and Peter C. Ordeshook. 1968. A Theory of the Calculus of Voting. *American Political Science Review* 62:25–43.

———. 1973. *An Introduction to Positive Political Theory.* Prentice Hall Contemporary Political Theory Series, ed. David Easton. Englewood Cliffs, NJ: Prentice Hall.

Stigler, George J., and Gary S. Becker. 1977. De Gustibus Non Est Disputandum. *American Economic Review* 67:76–90.

# Comment    Roger G. Noll

Paul Romer's essay has three objectives: to develop an economic theoretic explanation for why a genetic predisposition to vengeful behavior has survival value for the human species; to apply the theory of revenge as a conditional argument of an individual's utility function to voting behavior; and to explore the implications of this type of behavior with respect to the politics of Social Security. The specific line of reasoning in the paper proceeds as follows: humans are genetically predisposed to derive utility from revenge when another human abrogates an agreement to cooperate; legislative entitlements are analogous to bilateral cooperative agreements; and hence attempts to roll back entitlements would trigger vengeful responses by voters. This reasoning is then used to explain why Republicans proposed, and Democrats rejected, an attempt to reorganize Social Security as a universal old-age assistance program. According to Romer, the Republicans cleverly proposed these changes in the hopes that they would make Social Security easier to kill in the future, and the Democrats equally cleverly saw through this strategy and so opposed what would seemingly be part of their agenda—to expand the coverage of transfer payments.

Romer's work is an example of both the strengths and the weaknesses of what scholars in other disciplines have called "economics imperialism." The term refers to the invasion of the provinces of other social sciences—anthropology, political science, psychology, and sociology—by economists applying their toolkit of optimizing decision-theory models to traditional problems of other disciplines, and claiming to provide simpler, better, more comprehensive explanations than have been supplied by generations of scholars in sister fields. Much of the criticism of the exportation of economic methodology to other fields is defensive and wrong-headed, reflecting a lack of understanding about decision-theoretic models. But some of this criticism is on target. Economists frequently do overinterpret their results (most commonly, interpreting a qualitative, partial-equilibrium finding as a dominant, if not comprehensive, explanation for an observed phenomenon). And economists are notorious for ignoring previous research on the same issue by noneconomists and for testing their theories against a null hypothesis of chaos (e.g., the absence of a competing explanation) rather than against other plausible explanations that have been developed by scholars in other disciplines.

## The Core Theory

The core of Romer's paper is a game-theoretic explanation of how natural selection favors humans who are willing to make and accept promises for co-

Roger G. Noll is the Morris M. Doyle Professor of Public Policy in the Department of Economics at Stanford University.

The author gratefully acknowledges extremely useful guidance from Morris Fiorina in writing these comments.

operation but who, when a promise is abrogated, derive personal satisfaction from extracting an eye for an eye and a tooth for a tooth. The novelty in Romer's conceptual model is the intertemporal asymmetry of the cooperation: the sacrifices and rewards of the parties to an agreement are not distributed in the same way over time. Regarding Social Security, a working-age adult interprets the entitlement feature of the program as an intertemporal commitment to reward current sacrifice (the payroll tax on current wages) with a proportional pension upon retirement at some time in the distant future.

Romer's core theoretical model is an interesting contribution to an important and influential body of literature about, to use Robert Axelrod's provocative term, the "evolution of cooperation." This literature as much as any demonstrates the best of multidisciplinary research, and convincingly refutes the wrong-headed critics of the application of optimizing models outside of economics. Moreover, scholars from many disciplines have made important contributions, including political scientists (e.g., Axelrod), philosophers (e.g., Jon Elster), sociologists (e.g., James Coleman), and, of course, many economists. To say that Romer has contributed to this literature is not a small compliment.

My concern about Romer's essay is his exuberance in using his theory to explain voting behavior and its policy implications regarding entitlement programs. Romer's core accomplishment is really a "possibility theorem" in that it demonstrates that one among many human emotions could motivate behavior that, while seemingly irrational on the surface, is rational because it leads to mutually beneficial cooperation among egoistic actors. Stated this way, the model illustrates a standard game-theoretic result: a commitment to irrational out-of-equilibrium behavior supports the cooperatively rational equilibrium. Romer's twist, of course, is the suggestion that genetic preprogramming twiddles our utility functions in a way that makes the irrational out-of-equilibrium action in fact rational because we derive pleasure from entering the punishment phase of a cooperative game.

A single-effect, single-cause plausibility argument of this form suffers from two pitfalls. The first is that it borders on tautology: assume a level of utility, $R$, from punishing a defector that is sufficient to prevent most defectors from defecting, but is not so large that humans regularly bash each other for the slightest disappointment. Romer escapes the tautology by invoking sociobiology: because humans survived, $R$, like Baby Bear's porridge, must have been just right. The second is that it ignores all but one dimension of human motivation and behavior. Two others that come immediately to mind are altruism and rational foresight.

First, humans seem to have interdependent utility functions (i.e., they are quasi-altruistic). Thus, one alternative to revenge as the mechanism that polices the fulfillment of promises is that humans actually care about each other enough not to renege on promises when doing so is not too costly (Harsanyi's principle of "low-cost objectivity" [1969]) or when the benefits to others from altruistic behavior are enormous (Monroe's conclusion based on her study of Germans who protected Jews during the Holocaust).[1] Altruistic theories can also be defended on evolutionary grounds as attributes that enhance the survivability of the human species.

Second, the key to human survivability as a species, given that we are slow, weak, soft, clawless, long in maturing, and tasty, may be that we are good problem solvers who, among animals, are exceedingly unlikely to let autonomic emotional drives dictate our behavior. Moreover, humans probably are smart enough to recognize that life is a repeated game and that fulfilling a promise today enables one to make a similar beneficial agreement tomorrow. The advantage of this view of humans is that it avoids the fatalistic inexorability of genetic theories, leaving room for true choice and learning. The challenge to Romer is not just to demonstrate that revenge can explain cooperation, but that it predicts some behavior that other respectable theories cannot explain.

### Applications to Voting Behavior

Romer's immediate application of his theory is to voting behavior. Not surprisingly, a preoccupation of political scientists for an entire century has been to explain why and how citizens vote (given that voting is costly but is unlikely to affect outcomes and so to generate instrumental benefits). In the mountain of explanations for this seemingly irrational behavior, decision-theoretic models are a fairly late entrant. Initially, practitioners of rational-choice models in political science simply assumed that the act of voting was consumption, with citizens simply "feeling good" about engaging in participation. The tautological assumption that each citizen can capture $R$ utils from voting even offered to escape tautology by actually explaining something: differentials in turnout rates by income groups and age groups.

Romer's work can be interpreted in the context of this literature as providing an explanation for $R$, but one that is conditional on circumstances. In particular, $R$ is larger if voting enables the citizen to cast a vengeful vote against a candidate who has broken an intertemporal agreement of the form modeled by Romer.

Of course, hypotheses like Romer's are hardly new. Political scientists even have a term for it: negative voting. Indeed, for two decades a quite interesting debate has taken place concerning whether negative voting actually exists, and if so, whether psychological or rational-actor accounts provide a better explanation. A leading exponent of psychological theories is Richard Lau (1982, 1985), who provides two reasons for expecting that citizens are more likely

---

1. These and other extensions of the rational self-interest model of political behavior are discussed in various essays in Monroe (1991), many of which are written by proponents as well as opponents of rational-choice theory.

to respond negatively to political disappointments than positively to desirable political events.[2]

Lau's first explanation is tied to the idea of an altruistic superego governor of behavior: humans generally are thoughtful of each other, and derive pleasurable and rewarding experiences from their interactions; as a result, a failure to behave in a pleasant, cooperative, reliable way draws special attention and causes others to have serious doubts about the integrity of the person whose behavior is nonstandard. (This assumption certainly makes me wish I were a member of Lau's department!) Hence, a citizen who observes noncomplying behavior by an elected official will be prone to conclude that the official is untrustworthy, engaging in noncompliance when behavior is unobserved, and to vote accordingly. This form of response can be interpreted as reflecting the "availability heuristic"—a cognitive pathology whereby an individual overreacts to unusual events.

Lau's second explanation is, like Romer's, sociobiological. Lau argues that the "survival of the species" is promoted if people behave according to the precepts of Amos Tversky's prospect theory—that is, if humans go to greater lengths avoiding significant costs at the sacrifice of pleasurable gains than would be predicted from an expected utility calculation. Survival requires avoiding catastrophes, not having a good time. Hence, Darwinian natural selection causes us, when scoring our political leaders, to give them unusually large negative scores for their mistakes in comparison to the positive scores we assign to their successes.

On the rational-actor front, among the leaders of the analysis of negative voting are Morris Fiorina and Kenneth Shepsle (1989, 1990). Their approach is to use decision theory under conditions of incomplete information to analyze whether negative voting is plausible. They offer two different arguments.

First, Fiorina and Shepsle argue that one must be careful in asserting that negative voting has been detected because of a form of selection bias in elections. If voters underestimate the worth of a candidate, the candidate is likely to lose and, therefore, not to have the opportunity to generate more information that would change voters' minds. But, if voters overestimate a candidate's worth, the candidate is more likely to be elected, voters will then update their beliefs after observing poor performance in office, and the candidate will do less well in the next election. Indeed, if voters are Bayesian, the candidate will tend to do worse in every subsequent election until defeated.

Second, Fiorina and Shepsle develop a game-theoretic model of voter behavior in which a voter can decide how to weigh good news against bad news about performance in office. They demonstrate that a rational voter, facing imperfect observability of an office holder, will overweight the bad news relative to the good news because to do so causes less shirking by the elected official.

---

2. For a variety of other psychological theories of voting, see the symposium in the *American Political Science Review* 85 (December 1991).

This model is very similar to both standard trigger strategies and to Romer's, differing from the latter in that citizens elect to behave vengefully because they see its consequences down the decision tree, rather than because they derive pleasure from seeking revenge.

Finally, as an empirical matter, no negative voting theory can explain most (let alone all) voting behavior. In all postwar elections, most voters have voted for incumbents, and most voters cast nearly all their votes for the same party. Votes against challengers who have yet to break their first promise, and for a party regardless of changes in the policies of either party, can hardly be explained as punishment. The most one can expect from negative voting theories is a more powerful explanation for shifts in behavior by marginal voters.

The preceding brief, highly selective literature review is intended to demonstrate a single point: neither psychology, sociobiology, game theory, nor the idea that some voters are prone to vote against one candidate rather than for another are new to the study of voting behavior. Romer's particular model, however, is different than the rest, but to demonstrate its usefulness requires that it be run against other attractive horses.

**Application to Entitlements**

The final step in Romer's logical chain is to argue that his version of negative voting sheds light on the politics of entitlement programs. In essence, Romer argues that the 1950s dance between Democrats and Republicans about changes in eligibility and financing of Social Security reflected rational response by each side to their partisan differences about the program and the reactions of voters to attempts to cut it. Vengeful voters, argues Romer, see the entitlement form of Social Security as a long-term agreement on which they have relied in making other long-term decisions (notably, about plans for retirement), and so would be more prone to punish a political official who reneged on this arrangement than another political official who simply cut a transfer program to all old people.

This account raises several important issues. The first is about the identity of the support constituency, based upon the simple calculation of costs and benefits, of the Social Security system as initially designed compared to a straightforward old-age assistance program. The pseudoinsurance feature of Social Security makes the program less redistributive by income categories than a standard transfer payment because it ties benefits to tax payments. And, because total benefits are tied more closely to current receipts than past payroll tax collections, a salient feature of the program is its intergenerational redistribution. A reasonable interpretation of the effect of Social Security on most working-age adults in the 1950s is that they picked a system in which their children would support them in retirement, but preferred one in which they would be more likely to live independently rather than on direct payments from children, perhaps within the same household. As a result, most working-age adults in the 1950s could expect a positive net benefit from Social Security (and this expectation has been fulfilled), whereas a similarly designed straight pension would cause the net benefits of some higher-income individuals to turn negative. The Democrats certainly favored greater coverage, and did, in fact, pass a sequence of bills that gradually made Social Security (or state counterparts) virtually universal, but by preserving the pseudoinsurance feature they retained the support of some voters with above-average incomes. Thus, to argue that "vengeful voters" provide an additional explanation for the episode reported by Romer, one has to find elements of attitudes about Social Security that are not explained by this simple model of self-interested behavior. I personally do not find anything surprising in the Democrats' behavior to sacrifice some progressive redistribution in order to secure broader political support for the program, particularly a few years after the rise of the Conservative Coalition stopped further extensions of the New Deal.

Another challenge to the vengeful voter theory is to make convincing distinctions between this particular entitlement program and other governmental activities that reflect intertemporal commitments. In a sense, the nature of political competition is for candidates for office to make promises about future performance. Each candidate offers a vector of positions on issues. For incumbents, performance in office provides voters with estimates of likely future performance, to be weighed against more uncertain promises of a challenger. Most likely, because of the centralizing tendency of electoral competition, voters—at least, the decisive ones—are not likely to see one candidate as strictly dominating another on all elements of the position vector. Hence, electing one over another has an opportunity cost—sacrificing the advantages offered by other candidates on some issues. If a challenger runs for office on the basis of asking voters to sacrifice welfare on some dimensions in order to obtain more welfare on another, and then fails to deliver on the latter, should not Romer predict vengeful voting—even when the net benefits delivered by the winner are slightly higher than the benefits promised by the loser? What, then, differentiates entitlements as sources of vengeful reaction from other campaign promises that go unfulfilled?

Perhaps the closest parallel to entitlements is a long-term public investment program. Suppose the government embarks on a project that is expected to take ten years to complete, and then cancels the project halfway through. Rational-choice political theory predicts more resistance to cancellation than support for initiation, ceteris paribus, because once the project is begun, some citizens will have occurred sunk costs in reliance upon completion of the project. Hence, the expected net benefits that are required to initiate a program exceed the amount that, in midstream, are necessary to continue it. Vengeful voter theory should apply here as well, so that some voters who derive net positive benefits from an incumbent's whole platform will nonetheless vote for the challenger because the project was cancelled. Specifically, a voter who would derive private benefits from the project would have made parallel tax payments to support it during initial construction, but would then not be rewarded in the end by the stream of benefits.

Perhaps the biggest challenge to the theory is to explain all Social Security programs (including disability insurance, survivors' benefits, and Medicare). These elements vary considerably in the degree to which benefits are even symbolically tied to contributions and in their generosity. Medicare, for example, is certainly the most generous, bears the least connection between contributions and benefit entitlements, and so corresponds most closely to a standard transfer program that would generate the least revenge from cancellation or cutback. It is also the element of Social Security that is growing most rapidly and the principal threat to bankrupt the system, yet it has been impervious to significant containment. How does vengeful voter theory explain this phenomenon?

These questions are important to testing vengeful voter theory because the latter predicts that, holding constant the magnitude and distribution of benefits from a program, negative voting is more likely for cuts in entitlements than for other programs. If this is not true, the theory cannot be distinguished from other negative voting theories. In reality, the degree to which a program can be regarded as an intertemporal commitment, requiring some sacrifice now for benefits in the future that could engender a sense that the later rewards had somehow been earned, varies among programs. My sense is that this variation is more continuous than dichotomous, but in any case, the argument that entitlements are somehow separate from all other programs seems to me to be insufficiently explained.

## Conclusions

The thrust of these comments is that my comfort with Romer's argument is far greater at the more abstract, general level of argument, and least at the level of an application to understanding the politics of a particular program like Social Security. Economic modeling is obviously highly useful in a number of contexts other than analyzing private economic decisions, and equally obviously can add to our understanding of how people solve collective action and coordination problems. Romer's focus on emotionally motivated behavior as plausibly having value to humans in these types of circumstances is interesting and promising as part of the agenda for economic theorizing. For the specific case at hand, Romer's argument makes a good case for explaining the existence of revenge and its likely partial-equilibrium effects.

My skepticism deepens as the model is extended to the specific applications of voting behavior and the design of a program. Both voting behavior and designing programs plausibly involve numerous human emotions and values. They are also consequential decisions that are made after a protracted period of information dissemination and consideration. Here much work remains to demonstrate that the motive of revenge is a dominant force, compared to rational pursuit of some combination of self-interest and interdependent utility.

## References

Fiorina, Morris P., and Kenneth A. Shepsle. 1989. Is Negative Voting an Artifact? *American Journal of Political Science* 33:423–39.

———. 1990. A Positive Theory of Negative Voting. In *Information and Democratic Processes,* ed. John Ferejohn and James Kuklinski, 219–39. Urbana: University of Illinois Press.

Harsanyi, John C. 1969. Rational-Choice Models of Political Behavior versus Functionalist and Conformist Theories. *World Politics* 21:513–38.

Lau, Richard. 1982. Negativity in Political Perceptions. *Political Behavior* 4:353–78.

———. 1985. Two Explanations for Negativity Effects in Political Behavior. *American Journal of Political Science* 29:119–38.

Monroe, Kristen Renwick, ed. 1991. *The Economic Approach to Politics.* Princeton, NJ: Princeton University Press.

# 8    Information, Responsibility, and Human Services

Kenneth J. Arrow

## 8.1    Introduction and Historical Remarks

The recognition of the importance of information has been one of the major achievements of economic analysis in the period since World War II. Of course, the state of knowledge of participants in the economy was long recognized as a major determinant of the state of the economy. Indeed, the idea of the production function, as it was articulated by late-nineteenth-century neoclassical economists (Walras, Stuart Wood, John Bates Clark, Wicksteed), came to be recognized as an expression of the technical knowledge available to the firm (or to the economy, in more aggregate analysis). What was not really analyzed was the idea of information as a *variable,* differing among economic agents or over time.

The formal analyses of economic behavior before World War II implied indeed that information, whether about technology or about tastes, was the same for all participants. There was in fact a curious duality. On the one hand, everyone knew everything relevant. On the other hand, the price system was praised for requiring an economic agent to know virtually nothing about the rest of the economy except as revealed through prices. The Austrians (Menger, Hayek) pursued further than most other economists the personal nature of knowledge.

This duality did not lead to any contradictions because in a competitive economy both viewpoints (that of universal common information and that of completely private information) led to the same outcome, competitive equilibrium. But it must be stressed that this equivalence is valid only under stringent conditions: (1) the economy is in equilibrium (in fact, the process of achieving equilibrium involves an exchange of information, if it is not already universal; the so-called stability problem, how the economy achieves equilibrium, has

Kenneth J. Arrow is the Joan Kenney Professor of Economics emeritus and professor of operations research emeritus at Stanford University.

never achieved a satisfactory resolution); (2) the individuals know what the commodities are (or at least are equally ignorant of their properties); (3) the economy is competitive; (4) there are no externalities.

To make a completely explicit study of the role of information was not really possible without an adequate theory of behavior under uncertainty. To summarize inadequately, information amounts to a reduction of uncertainty (the matter is a little more complicated than that) and hence is meaningful only in that context. Although probability theory has been known for three centuries and even the expected-utility theory of behavior under uncertainty dates from Daniel Bernoulli's paper of 1738 (which, among other things, contains a very good explanation of insurance), there were only the most sporadic attempts to give a systematic treatment of even such straightforward matters as portfolio choice (Edgeworth 1888, on bank reserves; Marschak 1938, on portfolios; rather vague remarks of Irving Fisher and Frank Knight; Allais 1943, on the demand for cash balances).

The vigorous revival of expected-utility theory by von Neumann and Morgenstern (1947) and Savage (1954), the latter with an accompanying axiomatization of probability theory, precipitated a vigorous set of applications to economic uncertainty. The general formulation of uncertainty as a system of state-contingent commodities (Arrow 1953; Debreu 1959, chap. 7), the systematic development of portfolio choice by individuals (Tobin 1958; Markowitz 1959), and the incorporation of portfolio theory into general equilibrium theory in the capital-asset-pricing model (Sharpe 1964; Lintner 1965; Mossin 1966) followed rapidly.

These theories were based, however, on the assumption of a given public body of information. The uncertainties were in most models the same for all participants. In some it was possible for individuals to have different probabilities for the same events, but these were purely subjective choices, not based on different observations or other objective and transmittable differences in knowledge.

Mathematical statistics (R. A. Fisher, Neyman and Pearson, Wald) had been developing as a discipline, and it was devoted precisely to the optimal use of information, that is, how best to use a set of observations to modify beliefs. From a somewhat different point of view, communications theory (Shannon) was also concerned with the transmission of information. With the aid particularly of Savage's work, the idea that economic decisions should be thought of as functions of information became widespread. One of the earliest effects was seen in Marschak's work on organization theory (1954). He abstracted from conflicts of interest within the organization but emphasized differences in information. Different members made different observations ("received different signals" in language derived from communications theory) and had to make decisions that were complementary with or substitute for those to be made by other members of the "team," based on different observations. The initial distribution of information might be modified by communicating some of the signals to other team members.

While team theory has not developed very much, this picture of differential or asymmetric information was applied during the 1960s to the operation of markets. Subsequent work put more emphasis on incentives. The asymmetric information not only existed but could be the basis for profitable actions, and those without the information would take protective steps. Arrow (1963) found differential information important in the field of medical care, both in the supply of medical care itself and in the workings of medical insurance. (Concepts like "adverse selection" and "moral hazard" were already very well known in insurance practice but had little theoretical development.) Recognition of similar issues in the securities markets, product quality, share-cropping, optimal income taxation, and employment contracts followed very rapidly with work of Radner, S. Grossman, Mirrlees, Ross, Spence, and Stiglitz, among others. One side development was the recognition that, under asymmetric information, prices revealed information about the knowledge of others. To my mind, this particular proposition, ingenious as it is, has deflected attention from the great variety of ways in which information is transmitted, to put all emphasis on one.

The formal analyses of the economics of information based on explicit use of probability theory and the updating of probabilities based on new information have been very fruitful in illuminating previous inexplicable economic institutions such as share-cropping and incentive contracts. But they are only part of the story. One quite different insight into the role of information came from attempts to document and explain economic growth. The fact of technological progress was quite evident and has been referred to casually by most economists at least since Adam Smith. Nevertheless, attention to its importance was dramatically increased by the empirical work of Solow (1957), preceded by similar but less influential work by Tinbergen (1942) and Abramovitz (1956). All showed that output rose more rapidly than an index of total conventional inputs; an obvious interpretation is that information about the ability to transform inputs into outputs is growing over time.

Separately, there had already been a literature, as much sociological as economic in origin, that studied the diffusion of technological and other information. The models were very much drawn from the theory of epidemics; informed and uninformed individuals met each other at random, and at each meeting there was a probability of transmission of the information. This led to a logistic curve for the spread of the new knowledge, an observation that had already appeared in A. F. Burns (1934). Though there was little economic basis, somewhat more sophisticated formulations in which costs and benefits of communication appeared were developed by Griliches (1957) and Mansfield (1968). These models have not been much developed, but they draw attention to two important facts about the state of information: (1) it is not uniform in a country and certainly not in the world, so that there is indeed asymmetric information about technology; but (2) information does migrate; its distribution cannot be taken as given.

Stigler (1961) introduced a new point of view into the implications of differential information for information seeking. He postulated information (in his work, price information) that could indeed be discovered but only at a cost to the searcher. Stigler's theory has been intensely developed, though in spurts, but has had only limited application to technical or other information other than prices.

Apart from transmission, technological progress requires of course the creation of information that is entirely new. In the models of Solow and Tinbergen, information simply appeared exogenously. To some extent, it is indeed the by-product of noneconomic forces such as scientific curiosity. But to a great extent the new information is the result of deliberate inquiry, which means there is a specific investment decision based on the expectation of reward. This decision may be public or private. The incentives for the creation of information needed examination, especially in view of the fact that information could only partially be made into private property. Many interesting papers were presented at a National Bureau of Economic Research conference (1962), and there has been much subsequent literature, particularly on patent races.

It is obvious and important to note that the cost of acquiring information is a fixed cost with respect to production quantities, and this of course has obvious implications for the organization of competitive industries.

## 8.2  Some Generalizations about Information

The slippery role of information as an economic good is of deep significance to economic behavior, especially in the relatively information-rich modern economy. It is an economic good in the traditional sense; it is valuable, and it is costly. But it has a peculiar algebra. Adding one ton of steel to another permits more to be done; repeating the same item of information does not add anything useful. On the other hand, supplying a ton of steel to another reduces the steel available to the supplier; supplying information to another does not reduce the information available to the supplier.

From these trivial remarks, a whole host of consequences follows, some of which have already been noted. I want to stress some aspects of the role of information especially relevant to the human services that are the subject of this conference. Some are very common knowledge; others are not so widely remarked in the literature.

### 8.2.1  The Location of Decision: Information versus Utility

Most of our economic theory takes a simple view of decision making; each entity has a natural sphere (household consumption or production decisions). It is assumed that the individual whose interests or utility (benefits or costs of both) are at stake is the same who has more information about it. But in many cases the information about the consequences of a decision may not be at all in the hands of the "natural" decision maker. This is notoriously the case with medical care and indeed typically with professions (lawyers). Our practice in education is similar. The actual conduct of a school (even of a private school) is not in the hands of the individual parent and not even in the hands of parents collectively. A university faculty, even today with its shaken confidence, considers that it is better able to determine a curriculum and the contents of particular courses than the students or the parents.

One principle that is clearly valuable in many situations is that of colocating information and decision. *Responsibility* can be based on knowledge. This is the sterling contribution of Calabresi in his classic analysis of liability for accidents (1970).

Health and education are indeed examples of asymmetric information, but in a way different from that posed in the usual analyses. The ordinary cases are those in which an individual has private information about himself or herself, for example, his or her capabilities or willingness to perform, and this information is not available to others, for example, an employer. The examples I have in mind here are ones where another individual may have better information. This viewpoint would lead to paternalism, and indeed, in spite of all ideological opposition, we do accept paternalism in many spheres.

It must be emphasized that asymmetric information, even in this case, does not necessarily lead to shifting the locus of decision making. The individual less informed about his or her own well-being may nevertheless have enough information to permit monitoring the choices. Further, the responsibility need not be all or none. The asymmetric information I described may be equally applicable to complex machines, such as automobiles. The producer in general has much better knowledge of the performance characteristics than the buyer. We do not feel it necessary to remove choice from the individiual. But we do have a principle of product liability. The more informed party does not make the decision but bears a responsibility concomitant with its superior knowledge.

There are a number of modes of information transfer that are sufficient to permit the less informed but concerned party to make adequate choices. One is *experience;* the repeated use of objects from the same source may give a reliable measure of usefulness even to the buyer who could not begin to design or build an automobile. A second is *reputation;* this does depend on inexpensive non-market-based transmission of information from others. A third is the use of *signals;* warranties or prices may be used to signal quality, though these have to be validated through experience and reputation.

These devices permit the creation of markets in which principals employ agents who are better informed than they are. Current principal-agent theory takes the relation as given and proposes contracts to reconcile the interests of the two parties. The usual theoretical contracts are in general much more complicated than those observed in practice. The published literature neglects the market in which principals and agents come together.

These three modes of information transfer are market-based or at least non-coercive forms of information transmission to mitigate the effects of not colocating information and decision. Another tool is *government regulation.* The government licenses physicians (and lawyers), thereby guaranteeing some minimum standards. In a similar vein, we have government regulation of securities issues, which set standards for information disclosure. These provide at least part of the information, so that the decision maker is closer to being adequately informed.

### 8.2.2   Incentive Problems

Obviously, when decisions are shifted from the person most concerned to the one most informed, there are incentive issues. As noted, much literature addresses incentive contracts, which have little relation to actual contract practices. What is noteworthy in the case of medical care is the extent to which professional standards rather than incentive contracts are still the main source of control.

Obviously, in the medical field, as noted from the beginning, the presence of third-party payers has weakened the incentive to economize. This has shifted the incentives to the insurance carriers, and they are certainly beginning to accept this responsibility. But they have of course their own incentives, which are not those of the patients. It is remarkable therefore that the system has worked as well as it has.

The clearest incentive failures in medical insurance have been the increasing exclusion of preexisting conditions and the constant threat to exclude those who have become ill. Any true insurance would have to take a lifetime viewpoint. Many apparent ethical dilemmas (such as making genetic diagnostic tests) would disappear if this were understood. The problem here is a conflict between the possibility of acquiring information about a patient's health, which may well have other useful purposes in diagnosis and treatment, and the competitive nature of the insurance market.

### 8.2.3   Economies of Scale in the Production of Information

From the fact that information can be reused at the cost of transmission, it follows that there is considerable economy of scale in the accumulation of information. Economies of scale in turn imply specialization. That is why it pays to have a relatively small number of individuals specialized as physicians. In short, it is precisely Adam Smith's explanation of specialization that explains why the problem of asymmetric information arises in the first place. (Of course, there can also be specialization based on differential abilities and interests, analogous to comparative advantage in international trade. For the contrast between Smithian and Ricardian specialization, see Houthakker [1956].)

Economies of scale arise in another way, which may be called *statistical economies*. Much information is essentially statistical in character; it finds regularities in large bodies of data. This process by definition requires large scale. If we are discussing the reliability of equipment or the principles of good education, there needs to be a large sample to get some reliability. The experience of a single individual does not offer enough opportunities to get reliable results. Hence, there is value in central data collection, and correspondingly an automatic degree of specialization.

### 8.2.4   Information Dissemination versus Paternalism

The presence of economies of scale in information explains the mismatch between the location of information and that of concerns. The colocation of information and decision may not accord well with the individual who undergoes the benefits and costs. The physician knows more than the patient, but it is the latter's welfare that is at stake.

This raises the possibility of replacing regulation or proxy decision making by dissemination of information. In the medical field, this can take a number of forms. (1) Instead of licensing physicians, simply inform a potential patient of their training and their record of accomplishment. (But who would provide this information?) (2) Confine the physician's role to giving information, and let the decisions be made by the patient. (3) Make it easier to get alternative opinions.

### 8.2.5   The Inevitability of Information Diffusion

To some extent, the spread of information will occur in any case, though its reliability may be in doubt. Knowledge about new medical developments and treatments becomes known through a variety of means, in which both personal contacts and media play roles. Medical decisions are made against a background of social knowledge, though undoubtedly very unequally diffused. This is even truer of educational decisions. The professional insulation is much weaker, and lay boards have even more authority.

In both cases, the word "information" may not be quite accurate. What is diffused is opinion, and, as we well know, this may be in some cases far from the most relevant observations. Cognitive biases are well known, but perhaps even more important is the bias toward ease of an interest in communication. In both fields, faddishness is not at all uncommon.

### 8.2.6   Information and Organization

The way decisions are made and information is used depends heavily upon the organizational environment for decisions. The medical field is in many ways very decentralized. The ultimate unit is the patient-physician encounter, so that knowledge is used on an individual basis. Education is almost invariably carried out in classes; for the sake of continuity and coordination, the classes themselves fit into larger entities, schools. This means that the knowledge is partly embodied in bureaucratic rules of procedure. These may change from time to time under evolving information or opinions, but they have to change in a coordinated manner. This makes each change much costlier. It also gives less room for learning from experience to feed back into the decisions about curriculum and teaching methods.

## 8.3    Responsibility for Medical Decisions

There is a whole hierarchy of decisions that have to be made to determine the course of medical practice. Physicians make individual decisions about care of their patients, subject of course in the first place to the patients' consent, but in a context where their decisions are constrained by the prospects for reimbursement and by the availability of resources to carry out the diagnoses and therapies.

The conflict of incentives and information is increasingly leading to a diffusion of responsibility for medical decisions. The simple picture of the physician making decisions for the patient has certainly become more complicated. Patients always had a role in choosing to seek medical advice and from whom. Their choices are becoming increasingly restricted as medical practice becomes more organized. The problems of cost control in an insured world are partly met by the increasing use of control of medical services through review by health maintenance organizations and insurance carriers.

A particularly important issue in assigning responsibility for medical choice is the control of decisions about the provision of diagnostic facilities and hospital facilities. These decisions are central not only because they affect an important area of costs directly but also because they indirectly limit the possibilities for medical procedures. To exercise control over facility decisions requires knowing not only the technological usefulness of the facilities but also the alternative sources of supply in the relevant marketplace. The forces of competition, which might otherwise serve as a control, are dulled by third-party reimbursement and may be made less effective by competition among insurance carriers. There seems to be no major informational reason why a central authority cannot set limits (for example, by preventing reimbursement of unnecessary overhead costs), but since such an attempt was made to regulate the introduction of CAT scanners, my impression is that there has been no effective control.

## 8.4    Responsibility for Educational Decisions

As already suggested, education differs from medicine in its more strongly organized form, although modern developments in the structure of medical practice may be reducing the difference. Within the school, education is essentially a public good; because of economies of scale in coordination, any decision on education cannot be finely differentiated according to the individual.

Education may also differ from medicine in that the degree of knowledge behind it is less. It is harder to understand social processes, in which genuine experimentation is lacking, than biological processes. As a result, professional status, though not entirely lacking, is much less strong, and lay control is much less inhibited.

Society has largely retained the premise that primary and secondary education is primarily a state responsibility, as to both financing and supply. Objections have been made to both kinds of state responsibility, though more usually to the central role of the state in supply. The many versions of voucher schemes seek to achieve private competition for the supply of education. I am certainly no expert in these matters. Decisions have to be made as to the degree of resource support, the particulars of the curriculum, the qualifications of teachers, and the standards to be imposed on the students. Within the framework set by these overall decisions, the teachers still have all the decisions inherent in running a class.

There are additional complications in analyzing the allocation of responsibility in education. The needs and abilities of students differ very much among themselves, so that the aims of the system are not as clear as they are in medicine.

As with medicine, the decision making has become increasingly complicated as the sources of finance become more varied. In particular, the state and even the federal government have become larger participants as compared with the traditional (in the United States) control by local authorities.

By definition, the students are not a very useful set of decision makers; if they were, there would be no need for education. Can the parents play a role? Obviously, some parents are well informed, but many others are not, for all sorts of reasons, rational and otherwise. As Hirschman pointed out long ago (1970), there is an instability associated with parental influence. If a public school system starts deteriorating, it is precisely the most aware and knowledgeable parents who will put their children in private schools and therefore cease to influence the public schools; in his terminology, they choose "exit," not "voice." Now, "exit" is the consumer's decision-making mode in the private competitive sector. This has suggested to many that competition through voucher systems will serve the same function in education. But Hirschman's argument should give pause.

For the voucher system to work, it would be necessary to have informed parents. One cannot be dogmatic without empirical evidence, but I would be surprised if the average parent has the time or patience or competence to digest the relevant information. Indeed, one wonders where the information is to come from and in what form it should exist. Do we use test scores, themselves affected by the selection processes of the students? Impressions of individual teachers or of the physical appearance of the school will tend to dominate.

## 8.5   Decisions on Child Care

Child care has grown up under different circumstances than education and probably for a mixture of reasons, good and bad. There are many systems of child care, some private, some public. As compared with primary and secondary education, there is clearly less need for coordination. The sequencing of classes is much less important. It would appear that the ability of parents to monitor the conduct of the child care activity is much greater because the activity is much closer to everyday experience and knowledge. Most of the informational and structural arguments for the public supply of education are absent in the case of child care. Reputation and experience may suffice for adequate monitoring.

It is also true that the utility of child care to parents is probably more determined by local considerations than is the case with primary education. In particular, questions of convenience of locality play an important role. On matters such as these, the parents have a natural informational advantage. There are some advantages to specialization based on noninformational scale economies, but these operate at a level well below the smallest local government. There may, for example, be room for initiatives to base a school on the employees of a moderate- or large-size firm. But there seems no reason not to believe that the market will take advantage of those economies.

Hence, there seems to be much less reason for government supply or at any rate for government monopoly of child care than there is for government near-monopoly of primary education.

Are there grounds for government *financing*? A case could easily be made against it. Working mothers should buy child care if and only if the value of the additional income plus whatever gain there may be in being relieved of child care activity covers the cost of child care plus compensation for forgone leisure. However, this argument is complicated by the taxes on income (and possible loss of other benefits) and by redistributionist arguments that take us beyond the scope of this paper.

In the absence of government financing, it is not very clear that the government has any advantage in regulating the quality of child care. If the government does finance child care, at least to some extent, then it begins to have a stake in the quality of care. The most natural manifestation of this concern is regulation, especially in the form of setting minimum standards and possibly licensing personnel.

I have tried to show how informational considerations play an important part in organizing decision making in social services. The crucial point is that information is frequently found in the hands of those with less personal interest. A social system works best when decision, information, and interest are located together. The practical problems of medical care, education, and, to a lesser extent, child care arise because these three variables are possessed by different groups.

# References

Abramovitz, Moses. 1956. Resource-output trends in the U.S. since 1870. *American Economic Review Papers Proceedings* 46 (May): 97–103.

Allais, Maurice. 1943. *Économie et interêt.* Paris: Imprimerie Nationale.

Arrow, Kenneth J. 1953. Le role des valeurs boursières dans la répartition la meilleure des risques. *Économétrie: Colloques Internationaux du Centre Nationale de la Recherche Scientifique* 11:41–47. English version, The role of securities in the optimal allocation of resources. *Review of Economic Studies* 31 (1964):91–96.

———. 1963. Uncertainty and the welfare economics of medical care. *American Economic Review* 53:941–73.

Bernoulli, Daniel. 1738. Specimen theoriae novae de mensura sortis. *Commentarii Academiae Imperiales Petropolitanae* 5:175–92.

Burns, Arthur F. 1934. *Production trends in the United States since 1870.* New York: National Bureau of Economic Research.

Calabresi, Guido. 1970. *The costs of accidents: A legal and economic analysis.* New Haven: Yale University Press.

Debreu, Gerard. 1959. *Theory of values.* New York: Wiley.

Griliches, Zvi. 1957. Hybrid corn: An exploration in the economics of technological change. *Econometrica* 25:501–20.

Hirschman, Albert. 1970. *Exit, voice, and loyalty.* Cambridge: Harvard University Press.

Houthakker, Hendrik S. 1956. Economics and biology: Specialization and speciation. *Kyklos* 9:181–87.

Lintner, John. 1965. The valuation of risky assets and the selection of risky investments in stock portfolios. *Review of Economics and Statistics* 47:13–37.

Mansfield, Edwin. 1968. *Industrial research and technological innovation.* New York: Norton.

Markowitz, Harry. 1959. *Portfolio selection: Efficient diversification of investment.* New York: Wiley.

Marschak, Jacob. 1938. Money and the theory of assets. *Econometrica* 6:311–25.

———. 1954. Towards an economic theory of organization and information. In *Decision processes,* ed. Robert M. Thrall, Clyde Coombs, and Robert L. Davis, 187–220. New York: Wiley.

Mossin, Jan. 1966. Equilibrium in a capital asset model. *Econometrica* 35:768–83.

National Bureau of Economic Research. 1962. *The rate and direction of economic activity: Economic and social factors.* Princeton, NJ: Princeton University Press.

Savage, Leonard J. 1954. *The foundations of statistics.* New York: Wiley.

Sharpe, William. 1964. Capital asset prices: A theory of market equilibrium under conditions of risk. *Journal of Finance* 19:425–42.

Solow, Robert M. 1957. Technical change and the aggregate production function. *Review of Economic Statistics* 39:312–20.

Stigler, George J. 1961. The economics of information. *Journal of Political Economy* 69:213–25.

Tinbergen, Jan. 1942. Zur Theorie langfristigen Wirtschaftsentwicklung. *Weltwirtschaftliches Archiv* 55 (Heft 3): 511–49.

Tobin, James. 1958. Liquidity preference as behavior towards risk. *Review of Economic Studies* 25:65–86.

von Neumann, John, and Oskar Morgenstern. 1947. *Theory of games and economic behavior.* 2d ed. Princeton, NJ: Princeton University Press.

## Comment    Glenn C. Loury

Four policy areas have been the main concern of this conference: child care, health care, education, and long-term care. Within each area two central questions have been explored: What are the *social responsibilities* for provision of assistance in these areas? And, how can programs be designed to deal with *implementation problems* likely to arise when trying to meet these social responsibilities? Kenneth Arrow's paper addresses these matters at a conceptual level by considering the role that *limited information* plays in helping economists distinguish individual from social responsibilities, and in thinking about the issue of program design.

There are three perspectives from which to view these questions. One concerns how individuals perceive risks and take decisions in the presence of uncertainty and/or ignorance. Another relates to contracting between private parties and the functioning of markets in the face of informational asymmetries. The third perspective considers the functioning of government regulatory and service-providing institutions under conditions of imperfect information. All three perspectives are involved when asking about the *what* and the *how* of social policy.

One way to look at the issue of individual versus social responsibility, natural for an economist, is through the "market failure" paradigm. There one posits an idealized world of complete markets, on which every commodity can be traded, at every date and under every contingency, through costlessly enforced contracts under competitive conditions. Under such ideal circumstances private contracting and the individual pursuit of self-interest lead to efficient resources allocation. Under this paradigm the presumption is that social responsibilities (beyond the simple redistribution of income) arise only when the efficiency of private contracting cannot be presumed. To the extent that real-world trading possibilities depart from the idealization, one identifies a *market failure;* it is to remedy such a breakdown that the people, through their governments, undertake social actions of various kinds.

Information figures importantly in this paradigm. For example, the fact that a buyer of goods and services may not be as well informed as the seller about the quality of what is being sold leads to market failure when it is impossible to write and enforce contracts contingent on the resolution of this qualitative uncertainty. Insurance markets and markets for professional services are plagued by this problem. Thus, the social provision of insurance and the public regulation or certification of professional competencies are collective responses that can be rationalized as necessary in the face of the inadequacy of markets.

Yet this market failure paradigm is not totally adequate for two reasons. First, people need not be competent to define and effectively pursue their self-

Glenn C. Loury is University Professor and professor of economics at Boston University.

interest. If they are not, even in the absence of market failure, reliance on individual responsibility alone may not be appropriate. Second, the institutions of government are not exempt from the same performance failures that plague markets under conditions of limited information. The possibility of *government failure* militates against the presumption that matters will necessarily be improved when social responsibility is assumed in areas where markets function imperfectly. The difficulty of making large, bureaucratic organizations responsive to the interests and needs of their clients, and the susceptibility of public agencies to political influence by interested parties, illustrate some of the possible pitfalls.

It is for these reasons that I stress the three distinct perspectives mentioned earlier—individuals' (possibly "irrational") behavior, market functioning, and government functioning. I do not believe that there exists any neat theoretical scheme that provides a general answer to the question of what (if any) human services should be provided via social policy. That question inescapably raises philosophical and ethical issues; it also involves matters of culture and politics. It is probable that different societies, equal in economic resources and in the development of market institutions, will and should answer that question differently.

To illustrate, a central theme arising in all four policy areas and raised in Arrow's paper is the matter of *paternalism*—the coerced substitution of a collective or expert judgment for the individual's assessment of his or her self-interest. Use of state power to affect such coercion is practiced to some degree in all four policy areas—education, child care, long-term care, and health care. Some limitation of information or knowledge on the part of the individual subjected to paternalistic governance—her lack of understanding about how best to socialize her children, for example—is the primary rationale for this extraordinary usurpation of individual autonomy. Yet paternalism always involves *values* as well as *information*. Education is not just the provision of facts; it is also the transmission of a set of convictions about how one *should* look at the world. This distinction between values and facts is inherently political. It inevitably involves social judgments, collectively enforced. It is not subsumed in the distinction familiar from decision theory between an agent's assesssment of probabilities and his valuation of outcomes (see, e.g., Savage, *Foundation of Statistics*). It is important to realize, to take one case in point, that behind the conviction that broad benefits to ghetto children will follow from the universal provision of child care lies the social judgment that the values transmitted to children within institutionalized settings are preferable to those likely to be communicated to the child by its parent.

More generally, Arrow's paper calls attention to the fact that, in matters of human service provision, the locus of decision making, the locus of concern, and the locus of information need not coincide with one another. The locus of decision making identifies the agent governing the choice of a course of action; the locus of concern refers to the parties bearing the cost and/or enjoying the benefits of the action; the locus of information indicates who has the factual knowledge needed to select an efficient (net benefit maximizing) action. Problems arise when these loci are not concentrated in the same party. And while these problems need not require socialized service provision, or even public regulation of private provision, the evocation of public authority can often be seen as a response to some lack of coordination between these three loci. This framework is attractive since it captures situations of market failure, but does not require a strictly economistic view of the problem of distinguishing individual from social responsibilities.

A principal benefit of socialized human service provision is that it permits the violation of individual rationality constraints. The economic theory of mechanism design with incomplete information proceeds from the observation that no outcome can be implemented that is not consistent with self-interested, privately informed agents' being willing to reveal what they know. Yet, if truthful revelation results in an agent being made worse off than in the status quo ante, that agent would not participate in the endeavor. For example, under conditions of adverse selection in insurance markets, a well-known unraveling phenomenon occurs in which better risks selectively withdraw from pooled insurance contracts that are priced at the cost of providing coverage to the average risk. As the better risks withdraw, the pool worsens, raising costs and thus prices, and inducing further withdrawals. Often the only way around this problem is to compel participation by those who would otherwise opt out. Such use of the coercive power of the state is only possible when the organization of the insurance market, if not the actual provision of coverge, has been socialized. Mandatory education laws, and vouchers for education or child care that cannot be augmented with private funds or that are limited to use in nonsectarian settings, can be viewed in a similar light.

A lack of coincidence between the loci of choice, concern, and expertise is also evident in the class of situations associated with the *principal-agent problem*. In the health care sector the interaction between patient and doctor illustrates the problem. Interests are not coincident; one party knows his preferences among alternative treatment strategies given their likely outcomes; the other party knows better the uncertain relation between treatment strategies and results. Mechanisms of accountability—such as professional licensing, standards of practice enforced within a relevant community of practitioners, threats of ex post legal action, and experience/reputation effects—are imperfect at best.

Another, less obvious, instance of the agency problem is the relationship between society as a whole and the parents responsible for the care of children. The social interest in effective child rearing is obvious, but seldom so compelling as to override the autonomy of the family. Thus, human service provision to children is necessarily mediated by parental choice. As mentioned, to the extent that the instruments available to induce parents to make the "right" choice are inadequate, the case is strengthened for socialization of some activities that complement child development, to ensure appropriate investments are made.

Another set of issues arises in the classical *moral hazard* conflict between the desire to provide individuals with security and the need to provide them with incentives. This is a central element of the health care debate, but it is important in long-term care as well. Politically, the demand for security has been an important motive behind the growth of welfare states in the industrial societies. Yet the negative implications of inadequate incentive provision for social budgets and health costs have become increasingly evident. While people rally for their governments to provide them with security, we do not observe them in the streets insisting that they be provided with the incentives to make economically rational choices. Therein lies a basic dilemma in the political economy of service provision.

Another moral hazard dilemma arises in the presence of socialized service provision, deriving from the government's inability to credibly threaten to withhold services. All helping relationships are troubled by the following problem: The provider of assistance (P) wants the one in need (N) to act responsibly so as to minimize the need for assistance. At the same time P, being unwilling to tolerate undue suffering by N, is compelled to provide help whenever N's need becomes too great. So N can rely on the fact that, even when N has taken inadequate precautions against the prospect of needing assistance, should disaster occur P will come to the rescue. P's inability to tolerate N's suffering fundamentally limits P's ability to control N's behavior. This is the Samaritan's dilemma. Of course this problem arises in private, consensual relationships as well. But it is exacerbated in the context of public provision by the political dynamics that expose public decision makers inclined toward a "tough-minded" stance to the risks of being portrayed as mean-spirited.

Finally I want to observe, in keeping with a prominent idea in Arrow's paper, that the lack of information creates a circumstance in which learning and innovation become important. Research and development in the drugs industry and exploration of the human genome are instances of this general observation. Public policy—regulatory, antitrust, research support, and patent policies, for example—affect the incentives of private agents to create new information. Moreover, deep problems arise about the ways in which information should be exchanged and disseminated into the marketplace. The issues of "preexisting conditions" in medical insurance and of the identification of genetic markers associated with higher risks of contracting certain ailments have recently focused public attention on this problem. There is also the matter of learning about the most effective methods of organizing and managing socialized human service provision. Here the question of which activities are appropriately undertaken at the federal level, versus at the level of state and local governments, is crucial. Greater devolution permits greater experimentation from which might arise new knowledge about which methods of public provision are most effective, though this diversity undermines the ability to enforce minimal standards of provision across the various jurisdictions.

Viewing the problem of how to divide responsibility for human service delivery between the private or public sectors through the lens of information economics is no panacea, but it can be extremely helpful. Kenneth Arrow's paper should stimulate useful reflection on a wide range of issues related to this general problem.

## Reference

Savage, Leonard J. 1954. *The foundations of statistics.* New York: Wiley.

# 9     The Changing Roles of Public, Private, and Nonprofit Enterprise in Education, Health Care, and Other Human Services

Henry Hansmann

## 9.1   Introduction

The basic human services—health care, education, day care, and old-age care—are characterized by a strikingly diverse range of organizational forms. All of these industries are populated with substantial numbers of firms exhibiting each of three fundamentally different ownership types: for-profit, private nonprofit, and public (i.e., government-owned). The market shares of these ownership types differ markedly from one service to another, however, as shown in table 9.1. Moreover, those market shares have been shifting in recent decades, and they have been shifting at very different rates in the various services and sometimes even in different directions. For example, the market share of for-profit firms has been growing rapidly in child care and at a modest rate in hospital care, but has apparently been constant or declining in primary and secondary education. The market share of public firms, meanwhile, has been declining steadily in hospital care, remaining quite constant in primary and secondary education, and growing rapidly in higher education.

Finally, there is also substantial diversity and change *within* each of the basic ownership types. In particular, there has been a clear tendency toward increased vertical and horizontal integration among both for-profit and nonprofit firms in all of the human services, and at the same time at least an incipient tendency toward *dis*integration among public firms.

I shall analyze here some of the important factors that have given rise to these ownership patterns, and I shall explore as well some of the ways that public policy can and should affect these patterns in the future. I shall begin with some general observations about the role and behavior of firms in each of the basic ownership types, and then proceed to discuss, in turn, each of the

Henry Hansmann is the Harris Professor of Law at Yale Law School and a member of the faculty at Yale School of Management.

Table 9.1          Distribution of Ownership Forms in the Human Services
                   (percentages)

|  | Public | Nonprofit | For-Profit |
|---|---|---|---|
| Health care |  |  |  |
| Hospitals[a] | 24 | 64 | 12 |
| HMOs[b] | 0 | 48 | 52 |
| Old-age care |  |  |  |
| Nursing homes[c] | 8 | 23 | 69 |
| Child care |  |  |  |
| Day care centers[d] | 7 | 56 | 37 |
| Education |  |  |  |
| Primary and secondary schools[e] | 89 | 10 | 1 |
| Postsecondary institutions[f] | 78 | 20 | 2 |

[a]Short-term beds as of 1992 (American Hospital Association 1993–94).

[b]Number of enrollees as of 1993 (Gray and Schlesinger 1994, 15).

[c]Number of residents as of 1985 (National Center for Health Statistics 1989).

[d]Number of spaces as of 1990. Percentage public is based only on programs sponsored by public schools, and may underestimate the total (Kisker et al. 1991, vol. 1).

[e]Enrollment as of 1990 (U.S. Bureau of the Census, 1993, table 221). See discussion in text concerning percentage for-profit.

[f]Enrollment as of 1990 (National Center for Education Statistics 1992). See discussion in text concerning percentage for-profit.

four principal human service industries. Because the organization of health care has received so much attention recently, I shall try to provide some balance by giving special emphasis to education.

## 9.2   Nonprofit Firms

One of the most singular facts about the organization of production in the human services is the large number of private nonprofit firms that these industries contain.

### 9.2.1   The Affirmative Efficiency Role of Nonprofits

The defining characteristic of a nonprofit firm is that it is subject to a "nondistribution constraint" that prohibits the firm from distributing its residual earnings to any individuals—such as members, directors, or officers—that exercise control over the firm. There is general scholarly consensus that the most convincing efficiency rationale for employing the nonprofit form, as well as the apparent reason why nonprofit firms in fact originally arose in most industries in which they are found, is that the nonprofit form serves as a crude but effective consumer protection device in severe situations of asymmetric information (Hansmann 1987a). More particularly, nonprofits restrain producer opportunism where consumers, owing either to the circumstances under which a service is purchased or consumed or to the nature of the service itself, are unable to evaluate accurately the quantity or quality of the service that a firm produces for them. The advantage of a nonprofit firm in such situations is that, by virtue of the nondistribution constraint, the managers of the firm are limited in their ability to benefit personally from providing consumers with fewer or lower-quality services than promised, and thus have less incentive to do so.

As a normative justification and positive explanation for the role of nonprofit firms, this asymmetric information theory is most obviously convincing when the services involved are either being purchased for third parties or are public goods, as is the case with most donatively supported philanthropies. When a person makes what we call a "donation" or "contribution" to a charity such as the Salvation Army or Oxfam, for example, they are in effect purchasing services from the organization that are to be delivered to a third party. The purchaser, however, has virtually no way of checking whether her payment was in fact used to provide services for the intended beneficiaries, much less how well or in what quantity those services were performed. Similarly, when a person makes a contribution to an organization such as the American Heart Association (which supports medical research), or to Friends of the Earth (which promotes environmental protection), or to a listener-supported radio or television station, they are in effect purchasing public goods for consumption by themselves and others. Yet the contributor has no way of determining whether his payment actually went to purchase an additional increment of the public good, or whether, conversely, the organization would have produced the same quantity even in the absence of his contribution. In these circumstances, the nondistribution constraint provides reasonable assurance that all or nearly all of the organization's receipts will be used to finance production of additional services of the type that the organization promises to provide. Consequently, donatively supported organizations are almost universally formed as nonprofit firms.

Many nonprofit firms, however, receive no meaningful amount of income in the form of donations, but rather are "commercial nonprofits" whose income derives almost exclusively from fees charged for private goods and services rendered directly to the payor, just as it does for a typical for-profit firm. It is sometimes argued that problems of asymmetric information both explain and justify the existence of commercial nonprofits just as they do donative nonprofits. Today nonprofit hospitals, for example, typically receive no meaningful amount of donative income. Yet, because consumers are frequently in a poor position to judge the quality of the services that a hospital renders to them, it has been suggested that the nonprofit form is appropriate or even necessary to protect patients from the type of opportunistic behavior that could be expected from a hospital organized as a proprietary firm. This assertion remains controversial, however, since both logic and the available evidence give reason to believe that, at least in industries such as the human services, commercial nonprofits do not offer consumers significantly higher quality than do for-profit firms that provide similar services at similar prices.[1] The nondistribution constraint is, after all, a rather blunt instrument for consumer protection. Moreover, there are a variety of other devices, both public (such as regulation) and private (such as reputation), that can be deployed to provide quality assurance to customers of for-profit firms who would otherwise be vulnerable to exploitation owing to asymmetric information.[2]

If commercial nonprofits do not provide significantly higher quality services than their for-profit competitors, then what accounts for their presence in such large numbers? One possibility is that they simply represent institutional lag: they were originally formed as donative nonprofits, and then remained in place as the industry's reliance on donative financing declined. Another possibility is that they are a response to public regulation or to public subsidies (such as tax exemption or access to tax-exempt bond financing) that have favored nonprofit firms, including commercial nonprofits, over their non-profit competitors.

In making public policy for the human services, it is important to know which of these contrasting views of commercial nonprofits is correct, since the nonprofit firms in the human service industries are frequently, and increasingly, of a commercial rather than a donative character. We shall review some of the evidence below when we examine the individual service industries.

### 9.2.2   Potential Inefficiencies

If nonprofit firms only offered potential efficiency advantages over for-profit firms, and no disadvantages, then there would be no reason for concern when they occupy a large market share in any given industry. There are, however, some potentially significant inefficiencies that may accompany the nonprofit form.

*Operating Inefficiency*

It is frequently argued that, since the managers of nonprofit firms cannot appropriate their firms' net earnings, they have less incentive to minimize costs than do the managers of proprietary firms. The resulting operating inefficiency may be outweighed by the countervailing efficiency advantages of nonprofits where there are severe problems of asymmetric information, as is presumably the case with donatively supported organizations. Where consumers are reasonably capable of policing producer behavior, however, as they may be when patronizing commercial nonprofits providing human services—this incentive problem will render nonprofits less efficient than for-profit firms.

---

1. Some of the empirical evidence is cited below. See, in addition to those sources, Gray (1986, surveying the literature on health care) and Clarke and Estes (1992, comparing nonprofit and proprietary home health care organizations).

2. This is not to say that commercial nonprofits can never serve as an effective response to problems of asymmetric information. A clear example—though perhaps the only clear example— of an industry in which commercial nonprofits have arisen to serve this function is consumer savings banking in the early nineteenth century. (See Hansmann in press, chap.14.)

On the other hand, it is not obvious that we should generally expect non-profits to be significantly less effective at cost minimization than are for-profit firms, particularly in industries such as the human services where, owing to low economies of scale, markets are frequently served by a number of competing firms. For-profit firms, like nonprofit firms, are often managed by individuals who have no claim to an appreciative share of the firm's net earnings, but rather serve as fiduciaries for the nominal owners, just as the managers of nonprofits serve as fiduciaries for the firm's customers. Moreover, the managers of nonprofit firms have a strong stake in their jobs and their salaries, and may derive substantial nonpecuniary returns from the success of their organizations, all of which give the managers an incentive to promote their organizations' survival, prosperity, and growth, which in turn call for cost minimization. Perhaps for these reasons, the available empirical evidence has failed to demonstrate clearly that commercial nonprofit firms in the human services are generally inferior to for-profit firms in cost minimization (Pauly 1987; Schlesinger 1994). There is therefore reason to believe that concerns about the operating inefficiency imposed upon the human services through their heavy reliance on nonprofit firms, while not entirely misplaced, are easily exaggerated.

*Supply Response*

A more serious inefficiency associated with nonprofit firms, arguably, is their sluggishness in expanding or contracting their services in response to changes in demand.

The empirical evidence indicates fairly clearly that, when demand increases rapidly in the human services, nonprofit firms respond by entering or increasing their capacity only slowly; for-profit firms are much quicker in entering or expanding to fill the gap (Steinwald and Neuhauser 1970; Hansmann 1987b). Lack of access to equity capital is probably one reason for this slow supply response; lack of incentives for entrepreneurs who create and manage nonprofits may be another.

Similarly, nonprofit firms appear to be slow to reduce their output, or to withdraw from an industry entirely, when demand for their services contracts. Rather, they continue producing even when their invested capital is producing a very low or negative return. One reason for this may be that legal constraints make it difficult (though not impossible) for a nonprofit firm to withdraw its invested capital from the purposes to which it is currently dedicated (say, provision of hospital care in a prosperous suburban community) and devote it to another purpose (say, child care for the indigent in the inner city). Another and perhaps more important reason is that nonprofit administrators have little incentive to downscale their firms.

This problem is compounded by the fact that, even in the absence of explicit or implicit subsidies, a nonprofit firm can maintain its capacity and even grow in circumstances in which a for-profit firm would not be earning a market rate of return on its capital. Or at least this is the case for nonprofits—such as those typically found in the human service industries—that have accumulated, either from donations or from retained earnings, some significant amount of net capital. For a nonprofit firm need not—indeed, cannot—pay out a market rate of return on its accumulated capital. Consequently, so long as a nonprofit is earning just a zero net rate of return on net capital (after depreciation), it can continue operating at its current scale indefinitely. And if it earns any positive rate of return, even if that rate is well below the opportunity cost of the capital, the firm will have retained earnings that it can reinvest in expansion of its capacity, or that it can use to subsidize consumption of services provided with its existing capacity.

Imagine, for example, that a given community is served by two hospitals, one investor-owned and one nonprofit. Neither hospital provides any research, education, free care for the indigent, or other public goods; rather, they both just sell private medical services to individuals capable of paying for them. Each hospital has $100 million in net assets, in the form of physical plant and equipment that could be sold on the market for that amount. The nonprofit hospital, let us suppose, benefits from no explicit or implicit subsidies, private or public. Rather, like the investor-owned hospital, the nonprofit hospital is subject to aggregate federal and state corporate income taxes of 50% on net earnings. The for-profit hospital has annual net earnings of $15 million, representing a 15% gross rate of return on its invested capital, which yields $7.5 million dollars, or 7.5%, after taxes. This rate of return is just equal to the market rate of return for similar investments, leaving the firm with no incentive to either expand or contract its investment. The nonprofit hospital is substantially less cost efficient, with annual net earnings of just $6 million, or 6% of net assets, yielding $3 million, or 3%, after taxes. If the nonprofit hospital were, instead, an investor-owned institution, this below-market rate of return would presumably induce the firm—if it could not otherwise improve its performance—to sell its plant and equipment to another firm that could make them yield a gross return of at least 15%, either in providing hospital services or in some other activity. But the nonprofit hospital is under little pressure to do this. Rather, its managers are free to, and have some incentive to, invest the hospital's net earnings in further plant and equipment. Thus the nonprofit hospital is in a position to expand by up to 3% per year, taking market share from its investor-owned competitor and ultimately, if it chooses, driving the latter out of business entirely, even though the nonprofit firm is clearly the less efficient producer (and even though it benefits from no publicly provided fiscal or regulatory advantages).

This is not to say that nonprofit firms, no matter how inefficient, will always expand their services so long as they are not actually losing money. A nonprofit may decide to use its net earnings, not to purchase inefficiently large capacity for the provision of private goods, but rather to provide undersupplied public goods such as research or free care for the poor. And, if the nonprofit is not an efficient manager of its existing assets, it may decide to sell those assets and dedicate the sale proceeds to the provision of public goods, or donate them to another organization that can do that effectively. But there is good reason to believe that the managers of nonprofit firms, like the managers of investor-owned firms, often have an inclination toward empire building. And, while investor ownership by no means provides a perfect check on this tendency, the nonprofit form provides very little check at all.

The result is that nonprofit firms can act as traps for capital. Although non-profits may be slow to accumulate capital, the capital they have accumulated tends to become embedded.[3]

In service sectors that are populated by both nonprofit and for-profit firms, and that present no artificial barriers to entry by for-profit firms, the inability of nonprofits to respond quickly to increases in demand need not be a serious problem: entry or expansion by for-profit firms can fill the supply gap. When demand for an industry's services is declining, however, or when demand shifts to types of services significantly different than the existing institutions have been providing, for-profit firms may be an inadequate buffer for the slow re-sponse of the already-existing nonprofits: once all the for-profit firms have exited in a given service area, the nonprofit firms may still remain.

In sum, although nonprofit firms may often manage their existing capacity at costs that are not conspicuously higher than those that a for-profit firm would incur in like circumstances, nonprofit firms appear to be much more prone than for-profit firms to operate with either too little or too much capacity, or capacity of the wrong kind.

## 9.3 Public Firms

Although debate about the respective roles of public and private enterprise has been a central issue in political economy for the past 150 years, and al-though privatization is at the top of the economic agenda throughout the world today, there is remarkably little consensus on either normative justifications for governmental ownership or on positive explanations of why, in fact, public enterprise has come to play a large role in some industries—such as the human services—and not in others. Those gaps cannot be adequately filled here. Rather, we can only point to some considerations that appear particularly im-portant in the human services.

### 9.3.1 Subsidization

There are a number of potential justifications for governmental sudsidies to private consumption of particular goods and services. For example, there may

---

3. The excess capital that a nonprofit accumulates is sometimes not invested in the firm's own productive assets, but is instead held in the form of financial reserves. The large endowments accumulated by well-established private universities are an example (Hansmann 1990). Since these reserves are invested in the debt and equity of other firms, they need not result in substan-tial inefficiency.

be positive externalities associated with private consumption, or the private risk involved in consumption may be lower than the social risk, or capital market imperfections may threaten underconsumption by consumers who are not highly liquid, or paternalistic concerns may cause redistribution to the poor to be limited to specific goods and services.

Whether the government subsidizes a given service for these or other motives, one way to provide the subsidy is to produce the service directly, through government-owned and -operated firms, either without charge or at prices that are below cost. In the past, simple subsidization of this sort has apparently often been the motivation for governmental ownership of enterprise. Public hospitals, which in the United States have frequently been designed to treat the indigent, are an example.

But public subsidies need not necessarily be confined to public firms. One alternative is to channel the subsidies to private nonprofit firms, where the nondistribution constraint serves to assure the government that the value of the subsidies will ultimately be passed through to consumers of the firm's services. In the three decades following World War II, for example, the federal government provided extensive capital subsidies directly to nonprofit hospitals and universities. Why would governmental ownership ever be superior to a system of nonprofit firms supported by public subsidies? Better supply response is one apparent reason. If government wants to expand supply of a service rapidly, it may be easier to create or expand a system of governmental firms than to seek to encourage expansion of the nonprofit sector, as I shall discuss further when I focus on higher education. Similarly, it appears easier to induce *contraction* of a sector when the firms are publicly owned than when they are private nonprofits, as I shall discuss further in connection with hospitals.

Another alternative to governmental ownership is to structure public subsidies as demand-side subsidies that consumers can use to purchase services from private firms that are either nonprofit or for-profit. In fact, over recent decades, one of the most distinctive changes in the production of human services in the United States has been a strong tendency for government to move from supply-side to demand-side subsidies. A need for public subsidies therefore translates into a justification for public ownership only when there is some reason that the subsidies cannot or should not be structured as demand-side subsidies.

One such reason may be that the transaction costs of administering public subsidies are high. Decreases in those transaction costs over recent decades, as systems of public administration have become sophisticated, may be one important reason for the current trend toward privatization.

### 9.3.2   Information Asymmetry

Whether or not there is a justification for public subsidies, governmental enterprise can serve the function commonly ascribed to nonprofit firms: to protect consumers from opportunistic supplier behavior in situations of severe asymmetric information. Might there ever be a reason to prefer governmental enterprise over nonprofit firms in this role? Better supply response is again the most apparent answer.

### 9.3.3    Equality of Consumption

Another reason to favor governmental enterprise over private firms, whether for-profit or nonprofit, is to encourage or enforce equality of consumption. With private-sector firms as suppliers, it is difficult to prevent individuals from choosing very different quantities or qualities of consumption. Also, it is difficult to prevent consumers from segregating themselves among different supplying firms according to various socioeconomic or personal characteristics. Where, for some reason, such self-sorting of consumers appears particularly undesirable, governmental enterprise has the advantage that it can be organized to avoid sorting—or at least this is the case if, through subsidies or other legislative preferences, public firms achieve a near monopoly. As I shall discuss below, this rationale for socialization is particularly strong for "associative" goods and services, such as education.

## 9.4    For-Profit Firms

The essential efficiency virtues and vices of for-profit enterprise are familiar. It is helpful to keep in mind, however, that there are various tactics available to for-profit firms to cope with the problems of asymmetric information that would otherwise lead consumers to prefer to patronize nonprofit or governmental firms. The most obvious is to offer a reputational hostage. Horizontal integration, which offers the reputation of all units in the system as assurance for the performance of each of the individual units, is one method. Franchising offers a similar reputational hostage while retaining strong incentives for cost minimization at the level of the individual service unit. Not surprisingly, both of these approaches have become common among proprietary firms in the human services in recent years.[4]

## 9.5    Health Care

There are three principal types of institutions that market health care to consumers: primary care providers, such as health maintenance organizations and

4. Consumer cooperatives are another ownership form that is sometimes successfully used to deal with problems of asymmetric information between consumers and producers. The form is sometimes found in the human services. Group Health of Puget Sound, for example, is a well-established health maintenance organization organized as a consumer cooperative, and there are apparently also a number of day care centers organized as consumer cooperatives. Aside from these examples, however, consumer cooperatives have made few inroads in the human services. An important reason for this, probably, is that governance costs (including both the transaction costs of decision making and the costs of inefficient decisions) are relatively high in cooperatives that provide goods or services as complex as those in the human services that concern us here. In general, consumer cooperatives achieve substantial success only in supplying relatively simple, homogeneous goods and services (Hansmann 1988, in press).

primary care physicians in solo practice or partnerships; hospitals; and insurers. It is convenient to begin with hospitals, which have been the subject of the most intense study in the literature on ownership.

### 9.5.1  Hospitals

Until late in the nineteenth century, hospitals were almost exclusively charitable institutions—in essence, sick houses for the poor, supported heavily by philanthropic contributions. It was therefore natural that nongovernmental hospitals were organized as nonprofit firms, in order to cope with the problems of asymmetric information facing their donors.

Over the past century, however, advances in medical technology have transformed hospitals into places where persons of means also go for treatment. Moreover, with the development during the twentieth century of first private and then public health insurance, the overwhelming majority of Americans have become capable of paying for the hospital services they consume. As a consequence, charitable donations no longer represent a significant source of income for most short-term acute-care hospitals; rather, nonprofit as well as investor-owned hospitals now rely almost exclusively on patient fees for their income.

There have been substantial numbers of for-profit hospitals in the United States throughout the twentieth century. Until twenty-five years ago, however, these proprietary hospitals were often small clinics owned by the doctors to whose practices they were connected (Steinwald and Neuhauser 1970). With the implementation of Medicare and Medicaid in 1966, the average hospital became a profitable enterprise, more than able to cover its costs with patient fees. As a consequence, large publicly held business corporations began entering the industry, creating substantial chains of hospitals by acquisition and construction. After twenty-five years of aggressive efforts at expansion by these proprietary chains, the market share of for-profit hospitals has expanded noticeably, though not spectacularly, from 6% of all short-term beds in 1971 to 12% in 1992. Nevertheless, nonprofit hospitals continue to account for the great majority of all beds. In fact, the market share of nonprofit hospitals has actually *increased* slightly over this period, from 63% in 1965 to 64% in 1992 (American Hospital Association 1971, 1993–94).[5] In terms of overall market share, the growth of the large for-profit hospital chains has come at the expense of smaller proprietary hospitals and of government hospitals.

Given the transformation of the hospital industry from a charitable to a fee-for-service basis, why do nonprofits continue to have such a large market share? There appear to be two potential rationales that are attractive in terms of social welfare. The first is that the nonprofit form protects consumers against

---

5. Prior to 1971, counts of short-term beds in federally owned hospitals are apparently unavailable. Among nonfederal hospitals, however, the market shares of nonprofit, for-profit, and governmental hospitals remained constant from 1960 to 1971, at 70%, 6%, and 24%, respectively.

opportunistic exploitation of informational advantages. Empirical scrutiny has failed, however, to produce clear evidence that the quality of care in nonprofit hospitals is, on average, higher than that in proprietary hospitals (Gray 1986). This is not surprising. It is not obvious that problems of asymmetric information are so severe in this sector that the nonprofit form is likely to be a useful antidote. Hospitals generally provide relatively simple services, such as room, board, medical supplies, and nursing care; it is the doctors that practice in the hospitals that provide the most complex services, and those doctors are generally independent contractors rather than employees of the hospital. Indeed, the doctors serve as sophisticated purchasing agents for their patients in the consumption of hospital services. Moreover, the large for-profit hospital chains have an important reputational stake in providing high-quality service.

The second potential justification for the continuing survival of nonprofit hospitals is that the nonprofit form is needed to assure that the remaining indirect public subsidies to the hospital sector, such as tax exemption, are actually utilized to finance the public goods for which they are intended, such as research, education, and subsidized care for those members of the population who remain uncovered by health insurance. Yet most nonprofit short-term hospitals undertake no meaningful amount of research or teaching (in particular, they generally have no interns or residents), and the available data do not demonstrate convincingly that nonprofit hospitals on average provide significantly more uncompensated care than do proprietary hospitals.

All of this suggests that the nonprofit form is largely anachronistic in the hospital industry, and that if that industry were to be re-created today from scratch, nonprofit firms would represent a much smaller share of total capacity than they do now. This suggests, in turn, that the continuing large market share of the nonprofits is in large part the result of capital embeddedness.

This holdover of large numbers of nonprofit firms does not necessarily result in serious inefficiency in the hospital industry. As we noted above, there is reason to believe that the operating efficiency of such commercial nonprofits is relatively high in a competitive industry such as hospital care. Rather, if there is inefficiency, it may well lie more in the maintenance of excessive capacity among the nonprofits, and in the use of that capacity to provide excessive services.

What problems does this create for public policy? If nonprofit hospitals are no longer providing a quantity or quality of service that is unavailable from proprietary hospitals, then it is hard to justify continuance of subsidies such as tax exemption. And, in fact, the tax exemption of nonprofit hospitals has already come under serious assault at both the local and national levels. Removal of tax exemption will not itself, however, solve the problem of capital embeddedness. As we noted above, even in the absence of such subsidies, nonprofit firms can survive and grow even if the implicit rate of return on their invested capital is well below its opportunity cost.

This suggests that there is reason to seek a method to facilitate the transfer of invested hospital plant from nonprofit to for-profit firms. Legislation forcing conversion of nonprofit hospitals to the for-profit form, even if it were politically feasible (which it probably is not), seems an unnecessarily strong step. An alternative is to impose on the managers and directors of nonprofit hospitals (and, indeed, of nonprofit corporations generally) stricter fiduciary duties in responding to purchase offers, similar to the duties that the courts have imposed on the managers of business corporations, over the past decade, in responding to takeover bids. Indeed, since the directors of most nonprofit hospitals are self-appointing, rather than (as in a business corporation) elected by the individuals whom they serve as fiduciaries, there is good reason to impose on those directors fiduciary duties that are significantly stricter than those imposed on the directors of business corporations. In particular, one could place a substantial burden on the directors of a nonprofit hospital to justify any decision not to sell their assests to another firm, nonprofit or for-profit, that makes a serious bid to purchase them, and give the bidders standing to bring suit to enforce that duty. (The money that the nonprofit received from such a sale of assets would presumably be placed in a fund to be used for charitable purposes, such as financing medical care for indigents or promoting medical research.)

We observed earlier that an apparent advantage of public over nonprofit firms is that public firms can sometimes exhibit faster supply response. The hospital industry offers evidence of this. The shift from supply-side to demand-side subsidies represented by Medicare and Medicaid, as we have noted, deprived both nonprofit and public hospitals of their unique role in providing subsidized services to the poor. Moreover, in the 1980s, hospital usage in the United States as a whole began to decline. Presumably as a response to these developments, the rate of capacity expansion in both public and nonprofit hospitals slowed in the 1970s, and by the mid-1980s the aggregate number of beds in both types of hospitals actually began to decline. This reduction and ultimate reverse of the growth rate was conspicuously more rapid in public than in nonprofit hospitals, however, with the result that, while the aggregate market share of the nonprofit hospitals remained roughly constant, the market share of the public hospitals contracted from 31% of all short-term beds in 1971 to 24% in 1992 (American Hospital Association 1971, 1993–94).

Does there remain a potential role for public ownership of hospitals? Cost control is the justification most forcefully argued today. Unavoidable imperfections in the market for health insurance, the argument goes, create strong incentives for excessive consumption of health care, and these incentives are amplified by public subsidies. The only way to avoid overconsumption, therefore, is to ration supply, and the easiest way to do this is simply to make the government the owner of the hospitals. Whether the extensive governmental ownership of hospitals characteristic of other developed economies has helped control costs in those countries is, however, a matter of dispute (Aaron 1991, 94).

9.5.2   Primary Physician Care

Prior to the early 1970s, primary care physicians were organized almost entirely in proprietary practices owned by the physicians themselves, either as sole proprietorships or as partnerships. Investor ownership was effectively illegal under state legislation sponsored by the medical profession, as was any form of prepaid group practice except for plans operated by nonprofit firms. The federal Health Maintenance Organization Act of 1973 swept away this restrictive state legislation, and created as well some affirmative incentives for the creation of health maintenance organizations. Initially, however, those federal incentives favored HMOs incorporated as nonprofits.

As a consequence of these developments, all HMOs established before 1973, and most HMOs created in the decade following 1973, were nonprofit. As HMOs became better established, however, and as the federal legislation was modified to be neutral concerning forms of ownership, for-profit HMOs gained market share rapidly. As of 1981, only 12% of all HMO enrollees were in for-profit plans; just twelve years later, in 1993, the figure had increased to 52% (Gray and Schlesinger 1994).

Unlike nonprofit hospitals, nonprofit HMOs in general have no history of donative support, but rather have been purely commercial nonprofits since they were founded. The only efficiency rationale that can be offered for the nonprofit form among these organizations, therefore, is apparently that problems of asymmetric information are so severe for the customers of HMOs that for-profit HMOs could not be trusted. This argument, a priori, seems more persuasive for HMOs than the similar argument is for hospitals, for several reasons. First, HMOs provide actual physician services and not, as is often the case with hospitals, just ancillary services that are ordered by a patient's doctor. Second, the financial structure of an HMO, unlike a hospital, gives the organization a strong incentive to economize on the care given a patient, since the organization itself, and not the patient or the patient's insurer, bears the full cost of the care it administers to its customers. Third, hospitals are more capital-intensive institutions than are HMOs, and consequently are handicapped more severely than HMOs by being denied access to equity capital, as nonprofits necessarily are. The fact that for-profit firms have a much larger market share among HMOs than among hospitals, therefore, offers further support for the conclusion, suggested above, that if the hospital industry, like the HMO industry, were to be created anew today, the ratio of proprietary to nonprofit firms would be much higher than it presently is.

To be sure, the large proportion of for-profit HMOs might be a disequilibrium phenomenon that simply reflects the slow supply response of nonprofits. Once the total supply of HMOs has matched demand, so that the rate of new entry and expansion is much smaller than it is at present, the market share of the nonprofit HMOs may begin rising again. But there is reason to believe that this will not be the case. Large chains of proprietary HMOs have begun to arise—the six largest chains together now have 25% of all HMOs (Gray and Schlesinger 1994)—and their reputational stake promises reasonable protection against opportunistic behavior. Moreover, many of the customers of HMOs are not individuals but rather large employers and unions that have considerable sophistication in purchasing medical care and thus are unlikely to feel that they will obtain important protection from patronizing nonprofit firms.

On the other hand, the substantial heterogeneity of structure among HMOs, and the ambiguity of the categories to which firms are assigned in the available data, make it difficult to draw clear conclusions about the recent evolution of the industry. Much of the growth in for-profit HMOs has been among independent practice associations (IPAs), which now account for 40% of all HMOs. But IPAs, unlike the more traditional group and staff model HMOs, maintain little direct control over their affiliated physicians, serving principally just as insurers rather than as direct providers of care. Consequently, IPAs arguably have less ability to engage in opportunistically excessive cost cutting than do pure group and staff model HMOs, which as of 1993 remained 80% nonprofit (InterStudy 1994).[6]

### 9.5.3   Insurance

Health insurance in the United States first became important with the advent of Blue Cross hospital insurance in the late 1920s. Blue Cross was originally established by nonprofit hospitals as a means of increasing the ability of patients to pay their hospital bills. Since the hospitals were themselves nonprofit and were more interested in having their own bills paid than in seeking profits in the insurance business, and because a nonprofit provider was more likely to convince consumers that they could trust this new insurance product, it made sense to organize Blue Cross on a nonprofit basis. Subsequently, Blue Shield plans to provide insurance for physicians' services were organized on the same model.

In the following decades, for-profit firms entered the health insurance business and captured a majority of the market from the Blue Cross/Blue Shield plans. This development brought some difficulties, however, since the resulting increased competition aggravated the problem of adverse selection by consumers and selective rating by insurance companies, recently forcing Blue Cross to abandon its traditional policy of broad community rating.

Elimination of these selection problems, and of the reduction in risk spreading to which they give rise, may have been one reason why the government itself stepped in as the insurer when, in 1965, the national government decided to subsidize health insurance for the elderly and the poor through the Medicare and Medicaid programs. (Administrative simplicity was perhaps another justification for socialization.) The selection problem remains a central issue now,

---

6. A particular difficulty is that the Interstudy data, which appear the best available, assign roughly a third of all HMOs to the ambiguous "network" and "mixed" categories.

as the nation debates the appropriate scope of direct governmental involvement in extending coverage to the remaining groups of uninsured Americans. Complete socialization in the form of universal federal health insurance, would greatly mitigate the problems involved in creating appropriately large insurance pools, potentially allowing health risks to be spread as broadly as the society chooses (although the nature of the political process might limit substantially the types of pooling that could realistically be chosen). But, to be effective, governmental health insurance would presumably have to place substantial limits on consumer choice concerning the types of coverage, and hence treatment, to obtain. The mandatory government-managed regional insurance pools featured in current health care reform proposals are an effort at an intermediate solution.

## 9.6   Nursing Care

As of 1971, nonprofit nursing homes accounted for only 18% of all nursing care, with most of the rest provided by for-profit homes. Fifteen years later, in 1985, the size of the nursing care industry had nearly doubled. Nevertheless, nonprofit nursing homes not only retained but even expanded their market share over that period, from 18% to 23% (National Center for Health Statistics 1974, 1989). This expanding market share in the context of a growing industry provides some evidence that, for at least a substantial minority of consumers, nonprofit firms are perceived as providing a meaningful degree of protection against opportunistic producers. In part, however, it may also be a consequence of indirect subsidies and of favoritism toward the nonprofit form among state licensing and regulatory authorities.

The nursing care industry provides evidence of a problem presented by nonprofit firms that is, in a sense, simply an exaggeration of their virtue: they have a distinct bias in favor of high-quality service. Nonprofit nursing homes serve disproportionately the high-quality high-cost end of the market (McKay 1991). This is presumably because nonprofit homes tend to serve the nonpecuniary goals of the professionals who manage them, seeking to provide the highest-quality service possible and choosing to provide no care at all rather than care of low quality—and hence failing to serve the large segment of the market that can afford to pay only for minimal care.

## 9.7   Day Care

It would seem that problems of asymmetric information are less serious in day care than in nursing care, since families presumably are much more willing and able to monitor closely the quality of care that is provided to their children than that which is provided to their parents. Consequently, one might expect that nonprofit firms would play a smaller role in day care than in nursing care. It is therefore interesting that the reverse is the case: as table 9.1 shows, nonprofit firms have more than twice the market share in day care that they do in nursing care.

The interpretation of the market-share data for day care centers is clouded, however, by the fact that the distinction between the nonprofit and for-profit organizational forms is much less clear in the case of the very small-scale, labor-intensive firms such as individual day care centers than it is in larger-scale and more capital-intensive enterprise. The nondistribution constraint ceases to have much bite when most of a firm's income goes to salaries, and in particular when a substantial fraction of that income goes to the wages of the persons who control the firm: the salaries paid by a small, nominally nonprofit firm, and particularly the salaries of the administrators, can simply be adjusted at intervals to absorb the bulk of the firm's income as that income rises and falls. Consequently, many small day care centers may have adopted the nonprofit rather than the for-profit form simply because the choice would have little effect on the way in which the center was operated, but might bring some benefits in attracting consumers, in taxation, and in regulation. When a firm operates a substantial chain of day care centers, in contrast, the nondistribution constraint imposes important limits both on the ability of managers to appropriate a substantial fraction of potential net revenues and on the ability of the firm to obtain additional capital. This may help explain why the larger child care organizations tend strongly to be for-profit. As of 1992, for example, seven of the eight day care firms that had a total capacity of more than 5,000 children were for-profit. The tendency toward larger size among the for-profit firms may also, of course, reflect an effort to use the system's reputation as assurance of quality. In any case, the largest for-profit firms are now quite large. The biggest of them, KinderCare, operated over 1,200 centers as of 1992, with a total capacity of 145,000 children (Neugebauer 1992; Stephens and Neugebauer 1992).

Although there has been much controversy over the expanding role of for-profit day care centers, to date neither quantitative nor qualitative surveys suggest that, on average, the for-profit centers provide a lower quality of care than do nonprofit centers with the same level of income per child (Kagan 1991). (As with nursing homes, nonprofit day care centers on average provide more expensive care than do for-profit centers, and for this reason on average provide higher quality care [Neugebauer 1992, table 2].)

There is reason to doubt, then, that nonprofit day care centers serve an important role in providing parents with reassurance about quality care. On the other hand, they may serve an important role in capitalizing on the willingness of parents and organizations to donate materials, space, and (most importantly) labor to day care. The value of these donations is substantial, and, although some of them go to for-profit centers, for reasons rehearsed in section 9.2 the nonprofit centers naturally attract most of the donative support (Coelen, Glantz, and Calore 1979).

Publicly owned and operated day care centers, as table 9.1 shows, constitute only about 7% of the total. This figure contrasts strongly with the large role of public enterprise in primary and secondary education. An even more striking contrast between day care and grade school is evident in the way that public funding, and particularly federal funding, influences patterns of consumption. The politically and academically popular national Head Start program currently pays for 6% of all children in day care (Kisker et al. 1991, table 3.5). The Head Start program itself does not own or operate day care centers; rather, it provides subsidies to private nonprofit centers that meet the program's qualifications (and sometimes as well to centers operated by local governments). Among the requirements that a day care center must meet to receive Head Start funding is, in effect, that the center serves only children whose care is subsidized by Head Start—which is to say, very poor children, and disproportionately members of minority groups. As a consequence, the Head Start program strongly promotes the segregation of preschool children, de jure by class and de facto by race. As I shall discuss below, the most consistently argued and perhaps the most persuasive argument for publicly provided primary and secondary education is that public schools help avoid the severe segregation of children by class, capacity, and previous acculturation that might be expected in a system of private schools. Consequently, public policy toward preschool children seems to be strongly inconsistent with policy toward children in grade school and high school.

This inconsistency is not an administrative necessity. It appears that no appreciable accounting burden would be placed on the Head Start program if day care centers serving Head Start–subsidized children were to enroll other children as well, so long as those other children were entirely paid for by fees or other income sources. Why, then, are Head Start children segregated in separate centers? One explanation that has been offered is that, since Head Start has never been funded at a level sufficient to provide day care to all children who nominally qualify for the program, some form of rationing must be employed. And it is relatively easy to deny access to the program on the grounds that all spaces at the local Head Start centers are occupied, while it would be harder to explain why there are quotas on the number of poor children that the government will sponsor to attend centers that also serve more affluent children, even when those centers have space available. Or, put differently, so long as Head Start centers are segregated from other day care centers, it is easier to maintain the principle that day care, unlike primary and secondary school education, is a privilege and not an entitlement.

Head Start is not, however, entirely typical of public subsidies to day care. Many state programs of day care subsidy, both demand-side and supply-side, are explicitly structured to encourage centers to enroll children from a range of income classes.

## 9.8   Primary and Secondary Education

Primary and secondary education is notable as the human service sector in which the role of public institutions is the largest, and the role of for-profit firms is the smallest.

### 9.8.1   For-Profit Schools

Nobody seems to know, even approximately, how many for-profit primary and secondary schools there are in the United States. Statistics collected at the national level break down primary and secondary schools simply into public and private, without distinguishing between private schools that are nonprofit and those that are for-profit. Moreover, out of ten states surveyed for this essay only one—California—maintains statistics on the number of private schools that are for-profit. Those data show that currently 1,273 out of 4,005 private schools in California, or 32%, are for-profit, and that those for-profit schools enroll 58,336 out of 574,243 private school students, or about 10%.[7] Given that California appears to have larger proportions of proprietary institutions in other service sectors than most states, it seems likely that the ratio of for-profit to nonprofit schools in the U.S. as a whole is lower than 10%, but at present there seems no way of knowing. The figure of 1% for nationwide proprietary primary and secondary school enrollment given in table 9.1 is a guess, based on the California data.

We have even less information on the characteristics and quality of proprietary schools. From the California figures, the proprietary schools are generally small, with only 46 students on average (as compared with an average of 189 students for the nonprofit private schools). This is consistent with anecdotal evidence suggesting that for-profit schools nationwide are predominantly small academies that are often run as family businesses.

Unlike the other industries discussed above—hospitals, HMOs, insurers, nursing homes, and day care centers—in primary and secondary education there are no large for-profit firms that have constructed regional or national chains of institutions. Recently, however, two firms have begun to try: Whittle Communications and Educational Alternatives, Inc. Neither of these firms has had significant success to date, and both are scaling back their ambitions for the moment, seeking only to obtain contracts from local governments to administer publicly owned schools rather than, as they initially planned, constructing or acquiring schools that the companies will own themselves. Possibly these companies made their plans in the anticipation that publicly funded school voucher plans will be widely implemented by national, state, or local government, and that this will create the same type of opportunity for proprie-

---

7. Telephone interview with Ron Reid, Demographics Office, California Department of Education, August 4, 1994. The other nine states surveyed were Connecticut, Florida, Illinois, New York, North Carolina, Massachusetts, Minnesota, Texas, and Wisconsin.

tary schools that Medicare and Medicaid created for proprietary hospitals and nursing homes a generation earlier. If so, it now appears that they must be patient.

### 9.8.2   Nonprofit Schools

Even in California, nonprofit schools strongly outnumber proprietary schools. It may be that this is a reflection of parents' concerns about quality— the problem of asymmetric information. Parents might well doubt their ability to evaluate the education that their child is receiving. On the other hand, it is not clear that this should be, or is, an important factor. The content and methods of primary and secondary education are not so esoteric as to be beyond many parents' ability to evaluate. Moreover, schools develop substantial reputations over time.

Another reason for the predominance of nonprofit firms may be that which I suggested above for day care centers. For small institutions, such as the forty-six-student proprietary schools in California, there may be little practical difference between operating as a sole proprietorship, partnership, or closely held corporation on the one hand, and incorporating as a nonprofit corporation on the other; the individuals who manage the school will be able to derive roughly the same income from it either way. But the nonprofit form has the benefit of tax exemption, a better public image, and probably easier accreditation. Indeed, there is anecdotal evidence that private schools are often founded as proprietary firms, and then convert to the nonprofit form once they become established.[8]

Another reason for a school to adopt the nonprofit form is to attract private donations and public grants. Surely this is a factor among the elite preparatory schools, which solicit contributions from their alumni. It is also obviously a factor among religiously affiliated schools, which often receive financial support from their parent churches. Whether donations and grants are a significant source of income for nonprofit schools in general, however, is unclear. It seems a reasonable guess that most are, instead, almost purely commercial nonprofits.

### 9.8.3   Public Schools

The market share of public primary and secondary schools has long been relatively constant in the United States. It was 91% of enrollment in 1930, fell

8. Note that this transaction can be accomplished with little sacrifice of control or earnings. The individuals who own the proprietary school—whether through a sole proprietorship, a partnership, or a closely held corporation—simply form a nonprofit corporation, with no assets and with themselves as directors and officers. They then sell the school's assets to the nonprofit corporation at a generous price, providing 100% financing and taking back long-term notes at a substantial rate of interest for the purchase price. They continue to control the school and pay themselves salaries for the services they render to it, as they did with the proprietary school. And they continue to derive a return from the capital they originally invested in the school, through the payments on the notes. Prior to the 1960s, this pattern—formation as a for-profit firm, and then a controlled sale to a nonprofit—was apparently also common for hospitals.

to 86% in 1960, and returned to 89% by 1990 (U.S. Bureau of the Census 1970, 1993).

It is not easy to offer a clear normative justification for this large public sector. Surely there has been, at least in the past, an efficiency justification for public subsidy. Education is presumably a worthwhile investment for most children, but in many families both the children and their parents (who are usually not yet in their peak earning years) may be relatively illiquid and, for familiar reasons, unable to borrow to finance the child's acquisition of human capital. Thus, without subsidy, there could be substantial underconsumption. And, at least until recently, it has probably been difficult for governments to administer school subsidies on a demand-side rather than a supply-side basis, so that governments had to own and operate the schools they financed. This argument does not, however, provide a strong justification for public schools if, as advocates of voucher plans have been arguing for some years, demand-side subsidies are now feasible.

In any case, there is an increasingly prominent debate today as to whether this large public share should continue—a debate that has been fueled by the popular concern with the seemingly low quality of American primary and secondary education. Most reform proposals call for putting more competition into the system. Comparison of American higher education, which is outstanding by world standards, with American primary and secondary education, which is not, offers some support for this judgment, since the most distinctive characteristic of the American system of higher education is its highly competitive character. Empirical comparisons of the quality of differently organized schools, and particularly of public and private schools, also tend to support the call for more competition. Although it is difficult to distinguish clearly between the effects of different types of schools and the consequences of the self-sorting of families among those schools, there is evidence that more autonomous schools, and particularly private schools, provide a better education (Chubb and Moe 1990).

The most conspicuous of the recent reform advocates, Chubb and Moe, call for maintaining public ownership of schools while decentralizing administration and giving families freedom to choose the public school they prefer, with funding to take the form of a demand-side subsidy. Those authors do not, however, explain their reasons for advocating public ownership. All the arguments they offer for structural reform seem strongly to favor private schools over public schools, and arguably also favor for-profit schools over nonprofit schools.

Does there then remain a justification for maintaining schools under public ownership? The best argument, it appears, and the one that has been most prominently offered in various forms, is that public schools are justified as a means of avoiding excessive stratification of schoolchildren across schools in terms of socioeconomic class, aptitude, and educational attainments. Rich children, or gifted children, or white children, it is argued, will tend to congregate together in schools, separated from their less privileged contemporaries.

Why is stratification more of a concern with education than it is with health care? Why, that is, do concerns about segregation and stratification not argue as well for public ownership of hospitals and primary health care clinics? An important answer, evidently, is that stratification is a much stronger phenomenon in education because education is, to an unusually pronounced degree, an "associative" good—that is, a good whose utility to a consumer depends, not just on the quality of the producer's performance, but also upon the personal characteristics of the other customers who patronize that same producer (Hansmann and Klevorick 1994; Hansmann 1985). Membership in a country club is a prototypical associative good: the attraction of membership in a given club depends not just on the quality of the golf course and the food in the club's dining room, but also, and often much more importantly, on the qualities of the other members, such as their personalities, skill at golf, socioecenomic status, and business contacts.

Similarly, when attentive parents pick a school for their child, they are interested not just in the quality of the classrooms, the curriculum, and the abilities of the teachers, but also, and importantly, in the other students who will be attending the school. The reason, of course, is that a child's classmates will have a strong influence on the education, reputation, motivation, values, and bruises that the child acquires from the school. When one chooses a doctor or a hospital to perform one's appendectomy, in contrast, one has little reason to put much weight on the personal characteristics of the doctor's or the hospital's other patients.

When associative goods are produced by private firms in the market, there is a strong incentive for consumers to sort themselves across producers. More particularly, to the extent that consumers share similar tastes, there is an incentive for consumers to become stratified across producing firms, with one producer serving all the individuals who make the most desirable customers, a second producer serving the second most attractive stratum of consumers, and so forth. Moreover, although this incentive for stratification exists whether the producing firms are for-profit or nonprofit, it is especially strong among nonprofit firms. Also, stratification is likely to be particularly pronounced if individuals' incomes are positively correlated with the characteristics that make the individuals particularly attractive as fellow consumers (as generally seems true in education), or if all individuals are constrained to pay the same price for the good or service (as they would be under some voucher plans).

A voucher-supported system of private schools could thus be expected to lead to substantial stratification of students across schools. Public schools are arguably less prone to such stratification, since (at least in the absense of freedom-of-choice plans) they generally throw together all children who inhabit a given geographic area. On the other hand, public education already permits the substantial stratification that results from parents' choice of the school district in which to live, and the additional stratification that comes from a system of largely private schools might not represent a qualitative change.

But is stratification such a bad thing? There are several potential arguments against it. First, stratification may lead to social inefficiency in education. Less talented students, for example, may gain more from attending school with other students who are more talented than the latter would lose from the association. (Perhaps talented students will gain a good education regardless of their environment, but less talented students need the challenge and example of talented students in order to learn.) Second, whether or not it is educationally efficient, stratification may tend to reinforce income inequality. And third, whatever the educational and distributional consequences of stratification, it may harm noneducational goals such as political integration of the population. At present, however, we do not seem to have a very clear idea of the potential seriousness of these concerns.

## 9.9    Postsecondary Education

Postsecondary education, like primary and secondary education, is heavily socialized in the United States. What is more, in contrast to primary and secondary education, and to the other service industries discussed here as well, the market share of public institutions has increased markedly in recent decades. The fraction of college and university students enrolled in public institutions was 53% in 1920, and still only 51% in 1950. After the latter date, however, the public share began rising rapidly and continuously, as shown in table 9.2.

### 9.9.1    The Role of Public Institutions

What accounts for this growth in the public sector? Perhaps the best explanation is the rapid expansion of the industry. A demographic bulge and rapidly increasing prosperity swelled demand for higher education quickly beginning in the 1950s. Given the sluggish supply response that characterizes nonprofit institutions, it would have been difficult to meet this demand through expansion of the nonprofit sector, regardless of the generosity of the demand-side or supply-side subsidies that government made available. A faster and more dependable way to expand supply was simply to have government build and operate most of the needed new capacity. Thus, as table 9.2 shows, the five-year period that brought the most rapid rate of increase in enrollments, 1960–65, also brought the greatest expansion in the public sector—from 57% to 66% of all students.

There has also been substantial expansion in spending on health care in recent decades, and particularly in public spending. Yet, unlike public higher education, the market share of public hospitals did not increase during this period; rather, it declined substantially. What accounts for the difference? A

**Table 9.2**          **Public and Private College and University Enrollments, 1920–1975**

| Year | Public | % | Private | % |
|------|--------|---|---------|---|
| 1920 | 315,382 | 53 | 282,498 | 47 |
| 1930 | 532,647 | 48 | 568,090 | 52 |
| 1940 | 796,531 | 53 | 697,672 | 47 |
| 1950 | 1,354,902 | 51 | 1,304,119 | 49 |
| 1955 | 1,484,000 | 56 | 1,177,000 | 44 |
| 1960 | 1,832,000 | 57 | 1,384,000 | 43 |
| 1965 | 3,624,000 | 66 | 1,902,000 | 34 |
| 1970 | 5,112,000 | 72 | 2,024,000 | 28 |
| 1975 | 6,838,000 | 76 | 2,185,000 | 24 |

*Sources:* U.S. Bureau of the Census 1960, 1977.

critical factor, perhaps, is that, despite the expansion in expenditure on health care, hospital usage never increased at the same rate as did college enrollment, so that there was much less need for rapid creation of new capacity in hospital care than in postsecondary education. The five-year period in which college and university enrollments expanded most rapidly, 1960–65, was also the period in which hospital usage expanded most rapidly. But the growth in average daily hospital occupancy over those five years totaled only 18%, while college and university enrollments expanded at four times that rate, or 72%, during the same period (American Hospital Association 1989). Indeed, the major problem during the 1960s and 1970s was not to encourage the construction of more hospital capacity, but rather to *prevent* hospitals from adding new capacity that was unneeded, a problem that led to the widespread adoption of hospital certificate-of-need regulation by the states.[9]

If the major reason to expand the public sector in higher education was to meet a sudden bulge in demand, then perhaps it is not necessary to maintain that large public sector when demand is no longer increasing quickly. Moreover, whether we maintain public ownership of the now-extensive state university systems or not, there are strong arguments for converting those systems from their current heavy reliance on supply-side subsidies to demand-side subsidies. Those supply-side subsidies, as commentators have long noted (McPherson and Schapiro 1991), are distributionally regressive (since they give the same tax-free tuition subsidy to rich students as to poor, and since the rich are also more likely to attend the universities). Moreover, the supply-side subsidies reduce competition among colleges and universities and limit student opportunities by making it much less expensive for students to attend their

9. To be sure, there may also have been other important factors that caused the public sector to expand in higher education but not in hospital care. One of these, suggested by Victor Fuchs (in private communication), is that doctors, who were self-employed independent contractors under the prevailing system of private nonprofit hospitals, feared becoming employees in publicly owned hospitals, while university professors already had the status of employees and thus had less, or perhaps nothing, to lose.

home state's university than to attend an out-of-state university or a private university in their home state.

Indeed, while most of the recent debate about expanded voucher programs has focused on grade school and high school, there seems to be better reason to shift from supply-side to demand-side subsidies, and from public firms to private firms, in higher education than in primary and secondary education. The market for higher education is effectively national, with thousands of colleges and universities potentially in competition with each other, while markets for primary and secondary education outside of major cities are likely to remain local oligopolies. Moreover, prospective college students and their families are probably, on average, much better informed consumers than are the families that patronize primary and secondary schools.

This is not to suggest, however, that there is no rationale for public higher education outside of the need to expand capacity rapidly. Like primary and secondary education, higher education is an associative good. And, in fact, one can see clearly the stratification of students among the elite private colleges, which has resulted in a clear and highly stable prestige ranking among those institutions. In contrast to these private colleges, which have generally remained relatively small, the state universities commonly operate huge campuses that are relatively unstratified, bringing together a broad spectrum of students both academically and socioeconomically. If, as we speculated above, stratification has costs in terms of efficiency or equity, then the present public university systems may have some virtues worth preserving.

### 9.9.2 For-Profit Higher Education

We are left to ask, finally, why private institutions of higher education have been overwhelmingly nonprofit, and whether there might be a larger role for for-profit institutions in the future.

The fact that private colleges and universities have always depended heavily on donative financing, either in the form of private contributions or public grants, is presumably the principal reason why those institutions have been nonprofit. And, why have they had to depend on gifts and grants? The reason is apparently much the same that we offered above for public subsidies to primary and secondary education. Although a college education has evidently been a worthwhile investment for most students, even in the narrow sense that it increased the present value of their lifetime earnings by more than its cost (McPherson and Schapiro 1991), capital market imperfections prevent many students from borrowing the amount needed to pay the full cost of such an education. Consequently, there has been a strong need for subsidy. Indeed, the pattern of the private college financing that has prevailed for the past century, under which the college makes up the gap between costs and tuition revenues by soliciting donations from prosperous alumni, can be thought of as a form of implicit loan program under which students pay less than the full cost of their education under the understanding that, if successful, they will make contributions to the college to repay generously the risky loan they were in effect given (Hansmann 1980).

If this is the principal reason that colleges have been nonprofit, however, then a sufficiently generous system of public demand-side subsidies should obviate the need for private and public grants, and hence eliminate as well the need for the nonprofit form. It is, in fact, hard to find other compelling reasons why proprietary colleges and universities could not succeed. University students and their families seem sufficiently sophisticated consumers, and institutional reputations a sufficiently strong signal of quality, that problems of asymmetric information should not be a fatal obstacle. Nor need the research functions served by universities necessarily suffer from organization of higher education on a proprietary basis. Most colleges, after all, conduct no significant amount of scientific research as it is. And, even for those institutions that find there are economies of scope in combining research with teaching, research could presumably continue to be financed through the current system of competitive federal grants even if the receiving universities were proprietary.

There is already a substantial amount of for-profit postsecondary education in the United States, consisting of roughly four thousand institutions that largely specialize in vocational training. Unfortunately, detailed information on these institutions is difficult to find. It appears, however, that many offer full-time courses of study of up to two years' duration, including some amount of general education. Moreover, students at these proprietary institutions now account for about one-quarter of the grants and one-third of the loans made under the federal student aid programs, demonstrating the high responsiveness of proprietary institutions to demand-side subsidies (Apling 1993).

Other countries, moreover, have gone substantially further than the United States in developing proprietary higher education. In the Philippines, for example, a majority of college and university students attend proprietary institutions. This is not a trivial example, since the Philippines not only has the highest rate of higher education among developing countries, but has apparently been sending about the same fraction of its youth to college as have Belgium and France. Some of the for-profit postsecondary institutions in the Philippines are merely trade schools. Several, however, are substantial universities with broad curricular offerings. And, although the smaller institutions tend to be family-owned, the largest have stock that is publicly traded (Geiger 1986).

One cannot know how successful for-profit firms can be in providing general higher education until further experience has been accumulated. But it is hard to see a priori reasons why the experiment should fail.

## 9.10  Conclusion

The recent expansion of proprietary firms in the human services forces us to ask what role is played by the public and nonprofit firms that so heavily populate those industries, and whether the latter firms remain efficient. The answers to these questions, it appears, differ somewhat from one service industry to another. In all of these industries, however, it appears that further evolution toward proprietary firms is in store. Most importantly, the continuing dominance of education at all levels by nonprofit and, particularly, public institutions, which sets the sector apart from the other human services, seems to lack a strong efficiency rationale. Consequently, education as an industry may be on the verge of dramatic changes in the ownership and structure of firms much like the changes that have swept health care over the past twenty-five years.

# References

Aaron, Henry J. 1991. *Serious and Unstable Condition: Financing America's Health Care*. Washington, DC: Brookings Institution.

American Hospital Association. 1971–94. *Hospital Statistics* (annual editions). Chicago: American Hospital Association.

Apling, Richard. 1993. Proprietary Schools and Their Students. *Journal of Higher Education* 64:379–416.

Chubb, John, and Terry Moe. 1990. *Politics, Markets, and America's Schools*. Washington, DC: Brookings Institution.

Clarke, Lee, and Carroll Estes. 1992. Sociological and Economic Theories of Markets and Nonprofits: Evidence from Home Health Organizations. *American Journal of Sociology* 97:945–69.

Coelen, Craig, Frederic Glantz, and Daniel Calore. 1979. *Day Care Centers in the U.S.: A National Profile, 1976–1977*. Lanham, MD: University Press of America.

Geiger, Roger. 1986. *Private Sectors in Higher Education*. Ann Arbor: University of Michigan Press.

Gray, Bradford. 1986. *For-Profit Enterprise in Health Care*. Washington, DC: National Academy Press.

Gray, Bradford, and Mark Schlesinger. 1994. HMOs and the Changing Control of American Health Care. Manuscript.

Hansmann, Henry. 1980. The Role of Nonprofit Enterprise. *Yale Law Journal* 89:835–901.

———. 1985. A Theory of Status Organizations. *Journal of Law, Economics, and Organization* 2:119–30.

———. 1987a. Economic Theories of Nonprofit Organization. In *The Nonprofit Sector: A Research Handbook*, ed. Walter Powell. New Haven: Yale University Press.

———. 1987b. The Effect of Tax Exemption and Other Factors on the Market Share of Nonprofit versus For-Profit Firms. *National Tax Journal* 40:71–82.

———. 1988. Ownership of the Firm. *Journal of Law, Economics, and Organization* 4:267–304.

———. 1990. Why Do Universities Have Endowments? *Journal of Legal Studies* 19:3–42.

———. In press. *The Ownership of Enterprise*. Cambridge: Harvard University Press.

Hansmann, Henry, and Alvin Klevorick. 1994. Competition and Coordination in Markets for Higher Education. Manuscript.

InterStudy. 1994. *The InterStudy Competitive Edge: HMO Directory*. Excelsior, MN: InterStudy.

Kagan, Sharon L. 1991. Examining Profit and Nonprofit Child Care: An Odyssey of Quality and Auspices. *Journal of Social Issues* 47:87–104.

Kisker, Ellen, Sandra Hofferth, Deborah Phillips, and Elizabeth Farquhar. 1991. *A Profile of Child Care Settings: Early Education and Care in 1990.* 2 vols. Washington, DC: U.S. Department of Education, Office of the Undersecretary.

McKay, Niccie. 1991. The Effect of Chain Ownership on Nursing Home Costs. *Health Services Research* 26:109–24.

McPherson, Michael, and Morton Schapiro. 1991. *Keeping College Affordable.* Washington, DC: Brookings Institution.

National Center for Health Statistics. 1974. *Nursing Homes: A County and Metropolitan Area Data Book, 1971.* Hyattsville, MD: National Center for Health Statistics.

———. 1989. *The National Nursing Home Survey: 1985 Summary for the United States.* Hyattsville, MD: National Center for Health Statistics.

Neugebauer, Roger. 1992. Status Report #3 on Non-Profit Child Care. *Child Care Information Exchange,* May–June, 49–53.

Pauly, Mark. 1987. Nonprofit Firms in Medical Markets. *American Economic Review* 77:257–62.

Schlesinger, Mark. 1994. Mismeasuring the Consequences of Ownership: External Influences and the Comparative Performance of Public, For-Profit, and Private Nonprofit Organizations. Manuscript.

Steinwald, Bruce, and Duncan Neuhauser. 1970. The Role of the Proprietary Hospital. *Law and Contemporary Problems* 35:817–38.

Stephens, Keith, and Roger Neugebauer. 1992. How's Business? Status Report #8 on For Profit Child Care. *Child Care Information Exchange,* March–April, 57–61.

U.S. Bureau of the Census. 1960. *Statistical Abstract of the United States, 1960.* Washington, DC: Government Printing Office.

———. 1970. *Statistical Abstract of the United States, 1970.* Washington, DC: Government Printing Office.

———. 1977. *Statistical Abstract of the United States, 1977.* Washington, DC: Government Printing Office.

———. 1993. *Statistical Abstract of the United States, 1993.* Washington, DC: Government Printing Office.

U.S. Department of Education. National Center for Education Statistics. 1992. *Digest of Education Statistics, 1992.* Washington, DC: Government Printing Office.

# Comment    Joseph A. Grundfest

Henry Hansmann's fine paper makes several significant points about the evolution of nonprofit institutions in the human services sector. Hansmann's observations regarding the presence of "trapped capital" in the nonprofit sector may, however, deserve more prominence than he suggests. Billions of dollars of trapped capital present in the nonprofit sector pose a significant threat to nonprofit's efficiency and present a fundamental challenge to the continued vitality of the nonprofit sector, particularly in the rapidly changing market for health care services.

Joseph A. Grundfest is professor of law at Stanford Law School and was a commissioner of the U.S. Securities and Exchange Commission from 1985 to 1990.

Hansmann explains that as long as a nonprofit entity earns a rate of return on its capital that is at least equal to real economic depreciation, the nonprofit can continue in operation at its current scale indefinitely. There is no pressure on the institution to strive for a competitive, risk-adjusted rate of return that recovers the opportunity cost of its capital had that same capital been invested in the for-profit sector. Indeed, even if a nonprofit fails to recover its economic depreciation, it can continue in existence for many years longer than an equivalent for-profit firm that would be required to earn a positive return on its capital.

Nonprofit institutions are thereby insulated from market signals that discipline the private sector and that provide powerful incentives for the efficient allocation of capital. In addition, because nonprofits cannot tap private equity markets and cannot provide equity-based incentives for their management teams, nonprofit firms typically do not respond to market signals as rapidly as for-profit firms. Hansmann also points out that nonprofit managers have incentives to preserve the size of their institutions, even if market forces signal that downsizing or reallocation of capital is in the best interests of the social purpose that the nonprofit was created to serve.

As a consequence of these forces, Hansmann explains, nonprofit organizations can become pools of "trapped capital." These trapped capital pools are inefficiently managed and are either too large or too small for the purposes they are designed to serve. They also cannot be reallocated to alternate purposes absent extraordinary events.

The dangers of trapped capital are obvious. When capital loses its flexibility and shifts from "putty" to "clay," its ability to contribute to economic growth is sharply diminished. Alternatively, viewed from the perspective of modern option theory, capital that cannot be reallocated in response to new information has a low "option value" and therefore is not as productive as capital that is invested in identical ventures but that can be reallocated in response to subsequently acquired information (Dixit and Pindyck 1994).

The adverse consequences of trapped capital are most significant at times of rapid technological and demographic change because those are precisely the times at which optionality is most valuable. Those are also the times when the costs imposed by trapped capital are greatest. Now is one of those times, particularly in the provision of health care services.

There are, no doubt, substantial advantages to nonprofit provision of human services. Yet, as Hansmann ably points out, these benefits must be balanced against the inefficiencies inherent in the nonprofit sector. This balancing exercise need not be conducted in the abstract because, despite the prevalence of trapped capital in the nonprofit sector, the market can send two distinct types of signals about the relative costs and benefits of nonprofit versus for-profit organizational forms. The power of these signals may be muted by a variety of factors described below, but when market forces favoring one institutional form over another are sufficiently strong, the market's message is unambiguous.

The first signal arises in expanding markets. When a market for human services is growing and when new capital entering the market is disproportionately of the for-profit form, the market may be sending a signal that the comparative disadvantage of the nonprofit form is substantial. Hansmann's data illustrating a shift to for-profit providers in the health care field is at least broadly consistent with this observation (Sacks 1994).

The second signal is sent by nonprofit organizations that seek to abandon their nonprofit status and transform themselves to for-profit enterprises. This signal is far less ambiguous and is a powerful indicator that the monitoring, tax, and other benefits associated with the nonprofit form are insufficient to overcome the costs imposed by trapped capital, by the lack of access to equity market, and by the inability to provide competitive, equity-based incentives for employees.

The power of this signal is compounded by the fact that a combination of federal and state restrictions make such transitions extraordinarily expensive and effectively require that the nonprofit enterprise leave all of the equity value of its operations in the nonprofit sector as the price of its conversion to for-profit status. Put another way, "you can't take it with you" when it comes to shifting capital from nonprofit to for-profit status, and the decision to invest capital in the nonprofit form is effectively an irrevocable election of an organizational form, at least as to the current value of that capital.

At the federal level, tax law provides that a tax-exempt foundation may terminate its tax-exempt status either by transferring all of its assets to another qualified tax-exempt organization, in which case all of the foundation's capital remains in the nonprofit sector, or by agreeing to pay a termination tax.[1] The termination tax is generally described as the lesser of (1) the aggregate tax benefit received by the foundation, its substantial contributors, and others with interest therein, or (2) the value of the net assets of the foundation. Thus, the bargain with the federal government is that a foundation and its major affiliates must repay to the government the value of all benefits received as a consequence of its tax-exempt status.

If marginal tax rates are 50% or more, and if all substantial contributors are in the top bracket, then the amount of tax to be paid by the foundation will equal at least the amount donated by substantial contributors. Thus, unless the value of the fund's assets have increased by an amount greater than the sum of the rate of interest charged by the government and the payout rate to beneficiaries, there would likely be nothing left to distribute after payment of tax. Indeed, it is commonly observed that "the aggregate tax benefit can exceed the fair market value of the property transferred, particularly when interest on all increases in taxes is added on" (Cesare 1994).

State law establishes yet another barrier to the free mobility of capital across

1. For a detailed explanation of the relevant provisions of the Internal Revenue Code, see Cesare 1994.

institutional forms. In California, for example, nonprofit enterprises wishing to convert to for-profit status "are required by state law to donate to charity an amount equal to their total assets . . . to repay the benefits the business derived while operating as a nonprofit, tax-exempt corporation" (Ellis 1995). A nonprofit seeking to convert to for-profit status can satisfy this requirement either by establishing a new charitable foundation to which the value of the converting enterprise's assets is transferred, or by donating the value of its assets to existing charities.

The incentives to convert to for-profit form in some sectors of the health care industry are apparently quite powerful. In the past decade, ten to fifteen California HMOs have converted to for-profit status, leaving only six nonprofit HMOs in the state (Ellis 1995). As part of this trend, Blue Cross, the state's largest health insurer, created a for-profit enterprise, Well Point Health Systems, and then sold a 20% equity stake to the public through an initial public offering of common stock. In addition, Blue Cross has proposed converting entirely to for-profit status and is in negotiations with the state corporations commissioner over the form of the transaction, which may require a contribution of the remaining 80% stake in Well Point to a new charitable entity as well as contributions to existing nonprofit institutions. The value of the Well Point equity still to be contributed has been estimated as in excess of $2 billion, and the required additional charitable contributions are in excess of $100 million (Ellis 1995; Garrison 1994; "Blue Cross" 1994).

The benefits of for-profit operations are evidently quite powerful if Blue Cross is willing to forgo so much capital as the price of a transition to the for-profit form. Indeed, this transaction, along with dozens of other conversions from nonprofit to for-profit operations, is perhaps the strongest evidence that the inefficiencies of the nonprofit form have become quite large—particularly in the dynamically changing health care sector.

This trend toward for-profit operation in a market that already has substantial nonprofit investment raises significant policy issues. In particular, what, if anything can be done to facilitate the efficient flow of capital back from nonprofit to for-profit structures? Also, how can nonprofit institutions coexist in markets with potentially more efficient for-profit competitors? Ideally, nonprofit institutions will recognize their comparative advantages and redefine their missions so as to capitalize on services that they can perform better than for-profit enterprises. Subsidies for the poor, support for certain forms of research and public health education, and measuring the quality of services provided by the for-profit sector so that informed consumers can promote efficient competition are among the services that nonprofits might be able to offer while retaining a comparative advantage over their for-profit competitors. The bricks and mortar business of actually providing health care coverage may not, however, be the best use of the nonprofit dollar. This transformation of the nonprofit mission in health care—a transition looking toward the intricate coexistence of nonprofit and for-profit forms—promises a series of practical and intellectual challenges ripe for further research.

## References

Blue Cross of California to Contribute All Its Assets to a New Foundation. 1994. *Business Wire,* September 15.

Cesare, Lauren Watson. 1994. *Private Foundations and Public Charities: Termination (sec. #507) and Special Rules.* 877 Tax Management, Estates, Gifts, and Trusts Portfolios. Washington, DC: Bureau of National Affairs.

Dixit, Avinash K., and Robert S. Pindyck. 1994. *Investment under Uncertainty.* Princeton: Princeton University Press.

Ellis, Kristi. 1995. HMO Conversions Shower Charities with Donation. *Los Angeles Business Journal,* January 30, A10.

Garrison, Jayne. 1994. The New Price of Health Care. *California Lawyer,* December, 32–88.

Sacks, Jennifer. 1994. Wall Street Finances Healthcare's Revolution. *Investment Dealer's Digest,* October 3, 14–24.

# 10 Government Intervention in the Markets for Education and Health Care: How and Why?

James M. Poterba

Education and health care are the two largest government expenditure items in most developed economies. In 1991, total government spending on primary and secondary education in the United States totaled $219 billion, and another $96 billion was spent on public colleges and universities. Educational outlays represent nearly 30% of government purchases of goods and services. Direct government health care spending totaled $316 billion, and another $60 billion of forgone revenue was attributable to deductions and exemptions of health-related items under the income tax.

There are fundamental differences in the government's role in the health and education sectors of the U.S. economy. State and local governments are the direct providers of the majority (92%) of primary and secondary educational services. The service providers are government employees, with salaries set through a partly political process, and decisions about methods of production such as classroom activities and curriculum are made by quasi-political government bureaucracies. Competition between alternative providers of educational services occurs largely through competition between communities for potential residents.

In health care, although federal, state, and local governments ultimately pay for more than 40% of health outlays, they are direct *providers* of relatively little health care. While state and local governments operate some hospitals, and the federal government administers the Veterans Administration (VA) medical network, most health care providers work in the private sector. Various

James M. Poterba is professor of economics at the Massachusetts Institute of Technology and director of the Public Economics Research Program at the National Bureau of Economic Research.

The author is grateful to David Cutler, Peter Diamond, Martin Feldstein, Claudia Goldin, Jonathan Gruber, Louis Kaplow, John Lott, Roger Noll, Julio Rotemberg, Richard Zeckhauser, and especially Victor Fuchs for helpful discussions and comments. This research was supported by the National Science Foundation and the Robert Wood Johnson Foundation.

government programs and policies nevertheless substantially reduce the cost of medical care for many consumers. Medicare and Medicaid, the federal government's programs to provide health care services to the elderly and the indigent, are essentially tax-supported systems of government payments for services provided in the private market. In addition, the current income tax code subsidizes medical outlays by households who are neither elderly nor poor, thereby altering the price of health services.

The contrast between public policies in these two markets raises a host of questions about the scope of government in a mixed economy. Even a cursory review of current policies yields paradoxes. For example, why is most child care for preschoolers in the United States provided through a system of family and private market transactions, while primary and secondary education is provided directly by the government? Why is the public sector's role in higher education substantially smaller than its role in elementary education? Why did the GI Bill, which provided health care and educational benefits for veterans of World War II, rely on a federal bureaucracy (the VA) to directly provide health care, while relying on a variant of a voucher system and private providers with respect to education? Why does the federal government directly produce health care services for veterans, while relying on private providers for those who receive benefits under Medicare and Medicaid? Why are there substantial differences across localities in the degree of public versus private provision of some services?

These questions relate broadly to the "choice of instrument problem," the question of *how* government should intervene in a market if such intervention is deemed necessary. Although public finance textbooks, such as Rosen (1992) and Stiglitz (1988), begin by explaining that market imperfections and redistributive considerations can justify government intervention in a market economy, there is remarkably little discussion of what types of policies are justified. There is virtually no evidence on the empirical magnitudes of many of the key parameters needed to guide policy in these areas. Empirical evidence on the importance of potential market imperfections, and the distributional consequences of various interventions in the markets for education and health care services, is particularly scarce. Moreover, economic factors alone are unlikely to explain the observed structure of public policy, which is due in significant part to historical and political influences.

This paper explores the "choice of instrument" problem with particular application to the markets for education and health care. It is divided into five sections. The first outlines the traditional market failure arguments that neoclassical economists marshal to support public intervention in private markets, and discusses the application of these arguments to education and health care. Section 10.2 explores the link between goals of redistributive justice and public policies in these areas. Both education and health care have been described as "basic rights" in some contexts, suggesting that these services should not be allocated on the basis of ability to pay.

Section 10.3 examines the comparative merits of three potential policy interventions: price subsidies, including the special case of full public payment for purchases in the private market; public mandates for private provision; and direct government provision. It highlights conditions under which each of these potential instruments will be successful in achieving particular policy objectives, as well as situations in which each instrument may fail. Section 10.4 describes the current structure and historical evolution of public policies toward education and health care in the United States, and considers the degree to which the market imperfections and redistributive considerations described in the earlier sections can account for these policies. The concluding section outlines areas of uncertainty where further work is needed to evaluate alternative policy instruments.

## 10.1 Market Imperfections in the Markets for Education and Health Care

Market imperfections may take many forms: the consumption of some goods may impose external benefits or costs that are not reflected in their market prices, informational asymmetries or other factors may lead to the nonexistence of markets for some products, or consumers may not have the information necessary to make appropriate choices. This section considers the sources of market imperfections in markets for education and health care.

### 10.1.1 Market Imperfections with Respect to Education

Many of the classical economists broke with their usual laissez-faire view of the appropriate role of government when confronted with questions of educational policy. In *The Wealth of Nations*, Adam Smith argued that "[t]he state derives no inconsiderable advantage from [the education of the common people. If instructed they are] ... less liable to the delusions of enthusiasm and superstition, which among ignorant nations, frequently occasion the most dreadful disorders" (book 5, part 3, article 2). This reference to societywide externalities associated with the education of each individual is only one of the potential market imperfections that might warrant government intervention in the market for schooling.

The first, and most commonly alleged, source of a market imperfection with respect to education is the presence of externalities from schooling. This argument has been made in many ways; Cohn and Geske (1990) provide an overview. Some claim that an educated electorate is vital to a successful democratic society, for example, because it permits individuals to keep records, file tax returns, and evaluate campaign material. Others argue that an educated workforce is critical for the adoption of new technologies and for improving, not just an individual's productivity, but that of his or her coworkers. Yet a third externality argument holds that there is a negative relationship between education and crime, so that widespread education will reduce crime and the associated social disruption.

A related externality argument, that applied with particular force to the nineteenth-century United States, is that education assists in socializing many diverse immigrant groups. This argument is probably specific to *public* education: providing the same level of education through various parochial schools might have a smaller effect on social integration. Widespread public education during this period probably helped the "melting pot" to function, and exposed groups from different national backgrounds to the civic structure and related aspects of the United States.

Each of these arguments suggests that private spending on education contributes to a public good. If parents ignore the externalities associated with education in deciding how much to spend on their child's education, educational spending will fall below the socially efficient level. Public policies designed to increase educational attainment therefore have some prospect for raising social welfare.

A second potential rationale for government intervention arises because minors, who are the usual recipients of education, are not responsible for deciding how much schooling they will obtain. This responsibility falls to their parents, who also bear the costs of education. Since the benefits of education accrue primarily to the children who receive it, the level of spending on education depends critically on the degree of parental altruism. If parents place a low value on improvements in their children's future earning potential, then they may underinvest in their children, and government intervention might be justified on the ground that it protects children from decisions by their parents.[1]

One difficulty with this argument is that it could be invoked to justify state intervention in virtually all aspects of child rearing. Can parents be trusted to feed their children properly? To provide the appropriate amount and type of playthings and other stimuli to early development? It is not clear, as West (1970) notes, that the risk of parental underprovision of education is any greater than the risk of underprovision of many other important developmental inputs.

A third market imperfection that may be relevant for educational decisions involves capital market constraints. If some households face borrowing constraints that limit their total access to credit or cause them to face borrowing rates above the economywide marginal product of capital, then even parents whose altruism matched that of the social planner might underinvest in their children. Because loans to obtain education are not backed by tangible collateral, they are often difficult to obtain in private credit markets.

1. It is at least possible that some parents may be *more concerned* with their children than a social planner would be. Parents may also misperceive the value of spending on their children, measured in terms of the corresponding increment to future income or utility, or be concerned primarily with the *relative* status of their children, as discussed in Frank (chap. 6 in this volume). Any of these factors might lead to overprovision of private education.

A fourth market imperfection, one that applies most strongly in small communities with a limited number of children to educate, is the presence of fixed costs in educational production. The marginal cost of adding another student to a classroom is lower than the average cost of each student's education. Such economy-of-scale arguments, which may also apply to consumption of some types of specialized services in large school districts, provide an efficiency argument for group consumption of educational services. This does not necessarily imply that the public sector must provide education.

Although it is relatively easy to construct a list of imperfections in the market for educational services, it is extremely difficult to *quantify* their importance. How many parents, for example, would neglect their children's education? Moreover, while there are undeniably some externalities associated with education, primary and secondary education also yield very high *private* returns. The central question is therefore whether there are externalities associated with education *above the level that parents would choose in a private market.* Yet virtually none of the empirical evidence on the economic returns to education, with the notable exception of Lazear (1983), is directed at this issue.

Optimal government policy must balance the gains associated with the partial or complete correction of market imperfections against the costs of the policy and its associated distortions. Virtually any government intervention, whether through price subsidies or through public production of services, distorts the behavior or private agents. Peltzman (1973) and Sonstelie (1982) are among the small group of studies that have explored the inefficiencies created by the current policy of free public provision of education. Peltzman (1973) shows that free public school can lead some parents who would otherwise have chosen schools better than their local public schools to send their children to those schools. This is because lower-quality, but free, public schools may on balance be more attractive to parents than higher-quality schools for which they must pay tuition. This change in parental behavior can shift the economy from one equilibrium level of educational spending to another equilibrium with lower total spending.

Sonstelie (1982) also concludes that there is a significant efficiency cost to free public schools, but his argument relies heavily on his assumption that private schools are more efficient providers of educational services than their public school counterparts.[2] Neither of these studies considers the potential costs associated with public rather than private production of educational services. Further work on the private demand for education is important for evaluating a number of current educational reform proposals, such as those for

2. It is difficult to control for the differences in the attributes of public and private school students in making such efficiency comparisons. Even if private schools appear to be more efficient when they are educating only a small and self-selected part of the population, they could be no more efficient than existing public schools if their student input was the same. Relatively few studies have developed convincing empirical strategies for correcting for the endogenous selection of students into public and private schools.

school vouchers and other means of introducing more competition into the educational marketplace.

### 10.1.2    Market Imperfections with Respect to Health Care

While potential market imperfections with respect to education center on externality issues, those with respect to health care focus on information. Arrow's (1963) seminal analysis emphasizes several potential sources of market imperfection, including asymmetric information between consumers and providers of health care services as well as uncertainty about current and future needs for medical services. Uncertainty leads individuals to demand health insurance, and raises the question of whether the insurance market satisfies the conditions of perfect competition. Health care suppliers may also be imperfectly competitive, creating a further potential market imperfection.

The first potential difficulty with the health care market arises from the limited information that patients possess about the benefits associated with various medical treatments. The effects of most treatments are random to some degree, and patients are not well equipped to evaluate the relevant information on treatment effects. Individuals rarely confront the same major illness several times, so there is little opportunity to acquire information about the relative performance of different treatment regimens. Moreover, since purchasing medical care typically involves purchasing the services of an expert, quality evaluation is critical but very difficult.[3] Combining information from many different patients is problematic because of potential differences in their presenting conditions, so consumers may have no objective measures of physician quality. These factors suggest that patients may not make rational choices about which health care services to consume.

The unpredictable nature of many medical expenses, which leads to a demand for insurance, gives rise to a separate set of market imperfections. Risk-averse individuals can raise their expected utility by purchasing actuarially fair medical insurance. But once they have insurance that shares in the cost of their medical outlays, their demand for medical care will be distorted because they no longer face the full cost of their health care services. The resulting moral hazard problem will lead private insurers to offer less than complete insurance in the second-best insurance market equilibrium. While moral hazard may lead to the absence of complete private insurance markets, it does not necessarily provide a rationale for government intervention in these markets; the same problems that result from private insurance policies will also arise if the government provides insurance.

A related problem with the private medical insurance market turns on ad-

---

3. Richard Zeckhauser (1986) also notes that most medical care is a "preclusive good." Choosing to have an operation performed by one physician effectively precludes other physicians from performing this procedure.

verse selection in the purchasing population. Rothschild and Stiglitz (1976) and Wilson (1980) have shown that when potential insurance buyers are heterogeneous, adverse selection can lead to the disappearance of the markets for some types of insurance, hence to market failure. The government has an important advantage relative to private insurers in creating health insurance policies: it can compel individuals to participate. Compulsion enables the government to insure everyone at the actuarially fair rate for the entire population.

There are other potential imperfections in the private health care market. Most medical services are not supplied under perfectly competitive conditions. Many hospitals and some specialized physicians may be monopolists in their local markets, there may be collusion among the various doctors in an area, and there are a range of government subsidies to the production of health care professionals that cause deviations from standard efficiency conditions. Externalities may also arise in the consumption of medical care. Although small for most kinds of health care services, such externalities are present with respect to inoculation against infectious diseases and potentially with some other types of care as well.

In the health care market, as with education, it is easier to list potential market imperfections than to quantify their substantive importance or to link them to potential market interventions. For example, while the 1994 *Economic Report of the President* cites evidence that a nontrivial fraction of medical procedures are not medically necessary, it is not clear that these procedures are the result of informational or other problems. While many analysts agree that there are imperfections in the health insurance market, and as Aaron (1994) notes, private insurers have evolved a variety of devices such as experience rating, coverage waiting periods, and exclusions of preexisting conditions to address adverse selection problems, quantitative evidence on the substantive consequences of adverse selection remains elusive.

The vast majority of U.S. citizens currently obtain health insurance in private markets. A significant number of the uninsured have access to insurance, but choose not to purchase it.[4] Long and Marquis (1992) show that low-wage, part-time workers are particularly unlikely to purchase employer-provided insurance. They observe that one reason small firms with substantial numbers of such workers do not offer health insurance may be that their workers do not demand such coverage. There is virtually no empirical evidence linking various types of market imperfections to the health care utilization decisions of households.

---

4. Adverse selection may lead insurers to offer some kinds of policies at very high loads relative to their actuarial risk. Even if consumers could in principle buy such policies, but do not, there may be a case for government intervention to improve the workings of such markets. Thus the availability of an insurance policy per se does not indicate that adverse selection is not a problem.

## 10.2   Redistributive Arguments for Government Provision of Education and Health Care

While efficiency concerns are one rationale for public policies that intervene in the markets for education and health care, they are not the sole or even the primary rationale for existing programs.[5] Redistributive concerns also play an important role. With respect to both education and health care, many subscribe to what Tobin (1970) labeled "specific egalitarianism": the view that access to these services should not be conditioned on income. This section explores the redistributive arguments for government intervention in these markets in more detail.

At the outset, one must ask why redistribution should be linked to particular goods, rather than carried out with income transfers. Since the utility gain from transferring a given bundle of goods to a recipient is always less than the recipient's gain from receiving the cash value of these goods, there is a strong a priori argument for separating redistribution from the provision of particular goods.

While this argument applies for each recipient, it may not apply to a transfer program as a whole. There are a number of reasons why in-kind programs or subsidies to the consumption of particular goods can be more efficient than income redistribution, even when the consumption of particular goods does not generate externalities. First, in-kind transfers may be better than comparable cash transfers at channeling resources to a target population. Nichols and Zeckhauser (1982) and Besley and Coate (1991) argue that in-kind programs may help the government to distinguish the truly needy from other potential program beneficiaries. Second, in-kind programs may be attractive policies when policy makers seek to impose their preferences on individuals. In education, for example, public policies specify the amount of schooling a child must receive.

A final explanation for the use of in-kind rather than cash redistribution is political, rather than economic. More political coalitions support in-kind programs than equivalent spending on cash transfers, because in-kind goods and services are supplied by identifiable industries. Thus, there are interest groups that benefit from in-kind redistribution. Teachers and health care professionals may support expanded government transfers in their respective markets, even if they do not support expanded income redistribution in general.[6] West (1967, 1970) argues that, even if public provision of education was needed in the United States in the mid–nineteenth century to overcome a lack of infrastructure for delivering educational services, it was not needed for long.

---

5. Zeckhauser (1986), in an essay that explores issues similar to those raised here, concludes that "only a small portion of [the vast subsidies and direct payments for health care and education] can be justified primarily on the basis that they provide public goods or remedy market failures" (47).

6. Doctors, however, opposed the passage of Medicare and Medicaid in 1965, on the grounds that these programs were the first steps to socialized medicine.

West (1967) identifies support from several organized interest groups, including teachers, as essential to the continued growth of public schools.

### 10.2.1   Redistributive Concerns and Education

Providing "equal opportunity" is one of the objectives of current policies with respect to education. Since parental resources are unequal, even if parents value their children's lifetime utility in the same way as the social planner and face well-functioning capital markets, there will be differences in the level of education that children receive in a private market for education. Such differences may translate into differences in lifetime earning opportunities, which some argue against as unfair because they are beyond the children's control. The public sector must therefore ensure access to adequate education for all, either by supplying a basic educational services package, or through a system of income-linked subsidies of the price of education. Zeckhauser (1986) notes that equality can be defined in many, sometimes inconsistent, ways: equality of the price at which different households can purchase a given service, equality of the quantity of service consumed by different households, and equality of the outcome of service consumption are three examples.

In the United States, public education has historically been a responsibility of local government, although there has been a trend in the last half century toward greater centralization of finance at the state rather than the local level. For the 1990–91 school year, local revenue sources accounted for 46.5% of public spending on primary and secondary education, compared with 47.3% from state governments and 6.2% from the federal government (U.S. Department of Education 1993, table 156). In 1947–48, local governments provided 57.9% of the money, while two decades earlier, in 1929–30, the local share was 82.7%.

Local financing raises important qualifications to the redistributive power of public spending on education. Because communities differ in their tax bases and their willingness to impose taxes, there is substantial variation across places in spending levels. Although a number of court decisions during the last three decades have weakened the link between educational spending and property taxes on the grounds that the property tax base is highly unequal across communities, disparities across jurisdictions remain. Wealthy communities spend more on schools than poor communities, so the existing system of locally provided education is not as redistributive as it would be if a higher level of government were the primary service provider.

Since the incidence of local taxes is primarily on the residents of local jurisdictions, at least when individuals are free to move, local public provision of education is tantamount to taxing all residents of a jurisdiction to pay for the average level of educational consumption in the community. This policy can redistribute resources within a community, but it is a weak device for redistributing resources between those in different communities. Milton Friedman (1962) argues that the present combination of local government provision of education and reliance on local property tax finance makes it more difficult for low-income families to purchase high-quality education. This is because consuming high-quality public education usually requires purchasing an expensive house in a school district with high-quality schools. This can require a much greater outlay of resources than simply purchasing higher-quality education.

### 10.2.2    Redistribution and the Government's Role in Health Care

"Specific egalitarianism" also applies to universal access to health care. The recent health care debate provides many examples of policy makers and political leaders who believe that access to adequate health care should not be conditioned on ability to pay, and there seems to be substantial popular support for this view. Whether the stronger claim, that those with higher incomes should *not* have access to better care than those with low incomes, commands support is less clear. In any event, redistributive objectives play a central part in the design of government health care policy. Gornick et al. (1985) report that in 1963, on the eve of Medicare's passage, only 56% of those over sixty-five years old had health insurance. The insurance rate for younger age groups was substantially greater, even though the need for medical care was greater among the elderly population, and this was one of the factors contributing to support for Medicare.

Government policies to subsidize health insurance and health care redistribute along at least two dimensions. First, as with most redistributive programs, such subsidies transfer resources to those with relatively low incomes. With respect to medical care, however, one must also distinguish between the ex ante value of government insurance, before learning about a household's medical needs, and the ex post value of the insurance, after such needs are observed. The second aspect of redistribution within government health programs is a transfer from those who do not require much medical assistance to those who do. Because health outlays are highly concentrated, with estimates for 1994 suggesting that 20.3% of all health spending will be accounted for by the 1.6% of the population with more than $30,000 in spending, and 51.3% of spending will be done by the 8.1% of the population with more than $10,000 in health care outlays, the second form of redistribution can be quite important.[7]

Even if government subsidies to health insurance were not age-related, the age-specific pattern of medical care demand would lead such subsidies to redistribute to the elderly. The current structure of health care programs in the United States, with eligibility for Medicare conditioned on reaching age sixty-five, accentuates this redistribution. Such policies raise the standard of living of elderly households, and they also may reduce the financial and other burdens

7. *Economic Report of the President 1995*, 143. These statistics include all medical care spending, including preventative, routine, and acute care. Spending on acute care is even more concentrated, with Aaron (chap. 4 in this volume) reporting that 5% of the population account for more than half of the outlays in a given year.

on the *children* of the elderly, who would otherwise need to devote attention and resources to their care.[8]

The intergenerational pattern of benefits associated with medical care for the elderly is an important but relatively unexplored issue, and one that may be critical to explaining the political support for these programs.[9] Most individuals in middle age have surviving parents. For example, Himes (1994) shows that in 1987, the probability that a thirty-five-year-old white woman had two living parents was approximately .60. The probability that she had at least one living parent was greater than .90, substantially higher than the probability that she had at least one child (.81). The probability that a white woman has at least one living parent does not fall below one-half until she reaches her early fifties. Thus altruism from children to parents can explain political support among middle-aged individuals with respect to health care policy for the elderly. It is also possible that part of the increased taxes required to finance such benefits will be offset by higher bequests from parents who received transfers and therefore did not have to spend down their wealth during retirement.

### 10.3    The Choice of Instruments: Subsidies, Mandates, and Government Provision

Why is the nature of government involvement in education and health care so different? In the health care market, the government plays a largely financial role, purchasing health care services provided by the private market, while in the market for educational services, it is the single largest supplier of the service in question. This section considers the structure of public-sector interventions in private markets, given that there is a market imperfection or redistributive justification for some market intervention.

The basic criterion that a social planner would use to choose a means of market intervention is clear: select the policy that provides the highest level of social welfare. In practice, policy choices involve important political aspects that may dwarf direct social welfare concerns. Suppressing political considerations for the moment, this section considers the factors that determine the relative merits of different policy instruments.

The choice among various alternatives depends not only on the market imperfection that motivates government intervention in private markets, but also on the costs of different methods of intervention and the capacity of government officials to obtain the information needed for successful intervention.

---

8. Davis and Schoen (1978) explicitly mention reduced burdens on middle-aged children of elderly households as one of the benefits of Medicare. Cutler and Sheiner (1994) show that government provision of nursing home care displaces a substantial amount of care that would otherwise have been provided by children.

9. This question may be even more central to analyzing public support for provision of nursing home care rather than medical care.

These latter concerns suggest that even if there is a market imperfection, it may be optimal for the government *not* to intervene because the cost of government action would exceed the gains from remedying market imperfections. This possibility, "government failure," has been discussed for example by McKean and Minasian (1966) and Wolf (1993).

This section compares price subsidies, government mandates, and direct government service provision. It discusses the advantages and disadvantages of each. The next section describes actual polices toward education and health care in the United States, and asks whether the various considerations described below can explain the structure of current policies.

### 10.3.1   Price Subsidies

The textbook remedy for externalities that are not reflected in private choices is a "Pigouvian tax" that alters the price individuals face, so that their private choices will yield the socially efficient level of consumption. In practice, a range of public policies are available to alter the private cost of purchasing services such as education and medical care. These include tax subsidies, direct subsidies such as Medicare that involve government financing of most or all service consumption, and incentives to the production of services, such as grants to medical schools or interest-free loans for medical students.

The efficacy of price subsidies depends critically on the price elasticity of demand for the subsidized service. When this elasticity is low, when there is uncertainty about this elasticity, or when there is a wide divergence across households in this elasticity, then price subsidies may be an unattractive form of market intervention. Weitzman (1974) develops an argument of this form in his comparison of "prices vs. quantities" as alternative means of regulation.

There is no consensus on the empirical magnitude of the price elasticities of demand for education and medical care. Studies of the demand for education typically compare local public spending in different towns, and invoke the median voter model to argue that each town's spending is the level demanded by the town's median voter. There are many potential difficulties with this approach, including the potential influence of political institutions such as Proposition 13 on local spending, and the problem of modeling the choice of local spending when jurisdictions are imperfectly competitive. Studies of this type usually yield relatively small estimates of the price elasticity of demand; Sonstelie's (1982) study of California, for example, suggests a value of $-.16$.

In the medical care market, the central problem is the potential endogeneity of health insurance, which has an important effect on the net price of medical care services. Some of the most convincing empirical evidence to date on the price elasticity of demand for medical care is based on the RAND Health Insurance Experiment, a systematic social experiment that was conducted in four cities during the mid-1970s. In analyzing the resulting data, Keeler et al. (1988) report an elasticity of demand for total medical care of $-.22$ for households facing copayment rates of greater than 25%. The estimated demand elasticity for well-patient care is greater, $-.43$, while the elasticity for hospital care is $-.14$.

Specific egalitarianism with respect to health care does not imply that all individuals should consume the same amount of medical care; some people need very little care in a given year. Rather, it implies equality of *access,* so that, conditional on need, individuals have the same opportunity to receive care. This suggests that, from the standpoint of public policy, a key parameter is the price elasticity of insurance demand rather than medical care demand. The demand for insurance is substantially more price sensitive than the demand for health care. Gruber and Poterba (1994) present evidence, based on changes in tax incentives for insurance purchase in the 1980s, suggesting that the price elasticity of insurance demand is between $-1$ and $-2$. These estimates, which are based on the effects within several years around a tax reform that reduced the after-tax cost of insurance for the self-employed, may somewhat overstate the long-run elasticity of demand for insurance. They are nevertheless consistent with earlier studies using different methodologies, which also suggest large price effects on insurance demand.

These elasticity estimates suggest that, while price subsidies may have substantial effects on the demand for health insurance, they are not likely to have large effects on the demand for education. This has direct implications for the choice of policy instrument: price subsidies to education may not be very successful in altering the quantity of services in the private market.

The principal advantage of price subsidies is that they preserve individual choice in selecting service providers and the level of services to be consumed. Such choice permits individuals to search for goods and services with qualities or other attributes that are well suited to their needs. If there is substantial heterogeneity in household tastes, than allowing individual choice can have a substantial positive effect on consumer welfare.[10] The difficult case arises when recognizing this heterogeneity may exacerbate the market imperfections or inequality that public policy is designed to address.

One drawback with price subsidies is that they create incentives for households to recategorize nonsubsidized expenditures in an attempt to qualify them for the subsidy. This problem, the dual of the tax-collection problem in which taxpayers redefine taxable income into nontaxable forms, has two consequences. First, it means that the revenue cost of a price subsidy may be greater than the subsidy rate times the actual amount of the subsidized activity. Second, and significantly if the government's objective is to ensure that everyone consumes a minimal service level, the private market may create "sham transactions" that qualify for the price subsidy but do not achieve the government's goals.

Education illustrates the potential problem with sham transactions. If parents received subsidies for school spending, but "schools" were not well de-

---

10. This argument presumes that consumers are capable of making rational demand decisions, an assumption that may not hold with respect to some aspects of medical care.

fined for this purpose, one could imagine a range of service providers who would commingle services for parents with educational services. Schools might, for example, organize family field trips that were of value to parents as well as children, and include the cost of these trips in tuition charges. The ease or difficulty of monitoring such sham transactions affects the desirability of using price subsidies to encourage service consumption.

Two additional problems deserve mention when subsidies are enacted as part of the tax system, as they are with some aspects of health care. First, because marginal tax rates are progressive, a subsidy that operates by allowing individuals to deduct certain expenditures from taxable income will have a larger marginal effect on the price paid by high-income households than on that paid by low-income households. Second, the effective subsidy rate in this case is affected by changes in the income tax system, changes that may bear no relation to changes in the rate of subsidy that is suggested by the underlying market imperfections.

### 10.3.2   Government Mandates

One alternative to price subsidies is a government mandate that all households purchase a particular good or service. The discussion of "individual mandates" in the recent health insurance reform debate provides an example: individuals would be required to purchase health insurance satisfying some criteria, but these policies could be purchased in the private market. Current requirements that employers purchase workers compensation insurance, and that children receive certain vaccinations before beginning elementary school, are examples of government mandates.

The primary advantage of mandates is that they ensure universal consumption, and they can be tailored to directly control levels of consumption. By mandating that all children in certain age groups attend an accredited elementary or secondary school, current legislation achieves at least one measure of equality in educational consumption. When concerns about equity in outcomes rather than opportunity motivate policies, mandates may be attractive policy instruments. Mandates can be open-ended, requiring all individuals to consume at least a certain amount of a service, or they may be close-ended, specifying precisely the good or service that is to be consumed. The latter achieves a greater degree of equality across individuals, at the welfare cost of denying individual choice.

It is important to contrast the effects of price subsidies with the effect of government mandates in the framework suggested by Weitzman (1974). With price-based instruments, at least ex ante, it is difficult to assess the quantity response to a policy. This makes such instruments unattractive in situations where there are substantial benefits to particular levels of service consumption, as might be the case with some levels of education or some types of inoculations. Mandates, with or without public service provision, solve this problem because they specify the level of service consumption, but they impose ex ante unknown costs on many individuals and firms.

A secondary advantage of mandates, which can be very important in the political economy of policy design, is that they can be designed to impose costs on individuals or firms without affecting government budgets. In times of fiscal stringency, such as the present, mandates may be particularly attractive to policy makers because they provide a mechanism for affecting real activity without spending money. Some popular discussions of public policy appear to exhibit confusion about the relationship between taxes and mandates, and there appears to be more political opposition to new taxes than to new mandates with economically equivalent effects. This is one of the reasons that mandates played a central role in the recent discussion of health care reform.

Mandates require a well-functioning private market for the mandated good or service if they are to succeed. Mandating that consumers purchase a service that is supplied under conditions of imperfect competition, for example, may have less favorable effects on social welfare than mandating purchase of a service that is competitively supplied. This issue arises with respect to health insurance mandates: if one of the market imperfections in health insurance is that adverse selection leads to missing insurance markets, a mandate without government insurance provision may be ineffective.

The economic analysis of government mandates is not as well developed as the analysis of taxes and price subsidies, but several points about the efficiency consequences of mandates nevertheless deserve mention. First, by mandating minimum levels of consumption but not altering the price of services for those who want to consume more than the mandate level, open-ended mandates avoid distorting the behavior of higher-consumption households. Summers (1989) emphasizes this point in his discussion of employer mandates. Second, assuming that individuals must pay to satisfy the mandate either by purchasing the mandated good or service, or through reduced wages if the mandate affects employers,[11] then a mandate is a form of "benefit tax." Leaving aside issues of efficiency in production, a mandate for individual consumption of a given commodity bundle is equivalent to government provision of this bundle, financed by a lump-sum tax.

The welfare cost of a mandate depends on the difference between the amount the individual values the mandated good and the cost of purchasing this good. At least in some cases, the efficiency cost of a mandate can be substantially smaller than the efficiency cost of tax-financed government provision of the service.[12] Mandates may therefore be attractive in situations where total private spending on a good is large, but the government wants to increase this

---

11. Gruber (1994) summarizes previous work, and presents new evidence, on how wages adjust to government mandates that firms provide certain benefits to their workers. When mandates apply only to a subgroup of employees, wages may decline for some workers who do not benefit from the mandate, and they may not decline by the full amount of the mandate's cost for some workers who do benefit.

12. Mandates can avoid the distortions associated with providing a given level of a good or service to all individuals, but they cannot avoid the distortions that follow from attempts to redistribute resources across households.

spending without transferring all of the initial outlays into the government sector.

### 10.3.3  Public Provision

A third means of encouraging consumption of particular services involves direct public production. This could be combined either with a regime in which service recipients do not pay, and costs of production are covered through tax revenues, as with education, or with a regime in which consumers are charged when they purchase government-produced goods and services. The Government Printing Office and state universities are examples of the latter system. Government production can be, but need not be, coupled with a mandate for consumption.

Public provision differs from price subsidies and mandates in that it gives government greater control over the nature of the services individuals consume. This can also be achieved in the other cases by regulating the product that is subsidized or mandated, but in some cases the costs of regulation may make this an unacceptable strategy. In the case of education, for example, one reason for substantial government production may be the difficulty of specifying a required school curriculum for nongovernment providers, although the existence of accredited private schools raises some question about this explanation. Public provision can also be a device for restricting potentially wasteful private competition among consumers, which Frank (chap. 6 in this volume) suggests may apply to some extent with respect to educational and other services consumed by middle- and upper-income households.

Government control may also be important when distributional issues that might be difficult to resolve in the private sector arise in the allocation of services. In education, for example, there may be important externalities across children within a classroom or school.[13] How would the private market handle the disruptive child who imposes negative externalities on other children? Possibly by excluding him from the school, or by charging him a premium to attend school. If these responses seem unacceptable to notions of justice or equal opportunity, it may be necessary for the government to control the production process.

A distinct reason for government provision of some services is that profit-making enterprises may place their bottom lines ahead of concerns about quality or appropriateness of service, undermining public confidence in their services. In such situations, nonprofit providers may emerge, or the public sector may assume responsibility for service delivery.[14] At a time when public confi-

---

13. The extent of peer-group effects and within-classroom externalities in the educational process is controversial. For example, Henderson, Mieskowski, and Sauvageau (1978) find positive externalities from being exposed to high-achievement students; other studies find weaker results.

14. Nonprofit providers avoid the charge of profit-maximization service delivery, but they may also be subject to some of the production inefficiencies that may characterize public production. Hansmann (chap. 9 in this volume) discusses the role of nonprofits in health and education and outlines potential sources of inefficiency in their operation.

dence in government seems very low, however, it is difficult to know whether consumers would prefer a for-profit hospital, which may deliver services that they don't need but that generate profits, or a public hospital, which may deliver low-quality versions of services they do need.

There are several arguments against public service provision. One is that the government is characterized by "production inefficiency" as a service provider. There have been numerous studies of the relative efficiency of public and private provision, surveyed for example by Vining and Boardman (1992). These studies, while not conclusive or uniform, suggest that government production is less efficient than private production, although the comparison between government production and nonprofit production, common in education and health care, is less clear. Bureaucrats who do not face the discipline of a competitive market may make inefficient choices with respect to factor inputs and their choice of output.

A brief summary of the state of research comparing efficiency at public and private health care facilities illustrates the lack of consensus. Lindsay (1976) compares various measures related to productivity at VA and private hospitals. The findings are mixed: lengths of stay for given procedures are longer at VA hospitals, but the staff-to-patient ratios are also significantly lower, in contrast to the inefficient input hypothesis. Becker and Sloan (1985) analyze data from the American Hospital Association's 1979 Survey of Hospitals on for-profit, nonprofit, and government hospitals. They do not find any pronounced differences in hospital costs across forms of ownership. Schulz, Greenley, and Peterson (1984) compare the costs of public and private mental health services, and contrary to the earlier hospital studies, they find substantially lower costs for private-sector providers. The existing literature on hospital costs is not conclusive, but it is far richer than the literature on the costs of public versus private education. Further work on the relative efficiency of different forms of ownership in both health and education therefore is needed to judge the cost of public production of services.

A second disadvantage to public provision is the absence of any objective standard for which services should be provided. For a profit-maximizing firm, services that generate profits will be provided. But for a tax-supported public institution, there are no such guidelines, and there is a resulting risk of overprovision of services, or of providing the wrong services.

A third disadvantage, which applies when publicly provided services are tax-financed, involves the efficiency cost of raising revenue. If total government spending to provide a given set services is $C$, but this amount is raised through taxes, then the cost imposed on the private sector is $(1 + \lambda)C$, where $\lambda$ is the marginal deadweight loss of raising tax revenue. For the current U.S. tax system as a whole, estimates suggest a value of $\lambda$ near .30. Ballard, Shoven, and Whalley (1985) provide support for this estimate. This efficiency cost of taxation compounds the efficiency lost in the production process.

## 10.4   Mixing and Matching Instruments: Current Policy toward Education and Health Care

Actual government intervention in the markets for education and health care involves each of the three policy instruments described above. This section describes the nature and evolution of government policies in both of these areas, and then tries to evaluate whether efficiency considerations, redistributive objectives, or other factors explain the nature of observed policies.

### 10.4.1   Government Involvement in Markets for Education

Public provision as well as mandates and price subsidies are evident in the market for education. Local governments are direct suppliers of most primary and secondary educational services. Yet with respect to preelementary education (child care), the government's role as a provider is limited. There are some price subsidies to consumers, and some regulations on private market providers. In higher education, there are price subsidies through a variety of student loan programs, which also alleviate capital market constraints, but state governments are also direct producers of higher educational services.

Before describing policies toward primary and secondary education, it is important to note that it is difficult to separate child care and education on any a priori basis. There is evidence that much of a child's performance in school is predictable from his or her preparation for elementary school, that is, from what would traditionally be labeled "child care." This subsection therefore describes government policies toward child care as well as primary, secondary, and higher education.

The vast majority of care for children under the age of five is provided in the home and/or by relatives. In 1991, 30.3% of children were cared for at home by a relative, 5.7% at home by a nonrelative, 13.1% in another home by a relative, 17.9% in another home by a nonrelative, and 23% in an organized child care facility.[15] The majority (62%) of the 2.9 million children enrolled in nursery school programs were in private-sector programs. Thus the overwhelming majority of care for children who are not yet old enough to attend elementary school was provided either by the private market or through nonmarket transactions within families or other social groups. This is paradoxical, since many of the arguments that might be advanced to justify public intervention in the market for education plausibly apply with even greater force to child care than to elementary education.

Child care for children in families where both parents work, or where a single parent works, is partly subsidized by the federal income tax code. The child care credit provides a credit of 30% of child care costs for families with

---

15. The remaining children were cared for in a variety of other arrangements. Data are based on the Survey of Income and Program Participation, as reported in the U.S. Bureau of the Census, *Current Population Reports P70-30.*

adjusted gross incomes (AGIs) of less than $10,000, and phases down to a credit rate of 20% for those with AGIs of more than $28,000. The maximum amount of expenditures to which the credit can be applied is limited to $2,400 for families with one child, and $4,800 for families with two or more children. There is also a federal tax provision that allows employees to pay for some child care expenses using dependent care accounts, which are offered by some employers as part of cafeteria-plan benefits. These accounts are more valuable than the child care credit for high-income households, but the total federal revenue loss associated with these accounts is small.

There is a sharp contrast between government involvement in the markets for child care and education. Most primary and secondary educational services in the United States are publicly provided. Primary and secondary education is both mandatory and free. In 1991, 90.7% of elementary and secondary school students were enrolled in public schools, and per-student expenditure averaged $4,622. At the college level, the public-sector role is weaker but still strong: 78.7% of college students are enrolled in public colleges (see the *Statistical Abstract of the United States: 1994,* Table 228). Real public spending has increased during the last three decades, due both to the rising real costs of educational inputs and to increased inputs per student. Hanushek and Rivkin (1994) report that the pupil-teacher ratio in U.S. schools, for example, has declined from 26.3 in 1950 to 20.5 in 1970 to 15.4 in 1990.

Table 10.1 presents data on the estimated cost of various government programs that affect children, as compiled by the House Committee on Ways and Means, augmented with information on state and local educational spending. The table includes information on outlays for programs that are targeted only to preschoolers, such as Head Start and other compensatory education programs, as well as the share of broader programs, such as food stamps and Medicaid, that is received by children. The table shows that, with the exception of spending on primary and secondary education, most of the programs targeted at children are relatively small. Moreover, most of these programs are targeted at children in poverty. The child care tax credit and the dependent care allowance are two of the few that are available to children in families above the poverty line.[16]

In light of the substantial flow of tax revenue to primary and secondary education in the United States, it is natural to ask whether concerns about market imperfections, a desire for redistribution, or other factors stimulated government support for education. The start of public education in the United States can be traced to a 1647 law of the Massachusetts Bay Colony directing any town with at least fifty families to hire a teacher, and any town with at least one hundred families to support a grammar school that could prepare young

---

16. This situation contrasts sharply with that in some European countries, where governments provide child care to a substantial fraction of households. Ohlsson and Rosen (1994) report that, in Sweden, 57% of preschool children were in public day care in 1992, while a very high fraction of the rest were home with parents who were on paid parental leave.

**Table 10.1          Government Spending Programs Directed toward Children, 1990**

| Program Description | Spending (billion $) |
| --- | --- |
| Cash transfers | |
| Social Security | 8.9 |
| Supplemental Security Income | 1.4 |
| Aid to Families with Dependent Children | 12.9 |
| Veterans Compensation | 0.5 |
| Earned Income Tax Credit | 4.0 |
| In-kind transfers | |
| Food stamps | 7.3 |
| Child nutrition | 7.1 |
| Medicare | 0.1 |
| Medicaid | 7.2 |
| Housing assistance | 7.5 |
| Low Income Energy Assistance | 0.6 |
| Federal educational programs | |
| Compensatory education | 4.5 |
| Impact Aid | 0.8 |
| Education for the handicapped | 1.6 |
| Other educational programs | 1.4 |
| Other federal programs | |
| Child support programs | 0.5 |
| Human development (Head Start and other) | 1.8 |
| Foster care/adoption assistance | 1.6 |
| Maternal and child health and immunization | 0.8 |
| Summer youth employment | 0.7 |
| Other | 0.6 |
| Revenue loss from tax credits | |
| Earned Income Tax Credit | 2.0 |
| Dependent care credit | 2.4 |
| Exclusion of employer-provided dependent care | 0.5 |
| Exclusion of benefits provided through cafeteria plans | 3.1 |
| State and local educational spending | 194.0 |

*Sources:* U.S. Congress 1993, 1566–67; author's tabulations.

men to attend a university. The introduction of this law, reproduced in Johnson et al. (1982), does not suggest concern with either market imperfections or redistribution: "It being one chiefe project of y ould deluder, Satan, to keeepe men from the knowledge of y Scriptures, . . . evy towneship in this jurisdiction . . . shall appoint one within their towne to teach all such children as shall resort to him to write and read" (252). While legislative language is not always a reliable guide to the factors that led to passage of a law, it may nevertheless be informative. This passage suggests a paternalistic desire to educate children. This was complemented by a concern that, without schools, the Massachusetts Bay Colony would not be able to ensure a future supply of ministers.

The Massachusetts law was a model for public school legislation in other New England colonies, but it did not diffuse throughout the United States until the nineteenth century. In the South, for example, with large plantations and few towns with critical population mass, schooling for the children of wealthy planters was usually provided by private tutors. In the middle Atlantic states, the school environment in the years following settlement involved a collection of private schools, many with religious affiliations. These states received many immigrants in the nineteenth century, and the growth of public schools in these states was justified in large part on the argument that such schools would facilitate assimilation of recent immigrants. Redistributive concerns did not appear to play an important role. The current concern about equality of access arose *after* public schools were well established in the United States.[17]

The evolution of public high schools in the United States also suggests that redistributive concerns were not central. When public high schools first became popular in the late 1800s, their incidence was regressive. Only the children of middle- and upper-income families could afford to remain in school beyond the elementary level, so they were the primary beneficiaries of these schools. Over time, the extent of participation in these schools grew, but similar arguments about regressive benefits have been applied to publicly financed colleges and universities in the period since World War II.[18]

The heavy reliance on local government provision of education in the United States, which contrasts with the situation in many Western European democracies, also undermines the importance of redistribution as an explanation for public provision of education.[19] Because local governments depended heavily on the local property tax base for their revenue stream, different towns even within small metropolitan areas have historically devoted very different levels of resources to their public schools.

### 10.4.2 Government Involvement in the Market for Medical Care

Government involvement in the market for medical care is even more diverse than that with respect to child care and education. The federal government's Medicare and Medicaid programs involve substantial government financing for private purchases of health care, while the VA and many state and local governments operate a network of hospitals. Unlike teachers, however, most health care professionals work for private firms or nonprofit institutions, although they are often subject to substantial government regulation.

Direct government spending on health services and supplies totaled $368

17. West (1967, 1970) describes the expansion of publicly provided education in the United States, emphasizing the role of a growing education bureaucracy in expanding the public sector's role.

18. Hansen and Weisbrod (1969) present evidence suggesting that the net benefits of the University of California system are greater for high- than for low-income households.

19. The apparently limited explanatory power of market imperfections and redistributive concerns to explain government provision of primary and secondary education suggests the need for alternative explanations. Lott (1987) considers a number of possibilities and discusses in particular the potential for "indoctrination" of particular values. This hypothesis is developed further in Lott (1990).

billion in 1992, 45.5% of total health care outlays (Congressional Budget Office 1992). The government's spending share was substantially greater for hospital care and nursing home services. Government funds also represented more than 60% of the costs of medical research and medical facilities construction.

The government's share of the aggregate health care budget has grown substantially in the last three decades. In 1965, government spending accounted for 24.7% of health care outlays in the United States, with state and local governments accounting for more than half of this total (13.2%). Since the enactment of Medicare and Medicaid in 1965, however, the federal government's role has increased. Federal spending accounted for 31.3% of all health care outlays in 1992, compared with 28% a decade earlier. Projections suggest even more rapid growth in the government's role in the future, as a consequence of both demographic change and continued growth in the relative cost of health care services.

Table 10.2 reports direct government spending on health care, as well as forgone revenue associated with several tax expenditures, for 1992. The single largest program supporting health care services is Medicare, which accounted for more than $130 billion and is projected to increase to more than $250 billion by the end of this decade. There are also substantial foregone revenues associated with the tax expenditures for health insurance ($45 billion), as well as substantial tax expenditures from the federal income tax deduction for medical expenditures in excess of 7.5% of adjusted gross income, and deductions for charitable contributions to health care institutions. Direct government spending on health care is substantially less important than federal payments for health care from others. Federal outlays on the VA health system, for example, were $14 billion in 1992, or 6.3% of total federal spending on health care.

The Medicare program has two parts. The first, Medicare Part A, provides hospital insurance for the elderly. This component of Medicare is funded with the revenues from a payroll tax on most employed workers, so it involves explicit intergenerational redistribution. Medicare Part B, or Supplementary Medical Insurance (SMI), provides insurance for outpatient services at hospitals and the costs of physician visits. SMI is an *optional* insurance program, although the vast majority of eligible households purchase it. Elderly individuals who choose to participate pay premiums that represent roughly one-quarter of the cost of this insurance. The balance of the cost is financed from general revenues. Since all elderly individuals are eligible for the same benefits under Medicare, this aspect of the program redistributes from high- to low-income elderly households. On a lifetime basis, this redistribution is partly undone, although probably not reversed, by the use of a regressive flat-rate payroll tax to finance Medicare benefits.

Tax subsidies for the purchase of health insurance and health care are the government provisions that affect the largest number of health care consumers. The exclusion of health insurance benefits from taxable income, and the tax

| Table 10.2 | Government Spending on Medical Care, 1992 (billion $) |
|---|---|

| | |
|---|---:|
| *Direct government spending* | |
| Federal | 253 |
|   Medicare | 136 |
|   Medicaid | 70 |
|   Other (VA, NIH) | 46 |
| State and local | 115 |
|   Medicaid | 53 |
|   Other (workers' compensation, public | |
|     hospitals) | 62 |
| *Tax expenditures on health (federal and state)* | |
| Exemption of employer-provided health | |
|   insurance | 45 |
| Untaxed Medicare benefits | 8 |
| Deductibility of medical expenses | 3 |
| Other (tax-exempt debt, charitable deductions) | ·4 |
| Total | 428 |

*Source:* Author's tabulations based on information in Congressional Budget Office 1992, tables 11 and B-2.

rules allowing households to deduct medical expenses in excess of 7.5% of AGI when computing taxable income, reduce the price of health care for most taxpayers. The reduction in the after-tax price of insurance raises insurance coverage among employed households. While the decision not to tax the value of employer-provided health insurance was taken with the recognition that this would spur private insurance coverage, some of the most rapid growth in employer provision of such insurance took place during World War II, when wage controls made it difficult for employers to raise compensation in other ways.

Tax subsidies may encourage private spending, but they are weak instruments for redistribution across households. Since marginal tax rates increase with household income, high-income households receive the largest percentage subsidy to their purchases of both health insurance and medical care.

Medicaid, the other major government direct outlay program, pays for health insurance for poor households. The program is administered by the states subject to federal guidelines. Federal Medicaid spending is the most rapidly growing government health care outlay, exhibiting an annual growth rate of 15% between 1987 and 1990, and 28% between 1990 and 1992, although these growth rates are not expected to persist. A substantial part of the rapid growth in the early 1990s was due to state gaming of federal reimbursement rules to maximize federal contribution to the state programs.

The history of government intervention in the medical marketplace suggests that redistributive concerns were the primary motivation for passage of the Social Security Amendments of 1965, which created Medicare and Medicaid. There is a long political history to the debate on public health insurance in the United States; see for example Starr (1982). A number of European countries, notably Germany and England, adopted universal health insurance laws in the late nineteenth and early twentieth centuries. There was active discussion of such proposals just before World War I in the United States, as part of a battery of policies supported by the Progressives. Their motivation appeared to be specific egalitarianism, the provision of health insurance as a basic human right. The outbreak of World War I derailed legislative interest in these proposals, however, and, facing some opposition from doctors who did not want government to infringe their professional sovereignty, these proposals did not attract much attention in the fifteen years after World War I.

The next wave of interest in national health insurance occurred during the New Deal, when President Roosevelt considered but rejected the idea of including health insurance in the legislation that became the Social Security Act of 1935. Once again, opposition from doctors was an important stumbling block. Although FDR never embraced national health insurance as a critical policy goal, President Truman did, and in 1948 he launched a major campaign to secure passage of a national health bill. The American Medical Association (AMA), by then a well-organized lobbying group, undertook an all-out campaign to block passage of this legislation. The debate took place during a period of great concern about Communist influence in the United States, and the AMA's labeling of the Truman proposals as "socialized medicine" and linking these proposals to Leninism proved successful in defeating them. The Social Security Amendments of 1950 did, however, stipulate that federal matching funds would be provided for medical payments to health care providers for medical care to those on public assistance. This was a first step toward federal provision of medical care for the needy, and it was expanded ten years later in the Kerr-Mills Act (1960).

The debate that led to passage of Medicare and Medicaid was joined in the mid-1960s, as part of the Great Society program. By this time, concern about access to health care for low-income and elderly households had become acute, in part because rising health care costs made it more difficult for these groups to obtain care. Only 56% of the elderly had health insurance prior to the passage of Medicare. The critical political maneuver in the Medicare debate was limiting the discussion to health care for the elderly. The evidence suggesting poorer access to health care for the elderly than for other age groups was difficult to dispute, and by focusing the program, objections from the AMA that this would lead to government control of doctors was blunted. Representative Wilbur Mills combined a Democratic proposal for mandatory hospital insurance (Medicare Part A) with a Republican proposal for a voluntary outpatient and physician care program (Medicare Part B) and produced legislation that was supported by a majority of Congress.

The critical element in the debate leading to Medicare was a distributional concern with access to health care among specific groups. On this dimension, Medicare achieved its objectives. Davis and Schoen (1978) present some evidence that the ratio of physician visits per year by those in high-income and low-income categories was more equal in 1975 than in 1964, before the passage of Medicare and Medicaid. The effect was less pronounced for the elderly than for younger groups.

To summarize this section, it is difficult to explain either the present structure of public involvement in education in the United States, or the historical evolution of the public sector's involvement, using either externality or redistributive arguments. Redistributive concerns do appear to play a greater role in defining government policy toward medical care. Concern about market imperfections in the medical marketplace does not appear to have played an important role in the rise of publicly financed medical care in the United States.

## 10.5  The Research Agenda

The questions of whether particular markets *may* exhibit imperfections, and whether redistribution could *in principle* be carried out, receive far more discussion among economists than the questions of whether markets are *actually* imperfect, whether government intervention in these markets improves or worsens matters, and whether various redistributive programs are *actually* successful. Yet the choice among various policies for government intervention depends on the actual performance of such policies. This concluding section outlines several areas where further research will yield high returns in informing the debate on choice of public policies in the fields of education and health care.

First, because externalities are invoked to justify intervention in both of these markets, there is a pressing need to document the magnitude of the externalities, particularly those associated with consumption of education. It is important in this regard to assess whether the generation of externalities changes as the level of consumption changes, that is, whether primary and secondary education yields larger or smaller externalities than higher education. If most externalities are generated by levels of educational input that individuals would choose to obtain *without government subsidy,* then the case for public intervention in the educational marketplace may be much weaker than is commonly believed. More generally, there is a need to quantify the importance of various imperfections that are listed as potential problems with the markets for education and health care, and to move beyond the discussion of reasons that *might* justify public intervention to reasons that *do* or *do not.*

Second, the efficiency of public providers of services, as opposed to that of private-sector providers, requires further attention, since this is a key determinant of whether governments should make or buy services. The range of organizational forms in the medical care sector—private hospitals, nonprofit hospitals, and state- and federal-government-run hospitals—provides a wealth of data for comparing input choices and productivity. While many studies of public versus private production conclude that the public sector is a less efficient producer of various goods and services, these studies are often contaminated by various selection biases in the set of services provided by the government. Zeckhauser (1986) argues that in higher education, public institutions tend to function more like their nonprofit competitors than like other government bureaucracies. Further evidence on this issue for primary and secondary education, and for hospitals, would be valuable.

A third important issue, involving political economy as well as the microeconomic analysis of government policy, concerns the basis of political support for redistributive policies toward children and the elderly. Spending on education represents redistribution to the young; spending on health care and health insurance transfers resources to the elderly. A number of commentators, including Preston (1984) and Kotlikoff and Gokhale (1993), have called attention to the rapid growth of transfers to the elderly, and the relative decline in society's investment in children.[20] This may reflect more effective political activities of elderly voters than those who are concerned with children, or it may reflect the fact that more middle-aged households are childless than without living parents. It is also possible that most middle-aged individuals know that they can expect to live well into their seventies and eighties, and to benefit from generous policies toward the elderly that are enacted today. These factors may explain the political reality of growing redistribution toward the elderly rather than toward children.

The current policy debates in both education and health care, including the discussions of school vouchers, increased state financing of schools, and a federal mandate for health insurance, suggest that the nature of government intervention in these markets is subject to continuing evaluation and potential change. This underscores the need for further investigation of both the arguments for government intervention in these areas, and the merits and demerits of alternative instruments for market intervention.

# References

Aaron, H. 1994. Issues Every Plan to Reform Health Care Financing Must Confront. *Journal of Economic Perspectives* 8:31–43.

Arrow, K. 1963. Uncertainty and the Welfare Economics of Medical Care. *American Economic Review* 53:941–73.

Ballard, C., J. Shoven, and J. Whalley. 1985. General Equilibrium Computations of the Marginal Welfare Costs of Taxes in the United States. *American Economic Review* 75:128–38.

Becker, E., and F. Sloan. 1985. Hospital Ownership and Performance. *Economic Inquiry* 23:21–36.

Besley, T., and S. Coate. 1991. Public Provision of Private Goods and the Redistribution of Income. *American Economic Review* 81:979–84.

Cohn, E., and T. Geske. 1990. *The Economics of Education.* 3d ed. Elmsford, NY: Pergamon Press.

---

20. This may be partly related to the nature of current policies toward children and the elderly: education is provided by a public bureaucracy, medical care by the private market with public subsidy. Voters may not like expanding the bureaucracy.

Congressional Budget Office. 1992. *Projections of National Health Expenditures*. Washington, DC: Congressional Budget Office.

Cutler, D., and L. Sheiner. 1994. Policy Options for Long Term Care. in *Studies in the Economics of Aging*, ed. D. Wise. Chicago: University of Chicago Press.

Davis, K., and C. Schoen. 1978. *Health and the War on Poverty*. Washington, DC: Brookings Institution.

*Economic Report of the President, February 1995*. 1995. Washington, DC: Government Printing Office.

Friedman, M. 1962. *Capitalism and Freedom*. Chicago: University of Chicago Press.

Gornick, M., J. Greenberg, P. Eggers, and A. Dobson. 1985. Twenty Years of Medicare and Medicaid: Covered Populations, Use of Benefits, and Program Expenditures. In *Health Care Financing Review: 1985 Annual Supplement*. Washington, DC: U.S. Department of Health and Human Services.

Gruber, J. 1994. The Incidence of Mandated Maternity Benefits. *American Economic Review* 84:622–41.

Gruber, J., and J. Poterba. 1994. Tax Incentives and the Decision to Purchase Health Insurance: Evidence from the Self-Employed. *Quarterly Journal of Economics* 109:701–33.

Hansen, W., and B. Weisbrod. 1969. *Benefits, Costs, and Finance of Public Higher Education*. Chicago: Markham.

Hanushek, E., and S. Rivkin. 1994. Understanding the 20th Century Explosion in U.S. School Costs. University of Rochester. Mimeo.

Henderson, J., P. Mieszkowski, and Y. Sauvageau. 1978. Peer Group Effects and Educational Production Functions. *Journal of Public Economics* 10:97–106.

Himes, C. 1994. Parental Caregiving by Adult Women. *Research on Aging* 16:191–211.

Johnson, J., H. Collins, V. Dupuis, and J. Johansen. 1982. *Introduction to the Foundations of American Education*. 5th ed. Boston: Allyn and Bacon.

Keeler, E., et al. 1988. The Demand for Episodes of Treatment in the Health Insurance Experiment. Report R-3454-HHS. Santa Monica, CA: RAND Corp.

Kotlikoff, L., and J. Gokhale. 1993. The Equity of Social Services Provided to Children and Senior Citizens. Working Paper no. 20. Boston University Department of Economics.

Lazear, Edward. 1983. Intergenerational Externalities. *Canadian Journal of Economics* 16:212–28.

Lindsay, C. 1976. A Theory of Government Enterprise. *Journal of Political Economy* 84:1061–77.

Long, S., and M. Marquis. 1992. Gaps in Employment-Based Health Insurance: Lack of Supply or Lack of Demand? In *Health Benefits and the Workforce*. Washington, DC: U.S. Department of Labor, Pension and Welfare Benefits Administration.

Lott, John R., Jr. 1987. Why Is Education Publicly Provided? A Critical Survey. *Cato Journal* 7:475–501.

———. 1990. An Explanation for Public Provision of Schooling: The Importance of Indoctrination. *Journal of Law and Economics* 33:199–231.

McKean, R., and J. Minasian. 1966. On Achieving Pareto Optimality—Regardless of Cost! *Western Economic Journal* 5:14–23.

Nichols, A., and R. Zeckhauser. 1982. Targeting Transfers through Restrictions on Recipients. *American Economic Review* 72:373–77.

Ohlsson, H., and S. Rosen. 1994. Public Employment, Taxes, and the Welfare State in Sweden. University of Chicago. Mimeo.

Peltzman, S. 1973. The Effect of Government Subsidies-in-Kind on Private Expenditures: The Case of Higher Education. *Journal of Political Economy* 81:1–27.

Preston, S. 1984. Children and the Elderly: Divergent Paths for America's Dependents. *Demography* 21:435–57.

Rosen, H. 1992. *Public Finance*. 3d ed. Homewood, IL: Irwin.

Rothschild, M., and J. Stiglitz. 1976. Equilibrium in Competitive Insurance Markets: An Essay on the Economics of Imperfect Information. *Quarterly Journal of Economics* 90:629–49.

Schulz, R., J. Greenley, and R. Peterson. 1984. Differences in the Direct Costs of Public and Private Acute Inpatient Psychiatric Services. *Inquiry* 21:380–93.

Sonstelie, J. 1982. The Welfare Cost of Free Public Schools. *Journal of Political Economy* 90:794–808.

Starr, P. 1982. *The Social Transformation of American Medicine.* New York: Basic Books.

Stiglitz, J. 1988. *Economics of the Public Sector.* 2d ed. New York: Norton.

Summers, L. 1989. Some Simple Economics of Mandated Benefits. *American Economic Review* 79:177–84.

Tobin, J. 1970. On Limiting the Domain of Inequality. *Journal of Law and Economics* 13 (October): 263–77.

U.S. Congress. House Committee on Ways and Means. 1993. *1993 Green Book: Overview of Entitlement Programs: Background Material and Data on Programs within the Jurisdiction of the Committee on Ways and Means.* Washington, DC: Government Printing Office.

U.S. Department of Education. 1993. *Digest of Education Statistics: 1992.* Washington, DC: Government Printing Office.

Vining, A., and A. Boardman. 1992. Ownership vs. Competition: Efficiency in Public Enterprise. *Public Choice* 73:205–39.

Weitzman, M. 1974. Prices vs. Quantities. *Review of Economic Studies* 41:447–91.

West, E. 1967. The Political Economy of American Public School Legislation. *Journal of Law and Economics* 10:101–28.

———. 1970. *Education and the State.* 2d ed. London: Institute for Economic Affairs.

Wilson, C. 1980. The Nature of Equilibrium in Markets with Adverse Selection. *Bell Journal of Economics* 11(spring): 108–30.

Wolf, C. 1993. *Markets or Governments: Choosing between Imperfect Alternatives.* Cambridge: MIT Press.

Zeckhauser, R. 1986. The Muddled Responsibilities of Public and Private America. In *American Society: Public and Private Responsibilities,* ed. W. Knowlton and R. Zeckhauser. Cambridge: Ballinger.

# Comment    Richard J. Zeckhauser

The government's actions on health and on schools,
Have little to do with economists' rules.

How should the government intervene in the economy? This is a central question for economics, be it Marxian or classical, liberal or conservative. Social policy—which includes the child care, elderly long-term care, education, and

Richard J. Zeckhauser is the Frank P. Ramsey Professor of Political Economy at the John F. Kennedy School of Government at Harvard University, a visiting scholar in the economics department of the Massachusetts Institute of Technology, and a research associate of the National Bureau of Economic Research.

health programs explored in this volume—offers fertile soil for the economist. Each year, dozens of dissertations and hundreds of articles attest to economists' abilities to identify market failures as the justification for social programs.

In his essay, James Poterba examines whether economics can effectively explain government's choice of instruments—subsidies, mandates, or direct provision—in intervening in markets for education and health care. He concludes, quite appropriately, that economics simply does not explain why the government so often directly provides education, yet relies on subsidies as its principal intervention in health care.

Poterba is best known for his carefully crafted empirical studies. Though studded with facts, this essay more reflects than distills, since "there is virtually no evidence on the empirical magnitudes of many of the key parameters needed to guide policy in these areas." Poterba provides a state-of-the-art overview of the rationales for alternative forms of intervention, and an insightful description of actual interventions in the health and education markets.

In his concluding pages, he turns to define a research agenda: he justifiably scolds economists for spending far too much time worrying whether markets may fail and whether interventions might work, and far too little time determining whether failures are significant or government programs successful. Then he briefly raises the flag of positive political economy, suggesting that political forces, more than economic logic, may explain the patterns of redistributive government interventions we observe. (For example, a population that has more voters with parents than with young children tips generosity toward elders and away from kids.)

## The Problem and Puzzles

Social policy borrows the metaphors of and an occasional empirical fact from economics, but otherwise ignores it. Economics, oblivious to reality, spins theories of how social policy should organize itself. It is no surprise that economics, notably the central tools of public finance, do not explain how governments actually intervene. Even if they did, economists, much less policy makers, rarely have sufficient information to know what magnitude of intervention is justified.

Economists' advice is mostly ignored on social policy issues. (Witness the dramatic shift in social policy thinking, despite no change in the underlying economics, with the election of a Republican Congress.) The concepts of economics at best serve as metaphors. Economic considerations do not explain government decisions on social policy. To illustrate:

Why do we have direct medical provision for veterans, but not for people who are poor (Medicaid) or old (Medicare)?

Why did we use vouchers, not direct provision, for the GIs' education?

Why is there so little direct government provision of care in nursing homes and child care, as compared to primary and secondary education?

Why does Massachusetts, an extremely liberal jurisdiction traditionally, have so little public higher education?

Why does Chicago have one public hospital, and New York many?

Using economics as the basis, the answer to any such question would be tortured, because there is sure to be another empirical scenario where nearly identical economic circumstances led to a quite different outcome, suggesting that the theory of market failure tells us little. Witness the United States and Canada on health care.

Fully informed answers to these questions, I believe, are idiosyncratic. Accidents of history, or hard work by political players—consider the insurance industry and health care reform—explain far more than the presence of an externality, or a substantially impeded information flow.

Poterba examines whether a concern for redistribution can justify policy. Redistribution can easily be thought of as a public good, thereby lending itself to a market failure justification for intervention. However, it does not explain the policy patterns we observe. If it did, the United States, with its relatively uneven income distribution, would have a bigger government sector than Sweden.

The only explanation for our haphazard pattern of social policy that is consistent with economics is that the optimum is broad; for example, it doesn't really matter whether the government or the private sector provides health care to veterans. Few observers, economic or otherwise, believe this. Sometimes we directly observe factors that lead to haphazard outcomes. For example, the Clinton health plan would have transformed one-seventh of our economy; it would have been the public finance–social policy example of the decade. In retrospect, the policy did not come close. Few health care experts—beyond our editor, who had already put his chips down in print—would have bet three to one against it a year before it failed. So, in the policy equivalent of chaos theory, we find that starting in nearly identical circumstances we can get dramatically different outcomes. It hardly makes sense after the fact to go back and find the clear economic factors that show why we ended where we did. Those factors hardly changed—what mattered were people's views of Clinton and his political strategy.

## Uncle Joe and "Aha, the Externality"

A great strength and weakness of economics is that it finds its concepts everywhere. Just as Aunt Martha always sees her beloved Uncle Joe in each new niece and nephew, so economists can find concentrated markets, inadequate information flows, and externalities whenever they look into a policy context. The danger is the "Aha, the Externality" syndrome: we find a market failure and discuss how to intervene. What is missing is any concept of the externality's magnitude, or much thought about how alternative measures, including doing nothing, would perform.

It is no surprise that with substantial support from economists, we have dozens of in-kind programs to support poor people that in sum dwarf cash assistance in their magnitude. Such programs, alas, make it virtually impossible to bring about welfare reform offering strong incentives to work.

### The Policy Loss

The failure of economics to describe suggests that our policies are far from optimal. Ruling out the Pollyannaish view that there is a broad optimum—for example, it does not matter whether the government or private sector produces, or a child care subsidy of $1,000 is about as good as one of $500—the design of policies is substantially in error. Good A is subsidized too much, B too little, and neither is produced in near the right quantity by the right party.

Poterba tells the moral right: Do the empirical analysis. Document the magnitude of the market failure, and assess the performance of any program that confronts it.

I would add that you should not be trapped by the lure of the lamppost: economic methods may shine most brightly where current policies are most reasonable. Where these methods are hardest to apply, as, say, when formulating policy to deal with the breakdown of the family, is where they may contribute the most.

### Concluding Thoughts

Chess masters can instantaneously memorize a pattern from actual play, but are just like the rest of us if some pieces are placed at random. Economists looking at social policy are like chess masters looking at random boards: the patterns make little sense, and it is hard to see what reasonable pattern of play could have led to what we observe.

The social policy game is hardly random, but neither is it driven primarily by the concepts that economists discuss. Economists need an improved knowledge of the real game, including both empirical realities and matters of institutional design and politics. With such knowledge, economists can speak more meaningfully, and help push our haphazard social policies in desirable directions.

# 11    The Politics of American Social Policy, Past and Future

Theda Skocpol

Debates about fundamental reworkings of national social policy are at the center of U.S. politics—and are likely to remain there for the foreseeable future. As the turn of a new century approaches, American are looking critically at the scope and purposes of their nation's social policies. Reconsiderations are inspired by the changing needs of a national population that includes increasing numbers of elderly people, employed mothers, low-wage workers not making incomes sufficient to support families, and employees without long-term job security. Yet today's policy discussions also grow out of unresolved political disputes from the past. Today's debates are new incarnations of ongoing battles over the expansion, contraction, or reorganization of public services and social spending in the United States.

Some debates are certainly hardy perennials. "Welfare reform," for example, has come up at least once a decade since the 1950s (Bane and Ellwood 1994, chap. 1), and President Bill Clinton's boldly declared intention to "end welfare as we know it" is only the most recent version of a long-standing aspiration to substitute wage-earning jobs for dependency by the poor on public aid. Of course today's version of "welfare reform" is informed by heightened worries about the growing numbers of single-mother-led families in America (Garfinkel and McLanahan 1986). Have governmental policies encouraged this trend? What reformed or new policies might encourage the stability of two-parent families and offer appropriate support for single-parent families?

Concerns about social protections for the elderly also recur, and nowadays they are sometimes coupled with calls to reorient our public policies toward "helping America's children." The rapidly rising cost of Medicare is decried by pundits and politicians, even as the elderly and many of their family members are asking for new public help to defray the costs of prescription drugs

Theda Skocpol is professor of government and sociology at Harvard University.

and long-term care for the partially or fully disabled. At the same time, conservatives argue that existing programs such as Social Security and Medicare are "too costly." According to the Concord Coalition (Peterson 1993), the United States is certain to "go bankrupt," and "our children and grandchildren" will be deprived of a chance to realize the American Dream, unless there are large cuts soon in taxation and spending for such "middle-class entitlements" as Social Security and Medicare.

The Concord Coalition has predominantly conservative backing and appeal, yet some of its arguments are meant to appeal to progressives. Some liberals are, in fact, willing to contemplate cuts in programs for the elderly out of desperation to free up tax resources to aid children and working-age families. Reviving a reform strategy used in earlier eras of American history, contemporary liberal groups such as the Children's Defense Fund dramatize the needs of the young (cf. Children's Defense Fund 1994). Pointing to rising rates of child poverty, children's advocates call for expanded public commitments to ensuring family health services, education, and day care.

Somewhat more surprising than ever-revisited public discussions about reforming welfare and ensuring security for the elderly and children has been the recent reconsideration of the U.S. federal role in health care. The issue of comprehensive health reform had all but disappeared from the national agenda after the late 1970s. Experts still worried about problems of access and rising costs, but politicians had given up on debating grand solutions after the Democrats under Jimmy Carter failed to make headway on health reform, and after conservative victories in the 1980s apparently made it impossible to talk about major new governmental ventures.

Then, in the fall of 1991, an obscure Democratic candidate, Harris Wofford, overcame a forty-point deficit in the opinion polls to win a special senatorial election in Pennsylvania (Blumenthal 1991; Russakoff 1991). Wofford ran television commercials promising that he would work for health insurance covering every American, and his surprise victory over a well-established Republican opponent was widely attributed to this emphasis on universal insurance. Suddenly, electoral politicians awoke to the worries about health coverage that were spreading among middle-class citizens (Starr 1991), who no longer feel secure about their jobs and employment-based benefits.

During his campaign for the presidency in 1992, Democratic candidate Bill Clinton picked up on the theme of comprehensive health care reform, even as he highlighted the need for new national policies to promote employment and economic growth (Clinton and Gore 1992). After President Clinton assumed office in January 1993, officials in his administration and task forces assembled around its edges set to work devising bold new plans for reworking America's social and economic policies. Some steps were taken quickly and quietly, such as the summer 1993 expansion of the Earned Income Tax Credit to boost the incomes of low-wage working families (Howard 1994). In other areas, such as job training and welfare reform, elaborate plans have been worked out, only to run up against draconian budgetary constraints that will probably prevent their full implementation. Democratic candidate Clinton had, after all, not only promised to reinvigorate national economic and social policies; he had also promised to cut the national budget deficit and trim back taxes for the broad American middle class.

Even in the face of powerful budgetary and political constraints, Clinton chose to stake much of his presidential prestige on a comprehensive "health security plan" unveiled in the fall of 1993 (White House Domestic Policy Council 1993). Echoing themes of universal protection reminiscent of former President Franklin Roosevelt's legislation for Social Security during the New Deal, President Clinton unabashedly hopes to make the 1990s a watershed for U.S. public social provision comparable to that of the 1930s. As the president declared in his September 22, 1993, speech to the Congress and the nation:

> It's hard to believe that once there was a time—even in this century—when retirement was nearly synonymous with poverty, and older Americans died in our streets. That is unthinkable today because over half a century ago Americans had the courage to change—to create a Social Security system that ensures that no Americans will be forgotten in their later years.
>
> I believe that forty years from now our grandchildren will also find it unthinkable that there was a time in our country when hard-working families lost their homes and savings simply because their child fell ill, or lost their health coverage when they changed jobs. Yet our grandchildren will only find such things unthinkable tomorrow if we have the courage to change today.
>
> This is our change. This is our journey. And when our work is done, we will have answered the call of history and met the challenge of our times.

Stirring presidential rhetoric aside, the specific proposals put forward in late 1993 by the Clinton administration were rejected or withdrawn not long after Congress began to consider them. No health care reforms at all were enacted prior to the congressional elections of November 1994, and any proposals reintroduced by the Clinton administration in 1995 are certain to be fundamentally reworked before anything becomes law. This is true not only for health care reform, but also for proposed changes in welfare, employment programs, and programs dealing with the needs of working families. Still, no matter how much—or how little—actually happens during the (one- or two-term) presidency of Bill Clinton, fundamental issues are not going to go away. Financing health care, caring for an aging population, retraining displaced employees, putting welfare mothers to work, alleviating child poverty or substandard nurturance, and making employment sustainable along with parenthood for all American families—all of these matters and more will require repeated attention from presidents, congressional representatives, state and local governments, and citizens. Well into the early twenty-first century, the United States seems certain to be reconsidering and revising its public social policies.

## 11.1   Understanding U.S. Social Policy Making

So how are we to make sense of the making and remaking of social policies in the United States? Many people would answer this query timelessly—in moral-ideological terms, or in supposedly value-neutral technical terms. For moralists, battles over U.S. social policy may be seen as clashes between advocates of "big government" versus "the market," or as combat between those who want to economically aid the needy versus those who want to control and reform their behavior. Meanwhile, for many professional experts, policy making is understood as a matter of doing objective research on the extent of societal problems, in order to devise optimal cost-efficient "solutions" for politicians to enact.

Moralists and technocrats thus look at social policy making in very different ways. But they have in common an almost total lack of historical and political sensibility. Both moralists and technocrats tend to look at policy formation outside of the context of America's historically changing governmental institutions, and without reference to broader political tendencies and alliances. Consequently, moralists are unable to understand why their version of "good" triumphs or fails to triumph over "evil" at any given moment. And technically oriented policy experts feel no responsibility to consider matters of governmental feasibility, or to take responsibility when the "efficient" solutions they propose either are not accepted, or lead to unintended and unwanted outcomes.

The lack of historical and political sensibility is, in a way, quite comfortable for moralists and technocrats alike. In the face of political failures, moralists can simply redouble their shrill, absolutist cries for good versus evil. And technocrats can retreat to academia or think tanks and continue working out perfect solutions for unnamed future politicians to adopt—with unforeseen consequences, for which the experts need take no responsibility. What moralists and technocrats both fail to achieve, however, are reliable insights into the political constraints and possibilities for making and remaking American public policies at any given historical juncture, including the present.

Even in a volume such as this, where most contributions appropriately focus on the technical and normative dimensions of ideal social policies, there is a place for a historically grounded analysis of the politics of social policy making. That is what this essay offers. It includes, first, an overview of the politics of U.S. social policy making from the nineteenth century to the present, and then a set of reflections on the lessons we might take from political history about constraints and possibilities at work in contemporary debates about social policies for the future.

## 11.2   The Political Formation of U.S. Social Policy

Modern "welfare states," as they eventually came to be called, had their start between the 1880s and the 1920s in pension and social insurance programs established for industrial workers and needy citizens in Europe and Australasia (Flora and Alber 1981). Later, from the 1930s through the 1950s, such programmatic beginnings were in certain countries elaborated into comprehensive systems of income support and social insurance encompassing entire national populations. In the aftermath of World War II, Great Britain rationalized a whole array of services and social insurance programs around an explicit vision of "the welfare state," which would ensure a "national minimum" of protection for all citizens against income interruptions due to old age, disability, ill health, unemployment, and family breakup. During the same period, other nations—especially the Scandinavian democracies—established "full employment welfare states" by deliberately coordinating social policies, first with Keynesian strategies of macroeconomic management and then with targeted interventions in labor markets.

Comparative research on the origins of modern welfare states often measures the United States against foreign patterns of "welfare state development." In such research, America is labeled a "welfare state laggard" because it did not establish nationwide social insurance until 1935, and an "incomplete welfare state" because it never enacted national health insurance or established full-employment programs coordinated with social policies. Certain insights can be gained from comparisons of this sort. But they overlook important social policies that were distinctive to the United States in the late nineteenth and early twentieth centuries, and direct our attention away from recurrent patterns in U.S. social policy and the political forces that have shaped and reshaped it over time. As I have argued in *Protecting Soldiers and Mothers: The Political Origins of Social Policy in the United States* (Skocpol 1992), it is important to break with the evolutionism and the socioeconomic determinism of most social-scientific research on the development of Western welfare states, particularly if one's objective is to understand U.S. social policies and politics.

Modern U.S. social policies did not start with the Social Security Act of 1935. Between the 1870s and the 1920s, U.S. federal and state governments established many policies aiming to protect, first, veteran Union soldiers and their dependents, and then mothers and their children. I label the first two (often-overlooked) eras of modern U.S. social policy the "Civil War era" and the "maternalist era." Recent eras are better known: the "New Deal era," and what I shall tentatively label the "era of controversies over the federal social role," which stretches from the 1960s to the present.

To make sense of these major phases of modern U.S. social provision from the Civil War to the present, I use a polity-centered theoretical framework, devised in critical dialogue with alternative social scientific theories that emphasize the sociodemographic, cultural, or class determinants of public social policies (for a survey of theories, see Skocpol and Amenta 1986). An essay such as this is hardly the place to go into great detail about this explanatory approach (for a full discussion of which see Skocpol 1992, introduction), but I can indicate its chief features.

I analyze social policy making in the context of the historical development of changing U.S. governmental institutions, political parties, and electoral rules. The United States started out with a federally decentralized "state of courts and parties" (Skowronek 1982), in which there were no centralized professionally run public bureaucracies. Instead, courts, legislatures, and patronage-oriented political parties held sway, with the parties competing for votes in the world's first mass democracy for males. Only around 1900 did U.S. governments at local, state, and federal levels begin to develop significant bureaucratic capacities. This happened as patronage parties and electoral competition weakened. Yet public bureaucratization in the United States has always proceeded in fragmentary ways, and the United States has never developed a strong, well-paid, or highly respected stratum of national civil servants. Nor is there any clear concentration of centralized governmental power in the United States. Divisions of authority among executives, agencies, legislatures, committees within legislatures, and state and federal courts are arguably even more pervasive within twentieth-century U.S. governance than they were in nineteenth-century party-dominated politics. What is more, U.S. national politics has always been rooted in congressionally mediated coalitions of local interests. From the time of patronage-oriented party politics in the nineteenth century, down to the more bureaucratically centered coalitions of today, public programs have an easier time of being enacted in U.S. national politics, and of surviving, if they distribute benefits, services, or regulatory advantages widely, across large numbers of local legislative districts.

To make sense of patterns of policy making in each major era, I consider the impact of changing U.S. governmental and electoral arrangements on the initiatives taken by officials and politicians. These political actors take initiatives of their own, and look for policies that will further their careers within given organizational contexts. I also look at the impact of institutional arrangements on the identities, goals, and capacities of the various social groups that have become active, at one period or another, in political alliances contending over the shape of U.S. public policies. Finally, my polity-oriented perspective highlights "policy feedbacks" over time: the influences that earlier social policies have upon the institutional arrangements and social groups that shape later social policies. Not only does politics make policies, the opposite is also true: policies make, and subsequently remake, politics, either by changing the fiscal and administrative capacities of government or by encouraging (or frustrating) group demands or alliances in the electorate and representative bodies.

Let me briefly illustrate how I use this sort of institutionalist, polity-centered framework to analyze patterns of policy and the politics that shaped them from the Civil War to the present. My treatment of each period here is breathtakingly succinct, but readers can easily find fuller elaborations of analytic framework and empirical discussions in other publications by me and my collaborators (see especially Weir, Orloff, and Skocpol 1988; and Skocpol 1992, 1995).

## 11.2.1   The Civil War Era

Early American "social policy" included state and local support for the most extensive and inclusive system of primary, secondary, and higher education in the industrializing world (Heidenheimer 1981; Rubinson 1986). Less well known, but even more telling, early U.S. social provision featured generous local, state, and (especially) federal benefits for Civil War veterans and their dependents. From the 1870s to the 1910s, there was an enormous expansion of disability, survivors', and de facto old-age benefits for veterans of the Union armies of the Civil War (for full details and documentation, see Skocpol 1992, chap. 2). By 1910, about 28% of all elderly American men, and nearly one-third of elderly men in the North, were receiving from the U.S. government pensions that were remarkably generous by the international standards of the day; many widows and other dependents of deceased veterans were also pensioners; and extra aid from state and local governments was often available to Civil War veterans and survivors. Union soldiers and their dependents, it was argued, had "saved the Nation" and should in return be cared for by the government, to prevent the possibility of their falling into dependence on private charity or public poor relief.

U.S. federalism, and its early electoral democratization, encouraged the competitive expansion of locally managed public education throughout the nineteenth century, while also allowing space for varieties of private schooling to flourish. Popular groups in America gained voting rights early, and farmers and workers alike saw education as a way to participate fully in a democratic polity and market society. No aristocracy, established church, or national bureaucracy held sway; thus schools and colleges and universities were free to proliferate competitively across localities and states. Early American public education was oriented more toward socializing majorities for citizenship than toward preparing elites for civil service careers (Katznelson and Weir 1985). During the Civil War, moreover, the ascendant Republicans enacted land grant subsidies to encourage public higher education and agricultural research to benefit farmers across many states.

In other ways, as well, the nineteenth-century U.S. polity encouraged inclusive social policies. After the Civil War, the expansion of benefits for Union veterans became rooted in competition between patronage-oriented political parties, as politicians used distributive policies to assemble cross-class and cross-regional electoral support from a highly mobilized and competitive male electorate (McCormick 1979). Union veterans and their dependents were seen as deserving of national support, but more than that, the old soldiers and those tied to them constituted critical blocs of voters, especially the tightly electorally competitive East and Midwest after the end of Reconstruction. Between the mid-1870s and the mid-1890s, the Republican Party in particular learned to combine tariffs and pension expenditures. Tariffs raised plentiful revenues for the federal government. In turn, the revenues could be spent on pensions, applications for which could be manipulated in ways that helped the Republicans to appeal to electorally competitive states just before crucial elections (McMurry 1922). Along with party politicians, thousands of veterans' clubs federated into the Grand Army of the Republic became key supporters of pension generosity from the mid-1880s onward, keeping congressmen across many northern legislative districts keenly interested in such social expenditures from the federal fisc.

### 11.2.2   The Maternalist Era

During the early 1900s, various policies aiming to help women workers and mothers and children proliferated (see Skocpol 1992, part 3). The federal government established the female-run Children's Bureau in 1912, and expanded its mission in 1921 through the enactment of the Sheppard-Towner program partially to fund state and local health care education to help American mothers and babies. Meanwhile, dozens of states enacted protective labor laws for women workers, arguing that their capacity for motherhood had to be protected. And forty-four states also enabled local jurisdictions to provide "mothers' pensions" to impoverished caretakers of fatherless children.

Around 1900, the nineteenth-century U.S. "state of courts and parties" was undergoing major structural transformations. The Democrats and Republicans became less electorally competitive in most parts of the nation, and elite and middle-class groups were calling for political reforms that would weaken patronage-oriented parties and create nonpartisan, professional agencies of government. At this juncture, reformers who wanted the United States to imitate early European social insurance and pension programs made little headway. Informed publics did not believe that turn-of-the-century American governments could administer policies honestly or efficiently, and reformers feared "corruption" among politicians if huge new social spending programs—reminiscent to them of Civil War pensions—were created.

Yet the same set of political circumstances that discouraged social spending for workingmen in the United States opened up opportunities for what I call "maternalist" reformers advocating social programs for mothers and children. Until 1920 (or a few years before in some states), American women lacked the right to vote, yet they were hardly absent from politics more broadly understood (Baker 1984). Elite and middle-class women formed voluntary organizations to engage in charitable, cultural, and civic activities. By the turn of the century, nation-spanning federations of women's voluntary associations had formed, exactly paralleling the three-tier structure of U.S. local-state-federal government. Women's federations allied themselves with higher-educated female professional reformers, arguing that the moral and domestic values of married homemakers and mothers should be projected into public affairs. Organized women urged legislators regardless of party to enact new social policies to help families, communities, and—above all—mothers and children. During a period when U.S. political parties were weakened, and when male officials and trade unions could not readily take the lead in enacting social policies for workingmen, U.S. women's voluntary federations were uniquely well positioned to shape public debates across many local legislative districts (Skocpol 1992, page 3; Skocpol et al. 1993). Thus the United States tended to enact maternalist regulations, services, and benefits at a time when European nations were establishing fledgling social insurance programs for industrial workers and their dependents.

Women's voluntary associations were more successful at setting agendas of civic debate and getting legislators to enact regulations or "enabling statutes" than they were at persuading governments to generously fund social programs. Mothers' pensions, in particular, were never adequately funded, and soon degenerated into new versions of poor relief. Ironically, too, after American women were admitted to the formal electorate by the Nineteenth Amendment in 1920, the civic engagement of many women's groups weakened. For this and a variety of other reasons—including the mobilization of the American Medical Association in opposition to Sheppard-Towner maternal health clinics—the expansion of maternalist social policies came to a halt by the later 1920s, and indeed was partially reversed. Then came the Great Depression, bringing with it social and political upheavals that ushered in the next great era of U.S. social policy innovation.

### 11.2.3   The New Deal Era

This watershed period featured various federal programs to help the (temporarily) unemployed, with the Social Security Act of 1935, which included national Old Age Insurance (OAI), federally required and state-run unemployment insurance, and federal subsidies for optional, state-controlled Old Age Assistance and Aid to Dependent Children (ADC, which was a continuation of the earlier mothers' pensions). In the public discourse of the 1930s and 1940s, the most "deserving" recipients of social benefits were said to be normally employed men who were temporarily forced out of work by the Depression, and the elderly. By the early 1950s, it was clear that social insurance for retired elderly wage earners and their dependents had emerged as the centerpiece of such generous and comprehensive public social provision as there would be in post-World War II America (Amenta and Skocpol 1988). The only other truly generous and comprehensive part of postwar national social provision was the GI Bill of 1944, which featured employment assistance and educational and housing loans for military veterans.

A number of structural changes and political developments set the stage for the policy innovations of the 1930s and 1940s. The federal government—and within it the Executive—came to the fore in the emergency of massive economic depression. State and local governments and charity groups exhausted their resources and literally begged for federal interventions, even as business groups and other conservatives lost their ability to veto governmental initiatives. Economic crisis also spurred the unionization of industrial workers as well as protests by organizations of farmers, the unemployed, and—perhaps most important—old people. Among the elderly, there emerged a widespread federation of local Townsend clubs demanding generous pensions for the elderly. Economic crisis also spurred electoral realignment, shifting votes from Republicans to Democrats—and transforming the Democrats from a warring camp of southern "dry" Protestants versus northern "wet" Catholics, into a nationwide conglomerate of local and state political machines all hungry for new flows of economic resources.

What the Depression, the New Deal, and even World War II did not do, however, was to remove contradictory local and state interests from "national" U.S. policy making. Even at their strongest, President Franklin Roosevelt and the assorted New Deal reformist professionals who flocked into executive agencies during the 1930s, all had to compromise with congressional coalitions rooted in state and local interests (Patterson 1967). Above all, they had to respect Southern Democrats' determination to protect their region's sharecropping agriculture and low-wage industries from actually (or potentially) unsettling "intrusions" by northern unions or federal bureaucrats. Southerners were happy to have resources from the federal government, but did not want either centralized controls or benefits that might undermine existing southern labor and race relations. And if the truth be told, congressional representatives of other localities and states in the nation felt pretty much the same protective way about whatever the major labor and social relations of their areas might be. There was a broad congressional consensus throughout the New Deal and the 1940s to preserve a great deal of federal variety in economic and social policy (Skocpol and Amenta 1985).

From this perspective, the shape and limits of the major social and economic programs of the New Deal era are not surprising. Federally run employment programs did not survive the mass unemployment of the 1930s, because efforts to institutionalize Executive-run "full employment planning" and "social Keynesianism" ran afoul of congressionally represented southern, business, and farm interests (Weir and Skocpol 1985). The Social Security Act included only one truly national program—OAI—enacted in an area where no states had previously established programs. Unemployment insurance, meanwhile, was made federal rather than national, not only because representatives of the South wanted their states to be able to establish terms of coverage, benefits, and taxation, but also because representatives of Wisconsin and New York wanted their "liberal" states to be able to preserve the terms of the unemployment insurance programs they had already established, prior to the Social Security Act (Amenta et al. 1987). Public assistance programs for the elderly and for dependent children were given federal subsidies under Social Security, but otherwise left entirely in the hands of the states.

During World War II, New Deal reformers tied to the National Resources Planning Board talked about permanently nationalizing and expanding both public assistance and unemployment insurance. But their proposals got nowhere at all, and Congress disbanded the National Resources Planning Board soon after they were made. Only OAI tended to expand coverage and become more comprehensive after 1935. Widows and orphans of wage-earning "contributors" were added to OAI in 1939, transforming it into Old Age and Survivors Insurance. During the 1950s, benefits for disabled wage earners were added to what was now known simply as Social Security, and coverage was extended to more occupations. The American "welfare state" that emerged form the New Deal and World War II was hardly comprehensive by the international standards of the day, yet it did eventually become relatively complete and generous for retired, disabled, or deceased regular wage earners and their dependents. The GI Bill and other World War II veterans' programs served as a kind of social support program for many young families in the 1950s. But of course, this was a temporary set of supports that "grew up" with the age cohorts that fought World War II, and has not been in place for the younger cohorts that have followed (Newman 1993).

### 11.2.4   The Era of Controversies over the Federal Social Role

A new period of innovation in U.S. social policy was launched in the aftermath of the civil rights struggles of the 1950s and 1960s, as southern blacks gained the right to vote and liberal Democrats very temporarily gained executive power and majorities in Congress (Patterson 1981, parts 3 and 4). Liberals dreamed of "completing" the social and economic agendas left over from the unfinished reform agendas of the 1930s and 1940s, and many activists hoped to rework U.S. social programs in ways that would aid and uplift the poor, particularly the newly aroused black poor.

Despite the extravagance of liberal hopes (not to mention radical demands) at the height of the War on Poverty and the Great Society, policy legacies and institutional features inherited from the New Deal era shaped and limited the openings available to policy makers. As Margaret Weir (1992) has explained, liberals, unionists, and civil rights activists were not in a good position to create public full-employment programs that might have jointly benefited the black poor along with white and black unionized workers. Instead, institutional and intellectual legacies from the New Deal and the 1940s encouraged public policies that emphasized "commercial Keynesian" macroeconomic strategies supplemented by small federal programs designed to reeducate the poor to make them "employable." Soon caught in political controversies and squeezed for resources during the Vietnam War, federally sponsored employment-training efforts never really succeeded.

As the War on Poverty gave way to the Great Society and Nixon reforms, the emphasis shifted from job training and community development programs, toward helping the poor through new or expanded categorical social benefits such as Aid to Families with Dependent Children (AFDC), food stamps, and Medicaid. Reasons for this shift are many, but they include liberal demands for more spending on the poor, the after-effects of urban rioting, and the preference of the Nixon administration for spending rather than subsidies for services and antipoverty agencies that were likely to be part of the Democratic Party's organizational base. For a time, expanded social spending on targeted welfare programs helped welfare mothers and their children, as more needy single-parent families than ever before were added to the welfare rolls. Yet during this same period, the Social Security Administration took advantage of the heightened concern with antipoverty policy to put through long-laid plans for Medicare, nationalized Supplemental Security Income, and indexed Social Security benefits. In due course, the elderly on Medicare, Supplemental Security Income, and Social Security after it was indexed in 1972 benefited most from the social policy innovations of the so-called War on Poverty era. Despite the focus of the rhetoric of this period on poor working-age people and children, the most generous and sustainable innovations of the period helped to pull most of the American elderly out of dire poverty for the first time in modern history (Danziger, Haveman, and Plotnick 1986, 61).

Nor was this the end of the story of how the War on Poverty and Great Society ended up shortchanging the poor. By the later 1970s, and particularly during the 1980s, political backlashes set in against the social policy innovations and extensions of the 1960s and early 1970s. Leaving aside important exceptions and nuances, one cay say that expanded "social security" provision for the elderly (poor and nonpoor alike) remained popular with broad, bipartisan swatches of American voters and politicians, while public "welfare" assistance to the working-age poor became an increasingly contentious issue among politicians and intellectuals, and within the electorate as a whole. The division between "social security" as a set of earned benefits and "welfare" as undeserved handouts to the poor had been built into the programmatic structure of federal social provision since the New Deal; in the wake of the policy changes of the 1960s and 1970s, this division became highly politicized along racial lines. AFDC, food stamps, Medicaid, and other targeted "welfare" programs expanded after the mid-1960s. But, argued conservative critics, America's social problems got worse, not better. Although few experts familiar with statistical arguments about poverty accept the accuracy of claims by analysts such as Charles Murray (1984) that federal antipoverty programs have actually "caused" increased in out-of-wedlock childbearing or crime, it is fair to say that this argument has expressed (and helped to create) a sea change in popular and expert opinion over the past couple of decades. After all, expansions of welfare in the 1960s and 1970s manifestly did not reverse or prevent such poverty-related social ills as increasing out-of-wedlock childbearing. Thus, even if the causal picture is not what Murray argues, the picture he paints can easily have a broader ideological resonance with general expert and citizen frustration about "welfare as we know it."

Attacks on expansions of federally mandated or subsidized welfare programs for the poor aided the electoral fortunes of Republicans and—more generally—of conservative critics of governmental social provision (Edsall and Edsall 1991). Various reasons can be cited why such attacks were politically successful. Some would argue that they appealed to tacit racism in the U.S. white majority (Quadagno 1994); others would argue that, racism aside, middle-class and working-class citizens were less and less willing to pay taxes for federal social transfers during a time of employment instability and declining real family wages. Whatever the reasons, conservative Republican Ronald Reagan used antiwelfare appeals as part of his winning campaign for the presidency in 1980. And after Reagan ascended to office, the rate of growth of federal social spending slowed. More pertinent, a sweeping tax cut was enacted in 1981, setting the stage for growing federal deficit that has since made it virtually impossible for new social programs to be funded. The persistence of a huge federal deficit also encouraged renewed conservative calls for severe cutbacks in federal social programs, including Social Security and Medicare (as well as "welfare," which after all accounts for only a tiny portion of the federal budget).

The Reagan administration of the 1980s did not eliminate many programs or cut absolute domestic social spending, but it did retard the growth of expenditures on targeted programs that had already lost considerable ground in the face of inflation during the 1970s. More important, the Reagan era signaled an ideological sea change. Both politicians' rhetoric and the actual squeezing and disrupting of governmental programs that occurred in this period helped to delegitimate governmental solutions to domestic social ills. Politicians became highly reluctant to discuss taxation as a positive means to the resolution of civic or individual concerns (Blumenthal and Edsall 1988). And the huge federal budget deficit created by Ronald Reagan's tax cuts itself moved to the center of public discussion as supposedly the leading problem for the nation to resolve in the 1990s—neatly directing attention away from the increasingly acute difficulties faced, not only by welfare recipients, but by less-educated *working* families in the U.S. national economy (Danzinger and Gottschalk 1993; Freeman 1994).

Many of the supporters of Bill Clinton hoped that the election of this moderate Democratic president in 1992 would suddenly undo the delegitimation of the federal social role that had progressed so far since the 1970s. It is by now apparent, however, that the policy initiatives of the Clinton administration often cannot assemble congressional majorities, and are invariably debated in a context of the continuing federal budget crisis and intense popular distrust of government. The decade of the 1990s is proving to be as ideologically contentious as any period in modern U.S. political history—especially on matters having to do with the extent and forms of federal government involvement in the regulation or funding of social benefits and services.

## 11.3  Opportunities and Constraints in U.S. Social Policy Making

Patterns in history are not just of antiquarian interest. They speak to issues that continue to animate U.S. political debates today. Although no one can predict the outcome of ongoing policy debates and political struggles, we can discern a number of interesting patterns across past eras of U.S. social policy and politics—patterns that at least cast light on alternative strategies, and on constraints and possibilities that matter for all of us as we debate policies for the American future, including debates about the particular kinds of policies featured in this volume.

### 11.3.1  The Popularity of Social Programs for the "Worthy" Many

It is often claimed that Americans are a people inherently opposed to taking "handouts" from government. But a full historical purview suggests that much depends on how benefits are understood and structured. Since the nineteenth century, large numbers of mainstream American citizens have been delighted to accept—and politically support—certain generous, government-funded social benefits. Public education, Civil War benefits, the Sheppard-Towner health program aimed at American mothers and babies, and Social Security insurance—all are examples of broad social programs that have done very well in U.S. democracy. Such programs have been aimed at beneficiaries culturally defined (at any given time) as "worthy" because of their past or potential contributions to the nation. Children have been understood as potential citizens and economic contributors, and military veterans as those who served and "saved" the nation. By the 1930s, the elderly were seen as worthy of support after a lifetime of "contributions," through both taxes and work. And back around 1900, interestingly enough, mothers were celebrated as "serving the community" through childbearing and rearing in the home.

By now, of course, things have changed for mothers. Since the 1960s, the labor-force participation of married American women, including mothers of young children, has grown sharply. Elite and middle-class Americans no longer celebrate the cultural ideal of the "stay-at-home mother," and this erosion of the original cultural understanding behind mothers' pensions/ADC/AFDC coincides with the racial tensions over poverty programs that I discussed above. More than ever before in U.S. history, welfare mothers have come to be defined as "not working," as taking "handouts." Not only are mothers on public assistance more likely to be unwed or divorced and disproportionately nonwhite, rather than the mostly white widows they once were; their work as child rearers in the home is no longer consensually valued in American culture. Indeed, the capacities of poor mothers to do an adequate job of raising their own children are nowadays very often questioned by professional experts and the middle-class public. Back in the 1910s, reformers argued that mother love in the home was the key to good child rearing, and that poor fatherless children should be taken out of the orphanages or foster homes to which they had been consigned. Today, reformers are just as likely to argue that poor children would be better off in day care centers, or maybe even in orphanages.

The structure of benefit programs as more or less universal matters, too (along with cultural understandings about which categories of people are worthy beneficiaries). Although middle-class and working-class Americans are typically reluctant to see public monies spent for the poor through welfare programs, they have repeatedly been willing to support politically and pay taxes for social benefits that are considered to be "earned" by citizens such as themselves. Aid to the poor has also been acceptable whenever such aid has been part of broader, more universalistic policies that also benefit middle-class citizens (Skocpol 1991). As Hugh Heclo (1986) has explained, perhaps the best way to help the poor in America is to do so without talking about them, in the context of social services or benefits that have a broader, more universal constituency.

Social Security benefits for the retired elderly are the best contemporary example of support by Americans for universal social policy. Because of the way the financing for Social Security was set up (a matter discussed below), and because of how the program was portrayed by its administrators after 1935 (Derthick 1979), retired wage earners are thought to "earn" pensions linked to their records of employment and the previous levels of their wages. Actually the system is financed from current taxes, and there is considerable redistribution toward lower-income retirees, but these features of the system have never been made politically visible to the average participant. Social Security now encompasses almost all employed Americans and their families, and since the 1970s it has become by far the nation's most effective antipoverty program, without being defined as such. In recent decades, Social Security has enjoyed strong bipartisan support across lines of class and race.

Conservatives who are opposed to large governmental programs of social provision understand well that Social Security is hard to cut back as long as it has middle-class support. It is therefore not incidental that contemporary conservative tactics for shrinking Social Security take the form of efforts, first, to convince young upper-middle-class employees that Social Security is a "bad deal" for them economically, that they would be better off to turn to private investments for retirement. Another tactic is to attempt to undermine the confidence of all Americans that Social Security will be there in the future, by suggesting that the system is "bound to go bankrupt" as the post-World War II baby boom generation ages. Actually, Social Security is currently in fine fiscal shape, and any problems for the long-term future could readily be addressed by the kinds of bipartisan commissions that have made adjustments in the past. Using lurid projections that presume no such adjustments will ever be made, conservatives propose to "save" Social Security by trimming it back into a program targeted especially on the most needy elderly, and taking better-off middle-class people out of the system.

Some critics of Social Security may honestly believe this is just a matter of fiscal responsibility, but many surely have learned a lesson from political history: Social Security has expanded and survived *because* it has middle-class participation and support. If middle-class Americans are removed from the system, they would soon resist paying taxes that are currently used to create proportionately more generous pensions for lower-income workers. Social Security would soon be gutted, turned into one more demeaning welfare program for the poor. Then it could easily be cut back even further, transferring resources to private investments controlled by the well-to-do while leaving millions of elderly Americans mired in poverty, as they were before the 1970s. Their children and grandchildren (especially the women among them) would also suffer, because any taxes they saved during their working lifetimes would be more than offset by the expense and disruption of caring for parents without adequate resources to live with dignity in retirement. Historical analysis suggests that this sort of scenario will very likely unfold if Social Security is changed from a relatively universal social benefit for the deserving majority, into a means-tested welfare benefit narrowly targeted on the most needy few.

11.3.2    The Problem of "Government Bureaucracy"

History also shows that arguments over particular social policies at given moments of U.S. history have been closely linked to perspectives on what U.S. government should do, and to beliefs about what it apparently *can* do effectively. Americans are recurrently skeptical that government can administer programs effectively. What is more, policy debates are influenced by the reactions of governmental officials, citizens, and politically active social groups to previous public policies. Prior policies may be seen as models to be extended or imitated, or they may be seen as "bad" examples to be avoided in the future. If policies that serve as an immediate referent for debates are seen as wasteful or corruptly or inefficiently administered, those perceptions can undermine efforts to create new or expanded policies along the same lines.

Back in the early twentieth century, for example, some politicians and trade unionists wanted to imitate Civil War pensions, extending them into pensions for most elderly working Americans. But most politically active middle-class groups in that era viewed Civil War pensions as a negative precedent. They were trying to reduce the power of the kinds of elected legislators and party politicians who had worked to expand Civil War pensions in the first place. And they saw Civil War pensions not as social expenditures that legitimately aided many deserving elderly or disabled people, but as sources of funding for "political corruption" (Skocpol 1992, part 2).

In the 1990s, some politicians and groups want to build upon existing parts of U.S. social policy—for example, moving from Social Security for the elderly to universal "health security" for all Americans. During the Medicare battles of the 1960s, reformers were successful in invoking the Social Security model to mobilize support for medical insurance for all of the elderly, rather than for benefits targeted on the poor elderly alone (Jacobs 1993, chap. 9). Today, however, the Social Security precedent may have less influence. Many people believe that the U.S. government bungles virtually any program it touches. They point to problems with the postal service, or with earlier federal regulatory programs, in order to argue that the quality of American health care will inevitably be undermined if the national government takes a stronger role in the health care system.

A historical and institutional perspective on the 1993–94 debate over health care reform helps us to understand why the comprehensive health security plan introduced by President Clinton in September 1993, apparently to great acclaim, so quickly became the target of rhetorically devastating attacks against "governmental bureaucracy." To be sure, President Clinton and his advisers tried to use lessons from U.S. political history in devising and arguing for their version of comprehensive health care reform. I have already noted the president's attempt to link up with favorable attitudes toward Social Security by emphasizing universal health coverage that "can never be taken away" from any American. In addition, the president and his advisers tried to be clever (to the point of obfuscation) about the issue of governmental power. They took it for granted that Americans are wary of giving "the state" a stronger role than "competitive market forces." Consequently, they proposed a version of health reform—called managed competition—that supposedly did not rely on taxes, and that allegedly would preserve and enhance market competition in the offering of health insurance "choices" to all Americans (Starr 1994; Hacker 1994).

Still, the president and the health care experts who advised him may have failed to notice a quite important—historically noticeable—nuance about American reactions to governmental power. Especially since the 1980s, conservatives have proclaimed that Americans invariably hate taxes. But history shows that middle-class Americans have been quite willing to pay taxes when they were sure that these monies would go for worthy purposes from which they along with other citizens benefit. At the same time, history also reveals that many sorts of proposed social policy reforms—including proposals for publicly guaranteed health coverage in the 1910s, 1930s, 1940s, and 1970s— have been highly vulnerable to ideological counterattacks against government "bureaucracy" (Skocpol 1993). Arguably, Americans resent government regulations even more than they may dislike taxes.

Of course, the Clinton health care reform plan of 1993 was very susceptible to the "bureaucracy" criticism. It tried to achieve universal coverage and cost control in health care by overlaying multiple existing private bureaucracies— hospitals, insurance companies, medical associations, state and local governments—with still more layers of federal bureaucratic regulation. Conservative critics were able to ridicule the proposed Clinton reforms for their regulatory complexity.

Although U.S. government has always been in many ways much *less* bureaucratic than the governments of other advanced-industrial nations, nevertheless there are understandable reasons why Americans fear public regulations. Precisely because the federal government in the United States lacks strong administrative bureaucracies that can reach directly into localities or the economy, national-level politicians tend to enact programs that rely on a combination of financial incentives and legal rules to get things done. The federal government partly bribes and partly bosses around state and local governments and nongovernmental groups—getting them to help the federal government do what it cannot do alone. Ironically, however, this sort of situation often gives rise to louder outcries against "federal bureaucratic meddling" than might exist if the national government were able to act directly, especially by using administratively unobtrusive financial transfers to cover a modicum of health insurance for everyone. Such outcries are especially likely to occur if the federal government proposes to regulate more than to subsidize.

Thus, in the debates over the Clinton health plan, lots of groups—including insurance companies, but also hospitals and state governments—feared that federal regulations might financially squeeze and forcibly remodel their operations over time, without giving them offsetting benefits in the form of generous federal subsidies to pay for currently uninsured groups of citizens. This worry about the "bureaucracy" of the Clinton health care plan was obviously enhanced by the fact that the president's declared objectives include "controlling costs" in the national health care system, as well as extending coverage to all Americans. The president promised to do all of this without raising new general tax revenues, and opinion polls indicated that people were (rightly) skeptical about "getting something for nothing." Ironically, by trying to quell worries about taxation, the president and his allies heightened even more deepseated—and historically very predictable—worries about "government bureaucracy" in the United States.

### 11.3.3   Will Americans Pay Taxes for Social Programs?

U.S. history gives the lie to a notion accepted as virtually sacrosanct in the early 1990s: Americans will not pay taxes to fund social programs. At the same time, history highlights how crucial the issue of taxes is. If programs are not linked to reliable sources of funds, they cannot readily expand into the sorts of generous, cross-class programs that gain broad popular support in American democracy.

Civil War benefits in the late nineteenth century had the luxury of being linked to a politically complementary and very generous source of federal taxation. Republicans in that era were not only the party that had "saved the Union" and wanted to do well by the veterans and their relatives. Republicans were also supporters of high tariffs on U.S. industrial and some agricultural commodities. Those tariffs rewarded carefully fashioned alliances of businessmen, workers, and some farmers in the North, while in effect punishing southern farmers, who did not vote for the Republicans (Bensel 1984, chap. 3). At the same time, tariffs generated a lot of funds for the federal treasury. Actual "surpluses" emerged at key junctures, and the Republicans needed politically popular ways to spend them. One of the answers, from the Republican point of view, was Civil War benefits, because these tended to go to people in their northern electoral coalition—such as farmers or residents of small nonindustrial towns—who were likely to have served (or had family members or neighbors serve) in the Union armies, but who did not necessarily benefit from tariff regulations (Sanders 1980). For a time, the Republicans ended up in the best of all possible policy worlds; they could support and expand politically complementary taxation, regulatory, and spending programs.

Maternalist social policies ended up being very limited in the public funding they could mobilize, and thus the benefits they could deliver to broad constituencies. As I pointed out earlier, the federated women's associations that had considerable success at influencing public opinion and the enactment of regulatory legislation in the states, often could not persuade legislators to raise taxes and generously fund programs for mothers and children. This was an era of attacks on taxes by advocates of business competitiveness, and those attacks were especially likely to be effective in local and state governments, where funding decisions were made about mothers' pensions. At the federal level, tariffs were raising proportionately less revenue, and the income tax, instituted in 1913, remained marginal and focused only on the wealthy.

The only maternalist program that managed to tap into expanded funding for a time was the Sheppard-Towner program of the early 1920s. This was the one maternalist program structured as federal subsidies for a set of services open not just to the poor but to all American mothers; consequently, women's groups were able to ally with the Children's Bureau to persuade Congress to increase the program's appropriations over its first years. But by the mid-1920s, Sheppard-Towner had come under fierce attack from conservatives, including doctors, opposed to federally supervised and financed social services. The original legislation, enacted in 1921, expired in 1926 and had to be reauthorized by Congress. While majority support still existed, opponents in the Senate were able to use the institutional levers available to determined minorities in U.S. governance to block reauthorization after 1928. Sheppard-Towner subsidies disappeared, and the Children's Bureau lost influence along with resources within the federal government.

It is well known, of course, that U.S. federal government revenues expanded after the Depression and World War II. During the 1930s, all levels of government were strapped for resources in a devastated economy, but the federal government gained relative leverage over local and state governments because of its continuing ability to borrow. Although the Roosevelt administration tried to cut taxes and reduce government spending, it also raised and deployed "emergency funding" to cover many economic and social programs. Then during World War II, the federal income tax was expanded to encompass much of the employed population. Automatic payroll withholding was instituted, a device that makes tax payments less visible to citizens, thus ensuring a regular and expanding flow of revenues to the federal government during the postwar economic expansion.

The various programs enacted in the Social Security Act of 1935 surely benefited from the overall growth of federal revenues starting in the 1930s and

1940s. Yet OAI, the part of the 1935 legislation that eventually became popular and virtually universal—and usurped the label "Social Security"—carried its own source of funding: an earmarked payroll tax that was supposed to be used to build up a separate "trust fund" to cover future pension obligation. Because of President Roosevelt's fierce insistence on "fiscal soundness" for nonemergency social insurance programs, retirement insurance actually kicked in as a set of taxes well before any benefits were paid. After 1939, the program became more of a pay-as-you-go venture than it was originally (Achenbaum 1986; Berkowitz 1987). Still, Social Security retirement insurance always benefited—ideologically as well as fiscally—from the existence of its earmarked payroll tax and nominally separate trust fund. Social Security taxes were deliberately labeled "contributions" and were treated as payments that built up individual "eligibility" for "earned benefits" (Derthick 1979; Zollars and Skocpol 1994).

As the system expanded to include more and more categories of employees, new taxes were collected ahead of the payment of benefits. Most retirees during the 1950s, 1960s, and 1970s actually did very well in terms of what they had paid into the system over their working lives. Increasing Social Security payroll taxes were accepted politically by most American citizens as the system expanded toward near-universal coverage. Once the coverage became very broad, the majority of citizens—the elderly and their children—gained a stake in promised benefits. Even today, Americans do not object as much as one might expect to Social Security taxes, despite their regressiveness and the large cut they take from average incomes. The Social Security system's trust fund remains relatively solvent within an otherwise severely strained federal budget, and this affords it a bit of political protection in the face of determined conservative efforts to cut social spending.

Taxes are arguably the pivot on which the future of federal social policy may turn. The Concord Coalition, Ross Perot, and other advocates of deficit cutting are determined to severely cut both federal taxes and federal social spending. The aim is to shift U.S. savings into private investment funds. Deficit cutters appeal to American middle-class citizens as taxpayers—especially as payers of property and income taxes—rather than as potential beneficiaries of existing or new broadly focused social programs. As I have already discussed, deficit-cutting conservatives are hard at work trying to reduce American middle-class faith in the viability and legitimacy of "middle-class entitlements" such as Social Security and Medicare. And of course, deficit cutters are determined to block broad new federal commitments to universal health care or long-term care benefits for the elderly.

On the other side of the political spectrum, progressives want to increase government-funded "investments" not only in the economy, but also in education, health care, and other social services. Progressives have already lost many battles to expand such social programs to the degree that they are narrowly targeted on the poor, on blacks, or on inner cities. They are still trying to expand programs for children. But many in the voting public remain suspicious that "children's programs" are a proxy for "welfare" expenditures or for make-work social service jobs (Taylor 1991). One way out is to advocate, as the Clinton administration has done, either "tax credits" for the less privileged (such as the Earned Income Tax Credit) or extensions of universal "security" programs (such as health care coverage) that are claimed to benefit the middle class as much or more than the poor. But such progressive strategies are badly hampered by the unwillingness of Democratic Party politicians to think creatively about—or talk publicly about—taxes. After all, tax-expenditure programs can hardly be expanded indefinitely as a tool of federal social policy, in an era of huge deficits and reduced overall tax revenues. And new universal social programs cannot work politically, as we have seen in the recent health care debate, unless they have some federally mobilized resources behind them.

### 11.3.4    Better Social Policies for the Future?

A historical-institution, polity-centered approach to understanding the politics of U.S. social policy making encourages us to consider macroscopic contexts, period effects, and interconnections among specialized "policy areas." Even so, implications can be drawn out for the particular policy issues addressed in this book. I have already discussed the implications of my approach for understanding the 1993–94 debates about President Bill Clinton's health security bill. Those debates sputtered to inconclusion in the fall of 1994, and comprehensive health financing reform is unlikely to come again soon onto the U.S. legislative agenda. I expect the next rounds of debate to focus on extending coverage for people leaving welfare, on extending insurance coverage to all or most American children, and—perhaps above all—on cutting Medicare as a way to relieve pressures on the federal budget. The constraints that will operate in these debates are well captured by the general discussions I have already offered. Consequently, I propose to say little more here about health care reform; I shall focus instead on long-term care for the elderly, educational reform, and issues about child care provision.

New policy ideas in each of these areas cannot be considered on economic-efficiency grounds alone. Any new proposals would necessarily be debated, enacted, and implemented within the context of the sorts of overall limits and possibilities I have already discussed, and against the backdrop of previously existing social policies about children and the elderly. The focus of this volume, moreover, is largely on social *services,* not simply monetary benefits financed privately or through government. That means that the politics of each of these areas activates actual or would-be service deliverers, as well as the social groups that do, or might, benefit from the services in question. Day care providers, teachers, school administrators, nursing-home operators, doctors, and insurance companies—all of these sorts of "providers" matter as much as, and usually more than, children and old people in the *politics* of designing and redesigning social services of the sorts we are considering here.

*Long-Term Care*

Possibilities for financing long-term care for the elderly are very much tied up by current national concerns about the federal budget deficit and the growing cost of commitments that have already been made to elderly health care through Medicare and Medicaid. (Although neither Medicare nor Medicaid offers sufficient coverage for long-term care, and certainly not for home-based care, Medicaid does cover nursing home expenses for the impoverished elderly and for middle-class retirees who "spend down" to the near-poverty level in order to attain eligibility.) Because of current citizen hostility toward government and public spending, proposed new cuts in federal expenditures for Medicare and Medicaid are likely to dominate debates about "health care reform" for the next few years. If recent trends toward squeezing physician and hospital reimbursements continue, we may expect that Medicare and Medicaid will function less and less effectively over time, spreading popular disillusionment with public health insurance, without addressing the actual social needs privately, either. Crises of coverage, cost shifting, and efficiency in America's current hybrid health financing "system" may simply deepen for a decade or so, as the aftermath of the failed debates of 1994 plays out politically.

As we have learned elsewhere in this volume, private insurance is unlikely to offer viable policies to help today's young and middle-aged adults plan for possible long-term care expenditures when they become very old. Yet enactment of a new comprehensive, non-means-tested federal guarantee in this area seems equally unlikely. An economically rational solution might be a federal requirement that each American "save" from private income for future long-term care, either in the home or in institutional settings. This sort of proposal would rely on federal regulatory power, but not spending, and it might attract support from nursing home operators and health care providers. However, any such mandatory requirement would be very much subject to political criticism as a form of "governmental coercion"—and as an additional tax burden on already hard-pressed working-age families. I conclude that such a mandatory savings plan could not succeed during the 1990s if proposed and debated in isolation. It might, however, succeed as part of an overhaul of Medicare or Social Security, or as part of a new approach to universal health care (which might come sometime early in the twenty-first century).

*Education*

Primary and secondary education in the United States remains centered in a publicly organized system of schools, almost entirely run at the local level and financed mostly through local and state taxes. As we have seen, institutional investments made long ago within U.S. federal democracy (rather than considerations of economic or social "efficiency" in the mid-twentieth century) have made the public educational system what it is today. This is true, even though the historical ideal of "schooling for all" has in recent decades been considerably eroded by the growth of secular private schools catering to the children of privileged middle-class professionals living in urban areas. The opting-out of certain upper-middle-class parents has no doubt reduced support for public school taxation. Yet financial allocation to public schools has, in the aggregate, grown steadily in recent decades, so it is hard to argue that American public schools are starved for funds.

Current ideas about "school reform" focus on organizational incentives rather than money as such. They range from proposals for empowering principals and teachers in individual schools, through plans for promoting competition among public schools within local areas, to calls for tax-financed vouchers that would enable parents to choose among public schools or (even) between public and private schools. Whatever their conceptual merits, such proposals have very different possibilities from a polity-centered perspective. Given the existing institutional arrangements within—or against—which reforms would have to be enacted and implemented, it seems very unlikely that Americans will suddenly decide to totally scrap public schools in favor of a private, market-oriented voucher system. Such a step would be seen by many voting citizens—and portrayed by providers employed in the current public school system—as little more than a vast tax subsidy to parents who are now paying for private schooling in addition to paying taxes for public schools. More public money would have to be raised and spent at a time when Americans are highly sensitive about raising taxes.

Reforms that rearrange administration or financing within the public school system seem much more likely, however, because U.S. public opinion is increasingly aware that there are problems with the quality of school performance. Significant rearrangements—including vouchers for public school "choice"—are being enacted within particular states or localities. If they prove attractive in politically visible ways—by lowering school-related tax costs and/or improving the educational performance of schools—such reforms could then spread by "competitive emulation" across many localities and states. That was the way that America's commitment to public schooling originally grew up in the nineteenth century: *not* from the top down at the behest of the national bureaucratic or professional elites, but from the bottom laterally through competitive emulation across many localities. I would expect school reform to happen again in this manner, to the degree that there are any significant modifications in the status quo.

## Child Care

Child care represents a politically conceivable new area for significantly expanded public financing in the United States, but probably not for direct provision of child care services by the federal government. Over the past several decades, U.S. women's labor-force participation has increased markedly, including the employment of mothers of infants and toddlers as well as school-age children. For better or worse, single parenthood is also very much on the rise; about half of all American children born today can expect to spend significant portions of their minority in single-parent (usually mother-led) households (McLanahan and Sandefur 1994). Such social trends increase the potential social demand for, and economic relevance of, preschool and after-school child care. Yet these trends are playing out in a U.S. polity that currently does less through government to provide for, or to finance, child care than many European nations do currently, or have done historically.

From the late nineteenth century through the 1950s, many conservative or social democratic nations in Europe got into the child care business for essentially demographic reasons, to ensure high enough birth rates to sustain labor forces and populations of potential military recruits (Bock and Thane 1991). As a country of immigration, and a nation in privileged geopolitical circumstances, the United States did not worry as much about encouraging more births or more labor-force participation by mothers. Such child care subsidies as the United States developed historically were mainly centered in the welfare system. Mothers' pensions from the 1910s, federalized as ADC/AFDC from the 1930s, encouraged impoverished widows or single mothers to care for their children in the home, while remaining at least partly outside of the wage-labor market.

Because of these historical legacies, any debates about new U.S. child care policies for the 1990s are inevitably tied up with the contentious politics of "welfare reform"—yet another round of which is currently under way. For reasons that I discussed above, a new consensus has emerged among most experts and citizens, an agreement that stay-at-home motherhood should no longer be subsidized for the poor. According to proposals form the Clinton administration and congressional Republicans, AFDC is supposed to be turned into a program promoting paid-labor-force participation by impoverished single mothers. At the same time, children's advocates are arguing that any state or national legislation to limit welfare benefits and move single mothers into the low-wage labor force must be accompanied by the substantial expansion of public provision of, or subsidies for, day care services, including those offered through the Head Start program. As Arleen Leibowitz explains in her contribution to this volume, less-privileged children might well benefit from expanded day care services in terms of cognitive development and social skills that prepare them to do better in school. But it remains to be seen whether legislators and the American voting public will be willing to pay the cost of such expanded social services for the poor alone. In past historical episodes of "welfare reform," the end result has been to spend less on the poor and coerce them more. And indeed, very conservative Republicans today argue that welfare benefits should simply be cut off and children placed in orphanages if single mothers will not or cannot find work to sustain their offspring.

Given recent family changes, coupled with Americans' long-term proclivity for universal rather than poverty benefits, there might well be a broad potential constituency for more universal forms of child care provision. This could be true particularly for nonbureaucratic and noninvasive financial transfers, such as refundable tax credits, or vouchers available to all families, or enhanced dependent allowances delivered through the tax system. Broad financial transfers could be designed to deliver proportionately more aid to lower-income families, while leaving choices about specific types of care to families themselves. But the more universal the system, the more costly it would be in terms of tax revenues. Because of the current fiscal and political climate in the United States, electoral politicians will probably not promote the discussion of universal child care subsidies, no matter how acute the social needs may be. Debate for the foreseeable future is likely to remain focused on poor mothers and their children. Only after the next round of "welfare reform" is completed is it likely that U.S. politics can begin to focus on more fundamental issues of how to support all American families in a world where paid employment and parental duties must be combined in very new ways than in the pre-1970s past.

Elsewhere (Skocpol 1991) I have advocated a set of family security programs aimed at working-age adults and their children—the groups that are not well served by existing social programs. Family security measures would include universal basic health care financing of some sort, job training available to displaced or potential employees across the class structure, benefits for working parents, and assured support for single-parent families. These programs could be financed in part by the transfer of resources now spent on other social programs, including welfare. New taxes would also be required, and they could include a consumption tax (such as discussed in Fuchs 1994) as well as payroll deductions from absent parents for child support (Garfinkel 1992). If history is any guide, American citizens might conceivably be more supportive of relatively universal family security measures than they are of social programs targeted on the poor alone.

Nevertheless, given the electoral and institutional deadlocks that plague the U.S. national government right now, it is an open question whether any new programs that include taxes could be enacted by Congress, even if rational proposals were to be devised by federal officials or extragovernmental experts. New U.S. social programs to enhance the security of the elderly, of children, and indeed of all American families will never come about until both intellectuals and politicians start to talk about the socioeconomic functions, as well as dysfunctions, of taxes. The U.S. federal state has nearly reached the limits of what it can constructively accomplish through regulation and mandates in the absence of stable new sources of public revenue.

American citizens might, or might not, respond to new, wide-ranging discussions about the uses of tax revenues for supporting the young, the old, and working-age families in the middle. Yet it is certain that the citizenry will not respond unless they begin to hear thoughtful arguments and nonideological debates that encompass all sides of the issue. What do Americans want local, state, and national governments to do to cushion insecurities for families at various phases of the life cycle? How should governments act in partnership with citizens and businesses and providers of social services? And who will pay—in part, through taxes—for what we decide we want? Social scientists should enter this sort of broad democratic conversation, not just as designers of efficient "policy instruments," but also as citizens conversing with their fellows about the kind of good government and society we want for the twenty-first century.

# References

Achenbaum, W. Andrew. 1986. *Social Security: Visions and Revisions.* Cambridge: Cambridge University Press.

Amenta, Edwin, Elisabeth Clemens, Jefren Olsen, Sunita Parikh, and Theda Skocpol. 1987. The Political Origins of Unemployment Insurance in Five American States. *Studies in American Political Development* 2:137–82.

Amenta, Edwin, and Theda Skocpol. 1988. Redefining the New Deal: World War II and the Development of Social Provision in the United States. *The Politics of Social Policy in the United States,* ed. Margaret Weir, Ann Shola Orloff, and Theda Skocpol, 81–122. Princeton, NJ: Princeton University Press.

Baker, Paula. 1984. The Domestication of Politics: Women and American Political Society, 1780–1920. *American Historical Review* 89:620–47.

Bane, Mary Jo, and David T. Ellwood. 1994. *Welfare Realities: From Rhetoric to Reform.* Cambridge: Harvard University Press.

Bensel, Richard Franklin. 1984. *Sectionalism and American Political Development, 1880–1980.* Madison: University of Wisconsin Press.

Berkowitz, Edward D. 1987. The First Advisory Council and the 1939 Amendments. In *Social Security after Fifty: Successes and Failures,* ed. Edward D. Berkowitz, 55–78. Westport, CT: Greenwood Press.

Blumenthal, Sidney. 1991. Populism in Tweeds: The Professor and the Middle Class. *New Republic,* November 25, 1991, 10–15.

Blumenthal, Sidney, and Thomas Byrne Edsall, eds. 1988. *The Reagan Legacy.* New York: Pantheon Books.

Bock, Gisela, and Pat Thane, eds. 1991. *Maternity and Gender Policies: Women and the Rise of European Welfare States, 1880s-1950s.* London: Routledge.

Children's Defense Fund. 1994. *The State of America's Children Yearbook, 1994.* Washington, DC: Children's Defense Fund.

Clinton, Bill, and Al Gore. 1992. *Putting People First: How We Can All Change America.* New York: Times Books, Random House.

Danziger, Sheldon, and Peter Gottschalk, eds. 1993. *Uneven Tides: Rising Inequality in America.* New York: Russell Sage Foundation.

Danziger, Sheldon H., Robert H. Haveman, and Robert D. Plotnick. 1986. Antipoverty Policy: Effects on the Poor and Nonpoor. In *Fighting Poverty: What Works and What Doesn't,* ed. Sheldon H. Danziger and Daniel H. Weinberg, 50–77. Cambridge: Harvard University Press.

Derthick, Martha. 1979. *Policymaking for Social Security.* Washington, DC: Brookings Institution.

Edsall, Thomas Byrne, and Mary D. Edsall. 1991. *Chain Reaction: The Impact of Race, Rights, and Taxes on American Politics.* New York: Norton.

Flora, Peter J., and Jens Alber. 1981. Modernization, Democratization, and the Development of Welfare States in Western Europe. In *The Development of Welfare States in Europe and America*, ed. Peter J. Flora and Arnold J. Heidenheimer, 37–80. New Brunswick, NJ: Transaction Books.

Freeman, Richard B., ed. 1994. *Working under Different Rules.* National Bureau of Economic Research Project Report. New York: Russell Sage Foundation.

Fuchs, Victor R. 1994. Health System Reform: A Different Approach. *Journal of the American Medical Association* 272, no. 7:560–63.

Garfinkel, Irwin. 1992. *Assuring Child Support: An Extension of Social Security.* New York: Russel Sage Foundation.

Garfinkel, Irwin, and Sara S. McLanahan. 1986. *Single Mothers and Their Children: A New American Dilemma.* Washington, DC: Urban Institute Press.

Hacker, Jacob S. 1994. Setting the Reform Agenda: The Ascendance of Managed Competition. Senior honors thesis, Social Studies, Harvard College.

Heclo, Hugh. 1986. The Political Foundations of Antipoverty Policy. In *Fighting Poverty: What Works and What Doesn't,* ed. Sheldon H. Danziger and Daniel H. Weinberg, 312–40. Cambridge: Harvard University Press.

Heidenheimer, Arnold J. 1981. Education and Social Security Entitlements in Europe and America. In *The Development of Welfare States in Europe and America*, ed. Peter J. Flora and Arnold J. Heidenheimer, 269–304. New Brunswick, NJ: Transaction Books.

Howard, Christopher. 1994. Happy Returns: How the Working Poor Got Tax Relief. *American Prospect,* no. 17 (spring):46–53.

Jacobs, Lawrence R. 1993. *The Health of Nations: Public Opinion and the Making of American and British Health Policy.* Ithaca, NY: Cornell University Press.

Katznelson, Ira, and Margaret Weir. 1985. *Schooling for All: Class, Race, and the Decline of the Democratic Ideal.* New York: Basic Books.

McCormick, Richard L. 1979. The Party Period and Public Policy: An Exploratory Hypothesis. *Journal of American History* 66:279–98.

McLanahan, Sara S., and Gary Sandefur. 1994. *Growing Up with a Single Parent: What Hurts, What Helps.* Cambridge: Harvard University Press.

McMurry, Donald. 1922. The Political Significance of the Pension Question, 1885–1897. *Mississippi Valley Historical Review* 9:19–36.

Murray, Charles. 1984. *Losing Ground: American Social Policy, 1950–1980.* New York: Basic Books.

Newman, Katherine S. 1993. *Declining Fortunes: The Withering of the American Dream.* New York: Basic Books.

Patterson, James T. 1967. *Congressional Conservatism and the New Deal.* Lexington: University of Kentucky Press.

———. 1981. *America's Struggle against Poverty, 1900–1980.* Cambridge: Harvard University Press.

Peterson, Peter G. 1993. *Facing Up: How to Rescue the Economy from Crushing Debt and Restore the American Dream.* New York: Simon and Schuster.

Quadagno, Jill. 1994. *The Color of Welfare: How Racism Undermined the War on Poverty.* New York: Oxford University Press.

Rubinson, Richard. 1986. Class Formation, Politics, and Institutions: Schooling in the United States. *American Journal of Sociology* 92:519–48.

Russakoff, Dale. 1991. How Wofford Rode Health Care to Washington. *Washington Post National Weekly Edition,* November 25–December 1, 14–15.

Sanders, Heywood. 1980. "Paying for the Bloody Shirt": The Politics of Civil War Pensions, 137–60. In *Political Benefits,* ed. Barry Rundquist. Lexington, MA: D. C. Heath.

Skocpol, Theda. 1991. Targeting within Universalism: Politically Viable Policies to Combat Poverty in the United States. In *The Urban Underclass,* ed. Christopher Jencks and Paul E. Peterson, 411–36. Washington, DC: Brookings Institution.

———. 1992. *Protecting Soldiers and Mothers: The Political Origins of Social Policy in the United States.* Cambridge, MA: Belknap Press.

———. 1993. Is the Time Finally Ripe? Health Insurance Reforms in the 1990s. *Journal of Health Politics, Policy, and Law* 18 (fall):531–50.

———. 1995. *Social Policy in the United States: Future Possibilities in Historical Perspective.* Princeton, NJ: Princeton University Press.

Skocpol, Theda, and Edwin Amenta. 1985. Did Capitalists Shape Social Security? *American Sociological Review* 50, no. 4:572–75.

———. 1986. States and Social Policies. *Annual Review of Sociology* 12:131–57.

Skocpol, Theda, Christopher Howard, Susan Goodrich Lehmann, and Marjorie Abend-Wein. 1993. Women's Associations and the Enactment of Mothers' Pensions in the United States. *American Political Science Review* 87, no. 3:686–701.

Skowronek, Stepen. 1982. *Building a New American State: The Expansion of National Administrative Capacities, 1877–1920.* Cambridge: Cambridge University Press.

Starr, Paul. 1991. The Middle Class and National Health Reform. *American Prospect,* no. 6 (summer): 7–12.

———. 1994. *The Logic of Health Care Reform: Why and How the President's Plan Will Work.* New York: Whittle Books and Penguin Books.

Taylor, Paul. 1991. Plight of Children: Seen but Unheeded: Even Madison Avenue Has Trouble Selling Public on Aiding Poor Youth. *Washington Post,* July 15, A4.

Weir, Margaret. 1992. *Politics and Jobs: The Boundaries of Employment Policy in the United States.* Princeton, NJ: Princeton University Press.

Weir, Margaret, Ann Shola Orloff, and Theda Skocpol, eds. 1988. *The Politics of Social Policy in the United States.* Princeton, NJ: Princeton University Press.

Weir, Margaret, and Theda Skocpol. 1985. State Structures and the Possibilities for "Keynesian" Responses to the Great Depression in Sweden, Britain, and the United States. In *Bringing the State Back In,* ed. Peter B. Evans, Theda Skocpol, and Dietrich Rueschemeyer, 107–63. Cambridge: Cambridge University Press.

White House Domestic Policy Council. 1993. *The President's Health Security Plan.* Introduction by Erik Eckholm. New York: Times Books, Random House.

Zollars, Cheryl, and Theda Skocpol. 1994. Cultural Mythmaking as a Policy Tool: The Social Security Board and the Construction of a Social Citizenship of Self-Interest. In *Political Culture and Political Structure: Theoretical and Empirical Studies,* vol. 2 of *Research on Democracy and Society,* ed. Frederick D. Weil, 381–408. Greenwich, CT: JAI Press.

# Comment    Seymour Martin Lipset

Many discussions of American public policy in a comparative context suggest, as Theda Skocpol notes in her paper, that the United States has been a "welfare laggard," or as some others have put it, an outlier among the developed industrial democracies. Much of Skocpol's previous work has raised questions as to

Seymour Martin Lipset is the Virginia E. Hazel and John T. Hazel, Jr., Professor of Public Policy at George Mason University and a senior fellow of the Hoover Institution, Stanford University.

how valid this generalization is. In her book *Protecting Soldiers and Mothers: The Political Origins of Social Policy in the United States* and other writings, she has noted that the United States adopted important welfare policies about the same time as a number of European countries. The earliest was the provisions for benefits for Civil War veterans and their families, which began in the last part of the nineteenth century and continued into the twentieth. Since the overwhelming majority of adult males in the North served in the Union Army, this meant that a very large proportion of the population outside of the South was covered. These benefits included old-age pensions, dealt with health problems, and provided for support of widows and children. As noted, the timing corresponded with the introduction of welfare programs in various European nations, such as those fostered by Disraeli in Britain and Bismarck in Germany. The second early American program to which Skocpol has called attention involved various maternalist measures mainly on the state levels, which provided benefits for mothers and children.

These programs demonstrate that Americans in the late nineteenth and early twentieth centuries were willing to pay for welfare programs for specific groups. Yet these do not, in my judgment, negate the conclusion that the United States was and remains a welfare laggard. The veterans' benefits were given as recompense for service in the army during wartime, not as a right for all citizens or in order to redistribute income or as an entitlement. The program, as Skocpol indicates, did not set a precedent for the extension of welfare benefits to the rest of the population. Advocates of such policies, who tried to use the veterans' benefits as a model, failed.

The maternalist policies do correspond somewhat to latter-day, or contemporary, welfare programs. They were fostered by middle-class women, active in the feminist or suffragette movements. They were concerned with the problems of children of single mothers, largely of widows and divorced women. These policies also did not last, ending either around the time of World War I or, in the case of the one federal program, in the 1920s. Like Civil War Veterans' benefits, they did not serve as a model or precedent for federal policies.

There was, it should be noted, a third early set of policies that had definite roots in American values and that has continued into later times: support for education. If the United States has been a welfare laggard, it has been the educational leader with respect to expenditures and coverage for the different age groups, reflecting the country's greater commitment to equality of opportunity. From early in the nineteenth century, America led the world with respect to attendance at elementary school, then with high school, and finally in more recent times with the proportions of the age cohort going to college and graduate school. For each level of education at any given moment in time there have been more people studying in the United States than in Europe. And Americans have been willing to pay for the costs involved. This emphasis on education continues down to the present. A review of public opinion data over fifty years by Ben Page and Robert Shapiro (1992, 128) notes that "education has long been an area in which most Americans want government to spend more money." The most recent data on governmental expenditures reveal that the United States is still behind most developed countries with respect to welfare, but not to education.

There have, of course been major changes in the preferences of Americans since the 1930s. The Great Depression and the New Deal led to an American welfare state including Social Security, unemployment insurance, and various entitlement and transfer programs, such as AFDC, Medicare, and Medicaid. But as noted, comparative data still show that the United States has not caught up to the European countries. The proportion of the gross national product that Americans pay in terms of taxes per capita is the lowest in the developed world.

Why the United States lags may be dealt with historically and comparatively. On one hand, many historians and, I think, Theda Skocpol prefer to answer the question historically or situationally. And they have pointed to past American movements in support of greater state intervention for more welfare. It is true that there has been interest in welfare programs and statist economic policies, but it is also true the advocates of these policies have had less success here than elsewhere, that they have failed repeatedly, as with the recent effort to extend health coverage.

The analysis of American behavior in the welfare area may be linked to the discussions of Why no socialism in the United States? The "why no socialism" debates refer to the fact that the United States is the only industrialized country that has not had a significant socialist or labor party. The subject must be treated cross-nationally. (To this may be added the fact that today America is close to having the weakest trade union movement among industrialized countries in terms of the proportion of the labor force who belong.) The discussion has been particularly important for Marxist theory, as well as politics, since Karl Marx stated explicitly in *Capital* that the most developed country shows to the less developed the image of their future, that political systems are a function of the level of technology of economies. What this meant to Marxists prior to World War I was that the United States, as the most economically advanced country, would be the first socialist country. Various prominent Marxists assumed this would happen. As it became clear that the United States was not behaving properly, they became very concerned about the implications the lack of a socialist movement in the United States had for the validity of Marxist theory. The subject, of course, has been addressed by many nonsocialists and has been researched by academic scholars.

Those who have written on the issue have suggested many explanatory variables, in fact so many that the outcome seems overdetermined. One of the most interesting sets of hypotheses was advanced by H. G. Wells in 1906 in *The Future in America* and elaborated on by the American political theorist Louis Hartz in *The Liberal Tradition in America*, published in 1955. Wells and Hartz emphasized the impact of the dominant ideology or creed, of America's organizing principles, which have been classically liberal, on the polity. Classical liberalism, now sometimes referred to as libertarianism, favors a weak government, is suspicious of or fears the state. It subsumes Jefferson's dictum, that government is best which governs least. This antistatist doctrine defines the conservative or national tradition of the United States. Conversely, in Europe and Canada the dominant organizing principles have been statist. Conservatism in many of these countries has meant Toryism, an emphasis on mercantilism, a powerful activist state, elitism, noblesse oblige, and communitarianism. Harold Macmillan, who served as a Tory prime minister of Britain, defined Toryism, the ideology of his branch of the Conservative Party, as "paternalistic socialism." The argument derivative from Wells and Hartz suggests that, where national traditions legitimate statism, both the egalitarian left and the hierarchical right endorse welfare policies. Europe produced a statist right and a statist left, while the liberals, squeezed between them, were the politically weak backers of antistatist ideology and policies. In America, Wells argued, two parties were missing, the socialists and the conservatives. He contended as of 1906 that both American major parties would be wings of the Liberal Party in Britain, the left and the right.

In various writings in Canada and the United States, I have emphasized, as have many Canadian scholars, that Canada is the country of the counterrevolution, which, retaining the monarchy and state-related church, produced respect for the mercantilist state, while the United States is the country of the Whig revolution, and therefore has been antistatist and classically liberal (Lipset 1990). The different outcomes of the American Revolution produced varying receptivities to state intervention. Canada, though never electing a socialist party to national office, has two, the New Democrats (NDP), and the separatist Parti Québécois (PQ), which have been strong in most of its provinces. Four, Manitoba, Ontario, Saskatchewan, and British Columbia, have been governed by the NDP; Quebec has a PQ government. And the country has been much more receptive to welfare state measures than the United States. Brian Mulroney, who served as Conservative prime minister for most of the 1980s, described the welfare state as Canada's "sacred heritage" in the 1988 election campaign. His successor, Kim Campbell, who held office briefly after Mulroney retired, noted that Canada is basically a social democratic country. The leader of what has sometimes been described as the Reaganite right in Canada, Preston Manning, of the Reform Party, said in 1994 that Canadians owe a debt of gratitude to the social democrats of the country, the NDP, who are responsible for Canada's health plan, its system of family allowances, its more extensive provisions for the unemployed than the American, and many other welfare measures. Clearly the orientation of Canada toward welfare policies is quite different from that of Republicans. The latter are the only major anti-statist party in the developed world.

This brief comparative look does not mean that Skocpol is wrong in her analyses, or in her contention that there has been considerable support for social welfare policies in the United States. She prefers to explain their relative weakness as the outcome of specific conflicts and political processes. She is basically correct on the details. But she underplays what I consider to be important, namely, that the larger value context within which American politics takes place makes it much more difficult to institutionalize statist economic and welfare policies here than in Europe and Canada. It does not make it impossible. As Gerhard Casper emphasized in his talk to our conference, America has an extensive regulatory state, one that is stronger than those in most social democratic systems and in Canada. Where Europeans and Canadians choose direct state intervention, ownership or control of industry, and redistributive policies to produce more equality of result, Americans favor education and regulation to enhance equality of opportunity and a more competitive society. I would contend that the regulatory emphases are also related to the greater moralistic streak in American society. This orientation derives in some considerable part from the fact that this country is the only Protestant sectarian nation, Methodist, Baptist, and a myriad of others. The Euro-Canadian hierarchical churches, Catholic, Anglican, Orthodox, Lutheran, which have been state-related, not only have contributed to statist orientations in their countries but also have made them much less moralistic and individualistic than the United States, with its congregationally organized sectarian denominations.

The Wells and Hartz approach does not account for the success or failure of any particular policy effort or the strength of different ideologies in the United States, Canada, or other countries. There are other important factors that I do not have the time or space to deal with, particularly the varying political systems; divided government; checks and balances; president and Congress; weak executive authority compared to the more unified, parliamentary strong executive polity; and the different stratification systems, one postfeudal with stronger, more visible social classes and the other a product of a new revolutionary society with less consequent deference for elites and the state. The American sociopolitical system favors limited government, the European a strong state. But it is necessary to analyze specific differences through detailed historical case studies. And this is what Skocpol has done thoroughly and eloquently. I would simply urge the need for both comparative cultural and structural analyses as well.

## References

Lipset, Seymour Martin. 1990. *Continental Divide: The Values and Institutions of the United States and Canada.* New York: Routledge.

Page, Benjamin, and Robert Shapiro. 1992. *The Rational Public: Fifty Years of Trends in American's Policy Preferences.* Chicago: University of Chicago Press.

# Contributors

Henry J. Aaron
The Brookings Institution
1775 Massachusetts Avenue
Washington, DC 20036

Kenneth J. Arrow
Department of Economics
Stanford University
Stanford, CA 94305

Francine D. Blau
School of Industrial and Labor Relations
Cornell University
Ives Hall
Ithaca, NY 14853

Martin Feldstein
National Bureau of Economic Research
1050 Massachusetts Avenue
Cambridge, MA 02138

Robert H. Frank
Department of Economics
Cornell University
Uris Hall
Ithaca, NY 14853

Victor R. Fuchs
National Bureau of Economic Research
204 Junipero Serra Boulevard
Stanford, CA 94305

Alan M. Garber
Stanford Medical School
204 Junipero Serra Boulevard
Stanford, CA 94305

Joseph A. Grundfest
Stanford Law School 334
Stanford University
Stanford, CA 94305

Henry Hansmann
Yale Law School
127 Wall Street
New Haven, CT 06520

Eric A. Hanushek
Department of Economics
238 Harkness Hall
University of Rochester
Rochester, NY 14627

Christopher Jencks
Center for Urban Affairs and Policy Re-
 search
Northwestern University
2040 Sheridan Road
Evanston, IL 60208

Arleen Leibowitz
RAND
1700 Main Street
Santa Monica, CA 90401

Seymour Martin Lipset
Institute of Public Policy
George Mason University
4400 University Drive
Fairfax, VA 22030

Glenn C. Loury
Department of Economics
Boston University
270 Bay State Road
Boston, MA 02215

Roger G. Noll
Department of Economics
Stanford University
Stanford, CA 94305

James M. Poterba
Department of Economics
Room E52–350
Massachusetts Institute of Technology
50 Memorial Drive
Cambridge, MA 02139

Paul M. Romer
Department of Economics
University of California
Berkeley, CA 94720

Amartya Sen
Department of Economics
Littauer Center
Harvard University
Cambridge, MA 02138

John B. Shoven
School of Humanities and Sciences
Stanford University
Stanford, CA 94305

Theda Skocpol
Department of Sociology
William James Hall 470
Harvard University
Cambridge, MA 02138

Timothy Taylor
Managing Editor
*Journal of Economic Perspectives*
Hubert H. Humphrey Institute of Public
  Affairs
University of Minnesota
301 19th Avenue South
Minneapolis, MN 55455

Richard J. Zeckhauser
Kennedy School of Government
Harvard University
79 JFK Street
Cambridge, MA 02138

# Author Index

# Subject Index